WAR AND IMPERIALISM
IN REPUBLICAN ROME
327–70 B.C.

D0171277

WAR AND IMPERIALISM IN REPUBLICAN ROME

327–70 B.C.

BY

WILLIAM V. HARRIS

CLARENDON PRESS · OXFORD

Oxford University Press, Walton Street, Oxford OX2 6DP

London New York Toronto
Delhi Bombay Calcutta Madras Karachi
Kuala Lumpur Singapore Hong Kong Tokyo
Nairobi Dar es Salaam Cape Town
Melbourne Auckland

and associated companies in
Beirut Berlin Ibadan Mexico City Nicosia

Oxford is a trade mark of Oxford University Press

First published 1979
First issued in paperback (with corrections) 1985

British Library Cataloguing in Publication Data

Harris, William Vernon
War and imperialism in Republican Rome,
327–70 B.C.
1. Imperialism—History   2. Rome—Foreign relations
3. Rome—History—Republic, 510–30 B.C.
I. Title
321'.03'0937   JV98   78-40490

ISBN 0-19-814866-6

Printed in Great Britain by
the Alden Press, Oxford

PREFACE TO THE PAPERBACK EDITION

Many typographical corrections have been made for this new printing. The Press has also been kind enough to offer me some space for substantive comments, but I shall make these very brief. A more extensive statement of my opinion about recent work on the imperialism of the middle Republic will appear as an article entitled 'Current Directions in the Study of Roman Imperialism', in *The Imperialism of Mid-Republican Rome*, a collection of papers edited by me which is due to be published in Rome later this year. The same volume will contain papers by Domenico Musti, Erich S. Gruen, Emilio Gabba, Jerzy Linderski and Guido Clemente, and comments by several other scholars.

I am still in the contented or complacent position of thinking that the approach and the arguments employed in this book are valid ones. I would not say the same, however, for all the theories attributed to it by reviewers and commentators, some of whom, particularly in English-speaking lands, have seen strange mirages. So I ought perhaps to reiterate that I do not maintain that the Romans planned the construction of their empire long in advance (see p. 107), or that they were the 'aggressors' in every war they undertook during the middle Republic (I admit, however, that I find nothing absurd in the notion that in this period Rome was an exceptionally aggressive state). I do not even deny that the Romans sometimes fought defensive wars; indeed it seems quite natural that a state with a determined grip on power over many peoples other than its own should sometimes have to defend that power. These are matters which can scarcely be misunderstood except by scholars with simple binary minds (Rome was guilty v. Rome was innocent).

It may be worth mentioning a few of the works published since 1977 (the year when this book was completed) which would condition any book I might write on the same subject now, together with two of the more perceptive reactions to the original volume. An important new paper was published by F. Hampl in his *Geschichte als Kritische Wissenschaft* (Darmstadt, 1979), iii. 48–119; 'Das Problem des Aufstiegs Roms zur Weltmacht. Neue Bilanz unter methodisch-kritischen Aspekten'. A very stimulating book for an ancient historian is Philippe Contamine's *La guerre dans le Moyen Age* (Paris,

Preface to the Paperback Edition

1980). The responses of John North ('The Development of Roman Imperialism', *JRS* 71 (1981), 1–9) and W. Eder (*Gnomon* 54 (1982), 549–554) were particularly valuable ones, though I found much to disagree with in the former; and some of the contributions to the forthcoming volume *The Imperialism of Mid-Republican Rome* will, I think, be seen as notable steps forward. Other contributions are in the press: I will simply mention the excellent paper by Stephen Oakley on the Roman tradition of combat-by-champions (adding other evidence to that listed in p. 39 n.1).

I hope before very long to say something in print about both earlier and later Roman imperialism, about the nascent phase before 327 (this date is of course an arbitrary dividing line) and about the later phases after 70 B.C. Both periods are in serious need of further study with regard to what North has called the 'expansion-bearing structures' and also with regard to the beliefs and ideologies of the Romans concerned. Is it really true, as is now so often maintained or assumed, that the major 'discontinuity' in the social and economic history of the Roman Republic occurred about 200 B.C.? Renewed investigation of the economic structure and of the role of war during the preceding centuries is essential. It is apparent that there were important changes during the fifth and fourth centuries, but the nature of these changes remains to be defined. As for the later period, after 70 B.C., some of the important structural questions have scarcely been asked. The imperialism of the 50s and of the 30s needs further discussion, and though light has dawned on the external policies of Augustus, largely thanks to P.A. Brunt and C. M. Wells, a great deal needs to be said about the subsequent period of the principate. Fergus Millar raised some important questions in his article 'Emperors, Frontiers and Foreign Relations, 31 B.C. to A.D. 378' in *Britannia* 13 (1982), 1–23, but there is much to clarify and much to disagree with there. Intensified debate is needed in the light of what has been learned in recent years about the imperialism of the Republic.

Columbia University   WILLIAM V. HARRIS
May 1984

PREFACE

To those scholars who helped me in the writing of this book I offer my warmest thanks. J. F. Gilliam, by arranging an invitation to the Institute for Advanced Study, was largely instrumental in providing an invaluable period of free time; he then tolerated my turning partially away from the intended subject of my research and towards the subject of the present work. Jerzy Linderski has been extraordinarily generous in applying his formidable learning to drafts of the manuscript. M. W. Frederiksen and, in a later phase, M. H. Crawford, Erich S Gruen, and M. I. Finley were also kind enough to read sections of the text and offer me their critical comments. They helped me to strengthen the argument at various points and saved me from some errors of fact; it is not of course to be presumed that they assent to my theories.

I also wish to acknowledge assistance from the research fund created by the late William A. Dunning for the benefit of members of the Columbia History Department.

The subject of this book is important, and I feel no inclination to apologize for writing about it. There have been moments, however, when I wished that fewer people had written about certain topics. To keep the footnotes within reasonable bounds, I have usually avoided mere bibliography and I have expressed many disagreements tacitly or tersely. I hope—probably in vain—that I have not missed anything of importance in the modern work published up to late 1976.

COLUMBIA UNIVERSITY   WILLIAM V. HARRIS
MAY 1977

CONTENTS

Contents

TO ANN SUTHERLAND HARRIS

ABBREVIATIONS

Most of the abbreviations are those of *L'Année Philologique* or are otherwise well known. For full references to modern books whose titles are given in abbreviated form, see the bibliography. The sign [→ Bibl.] has been used in the footnotes to show that the item referred to has been reprinted in a different publication, and that the original pagination is indicated (as it always ought to be) in the reprint; in such cases the citation of the reprint is reserved to the bibliography. In addition the following may be unfamiliar to some readers:

ANRW	H. Temporini (ed.), *Aufstieg und Niedergang der römischen Welt*
CAH	*Cambridge Ancient History*
CIL	*Corpus Inscriptionum Latinarum*
FGrH	F. Jacoby, *Die Fragmente der griechischen Historiker*
FIRA	*Fontes Iuris Romani Anteiustiniani*
HRR²	H. Peter, *Historicorum Romanorum Reliquiae*, vol. i (second edn.)
IG	*Inscriptiones Graecae*
ILLRP	A. Degrassi, *Inscriptiones Latinae Liberae Rei Publicae*
ILS	H. Dessau, *Inscriptiones Latinae Selectae*
Inscr. It.	*Inscriptiones Italiae*
MRR	T. R. S. Broughton, *The Magistrates of the Roman Republic*
OGIS	W. Dittenberger, *Orientis Graeci Inscriptiones Selectae*
OLD	*Oxford Latin Dictionary*
ORF³	H. [= E.] Malcovati, *Oratorum Romanorum Fragmenta* (third edn.)
PL	*Patrologia Latina*
RDGE	R. K. Sherk, *Roman Documents from the Greek East*
RE	Pauly–Wissowa–Kroll (eds.), *Realencyclopädie der klassischen Altertumswissenschaft*
SIG³	W. Dittenberger, *Sylloge Inscriptionum Graecarum* (third edn.)

INTRODUCTION

Historical analysis, not narrative, is the purpose of this book. Roman expansion in the period of the middle Republic has been narrated innumerable times—best of all, in my view, by Gaetano de Sanctis (down to 133). There is scope for further reasoned and scholarly histories of that kind. But all existing narrative accounts are founded on more or less explicit assumptions about Rome's customary behaviour in international affairs, and certain of these assumptions deserve to be questioned. Above all, it is my intention to analyse Roman attitudes and intentions concerning imperial expansion and its essential instrument, war.

Roman behaviour requires explanation. 'No sane man', wrote Polybius, 'goes to war with his neighbours simply for the sake of defeating his opponent, just as no sane man goes to sea merely to get to the other side, or even takes up a technical skill simply for the sake of knowledge. All actions are undertaken for the sake of the consequent pleasure, good, or advantage.'[1] He was thinking of the Romans' expansion. In the surviving part of his work, unfortunately, we have no discussion of their real purposes. They felt the ambition to expand, he believed; but the text does not explain why they felt it, or why so strongly, or why for so long a period. For various reasons the historian might have failed to answer these questions in ways which would satisfy us, but at least he saw the need for investigation.

The Athenians at Melos in 416 are made by Thucydides to say that 'of the gods we believe, and of men we know for certain, that by a necessary law of nature they always rule where they can.'[2] From this it seems to follow that every major state is unvaryingly imperialistic in its behaviour, and hence that there is no need for an investigation of the mentality of particular imperialists. Polybius did not, I think, regard that as a satisfactory premiss for writing political history (nor, for that matter, did Thucydides).[3] The theory was taken up by Hobbes and it sometimes reappears in modern works; according to A. J. P. Taylor's phrase, 'Powers will be Powers.' But the appeal of the 'Thucydidean' generalization is deceptive. In real international politics it is seldom that a state simply chooses to extend its power by effortless fiat. It must

---

[1] iii. 4.10–11.   [2] v. 105.2.   [3] Cf. below, p. 111.

exert itself to establish its claim to power, it must pay costs and make sacrifices. States vary widely in their willingness to exert themselves for the extension and maintenance of power. This can easily be seen both in the ancient and in the modern world. To take examples from ancient history, there is an obvious contrast between Rome of the second century B.C. and Rome after Augustus. We could also compare, for example, the attitudes of (on the one side) Athens between 479 and 411, Macedon for most of the period from Philip II to Philip V, or Mithridates VI of Pontus, and those of (on the other side) the Athens of Demosthenes, the Etruscan republics of the fourth century, or Carthage for most, but perhaps not all, of the last 200 years of its independent history. It would, however, be hard to find other ancient states as willing as Rome apparently was during the middle Republic to tolerate the casualties and hardships of imperial expansion for such a prolonged period.

During this period Rome went to war almost every year, and for most of the period the extent of the citizens' involvement in war was extremely wide. Yet historians have seldom asked, and never systematically answered, what should be the first major question: what were the attitudes of the Romans towards the phenomenon of war? In answering this question, we shall naturally give a large share of our attention to the aristocrats who in the main determined the policy of the Roman state. The attitudes of ordinary citizens were not insignificant, however, and they will also be examined. At neither social level is the answer immediately revealed by direct evidence. The Romans' regular warfare grew out of and was supported by the social ethos, above all by the ideology of glory and good repute. But this social ethos was no accidental growth, and in order to comprehend it we shall have to investigate the full range of functions which war served within the Roman state.

The advantages which the Romans, the aristocrats above all, derived from war, and from the expansion of power which resulted from successful war, deserve to be explored in their complex detail. It is an extraordinary fact that no scholar has seriously tried to gauge the significance of glory for the history of Roman imperialism. Even in the case of the economic benefits of war and expansion, many brief and dogmatic views have been uttered, but organized scholarly investigations of the general question are very few. And in discussions of the economic motives for Roman imperialism it has been almost standard practice to dress up one's political feelings as history and to pass over the counter-arguments of other scholars. The entire matter will be treated in chapter II.

Presented with the evidence for the multifarious benefits of war and expansion, some historians will respond by claiming that, whatever the effects of Roman policies, the Romans had in general no desire to expand their power, certainly not on any conscious plane. In truth the occasions for articulating such a general desire were probably not numerous, a common attitude being assumed among Romans. And the limitations of our source material are in this respect severe. None the less the desire was there: Polybius reported it correctly (contrary to some recent opinion), and other evidence, virtually ignored by modern narrators of Roman expansion, is to be found in appropriate sources. The entire problem will be examined in chapter III.

The view just outlined appears to conflict with the virtually unanimous opinion of scholars that the Roman Senate attempted to avoid the actual annexation of territory. This is held to have been a principle of the Senate's foreign policy through much or all of the middle Republic. In fact the supposed principle would not have conflicted at all directly with the Romans' desire to expand their empire, since they saw the empire as consisting not of the annexed provinces but of all the territory over which Rome exercised power. In any case the 'principle' of non-annexation turns out on a renewed examination (which is undertaken in chapter IV) to be largely imaginary. Many of the occasions when it is supposed to have operated were not in fact ready opportunities for the annexation of new provinces. Even on the very few occasions when the Senate did voluntarily decline to annex, the reasons can easily be found in straightforward calculations of Roman interest. Existing theories designed to explain non-annexation are largely misguided. The one period in which Rome's failure to annex territory more quickly requires a somewhat complex explanation is one in which, according to many historians, the 'principle of non-annexation' had been discarded for decades—namely the years from the 90s onwards when the opportunities to annex Cyrene, and later Egypt, were long neglected.

No over-all theory about the Roman imperialism of the middle Republic has received as much support from historians as the theory of 'defensive imperialism'. Briefly described, this is the theory that the Romans generally fought their wars because of what they perceived—correctly or incorrectly—as threats to their own security. The validity of this interpretation will be examined in the last chapter of this book, which will consequently contain a survey, mainly in chronological order, of the origins of the wars which Rome fought in the middle-republican period. It will also have to include, by way of prelude, discussions of the fetial law and its significance and of the changing meaning of the 'just war'. In this chapter I shall reduce the importance of 'defensive imperialism' to its proper level, thus making room for the other factors in Rome's drive to expand which I shall have described in chapters I and II.

Three important preliminaries remain. As to the word 'imperialism', its use in this context should need no defence. It is current usage, and its meaning is reasonably clear. We can define it as the behaviour by which a state or people takes and retains supreme power over other states or peoples or lands.[1] Attempts to define it more narrowly, for example as a phenomenon which occurs exclusively as a result of capitalism, are now entirely futile, at least in the English-speaking world. This is in the first place a matter of language, not of politics. Usage is meaning. Writers who artificially redefine imperialism as such-and-such, prove to their own satisfaction that Rome's expansion was not a case of such-and-such, and therefore was not imperialism,[2] have proved only what all Roman historians have long known, that Roman imperialism was not identical with any imperialism of the nineteenth or twentieth centuries. In fact the term is, despite its vagueness, indispensable.

The phase of Roman imperialism which I have chosen to

[1] A definition was recently offered by R. Zevin (*Journal of Economic History* xxxii (1972), 319): 'imperialism is activity on the part of any state which establishes or subsequently exercises and maintains qualified or unqualified rights of sovereignty beyond the previous boundaries within which such rights were exercised.' But the reference to sovereignty is obviously tendentious, and makes the definition inadequate both with regard to some modern imperialisms—and also with regard to Roman imperialism. Substitute the word 'power'.

[2] See, e.g., D. Flach, *HZ* ccxxii (1976), 37–42; R. Werner (*ANRW* i.1.501–63), whom Flach criticizes, was himself unwilling to see any Roman imperialism in 'the East' before 148.

discuss in this work extends from the beginning of the decisive wars against the Italian peoples beyond Latium, i.e. from 327 B.C., down to the year 70 B.C. The opening date is determined partly by events, but chiefly by the qualities of the source material. Meagre though the material is for the period from 327 to 264, some results can be obtained; as we look further away, the distances become gradually murkier. The closing date needs rather more explanation. Again the character of the source material carried weight, and I chose to exclude the very last decades of the Republic partly to avoid adding certain lengthy discussions which would have been necessary, notably concerning Caesar's commentaries. But the date was determined above all by changes in Roman imperialism itself, changes which for the most part took place in the last years of the second century and the early years of the first. These developments will emerge in the pages that follow. In essence, foreign wars and expansion gradually ceased to be the preoccupations of the Roman aristocracy and the citizen body, and became instead the specialized policy of certain 'great men' and their followers. In the interim there was a period, from the 90s down to 73, when the military energies of Rome were taken up with protecting the existing empire against internal and external enemies. Most of my discussion will concern the period before the Social War of 91, though certain themes will carry us down to the years immediately after the death of L. Sulla. Thus the subject is Roman war and imperialism during the period of Italian and Mediterranean expansion.

Finally, some brief comments are required about one particular source problem. This concerns not Polybius or Livy or Ennius or Plautus—what I have to say about them and about other individual writers will appear later. What requires some preliminary comment is the actual accessibility or otherwise of discussions about foreign policy in middle-republican Rome. Much of this book is concerned not with particular crises or decisions, but with more general questions of Roman habits, attitudes, and aims. None the less the validity of the extant evidence about specific situations is a problem which will constantly recur. It is easy to grow over-optimistic in this matter. We know, at least in a general way, what allowances to make for the prejudices of Polybius, Livy, and our other main sources. We know, at least in theory, that all but a few of the speeches inserted into their histories by Livy, Appian, and Cassius Dio are free compositions which are not to be taken as accounts of what was actually said. A difficulty which we underestimate, in my view, is the one which ancient writers themselves encountered in acquiring authentic information about the foreign-policy decisions of the middle Republic. Polybius was quite well placed to reveal the reasoning and the feelings that lay behind Roman foreign policy, at least for the period for which he had living informants. Unfortunately Roman historical writers of the second century (including Fabius Pictor) by and large failed, so it seems, to write adequately on this aspect of Roman history. Most of them were of senatorial rank, hence presumably well informed about the political mechanisms of the Roman state. But they were hindered by patriotism and (in some instances) by incompetence; in any case they were little inclined, as far as we can tell, to try to explain the real roots of Roman policy. The neglect of policy analysis on the part of the annalists evoked a complaint from the historian Sempronius Asellio, writing probably as late as the 90s or 80s.[1] That his complaint was justified seems to be confirmed by the extraordinary absence of convincing arcane information from the preserved fragments of his predecessors. However the obscurity surrounding many foreign-policy decisions was made worse, and made permanent, by the aristocracy itself. It ruled in a quite secretive fashion. Its members had no need to reveal their private opinions to citizens at large. Many matters must always have been virtually settled in private among the leading men of the state. It is worth emphasizing, too, that the past proceedings of the Senate were mostly inaccessible even to historians who lived in the second century and certainly to Livy and his successors. These proceedings were generally not even recorded, let alone published, before Caesar's innovation in 59.[2]

---

[1] Gell. *NA* v. 18.9 (given in a textually unsatisfactory form as fr. 2 in *HRR* i[2]): '... scribere autem, bellum initum quo consule et quo confectum sit et quis triumphans introierit, et eo libro, quae in bello gesta sint, non praedicare autem interea quid senatus decreverit aut quae lex rogatiove lata sit, neque quibus consiliis ea gesta sint, iterare: id fabulas pueris est narrare, non historias scribere.' This is P. K. Marshall's text; for other reconstructions see M. Mazza, *Siculorum Gymnasium* xviii (1965), 144–6.

[2] Suet. *DJ* 20.1: 'primus omnium instituit ut tam senatus quam populi diurna acta confierent et publicarentur' (an implicitly anti-optimate measure). Cic. *Sull.* 40–2 and Plu. *Cat. Min.* 23 confirm that recording the proceedings of the Senate was unusual in the preceding period.

On occasion a magistrate might give instructions for a record to be kept on so-called *tabulae publicae*—but even these were kept in private.[1] Some scholars have supposed that summaries of the opinions which senators expressed in the pre-Caesarian Senate were to be found in accessible records.[2] That is purely wishful thinking. Of speeches made in the second-century Senate and afterwards published, very few seem to have survived into the late Republic, apart from those of Cato (who preserved them by inserting them in the *Origines*). From the third century scarcely an authentic word survived. There was even a degree of confidentiality about the Senate's proceedings, at least on some important occasions. Its decrees must have been recorded from a very early date, and many of them, perhaps all, were made publicly known.[3] In Cicero's time one could consult in *libri* at least those dated from as early as 146.[4] But as to what was said in the Senate, this information was often screened from the outside world.[5] It is perhaps for this reason that Polybius, in the extant sections of his work, preserves not one speech delivered by a senator in the Senate. The third- and second-century Senate was extremely hard for later writers to penetrate.

Polybius did in fact succeed in discovering the substance of some senatorial debates.[6] Paradoxically the Achaean exile was probably the only writer actually read by Livy or later historians who had any good knowledge of what had transpired in the Senate in the part of our period prior to 146. Cato's speeches apart, there was very little for annalists such as Claudius Quadrigarius or Valerius Antias to read which would tell them about a senatorial debate in, say, 200 or 192. The significance of this darkness that envelops the Senate's deliberations will emerge in the following chapters.

[1] Cic. *Sull.* 42 ('more maiorum').
[2] J. E. A. Crake, *Archival Material in Livy, 218–167 B.C.* (diss. Johns Hopkins, 1939), 190, U. Bredehorn, *Senatsakten in der republikanischen Annalistik* (diss. Marburg, 1968), 34 n. 8. H. H. Scullard, *Roman Politics*, 251, supposed that records of the Senate's proceedings in the period 220–150 may have been transmitted into the historical tradition.
[3] R. K. Sherk, *RDGE* 4–10.
[4] Cic. *Att.* xiii. 33.3.
[5] See Additional Note 1.
[6] Cf. P. Pédech, *La Méthode historique de Polybe*, 272.

I

ROMAN ATTITUDES TOWARDS WAR

SINCE the Romans acquired their empire largely by fighting, we should investigate the history of their attitudes towards war.[1] When they went to war, did they for example have to overcome strong feelings of reluctance or hesitation in some or all sections of their society? Did they dislike war and find it a burdensome interruption of their ordinary lives? Or, again for example, did they, all or many of them, regard it as a normal and regular activity? Did they perhaps regard it as not only necessary but desirable, an opportunity to gain individual and collective advantages and to fulfil the most important moral imperatives? And further, how did their attitudes change, as they can hardly have failed to, during this 250-year period in which the medium-sized, quite vulnerable state acquired its enormous empire, its incontestable power, and its layer of Greek sophistication? Some parts of the answers to these questions will be reserved to later chapters. In this one I shall describe what I believe can be learned from the evidence that bears directly on the question of Roman attitudes towards war in general.

The Roman state made war every year, except in the most abnormal circumstances. At the beginning of our period the Romans mobilized their army every spring and went to war with one or more of the neighbouring states. There was an almost biological necessity about the event, as Nicolet has written.[2] An annual event of such importance was naturally reflected in the religious calendar of the state—hence the rites of the Equirria, Quinquatrus, and Tubilustrium at dates from 27 February to 23 March, and on 15 and 19 October those of the Equus October and the Armilustrium.[3] Annual rites of this kind are rare

---

[1] On the importance of a predisposition towards war cf. G. Bouthoul, *Traité de sociologie. Les guerres: éléments de polémologie* (Paris, 1951), 442–3.

[2] C. Nicolet in J.-P. Brisson (ed.), *Problèmes de la guerre à Rome*, 117.

[3] The facts are summarized by K. Latte, *Römische Religionsgeschichte*, 114–21. On the Equus October cf. also H. S. Versnel, *Triumphus* (Leiden, 1970), 373. The origins of these rites are in dispute (cf. U. W. Scholz, *Studien zum altitalischen und altrömischen Marskult und Marsmythos* (Heidelberg, 1970)).

elsewhere.[1] During the first eighty-six years from 327 onwards
there were, as far as can be seen from defective sources, at most
four or five years without war.[2] It was probably in 241 that the
doors of the temple of Janus were closed for the first time after a
very long interval,[3] to be opened again almost at once because of
the rebellion of the Falisci; then, as far as we know, 240 and 239
passed without campaigns, understandably after the exhausting
efforts of the war against Carthage.[4] 227 and 226 may possibly
have been years of peace.[5] However, while the seasonal character
of Roman warfare declined in the third century, particularly
after 218, war continued to be an utterly normal feature of
Roman public life. It is unlikely that Rome was again at peace for
a whole year in all theatres until 157, in which year, Polybius
says, the Senate decided to make war against the Dalmatians,
one of its reasons being that it did not want the people to be
enervated by a lengthy peace—it was the twelfth year since the
battle of Pydna.[6] Another generation elapsed before there were
further years of peace, 128, 127, and 116. Of course these wars
varied greatly in their importance to the Romans in the sense that
far greater issues were on trial on some occasions than on others,
but we should not assume that campaigns against Spanish and
Ligurian peoples lacked seriousness for the Romans who were
involved in them. In the first century foreign wars were almost as
regular, but their direct importance to Roman citizens was
usually less, and Cicero was describing a true characteristic of the
middle Republic when he referred to the time of the *maiores* as one
in which 'semper . . . fere bella gerebantur'.[7]

I. THE ARISTOCRACY AND WAR[8]

Warfare bulked large among the formative adolescent and adult
experiences of the Roman aristocrat until very late in the second
century, and he expected leadership in war to be the most

---

[1] For the spring lustration of the Macedonian army, still in use in 182, cf. F. W.
Walbank, *Philip V of Macedon* (Cambridge, 1940), 246 n. 5.

[2] See Additional Note II.   [3] On the date, see p. 190.

[4] Cf. Polyb. i. 62.7, A. Lippold, *Consules*, 122.

[5] Cf. p. 198. On the year 220: p. 199.

[6] xxxii. 13.6–8.   [7] *De off.* ii. 45.

[8] By 'aristocracy' I intend to refer not to the *nobilitas* but to the wider group of those who
were members of the Senate or were closely related to senators. This is not to deny the
disproportionate power of certain members of the aristocracy or the significance of the

important activity of his consulship, should he succeed in rising to the highest office in the state. Success in war was by far the most glorious kind of achievement by which he could demonstrate his prowess, and there were strong imperatives that urged him to pursue this success. Among other imperatives, it was often in his economic interest to favour a war-policy, and the importance of this factor—considerable, but not I think predominant—will be assessed in chapter II. The first task is to investigate the social ethos in its relationship to war.

No one can hold a political office at Rome, Polybius reports, before he has completed ten annual military campaigns.[1] Mommsen doubted whether this regulation was in effect even as far back as 214,[2] but his argument was faulty,[3] and even if he was right many seasons of military service were clearly required of virtually all candidates for political office throughout the middle Republic.[4] Mommsen and some others have also argued that the future politician merely had to complete the ten-year liability period of the *eques*,[5] which can seldom have resulted in ten years'

distinction between the *ordo equester* (to which all aristocrats belonged until the *plebiscitum reddendorum equorum* of the Gracchan period) and the rest of the citizen body.

[1] vi. 19.4: πολιτικὴν δὲ λαβεῖν ἀρχὴν οὐκ ἔξεστιν οὐδενὶ πρότερον, ἐὰν μὴ δέκα στρατείας ἐνιαυσίους ᾖ τετελεκώς.

[2] T. Mommsen, *R. Staatsrecht*, i[3]. 505 (he thought that it was part of the *Lex Villia* of 180, cf. i[3]. 565, 567). P. Fraccaro (in P. Ciapessoni (ed.), *Per il XIV Centenario della codificazione giustinianea* (Pavia, 1934), 486 [→ Bibl.]), suggested that it was introduced shortly after the Hannibalic War. The rule was not yet in force in 214, according to B. Kübler, *RE* s.v. magistratus (1928), col. 414, A. E. Astin, *The Lex Annalis before Sulla* (Brussels, 1958), 45 n. 1.

[3] It rests on Liv. xxv. 2.6–7, where Scipio Africanus' candidacy for the aedileship of 213 is said to have been opposed by the tribunes 'quod nondum ad petendum legitima aetas esset' (the tribunes later desisted, and he was elected), opposition unmentioned in Polyb. x. 4–5. If Polybius' rule had existed, it is argued, it would have been invoked against Africanus and mentioned by Livy. However Liv. xl. 44.1 states explicitly that there were no *legitimae aetates* before 180, and it is probable that the words quoted from xxv. 2 are an anachronism, resulting perhaps from the fact that *legitimae aetates*, but not ten military campaigns, were a familiar requirement in the first century. The actual objection may have been that Scipio's military service was still insufficient (cf. D. C. Earl, *Tiberius Gracchus, a Study in Politics* (Brussels, 1963), 57 n. 1). For the possibility that Liv. xxv. 2.6–7 was influenced by the more famous case in which Scipio Aemilianus broke the law in the consular election for 147 cf. Astin, l.c. In any case since there were so many irregularities in the magistracies during the Hannibalic War, the Africanus incident hardly shows that the rule had not yet been devised (cf. G. Rögler, *Klio* xl (1962), 78).

[4] A radical innovation in this respect in the early second century would be inexplicable.

[5] Mommsen, o.c. i[3]. 506 (followed by M. Gelzer, *Roman Nobility*, 7 (= *KS* i. 22 [→ Bibl.]), G. De Sanctis, *SR* iv. 1. 510; cf. A. Afzelius, *C & M* viii (1946), 276; against Mommsen's view: B. Kübler, l.c., and others—but refutation came only from Fraccaro, o.c. 487). Mommsen's argument was that it would have been absurd to give a consul the

real service; but more probably he did in truth have to serve in ten campaigns.[1] This admittedly is not established by the fact that some future office-holders did serve in ten campaigns, but we have no reason to give Polybius' words any meaning other than their obvious one; and it is significant that in the only statutory statement known to us of an obligation to military service as a qualification for office, in the *Tabula Heracleensis*, it is specified that the candidate (for local office) can only fulfil the requirement of service in any given year if he spends at least half the year in camp or in a province.[2] The season's experience was not always a severe one even in the second century, for one might spend one's time in what was in effect a garrison army. But with the exception of Scipio Africanus in 214, no one is certainly known to have run for office (the military tribunate aside) without ten years' military service behind him until Cicero ran for the quaestorship in 76.[3] The rule had lapsed a generation or so earlier,[4] but among Cicero's contemporaries most candidates for office had probably still done some military service. Under the traditional system exemptions were few, even if they were wanted.[5] Thus the normality of warfare in the experience of the candidate for office is well established: most of these young men had taken part in active warfare annually during a long sequence of years, beginning in, or somewhat before, the eighteenth year.[6]

opportunity to impede a citizen's political career by refusing to enlist him; but such an attempt is only likely to have been made in a case of extreme *inimicitia*.

[1] The statement of C. Gracchus, cited by Plutarch (*CG* 2), that he had served for twelve years, τῶν ἄλλων δέκα στρατευομένων ἐν ἀνάγκαις, can be interpreted in different ways and does not help here (cf. Astin, o.c. 42 n. 1).

[2] *FIRA* (ed. Riccobono), i, no. 13, lines 89–92, 98–102 (three years of cavalry service or six years of infantry service). Mommsen (o.c. i³. 506 n. 1) noted this point but failed to explain it. Cf. Fraccaro, o.c. 487.

[3] On supposed earlier cases see Additional Note III.

[4] If the rule had not well and truly lapsed, an ambitious *novus homo* like Cicero could hardly have afforded to evade it (though even he did some service: M. Gelzer, *Cicero, ein biographischer Versuch* (Wiesbaden, 1969), 5–6). Afzelius (o.c. 277–8) suggested that Sulla abolished the requirement, but a less formal change (as well as an earlier one) is more likely (cf. R. E. Smith, *Phoenix* xiv (1960), 11 n. 65). C. Nicolet (in J.-P. Brisson (ed.), *Problèmes de la guerre à Rome*, 128–9) points out the case of Pompey, who was asked by the censors of 70, as he gave up the *equus publicus*, whether he had performed the required military service (Plu. *Pomp.* 22, Zonar. x. 2).

[5] Cf. below, p. 37.

[6] The exact age is of significance, not least because we can assume that the lower the age at which the young aristocrat began military service, the greater its importance in forming his personality. For the seventeenth birthday as the beginning of the period of obligation

During this military service the man with a political future before him would usually rise either by election or by selection to the office of military tribune. Since there were only six in each legion and they often found themselves commanding separate detachments, the post was a highly responsible one.[1] It was almost closed to soldiers who were not already members of the equestrian order, as far as we can see,[2] and it was thus among other things a mark of rank. For most of our period it was probably a normal part of the successful young aristocrat's career. The clearest evidence of this is provided by the career inscriptions (epitaphs and *elogia*) that refer to this period.[3] The military tribunate was perhaps losing some of its appeal by 151,[4] but most aristocrats probably continued to seek it as long as they undertook prolonged military service. For complex reasons, of which I shall say more later, this service became less attractive to them during the second half of the second century, and the tribunate must have become a less regular feature of the career. The latter trend was probably hastened by changes in military organization carried out by Marius and P. Rutilius Rufus in 107–105.[5] However, having held the tribunate, most senators of the

see Gellius, *NA* x. 28, Liv. xxv. 5.8, xxvii. 11.15. P. A. Brunt, *Italian Manpower*, 16 n. 7, 399 n. 3, makes an odd mistake over this. Service before the seventeenth birthday was performed in crises (cf. Liv. xxv. 5.8), and since we happen to know that it was performed by both Ti. and C. Gracchus (Fraccaro, o.c. 481–3), it was probably common for the sons of aristocratic families in their time (Fraccaro, ibid.). Whether such service counted towards the *decem stipendia* need not be settled here.

[1] This is emphasized by the requirement that of the twenty-four elected tribunes of Polybius' time, fourteen had to have performed five years' service, the other ten ten years' service (Polyb. vi. 19.1). E. Badian (*JRS* lxi (1971), 108) apparently holds that this regulation was established after the Hannibalic War, but it is much more likely to date from the time when these twenty-four tribunes were the full complement of a normal year, i.e. before the Hannibalic War, and it may well be as old as the elective tribunate itself. On the duties of the military tribunes: J. Suolahti, *The Junior Officers of the Roman Army in the Republican Period* (Helsinki, 1955), 43–51.

[2] Gelzer, *Roman Nobility*, 4–5 (= *KS* i. 20–1), R. Syme, *JRS* xxvii (1937), 128, but there were exceptions—cf. Nicolet, o.c. 147–8.

[3] *ILLRP* 313, 316, *ILS* 48, 49, 54, 56, 57, 60 (cf. 59). The only inscriptions that give full careers, but omit to mention the military tribunate are *ILLRP* 309, 310 (Scipionic epitaphs), and *ILS* 45; but the Scipionic epitaphs only mention sub-aedilician offices if the subjects failed to reach the consulship. *ILS* 45 lists the offices of C. Claudius Pulcher (*cos.* 92: on his identity see *CIL* i². 1. p. 200), apparently beginning 'q. iiivir a.a.a.f.f.'. The date for his military tribunate, which he probably dispensed with, would have been c. 110–105, and by this date the custom may well have disappeared.   [4] See below, p. 36.

[5] Cic. *Planc.* 52 seems to treat it as having been an ordinary step in the career in the last decade of the second century, without showing that it was a requirement. T. P. Wiseman,

middle Republic had had experience of military command in the field.

Until late in our period the most serious schooling the young aristocrat experienced from the age of seventeen was in warfare and military command.[1] Naturally he acquired some knowledge of oratory and law, but it is unlikely that these were fields of study that took much of the time of such men until the second half of the second century. The opportunities for the serious study of oratory were still limited, and the Senate's attitude is shown by its decision to exclude *rhetores*, as well as philosophers, from Rome in 161[2]—though this also shows that there were some to expel. A fair knowledge of Greek was apparently a common accomplishment among aristocrats of Scipio Aemilianus' generation,[3] but educated skill in oratory was quite slow in appearing, in spite of the subject's usefulness. Even according to the kindly judgement of Cicero, Ser. Sulpicius Galba (*cos.* 144) was the first real orator at Rome, M. Aemilius Lepidus Porcina (*cos.* 137) the first to show strong Greek influence.[4] As late as 92 the censors closed a school which had been opened by *rhetores Latini* in the previous year.[5] Aristocratic specialists in law existed even at the beginning of our period,[6] and legally competent urban praetors seem to have been common in the second century,[7] but there is no definite sign of intensive legal study as a normal activity. As for philosophy, it could have great appeal, as the general reception of Carneades

---

New Men, 145, argues that the decline in the military tribunate can be seen in the Jugurthine war, when the tribunes were partially replaced by legates. For the parts played by Marius and Rutilius in changing the status of the tribunate see Wiseman, ibid.

[1] There is no recognition of this fact in the standard works on Roman education, such as H. I. Marrou, *Histoire de l'éducation dans l'antiquité*[6] (Paris, 1965), M. L. Clarke, *Higher Education in the Ancient World* (London, 1971).

[2] Gellius, *NA* xv. 11.1.

[3] Cf. W. Kroll, *Die Kultur der ciceronischen Zeit* (Leipzig, 1933), ii. 118. Plu. *Aem.* 6 emphasizes the Hellenization of Roman education that took place in Paullus' family between his generation (he was born in the 220s) and that of his sons; on the limits of Aemilianus' Hellenization cf. A. E. Astin, *Scipio Aemilianus*, 15–16.

[4] Cic. *Brut.* 82 (but note §295), 95–6. Later critics did not think much of pre-Ciceronian oratory (cf. A. E. Douglas on *Brut.* 82.1).

[5] One of the censors being the great orator L. Licinius Crassus. The sources for this event: *MRR* ii. 17. The hostility to oratorical training that survived into the 90s is detectable in Cic. *De orat.* ii. 1.

[6] A. Watson, *Roman Private Law around 200 B.C.* (Edinburgh, 1971), 7–8. Ti. Coruncanius (*cos.* 280) 'primus profiteri coepit' (*Dig.* 1.2.2. 38, cf. 35), whatever that involved.

[7] J. M. Kelly, *Roman Litigation* (Oxford, 1966), 85–9.

and his fellow-ambassadors in 155 shows,[1] but hardly any young aristocrats spent months, let alone years, in studying the subject. Polybius' poor view of Roman education, formed in the 160s and 150s, is entirely unsurprising.[2] It was not until the generation of Cicero and Caesar that young men went to sojourn in the intellectual centres of the Greek world expressly to improve their education.[3] The gradual and complex change in the upbringing of adolescent aristocrats which is summarized here presumably both reflected and contributed to a decline in their interest in warfare. In the traditional system, however, the aristocrat's training was above all military.

The rising politician often had further experience of war in his quaestorship,[4] sometimes in the praetorship (much more often so after the number of praetorships was increased in 227 and 197), and sometimes also as a *legatus*. Thus it must have been virtually unheard of for a man to approach the consulship without substantial experience of military command until the last years of the second century.

The consulship entailed not only political power and responsibility, but also warfare, and it was there that almost all consuls met their heaviest responsibilities and brightest opportunities. The military command was, in Mommsen's words, the real kernel of the office,[5] and the command was exercised in active campaigns. The importance of the consuls' wars varied greatly, but warfare there was during virtually every year, usually for both consuls. The occasional suggestion in the early books of Livy that it was normal for one of the consuls to spend his year in the city is merely an interesting anachronism on his part.[6] In the historical period Rome's almost continual wars usually involved both consuls, and even in the second century, as long as we have Livy's narrative, we can see that well over three-quarters of all consuls commanded in active warfare—and of those who did not, some were restrained against their will.[7] After 167,

---

[1] Plu. *Cat. Mai.* 22.3—perhaps exaggerating to point the contrast with Cato's hostility.
[2] His opinion is cited in Cic. *De rep.* iv. 3.
[3] Cf. L. W. Daly, *AJPh* lxxi (1950), 40–54.
[4] This was normal for the two consular quaestors as long as it was for the consuls (see below), and common for the 'provincial' quaestors. [5] *R. Staatsrecht*, i³. 116.
[6] See especially Liv. iv. 10.8. C. Nicolet has shown (*REL* xxxviii (1960), 252–63) that these passages are based on first-century, and in fact Ciceronian, ideas.
[7] See Additional Note iv.

when the source-material becomes much less satisfactory, there seems to have been a certain change taking place: though from about 158 the assignment of 'Italia' as one's province gave one little opportunity of going to war, none the less the province seems to have been assigned often. The road-building which such consuls sometimes presided over was usually of military importance, but the consuls of this period were perhaps less enthusiastic about going to war than many of their forefathers. (Certain other factors are relevant to this decrease in military activity, and they will be discussed in due course.) However it continued to be standard for at least one consul to go to war each year,[1] and it is not until 100, politically a most abnormal year, that we can say with confidence that neither consul attempted to go to war with Rome's enemies.[2]

It is conceivable that this experience of war was largely involuntary. To test that hypothesis, the politics of particular wars must be discussed, and this will be done in chapter V. But it is also necessary to test it by examining the direct evidence for the attitudes of Roman aristocrats to war in general. This has not often been attempted. In a famous lecture R. Heinze once argued that the Romans felt no joy in armed struggle, they were never 'kriegslustig', they did not value war as man's finest and highest achievement.[3] These statements were not absolutely mistaken, but as a summary of Roman attitudes they are highly misleading. Polybius was much nearer to the truth when he offered the

[1] 144 is a known exception, when both consuls wanted a Spanish command, but were effectively prevented by Scipio Aemilianus on behalf of his brother Fabius, who was proconsul in Ulterior (Val. Max. vi. 4.2).

[2] These facts have often been ignored: hence, e.g., H. Bengtson states (*Grundriss*[2], 127) that in 171 Rome's leaders knew war only from hearsay, J. Balsdon (*Historia* xxi (1972), 224) that M'. Acilius Glabrio (*cos.* 191) 'had little or no military experience' before his consulship.

[3] *Von den Ursachen der Grösse Roms* (Leipzig, 1921), 27 = *Vom Geist des Römertums*[3] (Stuttgart, 1960), 15 [→ Bibl.]; he was speaking of the period before 202. Two arguments were used: (i) there is absolutely no trace among the Romans of delight in the reckless staking of one's life, man against man—but see below, p. 38; and (ii) the Romans were not fond of hunting, the peacetime counterpart of war. The latter argument is not entirely trivial (cf. Arist. *Pol.* i. 1256^b for θηρευτική as a part of πολεμική), but the facts about early Roman hunting are obscure (the evidence is in J. Aymard, *Essai sur les chasses romaines* (Paris, 1951), 30–41, 54–7), and their significance even more so. Heinze's theme was taken up in a transparently propagandistic article by E. Burck, *Die Antike* xvi (1940), 206–26. According to H. E. Stier, *Roms Aufstieg zur Weltmacht und die griechische Welt* (Cologne–Opladen, 1957), 62–3, the Romans did not glorify war as man's most glorious task; it was merely reality.

generalization that the Romans relied for every purpose on βία, violent force.[1]

Military success was not only highly advantageous to the Roman state, it was of vital importance to the personal aims and interests of many, probably most, Roman aristocrats. It fulfilled definite functions for them within Roman society.[2] Since aristocrats exercised control indirectly, through elections and assemblies, prestige was indispensable to them. Military success allowed them to lay claim to, and to a considerable extent to win, the high esteem of their fellow-citizens—on one level *laus*, on a higher level *gloria*.[3] To explain Roman imperialism in terms of these attributes is of course to agree in part with Sallust, for his account of the growth of the empire makes *cupido gloriae* of central importance.

But it is incredible how much the state grew within a brief period, once freedom had been gained: so great was the desire for glory that had affected men. As soon as the young were old enough for war, they learned the business of soldiering by toiling in armed camp, and they took their pleasure more in fine arms and cavalry horses than in whores and partying. So to men of this kind no toil was unusual, no ground seemed rough or steep, no enemy under arms seemed frightening: courage (*virtus*) had gained complete control. But there was intense competition among them for glory: each one of them hastened to strike down an enemy, to climb the rampart, and to be seen doing such a deed . . .[4]

---

[1] i. 37.7.

[2] J. A. Schumpeter's theory that the fundamental cause of Rome's imperialistic wars in this period lay in the 'class interests' of the aristocracy, which needed a way of creating distractions from internal social problems, is discussed in Additional Note v.

[3] This is the normal distinction between the two terms. According to Cic. *De inv.* ii. 166, 'gloria est frequens de aliquo fama cum laude'. Note also *Phil.* i. 29: 'est autem gloria laus recte factorum magnorumque in rem publicam fama meritorum, quae cum optimi cuiusque, tum etiam multitudinis testimonio comprobatur'; *Planc.* 60; *De off.* ii. 31. But usage is not uniform: cf. *Cat.* iv. 21.

[4] *BC* 7. 3–6. He continues: 'eas divitias, eam bonam famam magnamque nobilitatem putabant. laudis avidi, pecuniae liberales erant; gloriam ingentem, divitias honestas volebant.' But Rome lacked historians to celebrate its achievements, its best citizens preferred 'sua ab aliis bene facta laudari quam ipse aliorum narrare' (8.5). 'Igitur domi militiaeque boni mores colebantur . . . cives cum civibus de virtute certabant . . .' (9. 1–2). 'Sed ubi labore atque iustitia res publica crevit, reges magni bello domiti, nationes ferae et populi ingentes vi subacti, Carthago aemula imperi Romani ab stirpe interiit' (10.1). For all its faults, this is undoubtedly the most thoughtful analysis of the imperialism of the middle Republic left to us by a Roman writer. In *BJ* 41–2 there is a slight change in his view (cf. E. Koestermann on *BJ* 41. 2): 'nam ante Carthaginem deletam populus et senatus Romanus placide modesteque inter se rem publicam tractabant, neque gloriae neque dominationis certamen inter civis erat.' Here the emphasis is on the new conflict between *plebs* and *nobilitas*; evidently what he means is that

Now when he depicts them as dominated by love of glory, Sallust is certainly oversimplifying the Romans of the time before 146,[1] with the result that he underestimates some of the more mundane factors in their drive to expand; yet his understanding of the dynamics of republican imperialism may have been fundamentally correct. He was certainly not alone in thinking that *cupido gloriae* had been a powerful force in the middle Republic.[2] And his theory at least has the advantage that it fits in well with the known facts about the Roman social and political system. The practical importance of *laus* and *gloria* for the history of Roman expansion now needs closer investigation.[3]

One fact that is clear about these attributes[4] is that in the view of the third- and second-century aristocracy the primary means of achieving them was by success in war.

It is true that there were other sources of *laus* and even of *gloria*. Cato went so far as to say that *gloria* would come to the man who established enough storage space on his farm to enable him to profit from price-rises,[5] a remark probably intended to jolt the aristocratic reader.[6] Public offices, especially the higher ones, and membership of the Senate in themselves naturally conferred *laus*, as is confirmed, if it needs to be, by the best-preserved funeral *laudatio* of the period, that of L. Caecilius Metellus, who died in 221.[7] Yet office-holding was perhaps more important as an

the *nobiles* did not previously struggle for glory by fighting the *populus* (cf. D. C. Earl, *The Political Thought of Sallust* (Cambridge, 1961), 15).

[1] On the idealization of this period see the important paper of F. Hampl, *HZ* clxxxviii (1959), 497–525 [→ Bibl.].

[2] Cf. Cic. *De rep.* v. 7.9.

[3] For discussion of desire for glory as a cause of war in primitive societies see H. H. Turney-High, *Primitive War* (Columbia, S.C., 1949), 145–9.

[4] The terms themselves have been analysed by U. Knoche, *Philologus* lxxxix (1934), 102–24 = *Vom Selbstverständnis der Römer* (Heidelberg, 1962), 13–30 [→ Bibl.]; A. D. Leeman, *Gloria, Cicero's Waardering van de Roem en haar Achtergrond in de hellenistische Wijsbegeerte en de Romeinse Samenleving* (diss. Leiden, 1949); H. Drexler, *Helikon* ii (1962), 3–36; J. Hellegouarc'h, *Le Vocabulaire latin des relations et des partis politiques sous la république* (Paris, 1963), 362–88 (inaccurate).

[5] *De agri culti.* iii. 2.

[6] Otherwise interpreted by G. Tibiletti, *Relazioni del X Congresso Internazionale di Scienze Storiche* (Rome, 1955), ii. 241–2.

[7] Plin. *NH* vii. 139–40 gives a summary (reprinted in *ORF*³, pp. 10–11). The whole text will be needed in what follows: 'Q. Metellus in ea oratione quam habuit supremis laudibus patris sui L. Metelli pontificis, bis consulis, dictatoris, magistri equitum, xuiri agris dandis, qui primus elephantos ex primo Punico bello duxit in triumpho, scriptum reliquit decem maximas res optumasque in quibus quaerendis sapientes aetatem exigerent

opportunity for winning *laus* and *gloria* than as a direct source of those attributes.[1] And the other standard sources were clearly less important than military achievement. For young men, one such source was the practice of speaking in aggressive prosecutions, a practice well established in the time of Scipio Aemilianus' youth, and possibly very much earlier;[2] this was evidently a means of establishing a name, not simply a means of carrying on political disputes. Because he did not speak in court, Scipio had the reputation at eighteen of being effete and un-Roman.[3] Among the ten great and excellent things which wise men spent their lives in seeking, according to Metellus' *laudatio*, was skill in oratory, but we should be careful not to attribute more than the correct amount of importance to oratory itself, as distinct from prosecutions and from the opinions the orator uttered, in the early part of our period. Indeed how much fame did Galba or Lepidus Porcina acquire among their contemporaries purely by their oratorical skills? Cicero certainly attests to the *laus* acquired by the orators he so much admires, M. Antonius and L. Licinius Crassus, through their youthful prosecutions,[4] but it may only have been in their generation that a man could first make, and not merely confirm, a great public name very largely by his own skill as an orator. Finally, *gloria* was certainly passed on in part from father to son—an important point which will recur later.

consummasse eum: voluisse enim primarium bellatorem esse, optimum oratorem, fortissimum imperatorem, auspicio suo maximas res geri, maximo honore uti, summa sapientia esse, summum senatorem haberi, pecuniam magnam bono modo invenire, multos liberos relinquere et clarissimum in civitate esse: haec contigisse ei nec ulli alii post Romam conditam.' On the capital importance of this text for understanding the *nobiles* see A. Lippold, *Consules*, 76–7. Other *laudatio*-like texts mentioning public offices are cited below, p. 20 n. 4.

[1] It is noticeable that the first-century texts cited by Hellegouarc'h, o.c. 366 n. 14, to show that *laus* came from office-holding do not amount to very much. *Gloria* had been achieved by scarcely a tenth of the 800 men who had held the consulship, according to Cic. *Planc.* 60.

[2] On Scipio's time, Polyb. xxxi. 29.8–12. Other evidence on this practice includes Cic. *De off.* ii. 47, 49 ('multique in nostra republica adulescentes et apud iudices et apud populum et apud senatum dicendo laudem assecuti sint, maxima est admiratio in iudiciis', etc.), Apul. *Apol.* 66.4 (referring to a case of 112 B.C. as an example). The best evidence for the time before Aemilianus is Plaut. *Trin.* 651; cf. also (though there are anachronisms) Liv. xxii. 26.1–2 (C. Terentius Varro), Plu. *Cat. Mai.* 3.3, *Aem.* 2.4 (?). The combative aspect of this practice is significant for an understanding of young Roman aristocrats.

[3] Polyb. xxxi. 23.11.

[4] *De off.* ii. 47–9, *Brut.* 159.

Through most of our period, however, military achievements were the pre-eminent source of *laus* and *gloria*.[1] This is how one could reach the greatest distinction, and for most young aristocrats warfare provided the accessible path to high reputation. ἀνδρεία, courage, is important in every state, but especially at Rome, says Polybius,[2] and no doubt he was aware of the emphasis which the Romans placed on *virtus*. *Virtus*, as early as we can trace its meaning, is quite a general term, but it very commonly means 'courage' in middle-republican Latin.[3] Hence it was of course in war that a man had many of the readiest opportunities to demonstrate *virtus*. The primacy of military achievements is reasonably clear in Metellus' *laudatio*,[4] and most of the monumental inscriptions to be seen in middle-republican Rome either exclusively concerned feats of war or heavily emphasized them. They commemorated dedications of temples and altars, which usually resulted from victories, or they commemorated triumphs or dedications out of booty; or they were affixed to prominent monuments such as the column of C. Maenius (the victorious consul of 338) or the *columnae rostratae* of C. Duillius (*cos.* 260) and M. Aemilius Paullus (*cos.* 255), or the triumphal arches which began to appear in the second century, or the statues of famous Romans in the forum. The paintings prominently displayed in public buildings in the city in this period celebrated military victories or were at least the plunder of war.[5] Almost wherever one looked in public areas one could see

---

[1] This fact is regularly neglected even by those who explicitly recognize the importance of fame to Roman aristocrats (e.g. D. C. Earl, *The Moral and Political Tradition of Rome* (London, 1967), 35).

[2] xxxi. 29.1. It is of interest that according to Polybius (29.9) Scipio Aemilianus won a surpassing reputation by his exploits in the hunting field, probably an exaggeration in favour of his hero (A. E. Astin, *Scipio Aemilianus*, 27) and his own favourite pastime. M. Gelzer (*Roman Nobility*, 83 = *KS* i. 87 [→Bibl.]) significantly blurs the role of ἀνδρεία in Aemilianus' reputation.

[3] The collection of material in A. N. Van Omme, '*Virtus*', *een semantiese Studie* (diss. Utrecht, n.d. [1947?]), 37–49, has been superseded by that of W. Eisenhut, *Virtus Romana* (Munich, 1973), 23–43, 208–11. However the latter seriously underestimates the 'courage' component in the meaning of *virtus* in this period; in Plaut. *Capt*, 410, *Cas.* 88, *Cist.* 198, *Pseud.* 581, e.g., 'courage' or 'valour' is the appropriate meaning (otherwise Eisenhut, 26–8).

[4] See also the *laudatio*-like text in Liv. xxx. 1.4–6 (on which cf. F. Münzer, *Römische Adelsparteien*, 190 n. 1). There is no mention of such achievements in the *laudatio*-like praise of P. Licinius Crassus Dives Mucianus (*cos.* 131) given by Sempronius Asellio in Gellius, *NA* i. 13.10 (= *HRR*² fr. 8), understandably in view of the manner of his death.

[5] For a survey of this evidence see Additional Note VI.

claims to glory put forward by aristocrats, and most of the claims were based on success in war. For example, from the *comitium*, the physical hub of political life, one could by the mid-third century see, among the monuments close by, the *rostra* with the beaks of the Antiate ships captured in 338, the columns of Duillius and Maenius, and the Curia Hostilia decorated with a battle-painting showing M'. Valerius Maximus Messala (*cos*. 263) defeating the Carthaginians and King Hiero. By the late second century the area running from the Circus Flaminius to the Forum Boarium was crowded with the monuments of victorious generals.

There is plenty of other evidence that the greatest fame stemmed from deeds of war. The significance of the old practice of taking an extra name from the site of one's victory ('Calenus', 'Messala', 'Africanus', and so on) is blurred by the fact that it did not happen very often. The triumph, however, was palpably the supreme moment of the individual Roman's glory. On a more intellectual plane, it is also relevant that in the second century Latin historiography was preoccupied with warfare to a degree which later seemed excessive even to Romans.[1] And to return for a moment to physical objects meant to impress the public, the primacy of military achievements is emphasized by the fact that when, about 137, the *monetales* began the custom of commemorating the deeds of their own ancestors on *denarius* and other types, the majority of the commemorations were military, though this was in a period when the preoccupation of aristocrats with war was beginning to decline.[2]

The central importance of war in the winning of *laus* and *gloria*

---

[1] Sempronius Asellio in Gellius, *NA* v. 18.9 (see above, p. 6 n. 1).

[2] Cf. A. Alföldi, *Essays in Roman Coinage Presented to Harold Mattingly* (Oxford, 1956), 72–4, M. H. Crawford, *RRC* 728–9 (commenting on the prevalence of victory themes in the coin-types of 136–124), and on the function of the coin-types, Wiseman, o.c. 4. Earlier types commonly of course had military motifs, but without reference to the moneyer's family (and such types continued to be issued). Certain or probable military commemorations: Crawford nos. 239/1, 247/2–3, 262/1 (the figure on the reverse is not Pax; see below, p. 35), 263, 264/1, 267/1, 269, 273/1, 281/1 (this type is to be understood as a reference to P. Furius Philus, *cos*. 223, who triumphed over the Gauls and Ligurians), 282 (?), 286, 290/1 (?), 291/1 (civilian also), 293/1, 295/1, 297/1 (presumably referring to a victor's building), 305/1, 314/1, 319/1. Civilian commemorations: 242/1, 243/1, 245/1 (but with Victory), 266/1, 270/1 (with Victory), 292/1, 301/1. (I omit some mixed types.) An added reason for caution in interpreting this evidence is that one of the purposes of minting coins was to pay soldiers.

is still evident from the first-century sources. Greater intellectual sophistication brought wider concepts of fame, as Sallust's prefaces demonstrate.[1] However even in his philosophical writings Cicero sometimes reveals the traditional Roman attitude. The three great things that a man can do are 'to make a practice of defending lawsuits, to guide the people at the political meetings, and to wage war',[2] but though he himself resists the idea, very many (*plerique*) hold that 'the affairs of war are more important than those of the city'. He sets out to disprove this, but his Roman counter-examples strikingly fail to show that civilian successes could bestow more fame than military ones, even in his time.[3] In other philosophical and rhetorical works he admits that military achievements are the pre-eminent source of fame at Rome, the most glorious of the three standard aristocratic occupations (the others being jurisprudence and oratory). 'For who would not put the *imperator* before the *orator* in any ranking of the skills of illustrious men as judged by the usefulness or greatness of their achievements?'[4] In his political rhetoric the normal standards of Roman citizens are naturally clearer. The

---

[1] *BC* 3.1–2, *BJ* 1.1–4.8. For further evidence see Knoche, o.c. 119–20 (= *Vom Selbstverständnis der Römer*, 27).

[2] *De off.* i. 121.

[3] *De off.* i. 74, 76–8. Among the Greeks Solon can be set against Themistocles, Lycurgus against Pausanias and Lysander. 'Mihi quidem neque pueris nobis M. Scaurus C. Mario neque, cum versaremur in re publica, Q. Catulus Cn. Pompeio cedere videbatur; parvi enim sunt foris arma, nisi est consilium domi, nec plus Africanus, singularis et vir et imperator in exscindenda Numantia rei publicae profuit quam eodem tempore P. Nasica privatus, cum Ti. Gracchum interemit.' The list culminates in the glorification of the *domesticae fortitudines* of 63. With these final partisan items cf. *Mil.* 34, 72. Obviously there were those who thought that in these disputes fame belonged to the other side; but in any case violent acts in domestic politics were not a regular source of *laus* or *gloria* in the pre-Sullan period.

[4] *De orat.* i. 7 (the traditional hierarchy of values, C. Nicolet, *REL* xxxviii (1960), 248 n. 2). Cf. *De off.* ii. 45: 'prima est igitur adulescenti commendatio ad gloriam, si qua ex bellicis comparari potest . . .' (consciously parading the traditional view; cf. H. Roloff, *Maiores bei Cicero* (diss. Göttingen, 1938), 97, G. B. Philipp, *Das Gymnasium* lxii (1955), 68). Cf. *De off.* ii. 26: in the pre-Sullan Republic 'nostri . . . magistratus imperatoresque ex hac una re maximam laudem capere studebant, si provincias, si socios aequitate et fide defendissent.' *Tusc. Disp.* i. 109–110: 'Sed profecto mors tum aequissimo animo oppetitur, cum suis se laudibus vita occidens consolari potest . . .' etc., 'etsi enim nihil habet in se gloria cur expetatur, tamen virtutem tamquam umbra sequitur. verum . . .' etc.; then follows the list of the most glorious Romans: Curius, Fabricius, Caiatinus, the two Scipios, the two Africani, Fabius Maximus, Marcellus, Paullus, Cato, Laelius. All except Cato qualified primarily by military success. Numerous other passages in the philosophical works that set *gloria* in its military context are listed by Drexler, o.c. 12.

truly famous men of the past, whose names are invoked on suitable occasions, are almost all victorious dictators and consuls, Camillus, M'. Curius, C. Fabricius, C. Duillius, Caiatinus, the Scipios, Fabius Maximus, Marcellus, Paullus, and Marius[1]—just as the *gloria* of the Roman people was said to be the greatest in *res militaris*.[2] When he argues in favour of the primacy of military achievements in the *Pro Murena*,[3] Cicero is of course making a case for his client, but the claim could carry conviction, and it would have been impossible to argue that jurisconsults or even orators had such a claim to *gloria*. Most peoples admittedly have their military heroes, but there is a definite uniformity about the great men of Rome: most of them scored spectacular victories in war.

The vital importance to Roman aristocrats of the pursuit of *laus* and *gloria* must be brought out in full. The Roman state, says Polybius, takes pains to turn out men capable of enduring everything for the sake of getting, in their own country, τῆς ἐπ᾽ ἀρετῇ φήμης, the good repute that goes with valour.[4] The point is illustrated with a detailed description of the aristocrat's elaborate and impressive funeral-rites. He clearly believed that his generalization had long been true in the past, and it should be noted that while he saw the period after the battle of Pydna as one in which young Romans, Aemilianus excepted, discarded self-restraint, σωφροσύνη, he does *not* say that the Romans in general were ceasing to value courage, ἀνδρεία.[5] Perhaps also Polybian in origin is the comment of Diodorus in the context of 167: among the Romans the most distinguished men can be seen competing with each other for fame; in other states men are jealous of one

---

[1] Such lists are common (cf. previous n. and H. Schoenberger, *Beispiele aus der Geschichte, ein rhetorisches Kunstmittel in Ciceros Reden* (diss. Erlangen, 1910), 15–18): note especially *Cat.* iv. 21 (a list of those who have achieved the greatest *laus*—Africanus, Aemilianus, Paullus, Marius—and Pompey), *Planc.* 60 (the consuls who have achieved great *gloria*—Curius, Fabricius, Duillius, Caiatinus, Cn. and P. Scipio, Africanus, Marcellus, Fabius), *Pis.* 58 (but this is specifically a list of great *triumphatores*), *Balb.* 40. Cic. *Sest.* 143 adds some 'domestic' notables to the list: Brutus, Ahala, 'Lentulus' (i.e. P. Lentulus, *cos. suff.* 162, who achieved fame and exile as an opponent of C. Gracchus), and 'Aemilius' (i.e. M. Aemilius Scaurus, *cens.* 109)—the last three representing a specialized taste in heroes.

[2] *Leg. Man.* 6.

[3] *Mur.* 19–30. Cf. Nicolet, o.c. 248–51.

[4] Polyb. vi. 52.11: ... τῆς τοῦ πολιτεύματος σπουδῆς, ἣν ποιεῖται περὶ τὸ τοιούτους ἀποτελεῖν ἄνδρας ὥστε πᾶν ὑπομένειν χάριν τοῦ τυχεῖν ἐν τῇ πατρίδι τῆς ἐπ᾽ ἀρετῇ φήμης.

[5] xxxi. 25, 29.

another, at Rome they praise one another—hence Roman success.[1] From these two passages it seems likely that Polybius explained the success of Roman expansion in part (he knew other factors of course) just as Sallust did.

In the earliest Roman literature *laus*, *gloria*, and related concepts are referred to with striking frequency.[2] Out of their Roman context such Ennian lines as

> nunc est ille dies quom gloria maxima sese
> nobis ostendat, si vivimus sive morimur,

and

> omnes mortales sese laudarier optant,

and the three lines about Fabius Cunctator ending

> ergo postque magisque viri nunc gloria claret

might seem banal.[3] So might a squabble over *gloria* between a dictator and his *magister equitum* set in the year 325 by Fabius Pictor.[4] So might the allusions to fame in the fragments of Cato's writings.[5] But the accumulation of evidence is decisive: good repute and glory were among the things most valued by middle-republican aristocrats.[6]

A single indication of the Roman attitude would be enough, Polybius wrote. This σημεῖον was the aristocratic funeral, at which the deceased was carried into the forum and a relative described his virtues and achievements before the 'whole people'.

---

[1] Diod. xxxi. 6. Cf. Kroll, o.c. i. 45 and n. 3.

[2] Cf. Knoche, o.c. 109–10 (= *Vom Selbstverständnis der Römer*, 19).

[3] *Ann.* 391–2V, 560 (the latter quoted in isolation by Augustine, *Epist.* 231. 3 (*PL* xxxiii. 1023) and *De trin.* xiii. 3.6 (*PL* xlii. 1018), but treated by him as an old Roman sentiment), 370–2 (on the nuances of which cf. A. Lippold, *Consules*, 369). Ennius evidently based his own claim to fame on his glorification of his patrons' ancestors (Cic. *Tusc. Disp.* i. 34).

[4] *FGrH* 809 F15 (= Liv. viii. 30.9).

[5] *ORF*³ frr. 141 and 252 are the most significant. Note also *Origines* fr. 83P, the story of the *tribunus militum* Q. Caedicius (Cato, however, complained that this man had received less *laus* than King Leonidas).

[6] The words given to Alcmena in Plaut. *Amph.* 641–5 also deserve to be quoted here: 'sed hoc me beat/ saltem, quom perduellis vicit et domum laudis revenit:/ id solacio est./ apsit, dum modo laude parta domum recipiat se . . .'—surely the attitude approved by Roman men for a Roman wife (cf. R. Perna, *L'originalità di Plauto* (Bari, 1955) 205–6). There is probably Greek influence here, but that does not make the passage irrelevant. In view of all the other evidence, Livius Andronicus' lines from his *Aiax Mastigophorus*, 'praestatur laus virtuti, sed multo ocius/ verno gelu tabescit' (*Trag.* 16–17W), were clearly unorthodox to a Roman audience.

The historian goes on to describe the *imagines* or wax masks which preserved the appearance of these dead aristocrats, and the ways in which the *imagines* were displayed, including the remarkable custom of using them to parade the apparently living ancestors at later family funerals. The ancestors on parade were all men who had held senior magistracies, many with more or less authentic claims to military fame. There is no need to repeat the details from this well-known Polybian text. It is enough to say that while he leaves unanswered some important questions about what was taking place at these rites (he was no anthropologist), he makes it quite credible that 'the young men are inspired [by them] to endure everything in the public interest, for the sake of achieving the glory that attends good men.'[1]

At one time it was probably also the custom to sing the *laudes* of famous Romans at formal dinners. However the practice cannot be safely invoked in the present context since, to judge from a puzzling statement of Cicero's, Cato apparently reported in the *Origines* that the practice had long since ceased by his time. 'If only there existed the songs praising the deeds of famous men that used to be sung, according to Cato's *Origines*, many centuries before his time by individual guests at banquets.' Yet the tradition that such songs were sung seems strong (part of it was independent of Cato), and it is hard to see how anyone could have known of them if they had really ceased to be sung 'many centuries' before Cato lived.[2]

The most impressive manifestation of the individual's glory

---

[1] Polyb. vi. 53.1–54.3. On the *pompa funebris* see A. Mau, *RE* s.v. Bestattung (1899), cols. 350–5 (with F. Bömer, s.v. pompa (1952), cols. 1980–4). Known *laudatio funebris* texts were collected by F. Vollmer, *Jahrbücher f. class. Philologie*, Supp. xviii (1892), 449–528; see further M. Durry, *Eloge funèbre d'une matrone romaine* (Paris, 1950), XIV–XXI (the recently discovered *laudatio* of Agrippa has not added much to our knowledge of the traditional institution). Polybius might have added to his description of the funeral a mention of the *praeficae*, women who were hired to mourn and sing the *laudes* of the deceased (Varro, *LL* vii. 70, Non. Marc. 92L; in spite of Non. Marc. 212. 25–6L, it is most unlikely that they were hired only for those who had no relatives). It is interesting that the hiring of *praeficae*, in practice in Plautus' time, had evidently died out by the Sullan period (E. Fraenkel, *Elementi plautini*, 20).

[2] Cic. *Brut.* 75. The other sources are *Tusc. Disp.* i.3, iv. 3, Varro, *De vita populi romani*, ii in Non. Marc. 107L (a different account from Cato's), Val. Max. ii. 1.10 and perhaps Hor. *Od.* iv. 15.26–32, Quintil. *Inst.* i. 10.20 (cf. A. Momigliano, *JRS* xlvii (1957), 109–10 = *Secondo contributo alla storia degli studi classici* (Rome, 1960), 79–80). In my view H. Dahlmann, *Zur Ueberlieferung über die 'altrömischen Tafellieder'* (*Abh. Mainz* no. 17 (1950)), fails to discredit the evidence for the existence of the songs.

was of course the triumph. Modern writers on Roman imperialism sometimes treat this phenomenon lightly, which leads to misunderstanding.[1] If he had fought *suis auspiciis* and with sufficient success,[2] and on certain other conditions, the triumphing general, adorned with the attributes of Jupiter and perhaps those of a king, entered the city and moved in procession with his spoils and his army to the temple of Jupiter Capitolinus. In Polybius' words, he brought the actual sight of his achievements before the eyes of his fellow-citizens.[3] Afterwards the exact date of the triumph was recorded in the pontifical annals.[4] Through most of the middle Republic about one consul in three celebrated a triumph, either in his consulship or in his promagistracy. It was not an inaccessible honour like the *spolia opima*, but while it was often awarded for victories of less than world-historical importance, it was not merely commonplace.[5] It was an honour jealously competed for, and one which must have given great psychological rewards as well as political ones.

The first-century sources reflect some changes in attitudes towards fame, but the traditional attitude of aristocrats is still readily discernible. In his philosophical writings Cicero could sometimes deny the value of *gloria*,[6] and there were philosophers (Epicureans above all) who seriously belittled it; but Cicero and

---

[1] E.g. T. Frank, *CAH* viii. 330, with supporting misrepresentations.

[2] The date of the law requiring 5,000 enemy dead is not known; Val. Max. ii. 8.1 attributes it to the *maiores*, but it seems not to have been in force in 180 (Liv. xl. 38.8–9; however 'nullo bello gesto' is probably wrong, cf. Additional Note iv); Oros. v. 4.7 says that it was in force in 143, but his evidence cannot be trusted (cf. R. Combès, *Imperator* (Paris, 1966), 81 n. 25). J. S. Richardson (*JRS* lxv (1975), 61–2) argues that the law was passed soon after 180. The fact that the reality of some victories was disputed (cf. Cato, *ORF*[3] frr. 58, 94, 97) supports the view that senators took triumphs seriously. The difficulties of deciding whether a victory had been adequate increased when armies could not be brought home at the end of each season (cf. Liv. xxxi. 49.9–11).

[3] vi. 15.8.

[4] The calendar dates in the Augustan lists are as authentic as the names; cf. K. J. Beloch, *Römische Geschichte* (Berlin–Leipzig, 1926), 86.

[5] When the slave Chrysalus says in Plaut. *Bacch.* 1072–3 'sed, spectatores, vos nunc ne miremini/ quod non triumpho: pervolgatum est, nil moror', the joke probably refers to a recent group of triumphs (F. Ritschl, *Parerga zu Plautus und Terenz*, i (Leipzig, 1845), 423–7, and others; the alternative explanation offered by E. Fraenkel, *Elementi plautini*, 227, seems less likely); but a joke it is. U. Schlag, *Regnum in Senatu* (Stuttgart, 1968), 17–19, interprets 'pervolgatum est' as a serious verdict on the triumphs of the whole period *c.* 204–184 but her attempt to show that many of the triumphs of 200–191 were undeserved by previous standards rests on mere assertion, as she virtually admits (68).

[6] Philipp, o.c. 66–9, Hellegouarc'h, o.c. 380. In Cic. *Marc.* 25 it is held somewhat inconsistent for a *sapiens* to like *gloriae avidissimus*.

Sallust very frequently mention *laus* and *gloria* as ends obviously desirable to Romans, and the theme was thought suitable not only for rousing speeches to juries and to the people, but also in philosophical and historical monographs and in private letters.[1] This attitude they present in various sophisticated forms, but its essence they inherited from the aristocrats of the second century and earlier.

We must return to the time of the Italian wars of the years between 327 and 264. Were Roman aristocrats already as obsessed with fame as they seem to have been in the second century? Some scholars have claimed that individual achievement was not held to be of much importance at Rome until the second half of the second century, and that before that time there was an age in some sense or other without individualism.[2] Vague though these claims are, they deserve some attention. The element of truth which they contain—the only one—is that aristocrats in the middle Republic generally did observe some moderation in the pursuit of power and recognized that there must be limits to the individual's glory. (One man above all in the middle Republic showed himself reluctant to accept these limits, Scipio Africanus, and he ended his career, partly as a result, in the shadows. Marius was the first to build up the position of the *imperator* in untraditional ways without suffering for it.)[3] But there is nothing else to be said in favour of the view that the struggle for individual fame began only in the second century. An attempt to show that individual fame had no importance in the previous century by means of an analysis of the etymology of *gloria* led nowhere.[4] Even if the etymology were known, it would be

---

[1] Speeches: *Font.* 35, *Leg. Man.* 7, *Arch.* 26 (cf. 14, 29), *Pis.* 57, *Mil.* 97, *Phil.* i. 38, etc. Other genres: *De off.* ii. 45, *Tusc. Disp.* i. 109–10 (both quoted in part in p. 22 n. 4), Sall. *BC* 7.3 (above, p. 17), *BJ* 1.3, 4.5–6, Cic. *Fam.* v. 12, x. 26.3, *QF* i. 1.43–4, etc. See in general Knoche, o.c. 112–14 (= *Vom Selbstverständnis der Römer*, 21–2). Greek influences are of course detectable in both writers (on Sallust cf. P. Perrochat, *Les Modèles grecs de Salluste* (Paris, 1949), 53–4), but it was not from Greeks that they learned the importance of fame.

[2] J. H. Thiel, *De Rol der Persoonlijkheid in de Geschiedenis der romeinsche Republiek* (Groningen–The Hague, 1930), 3–24, with emphasis on the *verbondenheidsbewustzijn* of the aristocracy; Thiel was even led to write (14) that Italy was conquered not only by unknown soldiers and unknown centurions, but by unknown commanders. His theory was accepted by H. Wagenvoort, *Roman Dynamism* (Oxford, 1947), 62, Leeman, o.c. 128, 133; cf. V. Pöschl, *Das Gymnasium* lxiii (1956), 197; *contra*, for the period back to 264, A. Lippold, *Consules*, 84.

[3] On Scipio's persona see (e.g.) Lippold, 278–80, 358–65. On Marius cf. J.-C. Richard, *MEFR* lxxvii (1965), 69–86.   [4] Leeman, o.c. 124–7.

irrelevant, for when the word first appears in Latin its meaning is independent and well developed.

Of course political and social conditions did change between 327 and the mid-second century. At the beginning of the period, when the leading plebeian families were still struggling to establish their claim to a share of political power, the patricians may have emphasized their family trees, even more than later *nobiles*, as the justification for their pretensions to office. However the efforts of the plebeian families to assert themselves, and the need for patrician families to reassert themselves in more competitive times, probably increased Rome's belligerence in the second half of the fourth century. War gave officers opportunities both to win personal distinction and to provide largesse for the soldiers. Intense struggle was still going on between patricians and plebeians in the last years of the Second Samnite War and the early years of the Third: it was only from 306 that the Senate regularly began to vote triumphs for plebeians, and in M'. Curius Dentatus' tribunate (298?) the attempt of an *interrex* to refuse the consular candidacies of plebeians was only overcome with difficulty. Thus in the period of the Italian wars competition between the leading families in the state was already vigorous. Contemporary texts are almost non-existent, but there is scarcely any reason to suppose that the ideology of *gloria* was peculiarly plebeian, and no historian has succeeded in finding any difference between plebeian and patrician aristocrats concerning their attitudes towards war. No one would guess from the earliest Scipionic *elogium*, that of Scipio Barbatus, the consul of 298,[1] that individualism had yet to be invented. And Sallust (or a pseudo-Sallust, it makes no difference) claimed to quote the view of another patrician of the same period, Ap. Claudius Caecus (*cens.* 312): 'fabrum esse suae quemque fortunae'.[2] It could be authentic.

That *laus* and *gloria* were already attributes of great importance in the time of the Italian wars is shown by the existence of the characteristic institutions previously discussed. Most elements of the aristocratic funeral described by Polybius are

---

[1] *ILLRP* 309. However most scholars hold that this text was composed several decades at least after Barbatus' death (F. Coarelli, *DA* vi (1972), 82–97).

[2] *Ep. ad Caes.* i.1.2 (= W. Morel, *FPL*, p. 6). For bibliography on this fragment cf. L. Herrmann, *Hommages à Jean Bayet* (Brussels, 1964), 256–7.

certainly as old as that, notably the *imagines* and the public laudation.[1] The triumph may perhaps have grown more elaborate under Hellenistic influences, but it would be hard to name an clement in the republican rite that is likely to have come from the Greek world in the early part of our period.[2] In the late fourth century the political system was already based on competition among aristocrats, in which personal and family reputation, as well as *clientela*, inevitably weighed heavily. There is no real evidence that aristocrats of this period preferred anonymity to cover their successes in war, as some have suggested.[3] On the contrary: families preserved the memory of their earlier members' deeds (with embellishments naturally),[4] which implies that the leaders of Roman armies claimed credit for themselves, and were given it. In the mid-second century there probably was a certain sharpening of the rivalry for office, with the result that Polybius prophesied that this rivalry would become excessive, and that ἡ φιλαρχία καὶ τὸ τῆς ἀδοξίας ὄνειδος, love of office and the shame of obscurity, would lead to a change for the worse in the Roman state.[5] But the *certamen gloriae* was already an old tradition.

---

[1] F. W. Walbank on Polyb. vi. 53.2, 53.4, 53.7–8. Note especially the comment of Dion. Hal. v. 17.3 that the laudation was 'Ρωμαίων ἀρχαῖον εὕρεμα.

[2] A scholar who sought for such influences detected one in the models of conquered cities which were carried in triumphs (Liv. xxxvii. 59.3): A. Bruhl, *MEFR* xlvi (1929), 87–8. The *toga picta* may have been a third-century innovation at Rome (Festus 228L; cf. L. B. Warren, *JRS* lx (1970), 64), but the appearance of something very like it in the François Tomb makes this uncertain.

[3] The fact that in Cato's *Origines*, books IV–VII (running from 264 to his own time), the author 'horum bellorum duces non nominavit, sed sine nominibus res notavit' (Nepos, *Cato* 3.3–4, cf. Plin. *NH* viii. 11) has sometimes been interpreted (e.g. by Thiel, o.c. 3) to mean that he adhered to an anti-individualist tradition. His intentions have been discussed repeatedly. The important points are that (1) Cato was very far from reticent in the *Origines* about his own activities (*HRR*[2] frr. 92 = Liv. xxxiv. 15.9: 'haud sane detractator laudum suarum . . .', 95, 106, 108); (2) he was unique among Roman writers in omitting generals' names, as far as is known (in spite of F. Bömer, *SO* xxix (1952), 39, who after B. Niese and H. Peter (*HRR* i[2]. XL) argued that Cato's omission of names was a characteristic of early annalists; but Naevius, *Pun.* 34 Strzelecki = 34 Warmington, shows nothing of the kind, and Liv. x. 37.14 (= *FGrH* 809 F16) cannot be generalized to show that this was Fabius Pictor's practice, which it certainly was not (cf. F. W. Walbank, *CQ* xxxviii (1945), 2–3, A. Klotz, *Hermes* lxxx (1952), 331, 334, V. La Bua, *Filino–Polibio, Sileno–Diodoro* (Palermo, 1966), 12–14 etc.)); (3) he remained acutely aware of his own lack of ancestors (Plu. *Cat. Mai.* 1.2, D. Kienast, *Cato der Zensor* (Heidelberg, 1954), 31–2).

[4] H. Peter, *HRR* i[2]. XLIII–LIX.

[5] vi. 57.5–6.

The ideology of *laus* and *gloria* served some definite purposes. It was, obviously enough, in the interests of the state that vigorous deeds of war should have great moral worth attached to them. But these attributes also had vital functions within Roman society, most clearly the function of distinguishing aristocrats from the rest of the citizens. The rank-and-file soldier could gain official recognition for prowess in battle, but *laus* and *gloria*, as far as we can see, were mainly the prerogatives of aristocrats. The mechanisms for spreading fame, the theatre and poetry as well as those already mentioned, were largely at their service.[1] *Gloria* helped to justify the position of those in power, who were mainly *nobiles*, and truly fame is in a sense the basis of *nobilitas*. Again etymology as such is irrelevant,[2] but the term *nobilis* had several interlocking meanings in republican Latin and meant not only men of a specific social rank—as is well known, the *nobiles* were in the Ciceronian period the descendants of consuls—but also 'the celebrated'.[3] The political and social system was supported by the almost inevitable notions that glory was inherited by sons from their fathers and was accumulated by distinguished families;[4] and it was supported in a more subtle way by the notion that inherited glory imposed a heavy obligation on the descendants to perform great deeds of their own.[5] Hence the right balance, from the point of view of the aristocracy, between inheritance and merit.

For the individual aristocrat the harvest of reputation gathered from war could have practical political advantages, helping

[1] Cf. F. Coarelli, *DA* iv–v (1970–1), 260–2.

[2] In spite of Hellegouarc'h, o.c. 376, and others who have connected *gloria* and *nobilis*.

[3] Its pre-Ciceronian meaning is disputed, but in the third and second centuries *nobilitas* was closely connected with the possession of, and the right to bequeath, *imagines*.

[4] Inheritance: Hellegouarc'h, o.c. 366, 377 (though not all his citations are relevant). For accumulation see *ILLRP* 316 (next n.).

[5] *ILLRP* 311 (the *elogium* of a P. Cornelius Scipio, probably the son of Africanus): '. . . honos, fama virtusque gloria atque ingenium, quibus sei in longa licuiset tibe utier vita facile facteis superases gloriam maiorum . . .'; *ILLRP* 316 (the *elogium* of Cn. Cornelius Scipio Hispanus, who died soon after 139): 'virtutes generis mieis moribus accumulavi, progeniem genui, facta patris petiei, maiorum optenui laudem ut sibei me esse creatum laetentur; stirpem nobilitavit honor'. Plaut. *Trin.* 642 f. (the virtuous *adulescens* Lysiteles admonishes Lesbonicus): 'itan tandem hanc maiiores famam tradiderunt tibi tui,/ ut virtute eorum anteperta per flagitium perderes?/ . . . LESB.: omnia ego istaec quae tu dixti scio, vel exsignavero,/ ut rem patriam et gloriam maiorum foedarim meum', and so on for the rest of the scene. The idea that inactivity and lack of achievements actually diminish a family's *gloria* naturally appealed to non-*nobiles* (cf. Cic. *Mur.* 15–17, Sall. *BJ* 85.22–3 (Marius speaking)).

him to win office. Closely connected with fame was the money which helped to spread and preserve it, by means, for example, of public buildings constructed from booty.[1] These financial benefits gained from war, and their political uses, will be discussed in the following chapter.

Nobiles can seldom have experienced great difficulty in winning the lower offices, the military tribunate and the quaestorship (though competition for the latter must sometimes have been warm when there were still only four positions); and for a man whose ancestors had not held curule office or entered the Senate, powerful connections, well cultivated, must usually have been the key.[2] Though some of the great military heroes are known to have won military reputations early,[3] they usually possessed other sources of political strength. Yet it is implausible to suppose that either the elective or the non-elective military tribunes were chosen without regard for their reputations as soldiers. The best-known election for this office is that of Marius, whose reputation as a soldier got him elected 'per omnis tribus';[4] of course his talents were exceptional. However the case does show that the assembly was capable of taking account of a military reputation. He was surely not the first *novus homo* who achieved office by his known prowess in war; indeed the rewarding of such prowess with office accorded well with traditional Roman ideas,[5] and it was expected of politically ambitious young men that they would show *ardor mentis ad gloriam*.[6]

For higher advancement our evidence is really no better until we come to the consulship. *Pro Murena* has already been quoted on the role of *rei militaris gloria* in winning this office, but a closer analysis is needed. The most sustained attempt to explain the consular elections of the best-documented part of our period,

---

[1] On the political advantages of manubial building cf. M. G. Morgan, *Klio* lv (1973), 223.

[2] A relatively well-known case is Cato, if Plutarch is to be believed (*Cat. Mai.* 3.3).

[3] Marcellus, five times consul, seems to be such a case (Plu. *Marc.* 2.1–2 has some circumstantial detail).

[4] Sall. *BJ* 63.3–4; Diod. xxxiv/xxxv. 38.1 does not outweigh this.

[5] Nicolet, in J.-P. Brisson (ed.), *Problèmes de la guerre à Rome*, 144–6; but the evidence for this before the first century is thin—most instructive is Liv. xxiii. 23.5–6 (membership of the Senate for those who had won awards for bravery).

[6] Again Cic. *De off.* ii. 45 and other passages cited by Knoche, o.c. 114 n. 68 (= *Vom Selbstverständnis der Römer*, 22 n. 68).

H. H. Scullard's *Roman Politics*, allows this factor very little weight.[1] However, not only do some famous careers show the effects of military repute very clearly, for example Africanus' election for 205, many other elections confirm its importance. The careers of praetors who celebrated triumphs offer a test—if military repute was important, hardly any *triumphator* should have lost a subsequent consular election.[2] Receiving the vote of a triumph from the Senate was admittedly in itself a sign of political strength, but triumphs do not seem to have been refused for purely political reasons as often as one might suppose.[3] In the years between 227 and 79 fifteen out of nineteen securely attested praetorian *triumphatores* reached the consulship—a very high ratio—and one or perhaps more of the four exceptions may have died before their turns came.[4] The praetorian triumph was a relatively rare event, but it reveals the practical value of the repute enjoyed by successful commanders. The celebration of an *ovatio* also increased the likelihood that a man would succeed in winning the consulship.

A new investigation of consular elections in the middle Republic, which would be well worth while, ought also to consider the effects of military reputation in elections in which *viri triumphales* were not involved. For example: when L. Cornelius Lentulus who had been a highly successful general in Spain from 206 to 201,[5] but had not held the praetorship, was elected to the consulship of 199, it is likely that he owed his victory over the other patrician candidates in good part to his performance as an army commander.[6] Similarly C. Cornelius Cethegus may well

---

[1] It is stated that 'distinction in oratory or law ranked with nobility of birth and military service [*sic*] as one of three claims to the consulship' (16), the evidence cited being Ciceronian. But in the body of the book military distinction is mentioned only exceptionally (283).

[2] Cf. Cic. *Mur.* 15: 'pater [L. Licinius Murena, *RE* no. 122], cum amplissime atque honestissime ex praetura triumphasset, hoc faciliorem huic gradum consulatus adipiscendi reliquit quod is *iam patri debitus* a filio petebatur'.

[3] The refusal suffered by C. Cicereius (*pr.* 173) (Liv. xlii. 21.6–7) may be attributable to his origins, which were exceptionally lowly by consular standards—the record of his triumph *in monte Albano* in the *acta triumphalia* (*Inscr. It.* xiii. 1. pp. 80–1) includes the notation 'qui scriba fuerat' (on this status cf. Wiseman, *New Men*, 73).

[4] See Additional Note VII.

[5] Liv. xxxi. 20 etc.

[6] Exhaustive analysis of this and other cases would take too much space. On the patrician candidates for 199 see H. H. Scullard, *Roman Politics*, 282–3, but of those he lists only L. Aemilius Papus (*pr.* 205), M. Fabius Buteo (*pr.* 201), P. Cornelius Lentulus

have been helped to the consulship of 197 by his victory in Spain in 200. Of the candidates for 192 two, L. Flamininus and P. Scipio Nasica, were the centre of attention, the reason being that they were both patricians, 'and fresh military glory strengthened the candidacy of each' ('utrumque commendabat').[1] The campaign was inflamed by the contest between T. Flamininus on one side and Scipio Africanus on the other—'Scipio's glory was greater, and so much the more liable to envy; Flamininus' was more recent, since he had triumphed that year'.[2] L. Flamininus was elected for 192, Nasica for 191. It goes without saying that many other factors were important in consular elections, but in determining both which members of the *nobilitas* obtained the consulship, and which few outsiders did, a good reputation gained in war could be of decisive value. It would be reasonable to suppose that this factor declined somewhat in importance during the second century; to the legal expert M'. Manilius (*cos.* 149) may belong the distinction of being the first consul elected in spite of demonstrable military incompetence.[3]

Given the desirability of fame acquired in war, it would not be surprising to find Roman aristocrats bellicose in their behaviour towards foreign states. In reality the *certamen gloriae* had complex effects. It did make aristocrats more bellicose, and many particular cases are known when one or both of the consuls

Caudinus (*pr.* 203), and P. Quinctilius Varus (*pr.* 203) are at all likely to have been candidates. Scullard (95–6) attributes L. Lentulus' election to the power of his 'Claudian-Servilian group' and the support of the candidate's brother Cn., *cos.* 201, while noting that L. 'had several years of efficient service in Spain to his credit' (283). (J. Briscoe, *A Commentary on Livy, Books XXXI–XXXIII* (Oxford, 1973), 32, makes these two Lentuli members of his 'Fulvian' group.) Cn. Lentulus' influence must have been felt, but the power of these 'groups' in the election is purely hypothetical. Africanus *may* have been antagonistic to L. Lentulus' candidacy (for this there is some evidence, though Lentulus presided over Africanus' election to the censorship, Liv. xxxii. 7.1–2), but any further speculations are idle. On the other hand L. Lentulus' military reputation surpassed that of any of the other patrician candidates. All this is by way of example.

[1] Liv. xxxv. 10.4.

[2] Liv. xxxv. 10.5 (but it is possible that this and the following description in Livy may merely be the product of annalists' imaginations). Discussing the influences at work in consular elections, A. E. Astin (*Scipio Aemilianus*, 28–9) rightly mentions this as an instance in which 'military ability' counted for something; but Livy's emphasis on 'rei militaris *gloria*' is probably more accurate.

[3] Cf. Astin, o.c. 55. It would be interesting to know more about the successful election campaign of L. Hostilius Mancinus (*cos.* 145), who explained his own role in the capture of Carthage to audiences in the forum, with visual aids, and by this *comitas*, so it is said, won election (Plin. *NH* xxxv. 23). Military achievements could still be electorally important in the very late Republic: cf. T. P. Wiseman, *JRS* lvi (1966), 114.

showed themselves to be powerful influences in favour of war during their years of office—for example, in 264, 200, 194, 172, and 110.[1] These and similar cases make it clear that the chief magistrates of the state frequently allowed their personal interests to influence their own views on state policy. However the aristocracy's collective idea of the interests of the *res publica* did much to keep the struggle for glory within bounds, so that simultaneous campaigning on too many fronts was avoided and Rome's expansion was usually carried out cautiously. And since commands in certain wars were jealously competed for, the *certamen gloriae* could actually favour the ending of a war—for a commander liked to gain the credit for successfully *completing* a war (in part because this meant a better chance of a triumph). This encouraged M. Atilius Regulus to try to make terms with Carthage in 255, Flamininus to make peace with Philip V in 197, M. Claudius Marcellus to seek peace in Spain in 152, and Sp. Postumius Albinus to do so in Numidia in 110.[2] None the less the central point should be clear: the ideology of *laus* and *gloria* was such that it required the opportunities offered by war to be more or less continually available. It would be paradoxical in the extreme if Rome, thus constituted, did not often pursue aggressive policies towards other states.

Roman aristocrats felt other powerful imperatives besides those of *laus* and *gloria* (though none perhaps that was as obviously and regularly relevant to decisions about war). The important economic imperatives will be discussed in the next chapter. Some comments have already been made about *virtus*, a concept which retained strong military connections during our period. *Fides*, by contrast, has sometimes been portrayed as an influence somehow or other contrary to Rome's drive to expand its power.[3] It is true that *fides* may have helped to restrain Rome from attacking a state with which it had a formal or informal agreement (though it did not always succeed in so doing); but *fides* was most often invoked in foreign affairs for a quite different purpose, to justify armed intervention on behalf of a state to

---

[1] These cases are discussed in chapter V.
[2] 255: Polyb. i. 31.4 (probably to be preferred to the versions of the other sources, in spite of Walbank ad loc.). 197: see below, p. 141. On 152: App. *Iber.* 49. On 110: Sall. *BJ* 36.1, 37.3. See also Polyb. xxxviii. 8.2–4, and on Scipio Africanus in 202 below, p. 138.
[3] J. Heurgon in J.-P. Brisson (ed.), *Problèmes de la guerre à Rome*, 31–2.

which Rome was bound.[1] It could be used in utterly specious ways, for example to justify helping the Mamertines in 264.[2] It certainly was not an ideal which tended generally to restrain Rome from going to war.

Absent from the quite long list of 'abstract' terms to which the Romans of the third and second centuries are known to have paid communal attention—*concordia, salus, victoria, spes, fides, honos, mens, virtus, pietas,* and others—are *pax* and related ideas.[3] The Romans seem in any case to have conceived of *pax* as a condition that could only result from successful war; and no one would infer from the fact that *res placida* seems to have been one of the claims traditionally made by the returning general[4] that the Romans were reluctant warriors. In the Roman literature of this period, in spite of negative comment about war in the *Annales* of Ennius[5]—a work devoted to celebrating Rome's victories—there is scarcely a trace of that craving for peace which can be encountered (in company with a glorification of successful war) in the Hellenistic world.[6] To transfer Cicero's most idealistic

[1] This fact is neglected by M. Merten in her study, *Fides Romana bei Livius* (diss. Frankfurt-a.-M., 1965).

[2] On 264 note Hiero's complaint, Diod. xxiii. 1.4: *'Ρωμαῖοι δὲ θρυλοῦντες τὸ τῆς πίστεως ὄνομα . . .*

[3] The figure sometimes identified as Pax on the *denarius*-type of *c.* 128, M. H. Crawford, *RRC* no. 262/1, is someone else, presumably Juno Regina. No one could have recognized her as Pax from her supposed olive-branch; and on the later republican coins showing olive-branches, they are offered by foreigners as tokens of submission.

[4] Cf. Plaut. *Pers.* 753–4 ('hostibu' victis, civibu' salvis, re placida, pacibu' perfectis,/ bello exstincto, re bene gesta . . .'), *Poen.* 524, *Truc.* 75 ('re placida atque otiosa, victis hostibus').

[5] *Ann.* 266–7V: 'postquam discordia taetra/ belli ferratos postes portasque refregit' (on the difficulties of interpretation cf. E. Fraenkel, *JRS* xxxv (1945), 12–13). With *discordia taetra belli* cf. Hom. *Il.* xiv. 389. The fragments do not make Ennius' attitude entirely clear. H. D. Jocelyn (*ANRW* i. 2.1015) writes of his 'less than total acceptance of the military virtues', but scarcely justifies this view. In any case *Ann.* 268–73V ('. . . pellitur e medio sapientia, vi geritur res,/ spernitur orator bonus, horridus miles amatur . . .') (cf. *Ann.* 181V for the contrast between *bellum* and *sapientia*) is not to be recklessly generalized, with H. E. Stier, *WaG* vii (1941), 13 n. 17, as the Roman attitude. Obviously 'pellitur e medio sapientia' is not a Roman aristocrat's conception of what happened in the Senate when war was decided, and G. Pascucci persuasively argues that these lines refer to the Carthaginians and their attack on Saguntum (in *Poesia latina in frammenti*, Univ. di Genova, Fac. di Lettere, 1974, 111–5). It was characteristic of Ennius that he added book XVI to the *Annales* out of admiration for the courage of a certain pair of brothers (according to Plin. *NH* vii. 101).

[6] On this cf. M. Rostovtzeff, *SEHHW* 192–3, 1358–9, D. Loenen, *Polemos* (*Med. Nederl. Akad.* xvi no. 3 (1953)), 74–7, P. Lévêque in J.-P. Vernant (ed.), *Problèmes de la guerre en Grèce ancienne* (Paris–The Hague, 1968), 282.

sentiments about war ('wars are to be undertaken for the purpose
of living in peace without injustice . . .') to the Romans in general
and back to 264 B.C.[1] is a cardinal error of method. Negative
theoretical statements about war probably became more and
more audible to the most highly educated Roman aristocrats of
the latter half of the second century, with Panaetius probably
(though it cannot be proved) making a contribution. But no
effects can be detected.[2] The bloody-handed Sulla, it has recently
been argued, was the first Roman to propagandize among
Roman citizens about *pax*, *pax* between Roman citizens.[3] At
about the same period the doctrines of Epicurus first began to win
wide acceptance in Italy. In Cicero's generation peace, and not
only peace between citizens, begins to be an ideal accepted in
varying degrees by a significant number of upper-class Romans.[4]

Until late in our period reluctance to go to war on the part of
individual aristocrats seems to be almost unknown. A change
could be seen in 151. Polybius describes the response to the
prospect of a difficult campaign against the Celtiberians: an
unexpected terror attacked the young men, so that not enough
volunteers came forward to be military tribunes, though previously, he says, many times too many suitable candidates for the
available places had customarily come forward; the legates also
refused to serve; the reasons for all this being the unpleasant
reports of the previous campaign and the fact that M. Marcellus
(*cos.* 152) himself was frightened by the war. Scipio Aemilianus
saved the situation.[5] Polybius' account of this incident must in the
main be accepted,[6] and so must his assertion that it was utterly
unlike the usual Roman response to forthcoming campaigns.

[1] As did M. Gelzer, *Hermes* lxviii (1933), 137 [→ Bibl.].
[2] φιλανθρωπία and πραότης are irrelevant here, since (in the Roman view) they could
only be applied in international affairs to the defeated. On the question of *humanitas* in the
second century cf. A. E. Astin, *Scipio Aemilianus*, 302–6, G. Perl, *Philologus* cxvii (1973),
esp. 59–61, 64–5.
[3] S. Weinstock, *Divus Julius* (Oxford, 1971), 267.
[4] Leaving aside philosophical texts one notes, e.g., how Cicero finds it reprehensible
that Metellus Celer (*cos.* 60) does not greatly rejoice that *otium* is announced from Gaul—
'cupit, credo, triumphare' (*Att.* i. 20.5). For *pax* as a praiseworthy aim in an official text see
CIL i². 2580, line 19 (58 B.C.). Lucretius eloquently begs Venus for peace in i. 29–40.
[5] Polyb. xxxv. 4; also Liv. *Per.* 48, Val. Max. iii. 2.6, Oros. iv. 21.1.
[6] Though his account of Aemilianus' role is obviously tendentious; and his comment on
Marcellus also lacks credibility (A. E. Astin, *Scipio Aemilianus*, 40–42), and must derive
from Scipionic propaganda.

Reluctance to go to Spain may have been increased by the expectation that there would soon be opportunities for military tribunes to serve in a much more attractive campaign against Carthage. It is to be noted that *vacatio militiae* was not a privilege much sought by aristocrats, as far as we can tell. Exemption from military duty was a right of the *pontifices* and augurs (and perhaps their children),[1] probably more because of taboo than because of their duties, but if the right was used we do not hear of it. Young members of these colleges seem to have normal careers.[2]

It is equally difficult to find much reluctance to go to war on the part of *imperium*-holding magistrates. Some of the second-century consuls who achieved nothing *memorabile*, in Livy's opinion, during a year's campaign in Liguria may have lacked enthusiasm for warfare. Three of the praetors of 176, the one assigned to Sardinia and the two assigned to the Spanish provinces, asked to be excused from their commands, an unparalleled incident which Livy leaves somewhat obscure.[3] It may have been peace rather than war which they found unattractive.[4] However, from the 150s it became commoner for one of the consuls to pass his year of office without going to war; the most important reason was probably the difficulty of recruiting legionaries, but a decline in enthusiasm on the part of

[1] Cf. Mommsen, *R. Staatsrecht*, iii. 242–3.

[2] For certain individuals of equestrian standing exemption from military service appears as a privilege in 215 (Liv. xxiii. 49.1–3) and 186 (xxxix. 19.4). C. Nicolet has argued, however, that the *ordo equester* as a whole maintained its interest in military service in the second century (in J.-P. Brisson (ed.), *Problèmes de la guerre à Rome*, 124–33).

[3] Liv. xli. 15.6–10, cf. 27.2, xlii. 32.1–3, *ORF*³ p. 83. H. H. Scullard (*Roman Politics*, 189) lamely suggests that the incident occurred because of 'the growing independence of some of the younger men against the Senate'. The Sardinian praetor argued in the Senate that it would be inefficient to replace the present governor (Ti. Sempronius Gracchus), but the details at least of this argument were probably invented by an annalist (cf. above, pp. 6–7). The Spanish praetors claimed to be prevented from going by sacrificial obligations, which only occurred to the second after the first had won his point in the Senate. It may not be irrelevant that the consuls had obtained exceptionally bad omens (Liv. xli. 14.7–15.4), but the sacrifices were probably pretexts (cf. F. Münzer, *Römische Adelsparteien*, 221, and next n.).

[4] M. Popillius Laenas, the Sardinian praetor, *cos.* 173 and *tr. mil.* in the Third Macedonian War, could not be accused of having a pacific nature. P. Licinius Crassus successfully sought the command against Perseus in his consulship in 171. M. Cornelius Scipio is little known—but two years later he was expelled from the Senate (Liv. xlii. 27.2). Though the exact chronology cannot be known, most of the fighting may have been over by the spring of 176 (cf. Liv. xli. 17.1–5). Spain had been relatively peaceful since the treaty Gracchus had made with the Celtiberians in 178.

the consuls themselves may have been partly responsible. The Jugurthine War illustrates several of the various attitudes that were to be found in the Senate by that time. Some senators wanted to go to war on behalf of Adherbal in 112, but the supporters of Jugurtha—for whatever motive—prevented it until the king had defied the embassy of Aemilius Scaurus. The consul Calpurnius Bestia made peace in 111 after a brief campaign, either because he was bribed by Jugurtha (so Sallust) or out of policy (so some modern scholars). The war was reopened in 110, the crucial factor being that one of the consuls (Sp. Postumius Albinus) was, according to Sallust, 'greedy to wage war'; but he was one of those commanders already mentioned who tried to complete the war on terms for the benefit of his own prestige. Having failed in this, he left his brother Aulus in command of the army in Numidia. When Aulus was defeated by Jugurtha and forced to surrender, Spurius, in fear of the resulting *invidia*, 'fervently desired to pursue Jugurtha'. His successor Caecilius Metellus, *vir acer*, pursued the war in vigorous fashion. Finally the war gave the great opportunity to a *novus homo* who was, according to Sallust's somewhat flattering description, 'a spirit heroic in war but moderate at home, who spurned lust and riches and was greedy only for glory'.[1]

Finally, how did Roman aristocrats view the grimmest realities of the battlefield and the captured city, realities which until the last years of the second century they almost all knew at first hand? Heinze, in order to show that the Romans were not 'kriegslustig', argued that they did not love hand-to-hand combat itself.[2] This is in interesting contrast with what Polybius and Sallust have to say. 'Many Romans', says the former, 'have willingly fought in single combat ($\dot{\epsilon}\mu o\nu o\mu \acute{a}\chi\eta\sigma a\nu$) to decide a whole battle, many have chosen certain death . . .'[3] 'Each man hastened to strike an enemy, to climb a rampart, to be seen in the doing of such a deed . . .', says Sallust, generalizing about the period before 146.[4] Combat-by-champions was an important tradition at Rome which was still alive in the second century.

[1] The passages quoted are Sall. *BJ* 35.3, 39.5, 63.2.
[2] Above, p. 16.
[3] vi. 54.4; cf. fr. 19B–W.
[4] *BC* 7.6 (cf. 9.4).

Scipio Aemilianus is the last known monomachist.[1] The difficulties of interpretation are considerable, but the tradition clearly testified to the admiration that was accorded to the personal heroism and personal fighting ability of the aristocrat. This is of course in tune with the renown which belonged to the winner of the rarest of all honours, the *spolia opima*. Similarly the first man to climb a rampart, singled out by Sallust, is an aggressively heroic figure.

To turn to more normal fighting, the impossibility of generalizing about aristocratic comportment in battle is almost complete. None of the sources on our period can be trusted in a battle-narrative except Polybius, and even his details are often open to question. And even when we find a consul engaged in hand-to-hand fighting, it may be much against his will. But the suggestion that officers tended to keep out of actual combat[2] is not, for most of our period, convincing. The commander, it seems, was generally protected by a surrounding swarm of Roman soldiers, except in severe defeats.[3] But the tribunes, not to speak of the young aristocrats who had yet to reach this rank, cannot have had such an advantage. Indeed in ancient conditions it was scarcely possible for the tribunes to maintain any influence over the course of battle, once it had begun, without

---

[1] Legendary cases: the Horatii and Curiatii, L. Siccius Dentatus (*tr. pl.* 454) (the case of Horatius Cocles, which Polybius recounts in vi. 55, is somewhat different). Semi-legendary: T. Manlius Torquatus in *c.* 361, his homonymous son in 340, M. Valerius Corvus in 349 (for the sources see *MRR* i. 119, 136–7, 129). Historical cases (no doubt with fictional additions in most sources on most cases): M. Claudius Marcellus (Plu. *Marc.* 2.1, a passing allusion), Claudius Asellus (presumably identical with Ti. Claudius Asellus, *pr.* 206) (Liv. xxiii. 46.12–47.18), T. Quinctius Crispinus who killed the Campanian Badius (Liv. xxv. 18.3–15), M. Servilius Pulex Geminus (*cos.* 202) (he claimed to have fought no fewer than twenty-three single combats, Liv. xlv. 39.16–19, Plu. *Aem.* 31.2; he is commemorated on *denarii* of *c.* 127 (M. H. Crawford, *RRC* no. 264/1) and *c.* 100 (Crawford 327/1)), Scipio Aemilianus (Polyb. xxxv. 5.1 and other sources listed by A. E. Astin, *Scipio Aemilianus*, 46 n. 4; Polyb. fr. 6B–W reports the reasoned opposition of some of Scipio's colleagues). The fictional account of combat between Hannibal and Scipio Africanus at Zama given in App. *Lib.* 45 may be a story dating from the second century B.C. (cf. De Sanctis, *SR* iii. 2.603). Marius and perhaps P. Licinius Crassus (*cos.* 97) prudently refused such invitations (Front. *Strat.* iv. 7.5, Diod. xxxvii. 23). J. Harmand, *L'Armée et le soldat à Rome* (Paris, 1967), 397, is somewhat misleading on the first century. The whole topic deserves a scholarly article; cf. F. Münzer, *Römische Adelsparteien*, 227, J. J. Glück, *Acta Classica* vii (1964), 25–31 (the best discussion of monomachy, but he scarcely touches the Roman evidence).

[2] G. Veith in J. Kromayer–G. Veith, *Heerwesen und Kriegführung der Griechen und Römer* (Munich, 1928), 439–40 (but he is quite guarded).

[3] Note especially Polyb. vi. 31.3 and as an example cf. iii. 65.11 end.

being very near to the fighting itself (but they will of course have benefited from having at their disposal the best horses and the best armour). The much-scarred bodies of certain veteran officers are some indication of the part this class of person often played in combat. More indicative still, if we could only discover it, would be the casualty rate. What were the chances of losing one's life during the ten *stipendia*? Consular war-deaths were rare, except during the hardest period of the Hannibalic War when twelve men of consular rank lost their lives in the space of ten years, but certain indications (not clear ones, it must be admitted) suggest that two or three tribunes out of the twelve who served in a pair of legions may quite commonly have lost their lives in the most severe battle of a campaign.[1]

In the next section something will be said about the relative brutality of Roman war-methods (which is not to be exaggerated, but not to be ignored either). This was to some extent the result of policy, aristocratic policy. Particular acts of frightfulness do not perhaps reveal very much about the Roman ethos which we are investigating. Yet it was one of the most enlightened leaders of second-century Rome, Scipio Aemilianus, who—among other brutalities—cut off the hands of 400 rebelliously-inclined young men of Lutia in Spain.[2] It cannot be denied that very many Roman aristocrats seem to have been able to order or permit such acts of horror. The continuous train of wars in our period created no known distaste or revulsion among them.[3] Not for them any feelings of melancholy at the battle won.

What bearing do these facts have on Rome's attitudes towards particular wars? A more complete answer will be given later. It is in theory conceivable that the ideology of *laus* and *gloria* was merely a useful response to a prolonged series of external situations which forced Rome to go to war. The reason why I have not so far said much about the important place occupied by *victoria* in Roman thought is that anyone who goes to war wishes

---

[1] In such rare notices as Liv. xxx. 18.14–15, xxxiii. 22.8, 36.5, xxxv. 5.14 I take it that the named casualties are an authentic element, but probably the only one. Usually Livy does not specify tribunician casualties, whether few or many. In the above cases three, two, two and three tribunes respectively were killed, these probably being the casualties from among the twelve tribunes of two legions.   [2] App. *Iber.* 94.

[3] On Aemilianus' famous tears at the destruction of Carthage cf. A. E. Astin, *Scipio Aemilianus*, 282.

to win. In other words, the ideas and practices concerning *victoria* which we know existed in third- and second-century Rome could conceivably have existed in a state which fought wars only with great reluctance. The question is whether the social ethos I have been describing was created by circumstances external to the Roman state, or whether Rome's distinctive behaviour towards foreign states resulted from the social ethos. Of course the dilemma is not as sharp as this, for social ethos and external circumstances worked on each other. The regular train of wars, continuing even in times when the Roman state was not seriously threatened from without, shows the importance of the social ethos; and even the Romans themselves, as will appear in chapter V, did not feel themselves driven into war by external circumstances as often as is commonly supposed by historians. Furthermore, much of the social ethos concerning war is, as we have seen, explicable in purely internal Roman terms.

It does not follow from all this that Rome eagerly sought to make war on every possible occasion—on the contrary, the Senate usually showed great caution in avoiding too many simultaneous commitments. But we do know that Roman aristocrats had strong reasons to allow disputes and conflicts of interest between Rome and other states to grow into war.

2. THE CITIZENS AND WAR

Aristocratic though the Roman state was, the political system allowed the ordinary citizens some influence over foreign policy. The most important of the powers reserved to the Roman people, says Polybius, is 'to deliberate about peace and war. Further it is the people who ratify or disapprove alliances, peace-agreements, and treaties.'[1] In reality, as Polybius knew, the effective decisions were almost always made in the Senate. No case is known in which a senatorial decision to make war was successfully resisted by the people, and even formal war-votes may have ceased not long after Polybius wrote.[2] The people probably did have a recognized claim, at least through most of our period, to ratify or reject formal treaties, but they very seldom succeeded in altering

---

[1] vi. 14.10–11. It is not necessary to repeat here the well-known facts about undemocratic voting procedures of the Roman assemblies.

[2] On war-votes in the *comitia centuriata* see Additional Note VIII.

the terms.[1] They had no power over the conduct of negotiations with foreign states, and no formal control over the continuation of a war once it had been started. However the Senate did not make its decisions about peace and war in entire disregard of the rest of the citizen body and then simply obtain automatic approval. In 264, in 241, in 222, and in 200, and probably on some less important occasions as well, there were disagreements about such issues, disputes (broadly speaking) between Senate and people.[2] Though the people's direct power declined somewhat after the Hannibalic War, ordinary citizens in the category of *assidui* came to exercise an important influence over external policy in the second century by means of their willingness or unwillingness to serve in person in particular wars. From the 160s at least, recruiting considerations must have entered into senatorial thinking. Later, in the Jugurthine War, we can see how citizens outside the aristocracy could in certain circumstances have a strong influence on external policy.

How bellicose then were ordinary Roman citizens? Was it against their will that they were conscripted for campaigns whose purpose may have been hard to perceive? Was it obedience to the stern demands of patriotism that drove them to serve? Or did they, like many aristocrats, find warfare in some ways an attractive alternative to their civilian existence? Historians have sometimes suggested that ordinary citizens were opposed to the more aggressive kind of Roman imperialism,[3] but in the sources this is far from clear. On the few known occasions when Senate and people (or predominant sections of them) differed over foreign policy, it was not generally the Senate which was more aggressive[4] (the initial refusal of the assembly to vote war against Philip V in 200 being an exception not difficult to explain). When the aggressive praetor M'. Iuventius Thalna wished to start a war against Rhodes in 167 he appealed in the first place not to the Senate or consuls, but to the assembly.[5] No popular leader is

---

[1] The *comitia tributa* normally voted on peace treaties (Mommsen, *R. Staatsrecht*, iii. 340–4). The assembly rejected the peace made by C. Lutatius with Carthage in 241 (Polyb. i. 63.1–3), presumably as not being severe or profitable enough.

[2] On 222 see Plu. *Marc.* 6.2.

[3] A. J. Toynbee, *Hannibal's Legacy*, ii. 95–6 (the reluctance of second-century peasants to enlist 'for the maintenance and extension of an empire').

[4] Cf. H. H. Scullard, *Roman Politics*, 29–30.

[5] Polyb. xxx. 4.4–6, Diod. xxxi. 5.3, Liv. xlv. 21.1–4.

known to have raised his voice against war until Licinius Macer's tribunate in 73.[1]

The surviving literature provides little direct information about popular attitudes towards war. The political exploitation of fame earned in warfare supports the view that successful war was strongly approved, which is scarcely surprising. More important is the value evidently attached by ordinary citizens to acts of valour by ordinary soldiers. The system of battle honours stimulates not only those who see them awarded, says Polybius, but also those who remain at home. Those who win them become famous, take the places of honour in processions when they return home, and put up their spoils in conspicuous places in their houses.[2]

For further information, Plautus is the most interesting author, since in spite of aristocratic patronage he comes nearest to reflecting popular feeling. He does not celebrate military glory— far from it—but he does seem to speak to an audience quite preoccupied with war. When in the *Amphitruo* the slave Sosia describes the hero's victory over the Teloboae, one is led to suspect that the very lengthy battle-narrative, all put in Roman language, had a strong and direct appeal to the audience.[3] Plautus' writing, as many have noticed, is shot through with military metaphors, often of a specifically Roman kind.[4] It is significant that at the end of the Plautine prologue, the speaker commonly wishes the audience well in one particular respect— that they should be successful in war.[5] More will be said later of Plautus' frequent allusions to the most regular benefit ordinary soldiers gained from war, namely booty.

[1] Sall. *Hist.* iii. 48.17–18. However such sentiments had probably been heard in the period since 151 (see below).

[2] A summary of vi. 39.8–11. Note also vi. 37.13: one of the reasons for the stubbornness of Roman soldiers in battle is that a man who has lost his shield or sword desperately tries to recover it rather than suffer τὴν πρόδηλον αἰσχύνην . . . καὶ τὴν τῶν οἰκείων ὕβριν.

[3] *Amph.* 188–262. E. Fraenkel felt an overwhelming violence in these lines (*Plautinisches im Plautus*, 350 = *Elementi plautini*, 333).

[4] Cf. Fraenkel, *Elementi plautini*, 223–6, R. Perna, *L'originalità di Plauto* (Bari, 1955), 179–203, P. P. Spranger, *Historische Untersuchungen zu den Sklavenfiguren des Plautus und Terenz* (Wiesbaden, 1961), 41. The presence of military characters would not by itself be significant, since they are common in New Comedy.

[5] *Asin.* 15, *Capt.* 67–8, *Cas.* 87–8, *Rud.* 82, *Cist.* 197–202 (but this was certainly produced during the Hannibalic War). However in *Amph.* 32 Mercury claims to bring the audience the gift of *pax* (a topical reference according to H. Janne, *RBPhH* xii (1933), 516). According to *Amph.* 41–5, tragic prologues had been pronounced on the Roman stage in which Neptunus, Virtus, Victoria, Mars, and Bellona had recounted their benefactions to the Roman people, obviously military successes in every case.

The crucial evidence, however, for ordinary citizens' attitudes towards war concerns the legionary levy. War-decisions often committed a large proportion of the *assidui* to take up arms. Writing before the 1914 war, De Sanctis argued that the proportion who took the field even to provide the two legions of the fourth century was extraordinarily high, higher than the proportion ever mobilized in any modern state.[1] In fact all Roman census totals down to 265/4 are in the highest degree suspect,[2] but when we begin to have trustworthy figures they seem to reveal (in spite of the problems of interpretation) a remarkably high level of participation in the legions. If we accept the totals for the period 252 to 223, the earliest ones which have a good chance of being correct, and if we accept Brunt's argument that at the beginning of the Hannibalic War the *assidui* comprised about 42 to 44 per cent of the *iuniores*, the Roman state habitually mobilized, to form the four consular legions, between 18 and 24 per cent of the eligible *iuniores*.[3] This implies six or seven campaigns as the average life-term service of the *assiduus*. The number was much higher for those who lived during the Hannibalic War and survived in a physical condition to serve longer. During the second century the number of Roman citizens in the legions was generally much larger than it had been before 218. The median total of legions for the period from 200 to 133 is seven.[4] Unfortunately, now that the economic conditions of free peasants were becoming more difficult and the qualification of the *assiduus* had been lowered, we do not know how many men were eligible to serve in these legions.[5] Some evidence suggests

---

[1] *SR* ii. 202–3.

[2] P. A. Brunt, *Italian Manpower*, 26–33.

[3] The census totals for 252–233 (there are no more until 209–8) vary between 241,712 (Liv. *Per.* 19) and 297,797 (*Per.* 18). I am accepting a series of hypotheses: that these totals included the *seniores* (cf. F. W. Walbank on Polyb. ii. 24.14, Brunt, o.c. 21–25), that the *seniores* amounted to about 25 per cent of the totals (A. Afzelius, *Die römische Eroberung Italiens (340–264 v. Chr.)* (Copenhagen, 1942), 100), and that the totals included the *proletarii* (Brunt, 22–5). The proportion of the *assidui* is argued from the fact that after about 108,000 men had served in the legions in 218–215 (Brunt, 417–20; 105,000 on p. 64 is a misprint), only somewhat more than 2,000 qualified *iuniores* had failed to serve (Liv. xxiv. 18.7–8); hence it is reasonable to suppose that 90,000–95,000 men were qualified in 218. The total of free adult males was probably about 285,000 (Brunt, 64–6). These are of course only rough calculations, but they are necessary ones. In normal years 18,000 *assidui* served (16,800 infantry and 1,200 cavalry).

[4] The known facts are tabulated by Brunt, o.c. 424–5, 432–3.

[5] Brunt, o.c. 77, supposes 'by way of illustration' that by Ti. Gracchus' time there may

that qualified citizens commonly had to serve in many more than six or seven years. Not only was the maximum obligation of the infantryman sixteen years in Polybius' time, but it was also, most significantly, thought necessary to specify that he had to serve twenty years if emergencies required it. Lucilius, who had served in Spain and knew what he was talking about, mentions a soldier's serving almost eighteen years there, clearly a reference to the longest period of service that could plausibly be imagined.[2] The view that legionary service still amounted to six or seven years is based on flimsy arguments, and a figure twice as high would be more credible.[3] The increase resulted in part from a trend towards 'professionalization' of the legions,[4] more specifically from the probable fact that with the *assiduus* qualification lowered, many men who owned little land spent much longer periods in the army than *assidui* had normally done before the Hannibalic War. All the same it is important that citizens were still willing to serve in such large numbers. And this service often consisted not of seasonal campaigns, as in the period before 218, but of year-long duty. The contrast with Carthage, with most Hellenistic states, and with Rome under the Empire is obvious.[5]

have been only 75,000 *assidui*; this would imply fifteen years of legionary service as the average burden for the qualified citizen.

[1] The figure in Polyb. vi. 19.2 (τοὺς δὲ πεζοὺς ἓξ † οὐ † δεῖ στρατείας τελεῖν κατ' ἀνάγκην . . .) must be sixteen. Twenty in emergencies: vi. 19.4. Such regulations would have made no sense unless it was common for men to serve at least ten or twelve years. In my view Brunt (o.c. 399–401) does not establish that Polybius' sixteen was anachronistic.

[2] 490–1 M: 'dum miles Hibera/ terrast atque meret ter sex aetatis quasi annos'. Brunt, o.c. 401, fails to explain this.

[3] A. J. Toynbee, *Hannibal's Legacy*, ii. 75–80, and even Brunt, o.c. 399–401, rest far too much weight on the length of time for which particular legions remained in service. What matters most is not the length of *continuous* service, but the total quantity of service that individuals performed. There is one, and only one, piece of evidence in favour of six or seven years as the norm: in 140, according to App. *Iber.* 78.334, the soldiers in Hispania Citerior were replaced—ἓξ γὰρ ἔτη διεληλύθει στρατευομένοις. This is somewhat mysterious, since a large army had been sent to Citerior as resently as 143 (App. 76.322). If we accept Appian's statement, it signifies no more than that by now the Senate thought it undesirable to keep soldiers in Spain for more than six years at once. (The passage is misinterpreted by Toynbee, o.c. ii. 79.) There is reason to suppose that these soldiers performed no other military service during their lives (see R. E. Smith, *Service in the Post-Marian Roman Army* (Manchester, 1958), 7 n. 4), and Spain was in any case felt to be the most arduous theatre.

[4] On which see E. Gabba, *Athenaeum* xxvii (1949), 175–97 = *Esercito e società nella tarda repubblica romana* (Florence, 1973), 3–30.

[5] For Carthaginian reliance on mercenaries cf. Polyb. vi. 52.4, G. T. Griffith, *The Mercenaries of the Hellenistic World* (Cambridge, 1935), 207–33; however the question of

The norms of Polybius' day seem eventually to have been changed. In response to the dislike which was now felt for extended military service, there were passed 'several laws by which the years of military service were reduced'. The text of Asconius, our only source for this fact, is defective at the relevant point, but he apparently dates the legislation 'per eos annos', that is in the years shortly before it was abrogated at the instance of M. Iunius Silanus during his consulship in 109.[1] These laws do not, be it noted, show that the levy was generally hated throughout the second century; in fact they may well result from an important decline in the ordinary citizens' attraction to warfare.

Were these exertions largely involuntary?[2] The distinction between a conscript and a volunteer is not a straightforward one. The *dilectus* was backed by compulsion, to be applied when necessary. Volunteers do not appear very often in the sources—but when they do, it is apparently for some special reason, and ordinary volunteers were too commonplace to mention.[3] It is hard to see how a widespread and deeply felt reluctance to serve could have been overcome, given the lack of elaborate governmental machinery. Historians should resist the presupposition that the citizens were generally reluctant to serve. Nor is the apparent willingness of recruits to be dismissed as simply a result of an oppressive social and economic system directed by the

Carthaginian population remains obscure, as does the extent of the citizens' service in the navy. For some Hellenistic comparisons cf. A. Afzelius, *Die römische Kriegsmacht* (Copenhagen, 1944), 99–108; for a survey of the population figures cf. M. Rostovtzeff, *SEHHW* ii. 1135–43. For some medieval comparisons cf. J. Beeler, *Warfare in Feudal Europe 730–1200* (Ithaca, N.Y.–London, 1971), 249–51, and for some modern ones Brunt, o.c. 67.

[1] Ascon. 68 C. Cf. Brunt, o.c. 401, 407.

[2] According to Toynbee, o.c. ii. 76, 'perennial distant overseas service had naturally soon become intensely unpopular'. Brunt, o.c. 391–415, discusses the problem thoroughly, but his conclusion that 'the government normally had to rely on sheer compulsion' (396) does not convince me as far as the first half of the second century is concerned. He admits (392) that 'conscripts were not necessarily unwilling soldiers'.

[3] In 200 Scipio's African veterans were exempted from service in the Macedonian war unless they volunteered (Liv. xxxi. 8.6), an undertaking which may not have been kept (xxxii. 3); their claim to have served many years (xxxii. 3.5) may well be true (cf. J. Briscoe on 3.3–4). About 5,000 volunteers (including allies) went to the East with L. Scipio in 190, in spite of the fact that they had fulfilled their obligations under Scipio Africanus (Liv. xxxvii. 4.3). In 171 volunteers for the Macedonian war were numerous, 'quia locupletes videbant, qui priore Macedonico bello aut adversus Antiochum in Asia stipendia fecerant' (Liv. xlii. 32.6).

aristocracy. There is obviously much truth in this,[1] and at Rome, as elsewhere, the comfortably off and the old were largely responsible for sending the poor and the young into battle. But such an explanation hardly seems to account for the smooth running of the levy.[2] Could legal compulsion and the force of *clientela* have made this system work against the will of the mass of citizens?[3] The Senate's foreign policy would have been futile without a measure of popular support, and by the years 109–108 its policy was in considerable danger partly as a result of a decline in the willingness of the *assidui* to serve.

The presumption that people in general naturally dislike war seems to be widespread among Roman historians. In the preface to *Hannibal's Legacy*, Toynbee wrote of the human devastation caused by the First World War, and that event produced in England and elsewhere a marked change in attitudes towards war.[4] Revulsion against war was intensified in many of us by Vietnam. But these twentieth-century attitudes can make it more difficult to grasp the mentality of the Romans of the middle Republic. In many societies men have from time to time regarded war as exciting, glorious, a good way of escaping from the grinding miseries of civilian existence, and as a possible means of getting rich. In the Italian wars many Romans must have fought in the hope of gaining land and booty, and the expectation of booty continued to affect citizen's attitudes throughout our period. Such narrow opportunities of social promotion as there were at Rome were provided by military service.[5] Other factors helped to make men overlook the personal

---

[1] As Malthus said (*An Essay on the Principle of Population* (London, 1803 edn.), 500), 'a recruiting serjeant always prays for a bad harvest, and a want of employment, or, in other words, a redundant population.' But before the Hannibalic War the legions were not normally open to the indigent, and in my view were hardly so in the first half of the second century (however cf. Brunt, o.c. 405–6).   [2] On which note Polyb. vi. 26.4.

[3] The role of *clientela* in normal recruitment is unclear (it had been very important in an earlier period, cf. Dion. Hal. ix. 15.2 etc., and undoubtedly still could be on occasion, as when Scipio Aemilianus took 4,000 volunteers to Spain in 134). Polyb. vi. 31.2–3 probably refers to *clientes* of the consuls as a normal and sizable contingent (τινες τῶν ἐθελοντὴν στρατευομένων τῇ τῶν ὑπάτων χάριτι—the last four words seem to imply *clientes* rather than ordinary *evocati*, contrary to F. W. Walbank's interpretation).

[4] Of the sources for earlier attitudes, S. R. Steinmetz, *Soziologie des Krieges* (Leipzig, 1929), 5–9, is worth citing on intellectuals. More generally cf. Bouthoul, o.c. 352–6. A vivid and articulate illustration of a nineteenth-century British attitude can be found in T. Seaton, *From Cadet to Colonel* (London, 1866).

[5] C. Nicolet in J.-P. Brisson (ed.), *Problèmes de la guerre à Rome*, 147–52.

risks inherent in war. Patriotism was one, and quite apart from those occasions when Rome was directly threatened in a most obvious way, as in 225 and 218, many Romans, during the periods of conflict with the Samnites, the Etruscans, the north-Italian Gauls, the Carthaginians, the Macedonians, and others, must have hated these enemies more or less bitterly. In short, we ought not to assume in advance that military service was generally repugnant in the period before 151. In my view, very many Romans outside the aristocracy were content to exchange their civilian lives for legionary service, until in the mid-second century their attitude began to change progressively, a change which culminated in the laws referred to by Asconius and in Marius' 'proletarianization' of the legions in 107.

In any state one can expect to find some enthusiastic volunteers for the army and some defaulters and deserters, but these groups are irrelevant to the present question unless they are large. Apart from the period of the Hannibalic War, which made unparalleled demands on Roman manpower, including, as we have seen, the virtually complete mobilization of the *assidui*, we have very little evidence of unwillingness to serve in the legions until the middle of the second century. In the last stage of the Struggle of the Orders, for which the sources are admittedly very thin, the levy seems not to have been a political issue. In fact the most important exception to the citizens' usual acquiescence was the occasion in 200 when the centuriate assembly at first refused to sanction the Senate's decision to make war on Philip V. The sources are silent about other recruiting difficulties among citizens (other than colonists) before 169; and the silence is not without force, since although annalistic writers might have preferred to concentrate on such figures as Sp. Ligustinus (who, after rising through the ranks in twenty-two years of service spread over thirty years, offered his service again in the year 171),[1] they were not too squeamish to describe mutinies or attempts to evade the levy. In the first decades of the second century, complaints about legionary service seem to have resulted mainly from well-founded grievances felt by particular groups.[2]

---

[1] Liv. xlii. 34.

[2] 193: soldiers in *legiones urbanae* who had served their *stipendia* or who were sick asked to be exempted from active duty against the Ligurians (Liv. xxxiv. 56.9). 191: citizens of

In 169, now that the initial enthusiasm for the Macedonian war had been dissipated by unexpected reverses, insufficient recruits could be found without compulsion, and legionaries assigned to the war were slow in returning from leave.[1] I shall be suggesting later that one reason why Rome did not annex Macedon two years later was the likely unpopularity of garrison service there. Much more serious difficulties became visible in 151: because of unattractive reports of the fighting in Spain, says Polybius, 'a sort of extraordinary terror overtook the young men, *such as the older men said had never occurred before*', and they sought to evade the levy.[2] The conflict grew so intense that tribunes threw the consuls into jail.[3] It was probably soon after this crisis that the qualification of an *assiduus* was lowered from 4,000 to 1,500 *asses*,[4] which would help to explain how in 149–146 the government could build up the number of legions to twelve (a total not seen since 188). However the recruitment problem had returned in an intense form by 140, and led to among other things the imprisonment of the consuls in 138 and the major political crisis of 133.[5] This renewed tension was doubtless caused in part by a continuing decline in the number of *assidui*, but it also indicates

maritime colonies tried to claim the exemptions to which they were normally entitled (xxxvi. 3.5). 184: a dispute arose about the replacement of troops in Spain, some of whom had and some of whom had not served their *stipendia*—but the facts are obscured by the evident desire of their commanders to *deportare exercitus*, something apparently still felt by a majority of senators to be necessary for a triumph (cf. Liv. xxxix. 29.5, Mommsen, *R. Staatsrecht*, i[3]. 129–30) (Liv. xxxix. 38.8–12). Liv. xxxix. 29.10 is relevant but cryptic.

[1] Liv. xliii. 14.2–15.1.

[2] Polyb. xxxv. 4.2–6.

[3] Liv. *Per.* 48: allegedly because they could not obtain exemption for their friends. As far as we can tell, this was the beginning of the period of serious difficulties in recruitment (cf. A. E. Astin, *Scipio Aemilianus*, 167–8).

[4] For determining the date the main evidence is Polyb. vi. 19.3 (provides a *terminus post quem* of *c*. 153–150), Cic. *De rep.* ii. 40 (may provide a *terminus ante quem* of 129), and what is known about the retariffing of the *denarius* (gives a *terminus ante quem* of 133–123 (Sydenham) or *c*. 141 (Crawford, much more credibly)). Recent discussion: Brunt, o.c. 402–5 (but it seems very improbable that the change was as early as 171), M. H. Crawford, *RRC* 625.

[5] 145: the consul Q. Fabius Maximus Aemilianus exempted from the levy those who had fought in the Punic, Macedonian, and Achaean wars and took only those with no experience of war (App. *Iber.* 65). 140: C. Laelius' agrarian proposal was clearly intended to alleviate the manpower problem; the tribune Ti. Claudius Asellus attempted to prevent the consul Q. Servilius Caepio from leaving for Spain, quite probably because of a dispute over the *dilectus* (Liv. *Oxy. Per.* 54, Astin, o.c. 168 n. 1); Ap. Claudius Pulcher seems to have prevented a second *dilectus* from being held in the same year (perhaps to deal with the beginnings of the Sicilian slave-rebellion, rather than to reinforce Caepio in Spain (as Astin suggests, 126)) (*Oxy. Per.* 54). 138: *MRR* i. 483. 134: Scipio Aemilianus was

that the citizens' willingness to serve in war was becoming much more selective. Whereas many volunteered for the potentially profitable war against Carthage, and a number for Scipio Aemilianus' Spanish campaign,[1] Spain generally had few attractions now and the slave war in Sicily even fewer. It is interesting to observe that after 133 *dilectus* difficulties disappear from the sources, even though as many as nine legions were once in service (124) and seven often were; this probably results from the greatly increased efficiency of the censors in registering citizens that is evident from the census totals of 124 and 114[2]—that is to say, the burden was spread more widely. None the less the increasing unpopularity of military service among ordinary citizens is clearly attested by the laws 'quibus militiae stipendia minuebantur' of the years before 109. The Senate's expectation that Marius would lose popularity as a result of the *dilectus* in 107 was disappointed, since the expectation of booty had a strong effect; but all the same it is probable that a general decline in Roman belligerence, paralleled by the change in aristocratic attitudes, lay behind Marius' decision to recruit from among the *capite censi*.[3]

The time of changing attitudes which began in 151 has had to be discussed, but it is worth reaffirming that for most of the period with which this book is concerned, ordinary citizens generally co-operated with a system which required them to serve in the legions year after year in remarkably high numbers.

Another, even more indirect, means of investigating Roman citizens' attitudes towards war is to consider the level of ferocity and brutality which they showed in warfare itself.[4] It may be objected that this method cannot provide a reliable index of eagerness to go to war. Actions of extreme ferocity were often officially ordered or approved, and it is a psychological possibility that the Romans who acted ferociously under the pressures of

apparently prevented by the Senate from taking any non-volunteers to Spain (Plu. *Mor.* 201a, Astin, 135–6). For further discussion cf. Astin, 167–72, Brunt, o.c. 397–8.

[1] App. *Lib.* 75, *Iber.* 84.

[2] Cf. Brunt, o.c. 78–81.

[3] Cf. Sall. *BJ* 84–6, Val. Max. ii. 3.1, Gabba, o.c. 199–200 = *Esercito e società*, 32–3, Brunt, o.c. 406–7.

[4] M. M. Westington, *Atrocities in Roman Warfare to 133 B.C.* (diss. Chicago, 1938), is a useful (though partial) collection of material, but my conclusions often differ from his. Cf. also W. Kroll, *Die Kultur der ciceronischen Zeit*, i. 24–5.

combat felt no ferocity of any kind as they decided on war or agreed to go to war.[1] In my view it is more likely that the regular harshness of Roman war-methods sprang from an unusually pronounced willingness to use violence against alien peoples,[2] and this willingness contributed to Roman bellicosity. But before a defence of this view, a brief summary of Roman practices is required.

Later Roman sources naturally tended to soften the historical record (Livy can be shown to have done so on several occasions, and presumably did so on many others).[3] But when all due allowances have been made for the inadequacies of the evidence and the difficulties of generalizing about two and a half centuries of warfare, the Romans do seem to have behaved somewhat more ferociously than most of the other politically advanced peoples of the Mediterranean world.[4] In the case of captured cities, for example, Roman armies normally behaved more violently than Hellenistic armies. Polybius remarked on this. When Scipio Africanus' forces had stormed New Carthage in 209, 'he directed most of them, according to the Roman custom, against the people in the city, telling them to kill everyone they met and to spare no one, and not to start looting until they received the order. The purpose of this custom, I suppose'—so continues the rationalist historian—'is to strike terror. Accordingly one can often see in cities captured by the Romans not only human beings who have been slaughtered, but even dogs sliced in two and the limbs of other animals cut off. On this occasion the amount of

[1] Cf. Bouthoul, o.c. 420.

[2] It should be remembered that *ferox* and cognate words do not necessarily have bad connotations in republican Latin; cf. Catull. 64.73, Cic. *De rep.* ii. 4, Liv. iii. 70.10, etc. V. Pöschl, *Grundwerte römischer Staatsgesinnung in der Geschichtswerken des Sallust* (Berlin, 1940), 70 n. 1, has it quite wrong; see K. Eckert, *Der altsprachliche Unterricht* xiii (1970), 90–106.

[3] For a good analysis of three passages in which Livy distorts Polybius to minimize Roman cruelty or exaggerate Roman *clementia* see E. Pianezzola, *Traduzione e ideologia* (Bologna, 1969), 68–73. He might have added the case of the Macedonians who tried to surrender on the field of Cynoscephalae, most of whom were slaughtered by the Romans (Polyb. xviii. 26.9–12—even this account may be too favourable to the Roman side); Livy attempts to diminish Flamininus' responsibility and the number of the victims (xxxiii. 10.3–5).

[4] It has been claimed that a society in which a relatively large proportion of the population participates in the armed forces tends to show itself highly ferocious in warfare: S. Andreski [= Andrzejewski], *Military Organization and Society*[2] (London, 1968), 117–18. Rome of the middle Republic appears to offer some support for this generalization.

such slaughter was very great . . .'[1] Elsewhere in Polybius a Rhodian speaker refers to the same Roman habit, and indeed plenty of instances are known (quite apart from the suppression of rebels, which was always draconian) in which Roman armies as a matter of course killed indiscriminately in captured cities.[2] It was the normal Roman practice. Even the city that surrendered was not necessarily safe from a massacre.[3] Captured cities were very often thoroughly destroyed.[4] The legionaries' actions in battle struck fear into even the best Hellenistic army: when the Macedonians saw the dismembered bodies of their companions who had died fighting in the campaign of 199, they were frightened at the prospect of fighting against such weapons (the Spanish sword) and such men.[5] It was of course commonplace in Roman as in much other ancient warfare for prisoners to be enslaved (women and children included), for women prisoners to

[1] x. 15.4–6 (in spite of the fact that there were known to be few soldiers in the city, x. 8.4–5). Notice, however, that nearly 10,000 prisoners were taken (x. 17.6). In such cases some were usually spared for the slave-market.

[2] The Rhodian: xi. 5.5–7. He was expecting even the Aetolians to be opposed to the violation (ὑβρίζειν) of the free-born in captured cities, and to the burning of cities. Such things certainly did happen sometimes in the Hellenistic world (e.g. when Antiochus III took Sardis in 214, Polyb. vii. 18.9), but killing even the male inhabitants was not standard (cf. P. Ducrey, *Le Traitement des prisonniers de guerre dans la Grèce antique* (Paris, 1968), 109–47—this, however, is a very incomplete survey). For other Roman instances see Additional Note IX.

[3] Note the cases of Myttistratum in Sicily in 258 (Zonar. viii. 11; but Zonaras is capable of exaggeration in such matters, cf. Westington, o.c. 75 n. 1), Orongis in Spain in 207 (Liv. xxviii. 3), Locha in Africa in 203 (App. *Lib.* 15—against the orders of Scipio Africanus, who deprived the army of its booty and executed three officers), Phocaea in 190 (Liv. (P.) xxxvii. 32.12–13), Cauca in Spain in 151 (App. *Iber.* 52—all of military age killed), the Lusitanians in 150 (App. *Iber.* 60—they had previously been guilty of ἀπιστία, it is said; Ser. Sulpicius Galba was charged for his action and narrowly acquitted (Liv. *Per.* 49), but subsequently he was elected to the consulship of 144; cf. A. J. Toynbee, *Hannibal's Legacy*, ii. 642–4), Capsa in the Jugurthine War (Sall. *BJ* 91.5–7—*puberes* were killed; Sallust says that the action was 'contra ius belli', but justified by military considerations; cf. below, p. 74 n. 5).

[4] A list is scarcely necessary. Hellenistic kings certainly did this on occasion (cf. Polyb. iv. 64–5), but Greeks regarded it as extreme behaviour (xi. 5.6). The Roman attitude, as suggested by one of L. Mummius' inscriptions (*ILLRP* 122: 'Corinto deleto'), seems rather to be one of frank satisfaction.

[5] Liv. (P.) xxxi. 34.4: 'qui hastis sagittisque et rara lanceis facta volnera vidissent, cum Graecis Illyriisque pugnare adsueti, postquam gladio Hispaniensi detruncata corpora, brachiis cum humero abscisis aut tota cervice desecta divisa a corpore capita patentiaque viscera et foeditatem aliam volnerum viderunt, adversus quae tela *quosque viros* pugnandum foret pavidi volgo cernebant.' (The original may have contained a still harsher description of Roman methods.) Toynbee (*Hannibal's Legacy*, ii. 438) was wrong to imply that this was mainly a question of weapons—note the italicized words.

be raped,[1] and for booty to be gathered in the most ruthless fashion.

It is sometimes stated or implied that Roman methods of warfare grew more brutal in the second century.[2] There is no solid evidence for such a view, and the apparent mildness of the Italian wars is due to the patriotism of the Roman sources and the inefficiency of siege warfare in that period. And much of our knowledge of the ruthless acts of the Hannibalic War and later years is owed to the relative objectivity of Polybius and his influence on other historical accounts.

The significance of Roman ferocity is hard to gauge. In many respects their behaviour resembles that of many other non-primitive ancient peoples, yet few others are known to have displayed such an extreme degree of ferocity in war while reaching a high level of political culture. Roman imperialism was in large part the result of quite rational behaviour on the part of the Romans, but it also had dark and irrational roots. One of the most striking features of Roman warfare is its regularity—almost every year the legions went out and did massive violence to someone—and this regularity gives the phenomenon a pathological character. As far as the symptoms are concerned, Polybius gave an accurate description: writing about the First Punic War, but using the present tense, he says that it is a Roman characteristic to use violent force, βία, for all purposes.

---

[1] That this was normal practice is evident from such passages as Polyb. x. 18, 19.3–5, xxi. 38.2.

[2] Cf. De Sanctis, *SR* ii. 536–7, for the view that methods were still relatively mild in the period of the Italian wars.

II

ECONOMIC MOTIVES FOR WAR AND EXPANSION

1. THE PROBLEM

HUGE tracts of land came into Roman hands, as did enormous quantities of gold and silver and plunder of every kind; millions of people were enslaved; tribute in different forms flooded in; the ingenuity of Roman officials and businessmen exacted its profits in large areas of the Mediterranean world. There is therefore something paradoxical in denying that economic motives were important in Roman imperialism. However the paradox has often been propounded,[1] and the whole question requires detailed consideration.

A full history of the discussion would require disproportionate space. In past generations some well-known historians adopted theories attributing more or less central importance to economic motives,[2] and even the masterly narrative history of De Sanctis offered economic interpretations of certain phases of Roman imperialism.[3] On the other hand such theories were not easy to combine convincingly either with Mommsen's or with Holleaux's interpretations of the Roman imperialism of the period before the mid-second century—not that Mommsen was dogmatically opposed to all economic interpretations.[4] Frank and Hatzfeld directed vigorous attacks against 'mercantilist' explanations of Roman imperialism,[5] explanations that owed too

---

[1] The extreme paradox of an idealist is that a people with 'Habsucht' *cannot* acquire an empire: R. Heinze, *Von den Ursachen der Grösse Roms* (Leipzig, 1921), 22 (= *Vom Geist des Römertums*[3], 10 [→Bibl.]).

[2] G. Colin, *Rome et la Grèce de 200 à 146 av. J.-C.* (Paris, 1905), Ed. Meyer, *KS* ii (Halle, 1924), 376–401.

[3] G. De Sanctis, *SR* iii. 1.113, iv. 1.26 n. 58, *Problemi di storia antica* (Bari, 1932), 197–9. Cf. also M. Rostovtzeff, *The Social and Economic History of the Roman Empire*[2] (Oxford, 1957), 6–23, who, however, avoided in this, as in his other works, any explicit attempt to explain Roman expansion by economic motives.

[4] He explained the destruction of Corinth as the work of an alleged *Kaufmannspartei* (*RG* ii[12]. 50).

[5] T. Frank, *AHR* xviii (1912–13), 233–52, *Roman Imperialism*, 277–97; J. Hatzfeld, *Les Trafiquants Italiens*, esp. 369–76 (he cited the war against Mithridates begun by Nicomedes IV of Bithynia in 89 as the first occasion when financiers exercised serious influence on Roman policy (375, cf. 49–50)).

much—as is clear in retrospect—to certain attempts to explain nineteenth-century imperialism. Since the 1920s, despite the distinction of some dissentients, the majority view among Roman historians has been that economic motives were not important—so much so that it has generally been thought sufficient to discuss the topic in a cursory fashion. It receives an extended treatment in hardly any history of Rome written in the last decades.

In recent work two trends are especially noteworthy. Some Italian scholars have been defending in varying degrees what can be roughly classified as 'mercantilist' theories,[1] the merits of which will be discussed later in this chapter. On the other hand the published views of scholars in the English-speaking world are better represented by Badian, who writes, in reaction against 'mercantilist' theories: 'no such motives can be seen, on the whole, in Roman policy'; 'strange as it may seem to a generation nourished on Marx, Rome sought no major economic benefits'; 'the whole myth of economic motives in Rome's foreign policy at this time [the second century] is a figment of modern anachronism, based on ancient anachronism.'[2] Economic motives were absent, allegedly, until a gradual change began in the very last years of the second century.[3]

The difficulties of the problem come from several sources. It might still be hard to solve even if the source-material were incomparably more extensive, as the continuing historical disputes about nineteenth-century imperialism show. Scholars' opinions about this problem of Roman history are in most cases more or less closely linked with their feelings about the politics of modern imperialism. We are deplorably slow to admit that this is so, with the result that historians of various political persuasions—in the English-speaking world, it must be said, mainly those of the right—have succeeded in distorting the Roman past in conformity with their views about the modern world.

Furthermore there are difficulties of formulation and definition. What counts as an economic motive? If a Roman

[1] F. Cassola, *I gruppi politici romani*, esp. 50–83, 393–404, D. Musti, *RFIC* xcviii (1970), 240–1, G. Clemente, *I romani nella Gallia meridionale (II–I sec.a.C.)* (Bologna, 1974), esp. 73–85; cf. F. Coarelli, *DA* iv–v (1970–1), 263–4.

[2] *RILR*[2] 17, 18, 20. The supposed ancient anachronism is in Cicero, *De rep.* iii. 16; see below, p. 85.

[3] O.c. 44–59.

aristocrat sought to accumulate wealth for its own sake, or for consumption, his motives were obviously 'economic'. But what if he sought to enrich himself for the sake of prestige, to be gained by judicious distribution of the profits of war?[1] Or if he did so in order to strengthen his political position? In practice such distinctions are seldom possible, and I shall in what follows treat motives as 'economic' whenever material benefit is sought, unless some clear case of altruistic motivation arises.

Yet another great difficulty is that the source-material does not reveal the answer to the problem at all directly. The reasons for this must be stated, since Roman historians sometimes assume that economic motives should only be diagnosed if they are visible on the surface of the historical record.

Economic gain was to the Romans (and generally in the ancient world) an integral part of successful warfare and of the expansion of power.[2] Land, plunder, slaves, revenues were regular and natural results of success; they were the assumed results of victory and power. This is not to say that these were the only things that impelled Rome to war and expansion—there were other, less material, advantages as well. Nor is it to deny that there were limits to the energy and ruthlessness with which the Romans extracted economic gains from victory and power. The point is that it was scarcely possible for a Roman to dissociate the expectation of gain from the expectation of successful warfare and expansion. No Roman senator had to convince other senators that victory was, in general, wealth-producing. Those who wish to argue that economic motives were unimportant might support their paradox by showing that the Romans did not perceive victory and power as sources of wealth (and indeed many wars were fought which cannot have been immediately profitable to the state). Or they can argue that Rome and Romans refrained in some significant ways from accepting the economic gains which war and conquest offered; this contention can be supported by the claim that the Roman aristocracy was traditionally indifferent to gain. We shall see, however, that as far as our period is concerned these arguments against the presence of economic motives are without validity.

---

[1] On plundering apparently for this purpose in primitive societies see H. H. Turney-High, *Primitive War* (Columbia, S.C., 1949), 175–7.

[2] Cf. Y. Garlan, *La Guerre dans l'antiquité* (Paris, 1972), 200.

Such discussions as took place among aristocrats about the economic gains to be expected are of necessity hidden from us. Even when such discussions took place in formal meetings of the Senate, the proceedings were largely unrecorded and were often meant to be confidential.[1] We have no reason to think that any private *commentarii* or documents ever provided later historians with any important information concerning the motive forces behind Roman policies. In any case it was not by consulting original documents that Livy formed his view of the outlook of the senators of the middle Republic. Fabius Pictor and the second-century senators who wrote annals in Greek naturally did not dwell on greed as a motive for Roman expansion; indeed, we know that as early as the period 197–194 T. Flamininus found it advisable (in his letter to the Thessalian Chyretienses) to disclaim such a motive on behalf of the Romans in strong language.[2] What Cato and the earliest Latin annalists may have had to offer on this subject we do not know; the comment of Sempronius Asellio on his predecessors, that they restricted themselves to simple military history, and neglected political analysis, is suggestive.[3] In any case, extant writers did not use these sources much.

When extant writers of the first century B.C. and later expressed opinions about Roman motives for expansion or wrote historical works about the period, they were in general inhibited from attributing economic motives to the Romans, in spite of the fact that greed as a motive for fighting wars was a respectable commonplace in some kinds of literature.[4] Many believed that before a certain date, usually set in the period 187–146, the Roman state had been more or less free of *luxuria* and *avaritia*, and this doctrine was schematically imposed on to the history of Roman expansion. It is true that in Sallust's view the *maiores* did desire 'divitias honestas',[5] but for him as for Cicero, Livy and others it would have been impossible in most contexts to ascribe explicit importance to economic motives in the early period of expansion. Cicero and Sallust were aware that *avaritia* was a

---

[1] See above, p. 7, and Additional Note 1.

[2] *RDGE* no. 33 (= *SIG*³ 593), line 12: τελέως ἐν οὐθενὶ φιλαργυρῆσ[α]ι βεβουλήμεθα.

[3] Gell. *NA* v. 18.9 = *HRR*² fr. 2 (see p. 6 n.1).

[4] Among Augustan poets: D. R. Shackleton Bailey, *Propertiana* (Cambridge, 1956), 222, J.-P. Boucher, *Etudes sur Properce* (Paris, 1965), 20.

[5] *BC* 7.6.

charge that could be levelled against Rome, but naturally they
did not accept it as a basic explanation of this expansion. Cicero
could allege it as a straightforward historical fact—though he
knew that some disagreed with him—that ambitious *nobiles* had
always despised money, preferring popularity and glory.[1] When
avaritia did appear in the Roman state, it was more easily
recognized by Romans in its domestic manifestations than in
foreign policy.

Even Polybius is somewhat disappointing. We have probably
lost some important comments of his that would be relevant,[2] but
in the surviving sections he offers no analysis of the desire for
dominion which he sees in the Romans. As individuals, he thinks
the Romans admired money-making as long as the means were
appropriate.[3] Collectively, they behaved as one would expect
people to behave who were aiming at a world empire (as he
believes that the Romans began to do in the late third century),
that is to say they seized the gold and silver of their enemies.[4]
There is some criticism, notably of the comprehensive Roman
plundering of Syracuse in 211.[5] There is some defensiveness too,[6]
which suggests, but does not prove, that charges of Roman greed
had some substance for the Greeks of his time. But the sustained
Polybian analysis is missing, or perhaps was never written. Even
if it was written, it might have been unhelpful, for the pro-Roman
historian probably tried to avoid giving credibility to Greek
charges of φιλαργυρία; this was a practical political matter, not
just an abstract question of historical judgement.

2. ITALY AND BEYOND, 327–220 B.C.[7]

Plundering was a normal part of Roman warfare, and this was so

---

[1] *Phil.* i. 29 (the argument had a special purpose in this context).

[2] In iii. 4 he promises an eventual analysis of Roman rule, including the ambitions of the
Romans as individuals and as a state (§6). No man of sense wars with his neighbours
ἕνεκεν αὐτοῦ τοῦ καταγωνίσασθαι τοὺς ἀντιταττομένους ... (§10).

[3] See p. 88.

[4] ix. 10.11: τὸ μὲν οὖν τὸν χρυσὸν καὶ τὸν ἄργυρον ἀθροίζειν πρὸς αὑτοὺς ἴσως ἔχει
τινὰ λόγον· οὐ γὰρ οἷόν τε τῶν καθόλου πραγμάτων ἀντιποιήσασθαι μὴ οὐ τοῖς
μὲν ἄλλοις ἀδυναμίαν ἐνεργασαμένους, σφίσι δὲ τὴν τοιαύτην δύναμιν
ἑτοιμάσαντες.   [5] ix. 10, esp. §3.

[6] Cf. vi. 56.1–5 on the financial probity of the Romans (with the apparently
exaggerated implication that one could really be put to death for electoral bribery).

[7] I choose this periodization because of the historiographical facts, 220/19 being the
starting-point of Polybius' thorough investigation (i. 13.7–8 etc.) and approximately the
earliest time of which any of his living informants can have had memory, as well as
coinciding approximately with the beginning of Livy's third decade.

in the period of the Italian wars. The known cultural and economic levels of the Romans make it entirely likely that some of Rome's Italian wars had to a great extent the character of plundering expeditions.[1] It is important to remember that we are still in a period when neither the state nor individuals are likely to have despised profits of the size that could be obtained on campaigns. When the Romans agreed, in the treaty with Carthage which Polybius counts as the second (348 or 306?), that they would not plunder beyond certain geographical points, the inference is reasonable that active plundering was a regular form of Roman behaviour and under official control.[2] If the figures recorded by Livy for the *praeda* gained in many of the campaigns of the 290s are authentic, as most of them may well be,[3] they show a degree of interest in measuring and recording that was not typical of that time. Plunder was indeed important, not an incidental. Its total extent cannot be measured, but a vivid impression can be gained from the fact that though the largest cities were seldom captured by siege, enslavements of some 60,000 persons in captured cities are recorded for the years 297–293 alone, the climactic years of the Samnite wars.[4] The number of adult male citizens at this time was probably below 200,000, so the economic impact of the new slaves must obviously have been very great. In a static agricultural economy many of them may not have been put to productive use (and some no doubt were sold

---

[1] Cf. the sensible remarks of F. Hampl, *HZ* clxxxiv (1957), 264–7 [→Bibl.], and also A. Alföldi, *Early Rome and the Latins* (Ann Arbor, 1965), 377. For Roman piracy in the fourth century see Diod. xvi. 82.3, Strabo v. 232.

[2] Polyb. iii. 24.4.

[3] The evidence was collected by T. Frank, *ESAR* i. 43 n.3 (and for a useful collection of all the Livian evidence on plundering see P. Fabia, *Mélanges Ch. Appleton* (Lyons–Paris, 1903), 305–68). On records of booty in the late Republic cf. I. Shatzman, *Historia* xxi (1972), 183 n. 26.

[4] Cf. Frank, l.c., H. Volkmann, *Die Massenversklavungen der Einwohner eroberter Städte in der hellenistisch-römischen Zeit (Abh. Mainz)* (1961), 40, 113. Neither lists all the enslavements for which Livy gives figures. They are as follows:

x.15.6	Cimetra	2,900	x.34.3	Milionia	4,700
17.4	Murgantia	2,100	37.3	Rusellae	more than 2,000
17.8	Romulea	6,000	39.3	Amiternum	4,270
18.8	Samnites	c. 1,500	(39.4	Duronia	fewer than 4,270)
19.22	Etruscans	2,120	42.5	Aquilonia	3,870
20.15	Samnites	2,500	43.8	Cominium	11,400
29.17	Samnites, Gauls	8,000	45.11	Samnites	c. 5,000
31.7	Samnites	2,700	45.14	Samnites	fewer than 3,000
					[say at least 2,500]

The total is at least 61,560. The validity of these figures cannot be proved or disproved, but they are not at all implausible.

to non-Romans), but well-to-do Romans must in the main have been pleased to have this labour available. And the benefits of plunder are also attested for the period 302–291 by the new temples—no fewer than nine of them—which were thus financed.[1]

Even more important as a fundamental cause of the Italian wars was the drive to acquire land. At the end of the fifth century the area of Roman territory was, in Beloch's calculation, some 948 square kilometres (having of course already expanded from a much smaller nucleus).[2] The subsequent growth of the territory in Italy that was farmed to the direct benefit of Rome and Roman citizens was enormous. Land expropriated and settled by Roman citizens, either through colonies or through individual settlement, must have amounted in the period prior to the Second Punic War to at least 9,000 square kilometres.[3] Other land confiscated as *ager publicus* and sold off (*ager quaestorius*) or rented out by one means or another must, in spite of some uninformed assertions to the contrary, have amounted to a very large extra area[4]—it could hardly be less than 10,000 square kilometres.[5] Indeed it is plain that desire for more farmland helped to drive the Romans, and other Italian peoples, into wars in the fifth and fourth centuries.[6] In the later stages of the conquest of Italy the desire seems to have persisted among the Romans. Since conquered land, even when distributed, gravitated into the hands of the rich, there remained in the time of C. Flaminius plenty of poor citizens eager for the distribution of the *ager Gallicus*.[7]

[1] Listed by K. Latte, *Römische Religionsgeschichte*, 415. Much of the construction was presumably done by slave labour. But some at least of the temples were vowed in moments of national danger.

[2] K. J. Beloch, *Römische Geschichte*, 620.   [3] See Additional Note x.

[4] In addition to App. *BC* i. 7.26–7 the most important evidence is that which shows that there was *ager publicus* in places not known to have 'rebelled' against Rome (cf. W. V. Harris, *Rome in Etruria and Umbria*, 106–7—an unduly diffident account). T. Frank, *Roman Imperialism*, 80–1, was at least perspicacious enough to see that he had to disprove this if he was to show that the conquest of Italy did not have an economic character.

[5] Allied territory totalled roughly 100,000 sq. km. (cf. Beloch, *Die Bevölkerung der griechisch-römischen Welt* (Leipzig, 1886), 391, *Römische Geschichte*, 100, P. A. Brunt, *Italian Manpower*, 54, 172).

[6] Naturally there is no *direct* evidence of this (Cassola, o.c. 157, was not justified in invoking Liv. ix. 36.11). Nor would it be contrary evidence if colonists were sometimes reluctant to serve in military outposts, which is what colonies often were, as is claimed for Luceria, Minturnae, and Sinuessa by Liv. ix. 26.4, x. 21.10—not that these statements have much claim to authenticity (cf. Brunt, o.c. 192).

[7] On the encroachments of the rich: M. Gelzer, *The Roman Nobility*, 19–21 (= *KS* i. 32–

After the heavy casualties of the Second Punic War, the situation was more complex. Certain colonies failed, and that has been taken as evidence that there was no longer a strong demand for land among citizens.[1] But the colonization in the 180s and 170s is unintelligible unless there were many citizens eager to obtain farms, or larger farms, in new territories.[2] Settlement on such a scale presupposes some considerable will on the part of the settlers. This whole history of individual settlement and colonization must be set in its political context. Even though the landless poor were politically powerless before 133, the aristocracy was presumably perceptive enough to see the advantages of settling the discontented and potentially discontented on new lands far away from the city, especially since this seemed likely to make more men available for legionary service. Colonies also accepted Latins and allies, and hence they conveyed the further political advantage of permitting Rome to reward selected men in these categories—at the expense of Italians and Gauls who had opposed Rome.

Any economic explanation of the Roman conquest of Italy may seem to conflict to some extent with the common view that the Roman system of control was, fiscally at least, a mild one.[3] No direct tribute was exacted, in money or in kind. It is a truism that the Roman political system in Italy, as it was established between 338 and 266, was a well-judged combination of severity and moderation. However the economic opportunities of power were in fact exploited. Much of Italy was not yet in any full sense a money economy, and so the exploitation was based directly on land. Colonial and viritane settlements speak clearly enough.

---

4 [→Bibl.]), Brunt, o.c. 28, 371. For the popular support for Flaminius' measure of 232 see Polyb. ii. 21.7–8 etc.

[1] The evidence is that in 190 some colonists had left Placentia and Cremona 'taedio accolarum Gallorum' (Liv. xxxvii. 46.9–10) and that Sipontum and Buxentum were *desertae* in 186 (Liv. xxxix. 23.3–4). These are scarcely abnormal events in the history of colonizing movements (cf., e.g., E. S. Morgan on Jamestown, *AHR* lxxvi (1971), 595–611). The tribune who proposed five colonies in 197/6, C. Atinius Labeo, was so popular that he was elected to a praetorship for 195.

[2] M. W. Frederiksen, *DA* iv–v (1970–1), 348–9. For a summary of the facts: A. J. Toynbee, *Hannibal's Legacy*, ii. 655–6; cf. ibid. 635 n. 1 on the popular attitude to the expulsion of the Statellates. The inadequacy of purely military explanations of the colonization in Italy at this time should be apparent from E. T. Salmon, *JRS* xxvi (1936), 53–4. On Saturnia cf. Harris, o.c. 155–8.

[3] See, e.g., Toynbee, o.c. i. 272 ('generosity').

The confiscation of land to be sold or let out as *ager publicus* was a common, perhaps standard, concomitant of the unequal *foedus*, the most widespread instrument of Roman organization. Other sums were exacted too, probably including *portoria*.[1] Most important of all, the allied states had to finance large contingents to fight for the Roman state, but had no prospect, as states, of obtaining plunder and indemnities. Nothing impedes the supposition that Rome took as much from the Italians as it was able to without the blessings of a standing army and a bureaucracy.

Mercantile interests, on the other hand, seem unlikely to have played any important part in driving Rome onwards to the conquest of Italy, in spite of Cassola's arguments. It is conceivable that the Roman aristocracy had quite far-reaching financial interests, and conceivable too that after the colonization of Ostia in the mid-fourth century these interests spread rapidly. To suppose that in that period they saw anything reprehensible in large-scale commerce cannot be much more than a hypothesis. But it remains more likely that the economic ambitions of most Romans, aristocrats as well as ordinary citizens, were limited to land and plunder. There is no good evidence that Rome's first treaty with Naples, or the coins minted there for Rome, reflected any mercantile ambitions at Rome.[2] The Via Appia was an investment in political and military control, but it was hardly likely to bring direct profits to Roman aristocrats.[3] Nor should Zonaras' interesting statement that P. Cornelius Rufinus, the wealthy consul of 277, had friends (ἐπιτήδειοι) in Croton, be

---

[1] The first evidence refers to 199: Liv. xxxii. 7.3, referring to *portoria* and *venalicium* (the standard texts of this passage are unacceptable, but I do not know what should be read). Capua, Puteoli, and an unidentified 'Castrum' are in question. It is possible that Rome had not exacted these taxes before 199 (cf. S. J. De Laet, *Portorium* (Bruges, 1949), 55–7), but the alternative is more likely.

The senatorial decree forbidding the working of *metalla* in Italy (Plin. *NH* iii. 138, xxxiii. 78) was probably a short-lived provision immediately following the conquest, similar in motive to the decision not to exploit certain Macedonian mines after 167.

[2] In spite of Cassola, o.c. 123–4. On the treaty cf. Harris, o.c. 103–4. The Greek legends of the first Roman coins are natural enough on coins which were minted by Greeks in Greek cities.

[3] As Cassola implies, o.c. 129. Ap. Claudius Caecus' intervention as censor in the cult of Hercules *ad Aram Maximam* simply does not 'prove his interest in commercial activities' (cf. R. M. Ogilvie on Liv. i. 7.12 for an alternative explanation), much less that his views about external policy were determined by this interest.

made into the foundation for an elaborate theory concerning aristocratic motives.[1]

Turning to Roman expansion outside Italy in the period from 264 to 219, we are still dependent on very fragmentary evidence. Polybius testifies that the First Punic War was advertised to the people as a source of profits,[2] as well a war against Carthage in Sicily might be. The actual profits in slaves and inanimate plunder cannot be measured, but the scale of some enslavements is known to have surpassed that of the Italian wars—25,000 at Agrigentum in 262, 20,000 in Africa in 256, 13,000 at Panormus in 254 (in addition to 14,000 persons who purchased their freedom at 2 *minae* each), nearly 10,000 at the Aegates Islands in 241, to mention only the extreme cases.[3] Once again, some Roman campaigns look like plundering expeditions, notably the expedition which the consuls led to the wealthy region of Meninx (Djerba) in 253.[4] For one season we even have credible evidence that the navy's ships were taken to Hippo for a private plundering raid.[5]

What matters here is how the Romans perceived the economic effects of war, and how they reacted to these perceptions. The influx of booty and slaves could not be missed, and especially for those Romans with sizable landholdings or the means to acquire land the ready availability of slaves was of obvious significance. The attractiveness of Sicily as a tribute-paying possession may only have appeared gradually, but the island's fertility was probably already known to senators before the war. The Carthaginian empire in general is likely to have had a reputation for being rich, which was eventually confirmed by its ability to produce annual indemnity payments of 320 talents.

If in fact the Romans did not exact more from Sicily than the Sicilians had previously paid in tax—as claimed by the scarcely impartial testimony of Cicero—this shows only that the Romans

[1] Zonar. viii. 6. Cassola's comments: o.c. 170.

[2] Polyb. i. 11.2, cf. 20.1, 49.5; below, p. 186.

[3] Agrigentum: Diod. xxiii.9.1. 256: Polyb. i. 29.7. Panormus: Diod. xxiii. 18.5. Aegates Islands: Polyb. i. 61.8 (cf. Walbank ad loc.). See further Frank, *ESAR* i. 67 (though, as Volkmann points out (o.c. 55 n.4), Frank's comment that the Greek citizens of Agrigentum 'could hardly have been sold' is mistaken).

[4] On this region: Polyb. iii. 23.2. On plundering as an aim: Zonar. viii. 18 (against Gauls in 237).

[5] Zonar. viii. 16 (247 B.C.), with plenty of circumstantial detail (note also the end of ch. 16).

knew how to keep a subject territory under control.[1] In Cicero's view, the great merit of the so-called *Lex Hieronica* was that it made it possible to exact every last grain that was owed.[2] As far as we know, Rome imposed taxes whenever and wherever it could: Syracuse apparently had to pay an annual tax as well as an indemnity for some time after 263, and tribute was levied from the Illyrians as soon as the First Illyrian War was over.[3]

The aspects of Roman behaviour in the First Punic War which the conventional view explains least adequately—the Senate's decision to extend the war after the fall of Agrigentum, and the sheer determination of the state as a whole (supported by a large investment from some of its leading citizens) to continue the war until all Sicily was conquered[4]—these become much easier to understand if we pay proper attention to Roman acquisitiveness.

Roman citizens evidently continued to want land. Not only was there popular demand, unsuccessfully resisted by most of the Senate, for the distribution of the *ager Gallicus*,[5] but plenty of colonists seem to have been ready to move to Cremona and Placentia in 218. These cities were founded with 6,000 colonists each on land taken from the Gauls.[6] The difficulties and dangers which the settlers experienced in the first twenty years of the colonies' life were greater than had been expected, but there is no

---

[1] Cicero describes the moderation of Rome's taxes in Sicily in *II Verr.* iii. 12–15. On the taxation of Sicily cf. De Sanctis, *SR* iii. 1. 196–7, V. M. Scramuzza in *ESAR* iii. 237–40. The supposition of A. Heuss, *HZ* clxix (1949), 508–11 = *Der erste punische Krieg und das Problem des römischen Imperialismus*[3] (Darmstadt, 1970), 78–81, that Rome did not tax Sicily in the first years after 241 is quite without evidence (and one might have expected Cicero to mention the fact in the *Verrines*). On the taxation of Sardinia: De Sanctis, o.c. iii. 1.284.

[2] *II Verr.* iii. 20.

[3] The explicit evidence for the annual payments made by Hiero is Zonar. viii. 16. How much was required we do not know—there is no real evidence for 25 talents (De Sanctis, *SR* iii. 1.117) or 100 (M. H. Crawford, *RRC* 634). The latter figure is from Polyb. i. 16.9, which seems to refer to an indemnity. Cf. further H. H. Schmitt, *Die Staatsverträge des Altertums*, iii. 137–40. There is, however, a good deal to be said for a reconstruction such as that of H. Berve (*König Hieron II.*, *Abh. Bay. Ak. Wiss.* N.F. xlvii (1959), 36), according to which Hiero simply paid 100 talents of indemnity, in one instalment of 25 talents and fifteen of 5. On Illyria: Polyb. ii. 12.3, an ambiguous passage which is often taken to refer to an indemnity, but Liv. xxii. 33.5 slightly favours the notion that tribute was imposed, and it is hard to see how the Illyrians could have paid much of an indemnity after the campaign of 229–8.

[4] Pp. 186–90. For special contributions by the rich see Polyb. i. 59.6–7, with the comments of J. H. Thiel, *A History of Roman Sea-power before the Second Punic War* (Amsterdam, 1954), 302–4.

[5] How many settled there we do not know; presumably thousands.

[6] Polyb. iii. 40.4 specifies the numbers.

sign that the original colonists had been unwilling to migrate there. There may have been some compulsion, and if the ordinary colonists were people who were previously sunk in poverty, their freedom of choice was limited; none the less the colonies could not have worked unless they met a popular need.

Several events in the period between the first two Punic Wars raise again the question of a mercantile element in Roman imperialism.[1] The Senate was not indifferent to those who engaged in foreign trade, as is shown by the embassy sent on behalf of some 500 traders who had 'sailed from Italy' and had been imprisoned by Carthage for supplying rebels in the Mercenary War,[2] and by the famous embassy sent to Queen Teuta in 230 as a result of the maltreatment of Italian merchants. In the latter case other factors were involved besides the wish to protect merchants, but their complaints against the Illyrians were without much doubt what attracted the Senate's hostile attention to Queen Teuta and her subjects at this date.[3] These events should be allowed their plain meaning, no more and no less: from time to time the Senate was prepared to use the power of the state in favour of large groups of merchants. But it might of course have been willing to act similarly on behalf of any group of Italians, whether merchants or not.

What do we really know about Roman reactions to the economic gains made in the wars of this period? According to a stereotype current by the last years of the Republic and reproduced in some modern historical writings, the Roman aristocrat of the third century was a man of few possessions and he did not regret it.[4] Not only did such men actually refuse bribes proffered by foreigners to betray the state,[5] they ate from

[1] Some possibly relevant background events are hard to interpret, e.g. the Latin colony at the island of Pontiae in 313 and the amicable relations with Rhodes probably established *c.* 306–5. For the evidence concerning Roman trade with the East before 230 see Cassola, o.c. 31.

[2] Polyb. i. 83.7–8. The treatment of these men was cited as an excuse for the seizure of Sardinia and the accompanying extortion practised on Carthage (iii. 28.3). If the Carthaginians released by Rome after the freeing of the 500 numbered as many as 2,743 (so Val. Max. v. 1.1a, Eutrop. ii. 27), the importance attached to the 500 is apparent.

[3] For further discussion see pp. 195–7.

[4] According to Machiavelli, *Discorsi*, iii. 25, if M. Atilius Regulus had expected to enrich himself on his African campaign, he would not have asked to be allowed to return to Italy to attend to his farm (Val. Max. iv. 4.6).

[5] M'. Curius Dentatus is a favourite subject, as is also C. Fabricius; what substance these legends had, if any, cannot be known. In Curius' case the story is apparently early (Enn. *Ann.* 373V).

vessels of wood or earthenware, not of gold and silver. They did their own farmwork, on minuscule farms, with hardly any slaves.[1]

By the standards of the wealthiest men of the late Republic, third-century aristocrats cannot have been rich, certainly not in cash or precious metals. They were not surrounded with sophisticated luxuries. None the less the stereotype is vastly misleading. It cannot be reconciled with the likely facts about census qualifications at Rome, or indeed with the known facts about Rome's expansion in Italy, or with such indicators of private wealth as the large numbers of slaves and freedmen to be found at Rome.[2] No more authentic is the view that aristocrats in general were uninterested in self-enrichment.[3] Though wealth acquired by certain means was almost certainly disapproved, and on a few occasions army commanders may have refrained from taking the usual share of booty for themselves,[4] there is no credible evidence at all for the view that the aristocratic ethos was opposed to self-enrichment as such. The alleged 'old principle'[5] that 'omnis quaestus patribus indecorus visus' ('all profit was thought unsuitable for senators') comes from Livy's description of the passing of the *Lex Claudia* in 218,[6] which forbade senators and their sons to possess sea-going ships of more than 300-amphorae capacity, and not from the third century. As an explanation of the law it is totally inadequate,[7] since senators were not thereby deprived of all financial gain, but only of one kind. The Senate as a whole resisted the law, which was far from reflecting senators' own views—though not more than a few of them are likely to

[1] See Additional Note xi.

[2] The value of the required censuses of the equestrian order and the first class in terms of land (or of wheat-equivalent) cannot be calculated, but the equivalent of 400,000 *asses* (the qualification of a third-century *eques* according to M. H. Crawford, *RRC* 623; for a figure of 1 million *asses* see C. Nicolet, *L'Ordre équestre*, i. 47–66) was clearly hundreds of *iugera*. On freedmen: by 209 the *aerarium sanctius* had accumulated 4,000 lb. of gold, much (rather than all) of it from the 5 per cent manumission tax (Liv. xxvii. 10.11–12). Cf. in general Brunt, *Italian Manpower*, 28 n. 5.

[3] The sources attribute such lack of interest to M'. Curius (Cic. *Cato Maior* 55, Val. Max. iv. 3.5: the apophthegm may be authentic) and to C. Fabricius (iv. 3.6).

[4] On third-century instances cf. A. Lippold, *Consules*, 90. On army commanders and booty see below, p. 75.

[5] P. A. Brunt, *Second International Conference of Economic History* (Aix-en-Provence, 1962; publ. Paris–The Hague, 1965), i. 126 [→ Bibl.].

[6] Liv. xxi. 63.4. The phrase was also misused by Mommsen, *R. Staatsrecht*, iii. 898, T. Frank, *Economic History of Rome*[2] (Baltimore, 1927), 115.

[7] Cf. Lippold, o.c. 93–5.

have been deeply involved in large-scale maritime trade.[1] The 'old principle', if it ever existed, is an anachronism for 218. Some much better evidence about the attitude of the aristocracy towards the acquisition of wealth is provided by a text often quoted but seldom brought into relationship with imperialism, the funeral eulogy of L. Caecilius Metellus delivered in 221.[2] In this speech 'pecuniam magnam bono modo invenire' ('acquiring great wealth by good means') is referred to as a conventional ambition—and this did not mean inheriting money, since the word for that would not be *invenire*.[3] Finally, we find no suggestion in the sources that acquiring wealth by means of war was anything other than normal and approved.

When Fabius Pictor looked back over the period we have been examining, it seems clear that though he did not point to greed as the motive force of Roman expansion, he did perceive the connections between military expansion and wealth, and some-times drew attention to them. So one would judge from sundry remarks in Polybius that are probably owed to Fabius, and from the fragment in which he asserts that the Romans first 'perceived wealth' when they gained power over the Sabines.[4] Apparently the aristocrat whose views are best known to us in this period (but poorly known, of course) did at least recognize that economic ambitions of a certain kind had been part of Roman motiva-tion.

[1] The opposition of all senators except C. Flaminius: Liv. xxi. 63.3 (the truth may not be literal). That few senators were deeply involved seems a sure inference from the fact that the law was passed; that some were is a probable inference from the fact that it was proposed. If it had been this law that forbade senators to participate in public contracts, the fact would probably have been mentioned by Livy (cf. below, p. 80). Scholars' opinions on the purpose of the *Lex Claudia*: Cassola, *I gruppi politici romani*, 216–17.

[2] Plin. *NH* vii. 140.

[3] Taken as an allusion to inheritance by D. C. Earl, *Historia* ix (1960), 238, *The Moral and Political Tradition of Rome* (London, 1967), 32 (referring also to investment in land). For *invenire* and money cf. Plaut. *Pseud.* 732, Ter. *Phorm.* 534, Cato, *ORF*³ fr. 208 (p. 85) (apparently in a military context). For wealth in *laudatio*-like texts see F. Münzer, *Römische Adelsparteien*, 263 n.1. An obituary notice in Tacitus contains an interesting echo of the traditional praise (*Ann.* iv. 44: 'magnae opes innocenter partae'—probably an allusion to booty, E. Groag, *PIR*² C1379. See also *Ann.* xiii. 30 end).

[4] See p. 186 n. 3. Small touches can be revealing: at the battle of Telamon the appearance of the Gauls frightened the Romans, but at the sight of their gold accoutrements the Romans were aroused by hope of gain and were twice as keen for the fight—Polyb. ii. 29.9, diagnosed as a Fabian passage by M. Gelzer, *Hermes* lxviii (1933), 135 [→ Bibl.]; Fabius, it will be remembered, took part in this campaign. Cf. also ii. 31.3–6. The remark about the Sabines is in Strabo v. 228 = *FGrH* 809 F27 = fr. 20P.

3. DURING THE RISE TO WORLD POWER, 219-70 B.C.

A more detailed analysis is possible for the period which begins in the year 219. First I shall deal with the finances of the Roman state, then with the finances of Romans of different kinds, considering in each case the known effects of imperialism but also the possibility that the effects were incidental or accidental.

a. THE STATE

No useful balance sheet can be constructed for the finances of the Roman state in this period, in spite of Frank's efforts in that direction.[1] On a reasonable calculation, the ordinary annual income from direct taxation of the property of Roman citizens (the *tributum simplex*) did not in the period of the Second Punic War exceed the equivalent of 3·6 million HS, and may have been lower,[2] but the revenue from *ager publicus*, from the provinces, from booty, and from other sources cannot be calculated. Similarly, while the theoretical cost of paying one legion for one year amounted to some 2·4 million HS,[3] and the number of legions under arms can usually be known or inferred, the actual cost to the state of maintaining the army and of other normal activities is beyond our knowledge.

But what did senators expect the fiscal consequences of war and expansion to be? The majority of them must have had a clear notion of the size and main sources of Rome's revenues and liabilities. Most of them had been quaestors. Each year the Senate was probably presented with a computation of the treasury's contents and with a motion concerning the coming year's expenditure.[4] Of course they could scarcely work out with any precision the real net effect on the treasury of past (not to mention future) courses of foreign policy. But expansion before the Second Punic War had greatly increased public revenues without a comparable increase in regular liabilities. Once the war was over, the impression must have returned to senatorial minds that in general both war and expansion were profitable to

---

[1] T. Frank, *ESAR* i. 126–46, 222–31; cf. M. H. Crawford, *RRC* 633–707.

[2] Cf. De Sanctis, *SR* iii. 2. 623–31. I refer to sesterces throughout this section for the sake of uniformity.

[3] Cf. Frank, *ESAR* i. 76, Brunt, *Italian Manpower*, 411, Crawford, *RRC* 696–7.

[4] Crawford, o.c. 617.

the state. Modern writers sometimes claim that Sicily was the only province that 'paid its way' before the acquisition of the province Asia,[1] but this is an unsupported assertion. Its main relevance is to Sardinia and to the Spanish provinces. Without entering into a full and unnecessary discussion of the revenues drawn from the latter, we must admit that at a time when the mines near New Carthage produced 25,000 drachmae a day (i.e. some 36·5 million HS a year) for the Roman state[2]—this being only one of the sources of public revenue in the peninsula[3]—the occupation of Spain was profitable. Some of the sums that flowed into the *aerarium* in the early second century as a result of the expansion of Roman power must have been very impressive, especially to those who had experienced the financial difficulties of the Hannibalic War. One thinks not only of such items as the income from the Spanish mines, but also of the large indemnity payments (a misleading expression, at least in some cases where the 'indemnity' far exceeded the cost of the preceding war) exacted from some of the defeated. In the fifty years after the Punic treaty of 201, known payments of this kind came to approximately 27,000 talents (the equivalent of 648 million HS) ;[4] and in the period immediately after the treaty of Apamea the equivalent of 30 million HS a year was being obtained by this means.

The growth of the revenues which the Roman state derived from the provinces cannot be traced in satisfactory detail throughout the rest of our period. Frank gathered most of the evidence that deserves consideration. Growth was spectacular in

---

[1] Badian, *RILR*[2] 8. Cic. *Leg. Man.* 14 ('nam ceterarum provinciarum vectigalia, Quirites, tanta sunt ut eis ad ipsas provincias tuendas vix contenti esse possimus, Asia vero tam opima est ac fertilis . . .' etc.) is an exaggeration in the interest of Cicero's argument before the people (cf. R. Thomsen, *Third International Conference of Economic History*, iii (Paris–The Hague, 1969), 106) and tells us nothing useful about the period before 133, least of all what the Romans of that time expected the fiscal results of expanding the empire to be.

[2] Strabo iii. 148 = Polyb. xxxiv. 9.9. Polybius was presumably reporting from his own visit to Spain (on which cf. P. Pédech, *La Méthode historique de Polybe*, 555–9). Badian's assertion (*Publicans and Sinners*, 34) that the figure must refer to output rather than, as Strabo says, income to the state is entirely arbitrary (cf. J. S. Richardson, *JRS* lxvi (1976), 142).

[3] For references to other mines see Frank, *ESAR* i. 262.

[4] Cf. Frank, *ESAR* i. 127–38. The 600 talents of φόρος exacted by M. Claudius Marcellus from the Celtiberians in 152/1 (Strabo iii. 162, citing Poseidonius, *FGrH* 87 F51) are to be included here (cf. H. Simon, *Roms Kriege in Spanien, 154–133 v. Chr.* (Frankfurt-a.-M., 1962), 45).

the period from 146 to about 120 because of the territories newly subjected to tribute. In conjunction with Sicily and Spain, they produced most of the annual 200 million HS which appears to have been the annual income of the state just before Pompey's settlement in the East in the years 66–63.[1]

Little information survives about the total content of the treasury at any particular date within our period. The manuscripts of the elder Pliny inadequately preserve figures which he gave for the years 157 and 91, and something about the sum 'withdrawn' from the treasury by Caesar when he first entered Rome in 49. As far as one can judge from Pliny's vague language, these were peaks in the size of the treasury's balance—probably progressively higher peaks.[3] However we learn little from this source, for the only total which is clear is that for 157, the equivalent of 100·3 million HS,[4] which was a substantial sum by earlier standards, but by no means spectacular. In fact the most important conclusion to be drawn from this statistic is that the state had no difficulty in devising ways to dispose of its revenues; this weakens the claim that they were regarded as in some way incidental.

The Romans in fact made use of the contents of the public treasury. From 215 to 187 it was in debt to great numbers of citizens primarily because of the expenses of the Second Punic War. The debt was a large one, equivalent to twenty-five and a half years of the *tributum simplex*, and it was repaid out of the booty Cn. Manlius Vulso' brought from Asia. Shortly afterwards Rome began to find itself able to afford public expenditures unimaginable in the third century. Some of these must have impressed contemporary minds strongly. After Aemilius Paullus brought

---

[1] Plu. *Pomp.* 45.

[2] Plin. *NH* xxxiii. 55–6; 'Auri in aerario populi R. fuere Sex. Iulio L. Aurelio cos., septem annis ante bellum Punicum tertium, pondo XVII CCCCX, argenti XXII LXX, et in numerato ⌐LXI⌐ XXXV CCCC. Sexto Iulio L. Marcio cos., hoc est belli socialis initio, auri [here there must be a lacuna in the text] ⌐XVI⌐ XX DCCCXXXI. C. Caesar primo introitu urbis civili bello suo ex aerario protulit laterum aureorum XV, argenteorum XXX, et in numerato ⌐CCC⌐. nec fuit aliis temporibus res p. locupletior.' The problems raised by this passage cannot be fully investigated here.

[3] See the last sentence quoted in the previous note. Two of the chosen dates preceded expensive wars, which makes this more likely. That the total should have been very high in 49 is clear, given an income equivalent to 540 million HS (Plu. l.c.) (Crawford's analysis of this situation, *RRC* 695, is questionable).

[4] Crawford, *RRC* 635; not exactly 25·5 million *denarii* as said by Frank (*ESAR* i. 127) or 104 million HS as said by me (*AHR* lxxvi (1971), 1374).

home from Macedon an immense quantity of booty, to the value of 120 million HS or perhaps much more,[1] and Macedonian revenue began to flow into the treasury at a rate of some 100 talents (2·4 million HS) a year, direct taxation of Roman citizens ceased.[2] The citizen's *tributum* had perhaps not seemed as light a burden as it would seem to us.

The vast new expenditures on public works, especially from the censorship of 184/3 onwards,[3] were financed from imperial revenues. The censors who took office in 199, 194, and 189 were restrained in their building activities,[4] but their successors in 184, Cato and Valerius Flaccus, probably spent 24 million HS simply on improving the drainage system,[5] in addition to other projects. The censors of 179 were assigned the *vectigal* of a whole year for public works,[6] a far from normal level of expenditure. Their immediate successors likewise carried out a highly elaborate building programme.[7] The most expensive single project known to us in the second century is the Aqua Marcia, constructed in 144–140 at a cost of 180 million HS.[8] The censors of 142 completed the Pons Aemilius, the first stone bridge across the Tiber.[9] This was also a great period of road-building in Italy, and though some important dates are open to discussion, it was in the second century, in my view, that most of the major trunk roads of Italy were constructed.[10] A great array of other buildings

[1] For the amount see Walbank on Polyb. xviii. 35.4.

[2] Cic. *De off.* ii. 76, Plin. *NH* xxxiii. 56, Plu. *Aem.* 38.

[3] These works are listed by Frank, *ESAR* i. 183–7, 258–61, 286–7. Fuller references to particular buildings can be found in S. B. Platner–T. Ashby, *TDAR*. For the period after 167 see F. Coarelli in P. Zanker (ed.), *Hellenismus in Mittelitalien* (Göttingen, 1976), 21–31.

[4] Liv. xxxii. 7.3 (199), xxxiv. 44.8 (194), xxxviii. 28.3 (189).

[5] The sewerage works referred to in Liv. xxxix. 44.5 are presumably those said by C. Acilius, fr. 6 Peter (= Dion. Hal. iii. 67.5), to have cost 1,000 talents, probably an approximation, or perhaps in fact the cost of the censors' whole building programme.

[6] Liv. xl. 46.16.

[7] Liv. xli. 27.5–13. On the text of this passage cf. W. Richter, *RhM* civ (1961), 257–69; on its content, E. Gabba in Zanker, o.c. 316 n. 3 (but problems remain).

[8] Frontinus, *De aq.* i. 7. It had been begun earlier (cf. A. E. Astin, *Scipio Aemilianus*, 109).

[9] Liv. xl. 51.4.

[10] Cf. W. V. Harris, *Rome in Etruria and Umbria*, 163–8, where the Via Aurelia is dated to 144 (with 200 as an alternative possibility), the Via Cassia to 171 or 154 and the Via Clodia tentatively to 183. Other second-century roads: that built by the younger C. Flaminius from Bononia to Arretium in 187 (Liv. xxxix. 2.1–6), the Via Aemilia of 187 from Ariminum to Placentia (Liv. xxxix. 2.10; cf. T. P. Wiseman, *PBSR* xxxviii (1970), 126–8), the Via Aemilia of 175 from Bononia to Aquileia (Strabo v. 217), the road built by T. Quinctius Flamininus (*cos.* 150 or *cos.* 123) from Pisa to the upper Arno (*ILLRP* 458), the Via Postumia of 148 (*ILLRP* 452), the Via Aemilia Scauri of 109, at least one Via Annia and one Via Popillia—and possibly others (see in general Wiseman, o.c. 122–52).

was owed to the generosity and ambition of individuals.[1] Furthermore, building styles were becoming more luxurious: in 146 the first marble building in Rome was erected—the temple of Jupiter Stator in the Campus Martius, vowed by Q. Caecilius Metellus, the conqueror of Macedon, and paid for from his spoils, and in 142/1 in the Capitolium the first gilded ceiling was constructed.[2] This extraordinary growth of spending on public works is reflected in the well-known passage in which Polybius comments on the large number of contracts let by the censors throughout Italy, so many that 'one could hardly count them', with the result that almost everyone was involved in the sale of these contracts and the business that arose from them.[3] Even in Italian cities outside Rome much new public construction can be detected.[4]

Public expenditures on subsidizing the grain-supply for citizens also deserve mention in this context. There were instances in 203, 201, 200, and 196,[5] but the systematic programme begins with C. Gracchus' law in 123, and continues with the law of Saturninus, the less generous one of M. Octavius (probably to be dated to the 90s),[6] the *Lex Aemilia* of 78, and the *Lex Terentia Cassia* of 73. Add the cost of the state granaries initiated by C. Gracchus.[7] So little is known about these laws, about the price of grain, and about the number of beneficiaries, that the cost to the state is hard to estimate. The disapproval directed against Gaius' law by later conservatives may have been not only partisan but ill informed (on other occasions also they were too quick to announce that the treasury was being exhausted), but it probably

[1] See below, p. 76.

[2] Metellus' marble temple: Vell. i. 11.5, cf. Varro ap. Macrob. *Sat.* iii. 6.2, Plin. *NH* xxxvi. 40, *CIL* i². p. 252, Festus 496L (for an up-to-date plan see F. Coarelli, *DA* iv–v (1970–1), 243, drawing on the work of G. Gatti). The temple of Juno Regina in the 'Porticus Octavia', which is supposed by Platner–Ashby (*TDAR* 304), Frank (*ESAR* i. 286) and others to have been of marble and also built by Metellus, was probably the earlier temple of Juno Regina referred to by Liv. xl. 52.1–3 (in spite of the possible implication of the coin-type *RRC* no. 262/1) and not of marble (cf. B. Olinder, *Porticus Octavia in Circo Flaminio* (Stockholm, 1974), 123). *Laquearia inaurata*: Plin. *NH* xxxiii. 57. After 189 wooden and terracotta cult statues began to give way to metal ones: Plin. *NH* xxxiv. 34.   [3] vi. 17.3–4.

[4] On the second century: G. Lugli, *La tecnica edilizia romana* (Rome, 1957), i. 413–14, 468–9. On Campania cf. M. W. Frederiksen, *PBSR* xxvii (1959), 123–4. The dependence of such construction on imperialism is of course more tenuous.

[5] Liv. xxx. 26.6, xxxi. 4.6, xxxi. 50.1, xxxiii. 42.8.

[6] On its date cf. J. G. Schovánek, *Historia* xxi (1972), 235–43.

[7] Plu. *CG* 6, Festus 392L.

was and was meant to be a *magna largitio*. The cost of grain distribution in the year 70 can hardly have been much more than 6·25 million HS,[1] and this was not a great sum by the standards of the contemporary Roman treasury, but by the standards of the early second century, or of most other ancient states, it was a heavy expense. It could only be sustained by the treasury of an empire.

To set in the other scale, what arguments can be offered by those who deny that additional public revenue was a motive of any significance in leading Rome into war and expansion? Allegedly Rome did not put much effort into increasing its revenues.[2] Only two specific instances of this neglect can be cited before the crisis period of the late Republic, both concerning Macedon in the years after the battle of Pydna—and both these instances are illusory. Rome apparently exacted from the four newly created Macedonian 'districts' an annual sum about half the size of the revenue that had been exacted by the Macedonian kings. This, however, proves nothing. With no direct Roman control and no Roman garrison, with local resources depleted by war and by loss of territory, and with the governments of the new republics also requiring revenue (three of them had to maintain military forces), it is easy to believe that Roman taxation was set at the maximum level possible.[3] For a decade, admittedly, the Senate preferred to have the Macedonian gold and silver mines (though not those for iron or copper) closed rather than enriching Rome, but nothing can be built on this, since the year 167 is known to have been a time of bad relations between Senate and

---

[1] Cf. Cic. *II Verr.* iii. 72. The laws of the younger Cato (62) and Clodius (58) cost much more.

[2] M. Holleaux claimed (*Etudes*, v. 430; cf. *CAH* viii. 238) that since the Romans imposed no tribute on any of the peoples they conquered in the East in the period before 188, therefore they were very little concerned with profit; but as we shall see (pp. 140–3) their 'conquests' in the Greek states were not such as to ensure more than the so-called indemnities, of limited term, which were imposed.

[3] The level of taxation: Liv. xlv. 29.4, Diod. xxxi. 8.3, 5. According to Plutarch (*Aem.* 28.3) they were to pay 100 talents (= 2·4 million HS) a year, *less than half* of what they used to pay to the kings. Livy must have made the Roman terms at least as mild as Polybius made them, hence the 100 talents are to be regarded as half, rather than less than half, of the royal taxation. There is no reason to suppose that the Macedonians' taxation had been (by ancient standards) mild (as De Sanctis claimed, *SR* iv. 1.338; Polyb. xxxvi. 17.13 rather suggests the contrary); and Philip V had increased it in 185 (Liv. xxxix. 24.2). Aenus, Maronea, and Abdera were excluded from the new republics (Liv. xlv. 29.6) : on other territory lost cf. P. Meloni, *Perseo e la fine della monarchia macedone* (Rome, 1953), 419–20. A garrison of two legions would have cost at least 4·8 million HS a year.

publicani,[1] and any local control over the mine revenues contained palpable political dangers. In 158 the mines were in any case reopened.[2]

During the second century the political and economic interests of the state coincided fairly well, but at least from the time when Cyrene was bequeathed to Rome in 96 the issues became more complex. The arguments and interests opposed to the annexation of Cyrene and Egypt for many years outweighed those that favoured it, including the additional revenues to be expected.[3] Evidently the desirability of additional revenues—even Egyptian revenues—declined as the state grew richer, and the attitudes of the late 60s, when Egypt could have been annexed, must not be transferred back into the period before the annexation of Asia. For *that* period it is at best meaningless to say that Rome continued to collect revenues in the provinces 'as much from inertia as from conscious choice'.[4] Tax revenues were indeed a natural result of the expansion of Roman power, but that expansion was not brought about by inertia. Nor is the state which imposed an 'indemnity' of 15,000 talents on Antiochus III and in a single day enslaved 150,000 Epirotes to be called inert in enriching itself.

b. SENATORS

How important a causative factor were the gains that senators made for themselves? We have seen how their psychological and political needs were served by warfare, and we shall be considering later their perceptions of the political needs of the state. Was their drive to serve their own economic interests also an important element in Roman imperialism?

Acquiring booty was, to the Romans, as it was for most ancient peoples, a normal part of warfare. Not only was movable private property, including slaves, treated as booty, but prisoners, unless as an exception they were ransomed, were generally enslaved.[5]

---

[1] The closing of the mines: Liv. xlv. 18.3, 29.11, Diod. xxxi. 8.7. The sources explain this as resulting from the Senate's reluctance to entrust the provincials to the *publicani*, and its fear that Macedonian administration would lead to *seditiones* and *certamen* (Liv. xlv. 18, Diod.).

[2] Cassiodorus, *Chron.* p. 616M.

[3] See pp. 154–8.

[4] Badian, *RILR*[2] 18.

[5] See K. H. Vogel in *RE* s.v. praeda (1953), cols. 1200–13, A. Lippold, *Consules*, 90–1. Offering prisoners for ransom had not been usual Roman practice: Polyb. ix. 42.5–8. For

Surrender by the enemy did not necessarily bring the gathering of plunder to an end, and it was not only enemies who suffered.[1] The impressively organized Roman method of plundering captured cities which is described by Polybius[2] incidentally reveals that the whole business was taken very seriously by those who commanded Roman armies. As for the actual division of booty, the soldiers normally received a share, and the state very often did so. The problem of the shares received by army commanders, which a first inspection of the sources does not clear up, has been discussed in detail by Shatzman,[3] who confirms the conclusion that the normal and legitimate practice was for them to take substantial shares for themselves—such a share being known as *manubiae*—and that there was no presumption that this share would be used for purposes that were even ostensibly public.[4]

In the second century, it is true, there were some famous instances of self-restraint. When Cato was faced with his army's

specific political reasons prisoners were sometimes released gratis (e.g. Liv. xxvii. 19.2–6, xxx. 43.8, xxxi. 40.4). On the normality and legality of enslavement cf. Liv. xxxi. 30.2–3. When Marius took Capsa during the Jugurthine War, burnt it, slew the adult male Numidians, and sold the rest of the inhabitants into slavery and divided the booty, this seemed to Sallust (*BJ* 91.7) to be 'contra ius belli' (but justifiable). This remark is used by E. M. Štaerman, *Die Blütezeit der Sklavenwirtschaft in der römischen Republik* (Wiesbaden, 1969 [→ Bibl.]), 42, as proof that by now the Romans claimed no right to sell those they defeated; but she fails to notice the *deditio* that had been offered, and it is only the *deditio* that could make 'id facinus' (the whole treatment of Capsa) 'contra ius belli' (in spite of W. Dahlheim, *Struktur und Entwicklung*, 15).

[1] Plundering after surrender: Polyb. x. 15.8, xxi. 30.9, Sall. *BJ* 91.6–7 (e.g.). Not only enemies: cf. De Sanctis, *SR* iv. 1.112, on the booty T. Flamininus brought back from the Second Macedonian War.

[2] x. 16.2–9. These rules did not preclude all acts of undisciplined plundering: below, p. 102.

[3] I. Shatzman, *Historia* xxi (1972), 177–205.

[4] Shatzman, o.c. (though some points are open to argument; e.g. Cato fr. 203 (*ORF*[3] p. 82) should not have been invoked, o.c. 184, to support the view, itself probably correct, that generals were not obliged to spend any of their booty in the public interest). Modern works are often misleading about this matter; in addition to those cited by Shatzman, note the incorrect formulation of H. H. Scullard (*Roman Politics*, 14), who while admitting that there were some private profits for commanders asserts that 'the bulk of war booty went into the treasury' and that generals were 'expected to use their portion for religious dedications or public Games'; cf. also R. G. M. Nisbet on Cic. *Pis.* 90 and R. M. Ogilvie on Liv. ii. 42.1. On the level of other officers' profits see Shatzman, o.c. 203. On distributions to *equites* see the references gathered by M. Gelzer, *Roman Nobility*, 7 n. 38 (= *KS* i. 22 n. 38 [→ Bibl.]). The contrast between the gains made by Roman commanders and by Greek is pointed out by M. I. Finley, *The Ancient Economy* (Berkeley–Los Angeles, 1973), 55.

booty in Spain in 194, he himself took none of it, Plutarch reports, 'except what he needed to eat and drink'.[1] A characteristic saying is attributed to him : 'I do not blame those who seek to profit from such things, but I wish rather to strive in bravery with the bravest than in wealth with the wealthiest or in greed with the greediest.'[2] The story is suspect, however. Better attested are the two cases mentioned by Polybius: after the battle of Pydna Aemilius Paullus did not desire any of the booty, or even wish to look upon it; and after the capture of Carthage Scipio Aemilianus took nothing for himself.[3] This was exceptional behaviour and remarked on for that reason. What was quite common was for the victorious general to spend at least part of his own share of the booty on temple-building or some other public purpose, with obvious benefit to himself—the prestige to be gained from manubial building is clear, at least in a general way.[4] The case of L. Mummius, *cos.* 146, is an interesting one, though perhaps extreme. Cicero praises him for his self-restraint with regard to the rich booty of the Achaean War, but it can be seen how this self-restraint could be shrewdly combined with self-promotion: Mummius used his *manubiae* to 'adorn' Italy and the provinces, as is confirmed by inscriptions commemorating his gifts to various towns.[5]

In an earlier period, it has been argued, the leaders of the Roman state must have regarded plunder as an important consideration. As the level of Roman wealth rose by comparison with that of other peoples, so some Roman aristocrats must have come to regard the proceeds of plunder as negligible. That booty retained great importance in second-century Rome is suggested by Livy's insistent references to it in his fourth and fifth decades,

[1] Plu. *Cat. Mai.* 10 (cf. the allusion in Sall. *BC* 54.6). Cf. D. Kienast, *Cato der Zensor* (Heidelberg, 1954), 31–3. In Shatzman's view (o.c. 198) Cato wished to reform existing practice concerning the general's prerogative over booty.

[2] It conforms very tidily with the picture of Cato as a Stoic sage, which eventually reached the absurd point of describing him as 'contemptor divitiarum' (Liv. xxxix. 40.10); cf. Kienast, o.c. 20.

[3] Polyb. xviii. 35.4–5 and xxxi. 22 (Aemilius Paullus) and xviii. 35.9–12 (Aemilianus). For instances when all the booty was distributed to the troops see Shatzman, o.c. 202 n. 115.

[4] Cf. M. G. Morgan, *Klio* lv (1973), 223.

[5] Cic. *De off.* ii. 76; *ILLRP* 327–31. On the alleged moderation of the man who obliterated Corinth: Polyb. xxxix. 6. His subsequent lack of funds was celebrated: Cic. *II Verr.* i. 55, Plin. *NH* xxxiv. 17, Frontin. *Strat.* iv. 3.15. The destruction of Corinth was official policy, but Mummius perhaps felt some sort of doubt that it was justified.

but its precise significance for aristocrats is hard to recover. The only second-century commander explicitly said by an ancient writer to have made war for the sake of plunder is L. Licinius Lucullus (*cos.* 151), who, Appian claims, attacked the Vaccaei in Spain 'out of a desire for glory and a need for money'.[1] Though he says that Lucullus was poor, he apparently mentions these motives not because he thought them unusual, but in order to explain why Lucullus made his attack illegally, without the authority of the Senate. Cato claimed in his speech on behalf of the Rhodians (167) that plunder was what made many of the *summates viri* eager to make war against the islanders.[2] This might be interpreted simply as the attribution of a disreputable motive, but it should rather be seen as the confirmation of an important truth which was uncomfortable in this case because the Rhodians had a claim to Roman benevolence.

The necessity of obtaining extra funds by non-banausic means persisted in the second and first centuries, and indeed grew more intense as the costs of a political career increased. Some still sought to solve this problem by going on campaign—Caesar and some of his officers are familiar examples[3]—but especially after 146 plunder became less important than the opportunities for peaceful enrichment in the provinces.

The opportunities for self-enrichment open to provincial governors and their immediate subordinates were very extensive even in peaceful conditions.[4] A short account of this matter will be sufficient here. Verres showed remarkable energy in exploiting Sicily for his personal advantage, and though senators gained some notion of what was happening (the consuls of 72 even tried to restrain him in one judicial matter),[5] his governorship was afterwards renewed. Exaggerated as Cicero's charges may well

---

[1] App. *Iber.* 51. Ser. Sulpicius Galba, praetor in Further Spain, was even greedier than Lucullus, in spite of his wealth (*Iber.* 61). Other second-century campaigns with an important plundering element in them: Cn. Manlius Vulso's war against the Galatians in 189, L. Mummius' in Achaea in 146.

[2] Gell. *NA* vi. 3.7 (cf. *ORF*[3] p. 63).

[3] Cf. M. W. Frederiksen, *JRS* lvi (1966), 130.

[4] R. O. Jolliffe, *Phases of Corruption in Roman Administration in the Last Half-Century of the Roman Republic* (diss. Chicago, 1919), 1–76, surveyed the evidence, though not critically enough. Most of the practices of the late Republic were probably well known long before 70.

[5] Cic. *II Verr.* ii. 95. According to Badian (*RILR* 10), this was an occasion when 'the Senate as a whole' showed that it 'took its responsibilities [sc. to the provincials] seriously.'

be, they show what was considered possible—extortions to the total of 40 million HS in three years.[1] However some of the most significant Ciceronian passages on the exploitation of the provinces concern acts which he treats as perfectly normal.[2] The amount of direct evidence for the behaviour of second-century governors is unfortunately slight,[3] but an exploitative attitude is to be assumed. It is true that a certain willingness to listen to provincial complaints developed, and in 171 envoys from some allies in the Spanish provinces complained to the Senate about the greed and cruelty of certain Roman magistrates. Senatorial *recuperatores* were appointed to hear charges against three officials, and the affair ended in one acquittal and the voluntary and not very arduous exile of two of the defendants in Latium.[4] Evidently the Spaniards recovered nothing. In the period 159–154, we are told, several praetors were accused by provincials of *avaritia*, and condemned.[5] L. Cornelius Lentulus Lupus, *cos.* 156, was convicted of a *repetundae* charge under a tribunician *Lex Caecilia* about 153, and in 149 a tribune made an unsuccessful attempt to set up a court to try Ser. Sulpicius Galba, recently praetor in Hispania Ulterior, on the same charge.[6] The effort that had to be exerted to save Galba evidently disturbed the Senate. There followed in the same year the *Lex Calpurnia*, which set up a permanent court, with a senatorial jury, to deal with such charges, an action which is to be interpreted primarily as an attempt to take such proceedings into the gentle hands of fellow-senators,[7] rather than as evidence

---

[1] Gelzer, *Roman Nobility*, 112 n. 404 (= *KS* i. 112 n. 404 [→ Bibl.]). The figure is in *I Verr.* 56 ('... quadringentiens sestertium ex Sicilia contra leges abstulisse').

[2] E.g. *II Verr.* i. 44 (money demanded from Sicyon by magistrates on their way to Cilicia), *Leg. Man.* 37–8 (war funds distributed to fellow-magistrates or privately invested at Rome), *Att.* v. 21.7 (large sums extorted from provincial cities in exchange for exemption from billeting), *QF* i. 1.8–9. One of the most startling cases is that of Caesar in Spain in 61/0, where he must have acquired the 830 talents needed to satisfy his most urgent debts (cf. Plu. *Caes.* 11), and much of this by 'peaceful' means.

[3] There is scarcely any evidence of value for the third century; but cf. Lippold, *Consules*, 91.

[4] Liv. xliii. 2. Certain reforms resulted (sect. 12). Cf. Ps.-Asc. p. 203St = Cato, *ORF* [3] fr. 154 (p. 59).

[5] Liv. *Per.* 47 ends with the notice 'aliquot praetores a provinciis avaritiae nomine accusati damnati sunt.'

[6] On Lentulus: Val. Max. vi. 9.10, Festus 360L. On Galba (whose greed has already been mentioned): *MRR* i. 457, E. S. Gruen, *Roman Politics and the Criminal Courts* (Cambridge, Mass., 1968), 12–13.

[7] The view of W. Eder (*Das vorsullanische Repetundenverfahren* (diss. Munich, 1969), 50) that the Senate must have had some part in the proceedings against the praetors

of increased concern for the interests of provincials.[1] The *Lex Calpurnia* probably did have some restraining effect on provincial governors, but no one is known to have been convicted on a *repetundae* charge after 149 until C. Gracchus removed senators from the juries.[2] There may have been such convictions, but it is plain that offenders could only be brought to justice in the most exceptional circumstances, and in general the sole controls over a governor's behaviour in this respect were his own conscience and the disapproval of his peers. It is not to be doubted that many men of influence believed that certain restraints should be observed, and these controls must have had some effect.[3] C. Gracchus' claim that while he himself had gone as quaestor to Sardinia with his pockets full and had returned with them empty, others (other magistrates) had taken with them *amphorae* full of wine and had brought these home full of money,[4] has a certain value both as an indication that extreme *avaritia* was disapproved and that some profiteering was commonplace. It remains impossible to gauge the normal level of exploitation accurately, but throughout our period many must have seen provincial government as a major opportunity for self-enrichment. It was the idealistic maxim of a well-to-do and principled man late in his career to say that a good man should bring back from abroad only one thing, good repute.[5]

The private economic interests of Roman aristocrats in this period are notoriously hard to characterize. The assumption must be that most of their regular income came in one way or another from their landed estates. Scholarly investigation of

condemned in the 150s is based on fallacies (the notice in Liv. *Per.* 47 does not have to derive from the Annales Maximi, and even if it did the fact would be irrelevant); otherwise Eder's account of the *Lex Calpurnia* is a useful one.

[1] F. De Martino, *Storia della costituzione romana*, ii (Naples, 1964 edn.), 259–60, Gruen, o.c. 13–15, C. Venturini, *BIDR* lxxii (1969), 82; cf. W. S. Ferguson, *JRS* xi (1921), 94–6, Eder, o.c. 86–9. Gelzer, *Philologus* lxxxvi (1931), 286 n. 47 = *Vom Römischen Staat* (Leipzig, 1943), i. 166 n. 47 [→ Bibl.], was unable to find any substantial argument to set against this. However the fact that the proposer of the law gained the name 'Frugi' suggests that *his* motives may have been altruistic (cf. L. R. Taylor, *JRS* lii (1962), 24 n. 33).

[2] The cases are summarized by Gruen, o.c. 304–10. That of a certain Valerius Messala probably dates from about 119, that of M. Papirius Carbo ('fur magnus' and governor of Sicily, Cic. *Fam.* ix. 21.3) from about 112 (cf. Gruen, o.c. 111 n. 20, 132). It is not completely sure that Valerius was convicted.

[3] As is shown by the family judgement delivered against D. Iunius Silanus, praetor in Macedon in 141, and his subsequent suicide (cf. Gruen, o.c. 32).

[4] Plu. *CG* 2, Gell. *NA* xv. 12.4 (= *ORF*[3] frr. 23, 28).

[5] Cic. *De leg.* iii. 18. Something similar is attributed to the elder Cato in Plu. *Mor.* 199d.

other kinds of aristocratic business interests in the period before 70 suggests that lesser senators sometimes belonged to families with extensive non-agricultural economic interests, but that such interests were not characteristic of leading senators;[1] hence P. Rupilius (*cos.* 132), M. Aemilius Scaurus (*cos.* 115), and M. Crassus (*cos.* 70) were somewhat exceptional. The exclusion of senators from most public contracts was probably, at least until late in the period, real.[2] Yet there remains a large penumbra of uncertainty. The famous case of Cato is still the hardest: he is one of the very few personalities of the period about whose finances we know anything, and he seems to have evaded the law by making maritime loans.[3] Many other second-century aristocrats must have had cash surpluses from time to time. We happen to know that Scipio Aemilianus had fifty talents on deposit with a banker in 162.[4] How was such money invested? Did Aemilianus concern himself with the manner in which the banker invested it? These are unanswerable but important questions. The *Lex Claudia* was evaded, and by 70 was clearly among what Cicero called 'antiquae istae leges et mortuae'.[5] In so far as senators were involved in overseas trade, Rome's ability to protect its citizens helped them, yet it would definitely not be plausible to attribute much significance to this fact.

We must pay further attention to the interests that stemmed from the ownership and occupation of land. Did Roman governments pursue particular foreign policies designed to benefit large-scale Roman landowners? Large landowners did benefit enormously from war and expansion because of the effect these had on the slave supply. Slave labour was the best sort of labour for farming, as for many other purposes, and it is assumed in Cato's *De agri cultura* that slaves will form the core of the labour force on the properly organized farm.[6] Roman (and other) buyers

---

[1] T. P. Wiseman, *New Men*, 197–202, tabulates the material. Cf. also H. Schneider, *Wirtschaft und Politik, Untersuchungen zur Geschichte der späten römischen Republik* (Erlangen, 1974), 81–7.

[2] The most explicit evidence for the exclusion is Ascon. 93 C, Dio lv. 10 (cf. Mommsen, *R. Staatsrecht*, iii. 509–10, E. Badian, *Publicans and Sinners*, 120 n. 16). It is unlikely that this was a provision of the *Lex Claudia* of 218, as sometimes suggested (L. Lange, *Römische Alterthümer*, ii³ (Berlin, 1879), 162), since Livy does not mention it in that context, but this seems the right general period. Z. Yavetz (*Athenaeum*, xl (1962), 341 n. 61) less plausibly attributes it to the second century.

[3] Plu. *Cat. Mai.* 21.   [4] Polyb. xxxi. 13.

[5] Evasion of the *Lex Claudia*: Plu. *Cat. Mai.* 21, Cic. *II Verr.* v. 45.

[6] Cf. 2.2, 5.1–5, 56–9, 142.

seem to have devoured them voraciously. No over-all statistics can be calculated, needless to say, but the market was clearly able to dispose of slaves by the tens of thousands as early as the First Punic War. Some massive acts of enslavement are known: most of the Agrigentine captives of 210, 30,000 prisoners (a very round figure) at Tarentum in 209, a good proportion of the 80,000 killed or captured by Ti. Sempronius Gracchus' army in Sardinia in 177–175, 150,000 Epirotes in 167 [1] (this at a time when there were approximately 313,000 Roman citizens). This last action was not part of the normal procedure of a military operation, nor does it seem to have had any political rationale, though some scholars have striven to find one; [2] and even Frank had to admit that the action 'might support an inference that the Senate was eager to provide cheap labor in Italy.' [3] Prisoners of war went on being enslaved year after year: more than 18,000 prisoners were taken on Scipio's African campaign in 204–202, 10,000 were captured in three Spanish towns in 141, and so on. [4] The typical scale of the enslavements in successful campaigns is probably represented by the Istrian War of 177, in which one consular army (that of C. Claudius Pulcher) is known to have taken 5,632 persons. [5] A huge slave market flourished, depending in part on Rome's wars, in part on piracy, which was tolerated in the more distant seas, [6] and in part on other sources including ones far beyond the frontiers of the provinces. Strabo's testimony that Delos could handle the

[1] Agrigentum: Liv. xxvi. 40.13. Tarentum: xxvii. 16.7. Sardinia: xli. 28.8–9 (the figure is contemporary). Epirus: the figure is given by Polyb. xxx. 15 (= Strabo vii. 322), Liv. xlv. 34.5, Plu. *Aem.* 29 (and on the facts see N. G. L. Hammond, *Epirus* (Oxford, 1967), 634–5). Known enslavements in Spain are listed by J. M. Blázquez, *Klio* xli (1963), 178 (where some minor corrections are needed; and the figure of 30,000 in Suet. *Galb.* 3 is very suspect, cf. H. Volkmann, o.c. 110–11). The enslavement of 150,000 Cimbri and Teutones (Liv. *Per.* 68) was somewhat less gratuitous and therefore for present purposes less significant. A list of other acts of enslavement between 219 and 133 is given by Toynbee, *Hannibal's Legacy*, ii. 171–3. Note also Strabo v. 224 on the regular enslavements by Roman generals in Corsica, probably an allusion to second-century events.

[2] H. H. Scullard's contorted attempt to blame Charops (*JRS* xxxv (1945), 58–64) is to be rejected (cf. S.I. Oost, *Roman Policy in Epirus and Acarnania in the Age of the Roman Conquest of Greece* (Dallas, 1954), 134 n. 112).   [3] *ESAR* i. 188.

[4] Africa: App. *Lib.* 15, 23, 26, 36, 48 (the total is 18,200 or 18,800). Spain: App. *Iber.* 68 (500 were beheaded).

[5] Liv. xli. 11.8.

[6] Cf. H. A. Ormerod, *Piracy in the Ancient World* (Liverpool–London, 1924), 207. The interesting suggestion of E. Maróti, *Helikon* ix–x (1969–70), 36, that the change in Rome's policy on this matter at the end of the second century was influenced by the influx of Cimbrian and Teutonic prisoners collides with chronology, since M. Antonius' praetorian province for 102 was certainly determined before the battle of Aquae Sextiae.

importation, sale, and re-export of 10,000 slaves (a very rough figure) in a single day should not be taken to show that this was the regular daily traffic, but it probably derives from Poseidonius and it should not be discarded.[1] The period in question is that when Diodotus Tryphon was a power in Cilicia (142–137) and pirating for slaves flourished. What is most interesting is the fact that war itself did not satisfy the demand for slaves; so great was the demand that it created a trade with areas outside the provinces, and at least in the case of Bithynia in the years before 104 a trade of demographically significant size.[2]

Since demand was so vigorous it would be implausible to argue that slaves were a merely incidental result of war and expansion, or one little noticed by aristocratic landowners. The large-scale acquisition of slaves through war was already commonplace before 218, but the Hannibalic War gave a great impetus to slave-based latifundism, at least in certain regions of Italy;[3] we know that by 173 the tendency of landowners to engross excessive quantities of *ager publicus* was clearly perceived,[4] and at some date probably not long before 167 a *lex de modo agrorum* was instituted or revived to prevent such practices.[5] The *latifundia* of second-century Italy came into being partly because the rich took the opportunity offered by the slave supply. Appian's well-known description of the Italian situation deserves to be taken seriously:[6] the rich built up their estates and used slaves on them as farm-labourers and herdsmen, since free labour would have been drawn off from farming into the army. At the same time, he claims, the ownership of slaves brought them great profit because of the fertility of the slaves. Thus the powerful vastly enriched

[1] Strabo xiv. 668. He goes on to say that the cause of this slave market was the fact that after the destruction of Carthage and Corinth the Romans used many slaves; hence the pirates 'blossomed in profusion'. Poseidonius as the source: H. Strasburger, *JRS* lv (1965), 43. W. L. Westermann, *The Slave Systems of Greek and Roman Antiquity* (Philadelphia, 1955), 65, rejects the figure; in its favour cf. Y. A. Lentsman, *VDI* xxxi (1950), 58.

[2] Nicomedes III of Bithynia, when asked to contribute troops to Rome, replied that most of his subjects, having been seized by the *publicani*, were now slaves in Roman provinces— and the Senate took him seriously (Diod. xxxvi. 3).

[3] Cf. Toynbee, o.c. ii. 228–52 (not without distortions).

[4] Liv. xlii. 1.6 ('senatui placuit L. Postumium consulem ad agrum publicum a privato terminandum in Campaniam ire, cuius ingentem modum possidere privatos paulatim proferendo fines constabat'), 9.7 (he spent the summer doing this). Cf. in general G. Tibiletti, *Relazioni del X Congresso Internazionale di Scienze Storiche* (Rome, 1955), ii. 246–8.

[5] Cf. Toynbee, o.c. ii. 554–61. Livy's silence is a very strong objection to a new law.

[6] *BC* i. 7.29–31.

themselves, and the race of slaves multiplied throughout the country while the Italians declined. The land was held by the rich, who used slaves instead of free men on the farms.[1] The general validity of this description remains beyond reasonable doubt, in spite of the emphasis which some recent writers have placed on the evidence that in the Gracchan period some Italian land was still farmed in small units.[2]

A fertile slave supply had other advantages and attractions besides providing the preferred form of agricultural labour. Slaves were almost indispensable for certain other important economic activities—notably mining, in which tens of thousands of slaves were employed, who doubtless had to be replaced at frequent intervals.[3] And during the second century slaves were more and more in demand for other non-agricultural labour and for personal service.[4]

What is the ultimate strength of the claim made by traditional Marxists (and by J. A. Hobson) that the need for slaves was the true origin of the whole history of Roman war and expansion?[5] It can be no more than a doctrine. Unfortunately no well-informed Marxist writer has ever attempted to show in adequate detail how the entire phenomenon grew out of the production relations within Roman society. The attempt would be difficult, not least because Roman policy was created by an aristocracy which throughout its history devoted much of its energy to purposes other than self-enrichment, and which often, when it was concerned with gain, thought in terms of pillage and seizure

---

[1] Cf. Sall. *BJ* 41.7–8 (referring to the period between 146 and 133): '. . . populus militia atque inopia urgebatur; praedas bellicas imperatores cum paucis diripiebant; interea parentes aut parvi liberi militum, utique quisque potentiori confinis erat, sedibus pellebantur . . .', obviously a rough account, but not to be discarded.

[2] On small units see M. W. Frederiksen, *DA* iv–v (1970–1), 330–57, with the comments of A. La Penna, M. Torelli, F. E. Brown (359–62). The fact that the word *latifundium* is not attested in this period is entirely irrelevant.

[3] Cf. Badian, *Publicans and Sinners*, 33–4 (referring to Diod. v. 38.1 and 36.4).

[4] W. L. Westermann, o.c. 67–8, 73–4.

[5] For J. A. Hobson's view see *Imperialism, A Study* (London, 1938 edn.), 247–8. A 'traditional' Marxist exposition is offered by M. Dieckhoff, *Krieg und Frieden im griechisch-römischen Altertum* (Berlin, 1962). E. M. Štaerman, o.c. (above, p. 74 n. 5), 10–15, reviews various Soviet opinions. Some of these recognize that the desire for slaves was not in fact the sole cause of Rome's wars (e.g. V. S. Sergeev, *Ocherki po istorii drevnego Rima* (Moscow, 1938), i. 142.) Štaerman's own view, as sketched in o.c. 15–19, 36–70, emphasizes the importance of other economic factors. She was not, however, justified in relying on Cic. *Att.* iv. 16.7 (on the booty to be expected from Britain) as evidence that slaves were no longer valuable acquisitions in the late Republic.

rather than production; also because, when Rome's external policy underwent a profound change in the last years of Augustus' power, the reasons seem to have been mainly political. But historians opposed to Marxism are in danger of rejecting too much: for the slave supply was of very great importance to the well-being of the Romans of the middle Republic, to such an extent that it must have exercised a fundamental influence. Because the slave supply is not known to have been much discussed,[1] we tend to assume that it was of trivial significance. The subject was clearly a distasteful one in an aristocratic society, and even in Cato's work on agriculture, which gives plentiful advice about the purchase of farm-equipment, nothing is said about the purchase of the farm-slaves whose presence is assumed. Slave-dealing, as generally in the Graeco-Roman world, was a poorly regarded occupation. Yet slaves were bought in large numbers by, or at least on behalf of, the aristocratic leaders of the state. An adequate supply of slaves at reasonable prices was not likely to be forthcoming in peaceful conditions: demand presumably tended to rise in the second century, and perhaps throughout our period, and it cannot be supposed on any reasonable assumption about the fertility of slaves that slave-breeding, together with other internal sources such as foundlings, came anywhere near meeting this demand.[2] Thus there had to be an external supply: some of it could be obtained by purchase, as from Bithynia in the time of Nicomedes III, but most of it could more easily be obtained by war. Thus for a satisfactory slave supply war, or rather periodic successful war, was indeed highly

---

[1] But discussions are likely to have preceded such conscious decisions as the one that led to the requirement in the Aetolian treaty of 211 that those enslaved in joint Roman–Aetolian operations should belong to the Romans (Štaerman, o.c. 36–7, argues that this was dictated by the special shortage of slaves attested by Liv. xxvi. 35.5 and xxviii. 11.9), and the one that led to the enslavement of the Epirotes.

[2] The fertility of slaves as a group was probably low in the second century. The newly enslaved were disproportionately male, and some probably widespread methods of treating slaves hindered procreation—cf. Cato, *De agri cult.* 56, 57 (some of the *familia* consists of *compediti*). On the other hand another—perhaps less influential—writer on farming, Cassius Dionysius of Utica (cf. Varro, *RR* i. 1.10), advised that slaves should have 'coniunctas conservas, e quibus habeant filios' (*RR* i. 17.5; Toynbee, o.c. ii. 303 n. 8, was surely right to see the whole section as deriving from Cassius). And Appian does speak of the πολυπαιδία of the slaves in the pre-Gracchan period (*BC* i. 7.29), though this is often rejected. (It must be noted that Štaerman's arguments (o.c. 57–9, 65–70) in favour of relatively high fertility among slaves do not succeed in establishing much about the second century.)

desirable. This, however, was only one of the economic benefits which were assumed to grow from successful warfare, and there is no rational justification for reckoning it the only important one, still less for treating the demand for slaves as the root of Roman imperialism.

Did the foreign policies created by the aristocracy favour the interests of large landowners in other ways, besides improving the supply of slave labour? The Senate passed a decree at some date before 129—perhaps in 154—by which it banned the planting of olives and vines by the *transalpinae gentes*.[1] The general period was one in which the surpluses of large Italian estates were assuming greater importance, and at first sight the ban must have helped, and been intended to help,[2] Italian landowners in securing western-Mediterranean markets. Attempts have been made to avoid this conclusion and to show that the real purpose of the decree was simply to favour Rome's ally Massilia.[3] It seems likely enough that the Senate intended Massilia to benefit, but there is no adequate reason to doubt that landowners in Italy were also expected to gain by the measure. Cicero used it as a prime piece of evidence that the Romans had neglected justice in favour of their own interests (a line of argument he put into the mouth of the consular L. Furius Philus), and while this may conceivably be incorrect, it cannot simply be dismissed as an anachronism,[4] for such regulations were not characteristic of Cicero's own day; that

---

[1] Cic. *De rep.* iii. 9.16: 'nos vero iustissimi homines, qui transalpinas gentis oleam et vitem serere non sinimus, quo pluris sint nostra oliveta nostraeque vineae; quod cum faciamus, prudenter facere dicimus, iuste non dicimus, ut intellegatis discrepare ab aequitate sapientiam.' Existing olives and vines which had survived the campaign against the Oxybii and Deceatae in 154 could presumably continue to be cultivated (cf. A. Aymard, *Mélanges géographiques offerts en hommage à M. Daniel Faucher* (Toulouse, 1948), 38–9 [→ Bibl.]). The date 154 (supported recently by E. Badian, *RILR²* 19–20, G. Clemente, *I romani nella Gallia meridionale* (Bologna, 1974), 19, 132–3) is not entirely secure; it is just possible that Cicero was wrong to set it before 129, in which case a date after 124 would be more appropriate (and Aymard, o.c. 36–9, argued that it was part of the *lex provinciae*; cf. also P. A. Brunt, *Second International Conference of Economic History* (Paris–The Hague, 1965), i. 127 n. 4 [→ Bibl.]).

[2] It will not do to suggest (as Frank, *Roman Imperialism*, 280, appears to) that the Senate failed to understand what it was doing.

[3] Frank, Badian, ll.cc. These writers might have added the argument that since the Romans transferred ὅσην ἐνεδέχετο of the territory of the Oxybii and Deceatae to Massilia in 154 (Polyb. xxxiii. 10.12) and Massiliot territory must have been exempt from the ban, the actual decrease in olive and vine growing may have been slight.

[4] As by Badian, l.c. The policy was a milder version of one Carthage had followed in Sardinia (Ps.-Aristot. *De mirab. auscult.* 100), as may have been known at Rome.

is to say, he was not misled by some contemporary measure into interpreting the decree of 154 as he did. And to say that Rome had 'no interest whatever in southern Gaul' for another generation is seriously misleading, whether political or economic interest is meant.[1] The measure may not have been unique, but we know of no parallels. That is hardly surprising, since such a ban only made sense in an area where control could be exercised (no doubt the Massiliots were vigilant), but where direct Roman exploitation had still to be established. It is scarcely logical to argue that the Senate can have had no Roman advantage in mind in the case of the *transalpinae gentes* on the grounds that it did not damage the economies of the provinces by imposing similar bans.[2] It can, however, be agreed that the ban on the *transalpinae gentes* does not establish that the Roman aristocracy regularly subordinated the foreign policy of the state to their own interests as landowners.

Many Roman aristocrats did apparently succeed in enriching themselves very greatly in the second century, in spite of the rising cost of politics. That there was an immense growth of luxury is evident from contemporary evidence and needs no arguing. It was in the second century that they began to learn truly elaborate extravagances—the *villa expolita* on the coast, expensive foods, favourites of both sexes acquired at exorbitant prices, and so on.[3] The growth of Roman wealth after 167 struck a Greek as very swift.[4] Figures are as usual few and hard to interpret. When Aemilius Paullus died in 160 he apparently left property worth about 85 talents (the equivalent of 2·04 million HS), not an enormous sum; but as Polybius says, Paullus was not at all well off—indeed he cannot have been regarded as such in his own circle, given that funeral games might cost 30 talents (720,000

---

[1] Badian, o.c. 20. The lack of evidence for Roman landowning is immaterial. Clemente has collected the evidence for imports from Italy in the pre-conquest period at Entremont (o.c. 30–2) and a number of other sites (32–71); see further o.c. 23–9 on the important evidence of wrecked ships, of which the most striking is the well-known one from the Grand Congloué, perhaps best dated *c.* 175 (F. Benoit, *L'Epave du Grand Congloué à Marseille, Gallia* Suppl. xiv (1961), etc.). To what extent Roman citizens were involved in those commercial activities is of course unknown. On the exportation of wine by certain senators in the 120s see above, p. 79.   [2] Cf. Badian, o.c. 19.

[3] The *villa expolita* is an attested phenomenon from 164: J. H. D'Arms, *Romans on the Bay of Naples* (Cambridge, Mass., 1970), 1–17. References to expensive foods are numerous: Polyb. xxxi. 25.5–5a, Plin. *NH* viii. 223, x. 139, Plu. *Cat. Mai.* 8, Macrob. *Sat.* iii. 13.13, etc. Favourites: Polyb. xxxi. 25.4–5a.   [4] Polyb. xxxi. 25.7.

HS).[1] His son Scipio Aemilianus was adopted into the wealthier family of Africanus, but even Aemilianus, says Polybius, was a man of moderate property, *for a Roman*.[2] These words show that by the standards of the contemporary Greek world Polybius considered the Romans to be rich. Alexander the Isian, whom he judged to be the richest man in Greece, possessed something over 200 talents (the equivalent of 4·8 million HS).[3] The earliest Roman fortune we know which completely overshadowed this was that of P. Licinius Crassus Dives Mucianus, *cos.* 131, whose wealth was apparently set at 100 million HS, a very round but undoubtedly huge sum.[4] Such fortunes were rare even among the leading figures of the first century, and there were probably senators in all periods who barely satisfied the property requirements for membership. But wealth such as that of Alexander the Isian must have been quite commonplace in the Roman aristocracy from the mid-second century onwards.

We return to the problem of the aristocratic ethos. Roman aristocrats aspired to do other things besides make money; especially they aspired to win high office, to carry out its responsibilities successfully in peace and above all in war, and to receive the fame that resulted from these achievements. In the invective which he directed against M. Iunius Brutus in 91, L. Crassus suggested that it was not a mark of the *nobilitas* to increase one's patrimony,[5] and (though one might suspect the influence of assured prosperity here) this had never been a sufficient achievement for a *nobilis*. But the traditional outlook respected wealth,

---

[1] Aemilius' estate: 370,000 *drachmae* (Plu. *Aem.* 39), over 60 talents (Polyb. xxxi. 28.3). These sums presumably exclude the 25 talents of dowry returned after his death to his second wife (Polyb. xviii. 35.6, with Walbank's last n.). Polybius' view of Aemilius' possessions: xviii. 35.5 (οὐ περιττεύων τῇ χορηγίᾳ, τὸ δ᾽ ἐναντίον ἐλλείπων μᾶλλον), cf. xxxi. 22.3–4. Games: Polyb. xxxi. 28.6 ἐάν τις μεγαλομερῶς ποιῇ). Scipio Aemilianus pledged dowries of 50 talents for each of his two daughters (xxxi. 27.2), which he probably expected to pay without selling property (it was apparently unusual when this could not be done, xviii. 35.6).

[2] εἰς οἶκον εὐπορώτερον τὸν Ἀφρικανοῦ, Plu. *Aem.* 39; Polyb. xviii. 35.10 (οὐχ ὅλως εὐπορούμενος κατὰ τὸν βίον, ἀλλὰ μέτριος ὢν κατὰ τὴν ὕπαρξιν, ὡς Ῥωμαῖος), with Walbank's n.

[3] Polyb. xxi. 26.9, 14. But in third-century Greece there had been larger fortunes (F. M. Heichelheim, *An Ancient Economic History*, iii (Leiden, 1970), 124–5).

[4] Cic. *De rep.* iii. 10.17: 'cur autem, si pecuniae modus statuendus fuit feminis, P. Crassi filia posset habere, si unica patri esset aeris miliens salva lege . . . ?'

[5] Cic. *Brut.* 225–6 = *ORF*[3] fr. 45 (p. 255): '. . . quid te agere? cui rei, cui gloriae, cui virtuti studere? patrimonione augendo? at id non est nobilitatis. sed fac esse, nihil superest; lubidines totum dissupaverunt. an iuri civili? . . .'

and, as we have seen, acquiring it by certain means was a laudable achievement in an aristocrat. The contemporary evidence shows that this attitude continued to prevail in the second century.[1] 'Nos omnia plura habere volumus', said Cato in the Senate;[2] it was axiomatic. And Polybius is not likely to have over-stated Roman acquisitiveness—quite the reverse. In his view

the customs and rules about money-making activities are better at Rome than at Carthage. At Carthage nothing which results in profit is regarded as disgraceful, whereas at Rome the most disgraceful things of all are to accept bribes and to show greed for gain from disapproved activities; for no less strong than *their admiration for money-making from the proper sources* (καθ᾽ ὅσον γὰρ ἐν καλῷ τίθενται τὸν ἀπὸ τοῦ κρατίστου χρηματισμόν) is their disapproval of greed for gain from forbidden sources.[3]

(He goes on to exaggerate Roman severity towards bribe-giving political candidates.)[4] The same author reverts later to the exceptional tightfistedness of the Romans, and to their financial scrupulousness[5]—an attribute common enough in those intent on getting rich. Polybius certainly did not regard the Romans as other-worldly, and he does not say, as has sometimes been thought, that in the period before their overseas wars they were indifferent to wealth.[6] What he says is that *then* they would not accept bribes of the kind the Aetolians thought Flamininus had accepted from Philip V in 197; *now* (after 146, apparently) he would not say this about all of them, only about the majority. It is true that in order to show that they are still unbribable he illogically introduces the self-restraint shown by Aemilius Paullus and by Aemilianus with regard to booty in 168 and 146—evidence which is irrelevant, but which might be meant to show that some Romans scorned money. But Polybius does not make this latter claim.

Continuing pressures would have made it difficult for the aristocracy to set itself in any serious way against the more

[1] Cf. G. Tibiletti, *Relazioni del X Congresso Internazionale di Scienze Storiche* (Rome, 1955), ii. 240.

[2] Gell. *NA* vi. 3.37 = *ORF*[3] fr. 167 (p. 66).

[3] Polyb. vi. 56.1–3.

[4] In spite of vi. 56.4 we know of no one who was put to death for electoral bribery.

[5] xxxi. 26.9, xxxi. 27.10–11: '... for at Rome, so far from paying 50 talents three years in advance, no one will pay a single talent before the day it is due; such is their unparalleled carefulness about money and awareness of the financial value of time.'

[6] The passage in question is xviii. 35, misinterpreted by among others S. Mazzarino, *Il pensiero storico classico*, ii. 1 (Bari, 1966), 350.

respectable forms of self-enrichment. Certain kinds of lavish display were expected on a much larger scale than before the eastern wars. The sort of lavish gladiatorial games that were given to honour the death of Aemilius Paullus would, as we have seen, cost as much as 30 talents. Much more crucially, the level of expenditure required for the fulfilment of legitimate political ambitions tended to rise. This latter phenomenon has been adequately analysed by others, and the evidence does not need to be repeated.[1]

In parenthesis it is worth pointing out that we should not interpret the sumptuary regulations which were a characteristic of second-century Rome as evidence of hostility towards self-enrichment, though they resulted in part from the growth of private wealth. The regulations of Cato's censorship, and the *leges Orchia* (182), *Fannia* (161), *Didia* (143), *Licinia* (probably 131), and *Aemilia* (probably 115) were not directed against wealth, but against certain types of expenditure.[2] And while this policy derived in part from the fundamental moral beliefs of members of the aristocracy and from the psychological structures that underlay these beliefs, the legal stipulations against luxury seem to have had a quite straightforward political purpose, namely to reduce illicit influences in elections.[3]

There is no trace of obloquy attaching to the profits of war,

---

[1] Cf. Gelzer, *Roman Nobility*, 110–14 (= *KS* i. 110–14 [→ Bibl.]), H. H. Scullard, *Roman Politics*, 23–5, A. E. Astin, *Scipio Aemilianus*, 339. Cato, *ORF*[3] fr. 173 (p. 70), shows the direct connection between provincial extortion and political corruption (' "numquam ego pecuniam neque meam neque sociorum per ambitionem dilargitus sum." attat, noli, noli scribere, inquam, istud: nolunt audire').

[2] The *Lex Oppia* can be ignored as having had a quite different character. The *Lex Orchia* attempted to limit the number of guests at dinners; the *Lex Fannia* mainly attempted to limit the spending at dinners (but note the wide-ranging complaints of an advocate of the law, Macrob. *Sat.* iii. 16.14–17), as did the apparently less severe *Lex Licinia*; the *Lex Aemilia* forbade the serving of certain luxurious foods at dinners. The source material is listed in the relevant places by *MRR* and by I. Sauerwein, *Die leges sumptuariae als römische Massnahme gegen den Sittenverfall* (diss. Hamburg, 1970).

[3] It appears that there was some opposition to luxurious foods as such (Polyb. xxxi. 25.5 etc.); and for the hostility of certain aristocrats towards other forms of luxurious spending cf. Liv. *Per.* 48 (M. Aemilius Lepidus, *cos.* 187, 175, against expensive funerals). The connection of banquets with electioneering is strongly suggested by the *Lex Coloniae Genetivae Iuliae*, ch. 132 (*FIRA* ed. Riccobono, i. 197–8) and supported by the fact that the *Lex Orchia* was followed in 181 by the first law against *ambitus*, the *Lex Cornelia Baebia* (and on the *Lex Fannia* cf. Athen. vi. 274e). For D. Daube's ingenious theory that the sumptuary laws of the second century were intended to protect the finances of the hosts see *Roman Law, Linguistic, Social and Philosophical Aspects* (Edinburgh, 1969), 124–6.

though extreme greed could be criticized and generosity could be praised in this as in other contexts. Nor is it likely that the gains senators drew from more or less peaceful exploitation of the provinces were subject to any significant amount of dispraise from fellow-senators even in the second century, provided that the gains were not excessive.[1]

In one respect it seems likely that some senators became more willing during the second half of the second century to subordinate other traditional values to the desire for gain. Though the topic is inevitably surrounded by secrecy and political invective, they seem to have become more susceptible to bribes. In the period before the overseas wars, Polybius thought, Romans had generally been unwilling to accept bribes from foreign rulers.[2] The first important case we know is that of Timarchus of Miletus in about 161, who seems to have purchased from senators, especially those with weak finances, recognition for his position as a king in Media.[3] Polybius apparently believed that such things became commoner after 146.[4] Later the allegation of bribe-taking could be made with considerable plausibility against those senators who had shown themselves favourable to Jugurtha;[5] and to take a relatively sure example, the younger M'. Aquillius and others probably took a large sum between them in exchange for restoring Nicomedes IV to the throne of Bithynia.[6] A generalization on this topic is precarious, but some senators had become more willing to extract illicit profits from Rome's position of power.

It is true, and of great interest, that senators did accept certain specific limitations on their opportunities of profiting from the imperial system. Particularly striking is the rule that senators did not participate in the vast majority of the public contracts.[7]

[1] Cf. above, p. 79.

[2] xviii. 35.1.

[3] Diod. xxxi. 27a; cf. Gelzer, *Roman Nobility*, 114 (= *KS* i. 114 [→Bibl.]). What were the spells (γοητεῖαι) by which Timarchus' brother Heracleides won most senators over to the side of Alexander Balas in 153 (Polyb. xxxiii. 18.11, cf. xxxiii. 15)?

[4] Polyb. xviii. 35.2.

[5] The sources: Sall. *BJ* 13.5–7, 15–16, 20.1, 27.2, 28.1, 29, 32, 33.2, 40.1–2, etc. (see *MRR* i. 546). Sallust is excessively fond of this theme, but modern scepticism also goes too far (below, p. 250).

[6] App. *Mithr.* 11.36. On the question whether the elder M'. Aquillius (*cos.* 129) took a bribe from Mithridates V in exchange for Phrygia cf. App. *Mithr.* 12.39, 57.231, D. Magie, *Roman Rule in Asia Minor*, ii. 1049 n. 41, E. Gabba on App. *BC* i. 22.92.

[7] See above, p. 80 n. 2.

Eventually this gave rise to a somewhat strange situation in which senators were forbidden to benefit from what had possibly become the most profitable form of imperial exploitation; and by the last years of the Republic we know that some senators (it is very obscure how many) found this intolerable and acquired shares in the *societates publicanorum*.[1] Yet the original prohibition is perfectly intelligible and does not show that the aristocracy was indifferent to self-enrichment. It probably dates from the general period of the *Lex Claudia*. Public contracting meant selling goods and services to the state in what was probably felt to be an unaristocratic fashion, and the more properly aristocratic source of new wealth, success in war, was still regularly available. Furthermore some senators may well have been sensitive to the difficulties the state was likely to encounter in letting its contracts at reasonable prices if the bidders came from within the Senate itself. At the same time, as the *Lex Claudia* shows, there were well-to-do people outside the Senate who saw it as advantageous to keep senators out of this business and could rally substantial political support for their point of view.

Another limitation on the activities of senators deserves mention. While they were in their own provinces governors and legates were forbidden to buy slaves, except to replace slaves who had come with them and died in the province, because, Cicero says, the *maiores* thought it was robbery, not purchase, if the seller did not have a free choice.[2] This regulation, most necessary one would think, probably stems from the somewhat increased concern for the well-being of the provincials which can be detected from the 170s onwards.[3] It is not likely to have been observed with any rigour, and Cicero seems to admit that in using it against Verres, he is harking back excessively to *antiqua religio*.[4]

Plentiful allowance should always be made for individual

---

[1] The primary evidence is Cic. *Vat.* 29 ('eripuerisne partis illo tempore carissimas partim a Caesare, partim a publicanis?'); cf. E. Badian, *Publicans and Sinners*, 102. But when Cicero is directing unsubstantiated charges and innuendoes against his enemies, caution is required.

[2] *II Verr.* iv. 9–10.

[3] The regulation is not necessarily presupposed by the story told in Plu. *Cat. Mai.* 10.5, but seems to be presupposed by the one told of Scipio Aemilianus in Polyb. fr. 76B–W, Val. Max. iv. 3.13, Plu. *Mor.* 201a (referring to the period 140–139).

[4] 'Dicet aliquis: "Noli isto modo agere cum Verre, noli eius facta ad antiquae religionis rationem exquirere; concede ut impune emerit, modo ut bona ratione emerit, nihil pro potestate, nihil ab invito, nihil per iniuriam". Sic agam . . .' (*II Verr.* iv. 10).

divergences from the normal attitudes. If Polybius is to be believed on this topic, Aemilius Paullus and Aemilianus could both on occasion forgo easy opportunities of self-enrichment.[1] It may be that in the late Republic aristocratic prosperity, accompanied by philosophical ideas, changed the attitudes of some towards wealth.[2] The three men who, according to Athenaeus, observed the *Lex Fannia sumptuaria*—the only three— were the 'Stoics' Aelius Tubero, Mucius Scaevola, and Rutilius Rufus,[3] and they might be cases in point—not that the *Lex Fannia* opposed the acquisition of wealth. Yet in the last generation of the Republic it was the man who refused to enrich himself who was remarkable, Cato Uticensis—and investigation shows that even he connived at ruthless exploitation of Rome's subjects by his relatives.[4]

How then should we formulate the importance of economic gains in the Senate's policies? These policies were, within certain limits of prudence and within the capacities of the state, generally aggressive and often interventionist. The causes of this behaviour are manifold, and some of the most important had little to do with wealth. But to Roman senators economic gain, both public and private, was a normal concomitant of successful warfare and of the expansion of power. When the elder Ti. Gracchus' successes in Sardinia were commemorated by an inscription in 174, the text mingled the economic gains with the political ones as a matter of course.[5] We have seen how extensive and fundamental the economic gains were, and furthermore that according to the established ethos—which, however, underwent some modifications in the second century—private gain was desirable and important. Nor was economic exploitation confined to activities that were the incidental side-effects of military victory, as is shown most clearly by the enslavement of 150,000 Epirotes in 167 and by some other acts of enslavement. The presence of economic motives is not excluded by the fact that the stated reasons for war were of a quite different kind. Furthermore, if everyone in the

---

[1] On the latter (reader of Xenophon's *Cyropaedia* etc.) see A. E. Astin, *Scipio Aemilianus*, 118–19.

[2] For the philosophical influence cf. Cic. *De rep.* iv. 7.7, *Parad.* vi. 43.

[3] vi. 274c–e.

[4] S.I. Oost, *CPh* l (1955), 105–7.

[5] Liv. xli. 28.8–9 (booty, revenues); cf. Scipio Africanus' prayer at Lilybaeum in 204, Liv. (A.) xxix. 27.3.

Senate recognized the economic advantages of Rome's fundamental policies, these advantages did not have to be debated at
length. Meanwhile it can be conceded that some senators may
have been indifferent to personal enrichment. The best summary
formulation that is possible on the surviving evidence is that desire
for economic gain was a factor of the greatest importance in
predisposing senators to take aggressive and interventionist
decisions in foreign policy, and there is no reason to doubt that on
some occasions this desire played a more immediate part in
influencing policy.

c. OTHER CITIZENS

Two questions arise. To what extent did citizens outside the
Senate identify their economic interests with war and expansion?
And how much influence did their views have on the conduct of
the Roman state?

Many of the best-connected men outside the Senate, members
of the equestrian order, depended for their livelihoods on land,
and some of these must have benefited considerably from the
expansion of Roman power, like senatorial landowners. Many
non-senatorial members of the order still performed long periods
of military service,[1] and so shared proportionately in the
economic blessings of victory. Unmistakable advantages flowed
to Roman *publicani* on a huge scale through the collection of
Italian and provincial revenues, an activity which required the
participation of increasing numbers of people. Those who
contracted with the state for *ultro tributa* depended in large part on
the money Rome acquired by means of war and empire. The
furnishing of weapons and clothing to armies was in itself a steady
source of wealth,[2] for there was a mean total of seven legions in
service in the years between 200 and 91. As for profit margins,
there is no reason to think that in this (or any other) category of
the public contracts they were at all modest.[3] With regard to

[1] Above, p. 37 n. 2.

[2] Little is known of particular cases; cf. Liv. xliv. 16.4.

[3] As Badian argues, *Publicans and Sinners*, 21–5, 34–6, etc., without any good evidence
(cf. my review, *AJPh* xcvi (1975), 433–5). On the profits made from tax-farming in Sicily
in Verres' time (profits which were probably higher than those to be made from *ultro
tributa*) see A. H. M. Jones, *Third International Conference of Economic History*, iii (Paris–The
Hague, 1969), 85–7 = *The Roman Economy* (Oxford, 1974), 118–20.

public building, Polybius' well-known testimony as to the large number of people involved has already been quoted, and the dependence of such building on imperialism has been made clear.

In the wider category of *negotiatores*, anyone prepared to invest in trade outside Italy benefited from the growth of Roman power. The formal privileges which the Roman government sometimes secured for such people were only a part of the advantage. Not that these were negligible: the freedom from port-dues for Roman citizens and Latins in Ambracia, established by senatorial decree in 187, is likely to have been extended later to some other places.[1] The famous free harbour established in 167 at Delos proved highly advantageous and attractive to Roman and Italian traders, even though it gave them no privileges over traders of other nationalities;[2] nor can we suppose that Roman citizens were an insignificant part of the Italian community that grew up on Delos, as used to be claimed—quite the reverse.[3] It is also possible that the somewhat anomalous Roman seizure of Zacynthos in 191 was intended to help *negotiatores*, since it gave little political advantage to Rome.[4]

---

[1] Liv. xxxviii. 44.4: 'Portoria, quae vellent, terra marique caperent, dum eorum immunes Romani ac socii nominis Latini essent.' T. Frank, *Roman Imperialism*, 294 n. 7, was entirely wrong to suppose that this privilege was diluted by the inclusion of the Italian allies. There are no parallels (not with Abdera, in spite of Toynbee, *Hannibal's Legacy*, ii. 368), but there is little evidence against the existence of such clauses in later agreements and decrees. Admittedly the freedom of the *publicani* from *portoria* stipulated in the *Lex Antonia de Termessibus* (*FIRA* ed. Riccobono, i. 137) is evidence that other Romans did not have this privilege in Asia (Frank, o.c. 280). Cf. further J. Hatzfeld, *Les Trafiquants Italiens*, 322.

[2] Romans and Italians must have become more numerous at Delos than they were anywhere else in the Aegean before their penetration of the province Asia. The free harbour (Polyb. xxx. 31.10 etc.) has to be explained somehow: punishing Rhodes was an initial motive for establishing it, but after Rome agreed to an alliance in 165 (31.20), the cause of Rhodes' 85-per cent loss of port-dues (31.12—surely the correct interpretation; Toynbee, *Hannibal's Legacy*, ii. 365 n. 2) would have been removed if there had not been some reason for it. Note that Romans and Italians had apparently failed to establish themselves in considerable numbers at Rhodes (H. H. Schmitt, *Rom und Rhodos* (Munich, 1957), 132 n. 1). On the attractions of Delos cf. L. Casson, *TAPhA* lxxxv (1954), 180.

[3] See A. J. N. Wilson, *Emigration from Italy in the Republican Age of Rome* (Manchester, 1966), 105–11, F. Cassola, *DA* iv–v (1970–1), 317.

[4] Liv. xxxvi. 31.10–32.9. Epigraphical evidence for Roman penetration seems to be limited to *CIL* iii. 574; App. *Mithr.* 45 shows that there were Romans settled there by 86 (cf. J. Hatzfeld, o.c. 38–9). Cephallenia also deserves attention. Same, the chief town, was garrisoned by Rome after its capture in the winter of 189–8; rumours of expulsion had driven the inhabitants to resist and thus provoke a siege (Liv. (P.) xxxviii. 28.5–30.1). Rome's original policy in 189, whatever it was exactly, must have resulted from the piracy with which the Cephallenians had, in the previous year, closed the straits to *commeatus Italici* (Liv. (P.) xxxvii. 13.11–12).

What mattered more than these special privileges was the protection that the Roman state and the Roman name could give to citizens, and also to Italians, in places more and more distant from Rome—protection not often needed but always present in the background. Cicero claims in the *Verrines* that it is the Roman citizenship which protects Roman merchants to the ends of the earth,[1] and beneath the rhetoric there is a solid truth. A full and up-to-date account of the business interests of Romans and Italians is the provinces and beyond them is regrettably lacking. The great growth of these interests in the third and second centuries, outstripping anything that the reputedly more 'commercial' empire of Carthage had achieved, was a symptom of the dynamic energy shown by the Romans and by some other Italians; and to some extent it was supported by Rome's military strength.

In the provinces it was probably the *publicani* who benefited most, since they possessed some cohesive political strength, especially after their admission to the *repetundae* juries. Other beneficiaries were of course *negotiatores* in general, and Romans and Italians with large land-holdings in the provinces—though these were perhaps not an important phenomenon in many provinces until the first century.[2] Men in all these categories expected favourable treatment from Roman officials,[3] and it was especially common for *publicani* and financiers to look for official

---

[1] Cic. *II Verr.* v. 166–7.

[2] However there were already some such holdings in the second century (cf. P. A. Brunt, *Italian Manpower*, 213–14). The following evidence is relevant: Diod. xxxiv/v. 2.27, 31, 32, 34 (Italian landowners in Sicily in the period of the first slave rebellion; in § 31 he states that most of the large slave-owners were ἱππεῖς ἐντελεῖς τῶν Ῥωμαίων, a claim which is somewhat weakened by an anachronism in what follows; on these people cf. C. Nicolet, *L'Ordre équestre*, i. 292–4, and for an individual *eques* in 104, Diod. xxxvi. 4.1; G. P. Verbrugghe's attempt to show that Diodorus was wrong to suppose that there were Roman and Italian landowners in Sicily (*TAPhA* ciii (1972), 535–59) is not adequately argued); *Lex Agraria* (*FIRA* ed. Riccobono, no. 8), lines 43–96 (sales of *ager publicus* in Africa, evidently to large-scale Roman interests—cf. Brunt, o.c. 213 n. 9); *Lex Agraria*, lines 96–105 (*ager publicus* at Corinth). Roman landowners of republican date are known in Messenia from *IG* v. 1.1433 (cf. also 1432, 1434), but the exact date is controversial (cf. A. Wilhelm, *JÖAI* xvii (1914), 1–120, M. Rostovtzeff, *SEHHW* 753–4, Wilson, o.c. 150 n. 2). Concerning Chios in 86 see App. *Mithr.* 47. For Roman landowning in Gallia Transalpina in the very early years of the first century see Cic. *Quinct.* 12.

[3] Cf. Hatzfeld, o.c. 324–5. Specific evidence is not extensive for the second century, but Cato, *ORF³* fr. 173 (p. 71), lines 9–11, probably refers to private activities supported by governors.

support in obtaining money owed to them.[1] These sums included interest exacted at usurious rates on loans which cities had been compelled to seek by the financial demands of the Roman government itself. Sometimes the capital involved was not very large by Roman standards, as in the case of the Cloatii brothers, who three times in the 70s lent a few thousand drachmae to Gytheum, on one occasion at a rate of 48 per cent compound interest.[2] But on some occasions the scale was much larger, the extreme case being the 120,000 talents owed by Asia in 74–73 as a result of the 20,000 talent indemnity which Sulla had imposed.[3] Even when, as in the latter case, a Roman official eventually imposed a compromise settlement, it must be recognized that the existence of Roman power and the partial complaisance of Roman officials allowed profits to be made. Cicero was too benevolent to permit debt-collectors the actual command of troops within his province—though he allowed M. Brutus' agents to take troops to Cappadocia purely to exact interest from King Ariobarzanes—but it is clear that governors did sometimes grant this privilege.[4] In general the advantageous position of Roman financiers in the provinces is not to be doubted. It is true that relationships between Romans and Italians on the one side and provincials on the other sometimes seem to have been amicable and co-operative,[5] and some individual provincials prospered under Roman rule, but Romans and Italians must, at least in

---

[1] In the first century numerous cases are known in which provincial officials assisted in, or were at least asked to assist in, the collection of debts to Romans (e.g. Cic. *Mur.* 42, *Fam.* xiii. 56, 61, *Att.* ii. 1.12, vi. 1), or in unspecified *negotia* most of which were probably of this kind (Cic. *Fam.* xiii contains many such cases; note letters 27, 33, 38, 41–5, 53, 55, 57, 63, 74).

[2] *SIG*³ 748. Gytheum was not part of the province of Achaea, but the fact is immaterial here.

[3] 40,000 talents had already been paid on the Asian debt. Lucullus made himself unpopular with the lenders by imposing relative moderation, and the debts seem to have been cleared by the time he ceased to be governor (Plu. *Luc.* 20). But enormous profits had been made.

[4] No troops to be used against the Salaminians as Scaptius had requested: *Att.* vi. 1.5–6, 2.8–9. Troops to Cappadocia followed threatening letters from Cicero, which the latter wrote though he knew that Ariobarzanes could not pay, since he was already paying 33 talents a month of interest to Pompey (vi. 1.3–4, 2.7, 3.5–6). Scaptius had had troops from Ap. Claudius Pulcher, Cicero's predecessor, to use against Salamis, and this was clearly normal (vi. 1.6; cf. 2.8). M. Brutus was heavily involved in barely legal investment in the region of Cilicia, where he served as quaestor in 53 under his father-in-law (Ap. Claudius), an opportunity he had preferred to serving in Gaul (*De vir. ill.* 82.3–4). Cf. Badian, *RILR*² 84–6.

[5] On the Greek world, cf. Hatzfeld, o.c. 291–315.

certain provinces, have been aware of what might happen to them if Roman power failed. It did so temporarily in the province Asia in 88, and many thousands of Roman citizens lost their lives as a result.[1]

Beyond the provinces Roman and Italian business interests were certainly not negligible in the second century.[2] They were often more precarious than they would have been within the provinces, and it therefore seems likely that the Romans and Italians concerned regarded the ability and willingness of the Roman state to afford some protection in emergencies as vitally important. When a vigorous opponent of Rome appeared, such as Jugurtha or Mithridates VI, they necessarily preferred a Roman policy that was hard and assertive.

It has been claimed that the influence of provincial and extra-provincial *negotiatores* was not really in favour of Roman expansion. 'It is nothing short of absurd . . . to believe that this class [the *publicani*] could have been pressing for expansion of the Empire', wrote Badian,[3] commenting on the complaint of Nicomedes III in 104 that most of his subjects, thanks to the *publicani*, had been taken into slavery,[4] a result which the *publicani* could hardly have brought about in an annexed province. But most of the business in which Roman *negotiatores* engaged was even less likely than this one to encounter senatorial disapproval, and—more important—the sense of 'empire' with which we should be concerned is the primary Roman sense, namely the whole area in which Rome exercised power.[5] The question of annexation is subsidiary.[6] What we should ask is whether *negotiatores* in general had in the preceding decades, both before and after the annexation of Asia, favoured the extension of Roman power in Asia Minor and its extension to the point where Roman *publicani* exercised enormous power in the kingdom of Bithynia. The natural assumption must be that they did. Similarly in Numidia, while some *negotiatores* might have found the extension of annexed Roman territory after the Jugurthine

---

[1] On the number of casualties (80,000 or 150,000 in the sources) cf. P. A. Brunt, *Italian Manpower*, 224–7.

[2] On Transalpine Gaul see above, p. 86 n. 1. On the Greek world: Hatzfeld, o.c. 17–51, *passim*. On Numidia: Sall. *BJ* 26.1–3, 47.1. On Carthage before 146: see below, p. 99 n. 2.

[3] *Publicans and Sinners*, 89.   [4] Diod. xxxvi. 3.1.

[5] Below, p. 105.   [6] Cf. E. Gabba in *ANRW* i. 1.773.

War embarrassing, the supremacy of Roman power they must in general have supported, and indeed there is evidence that they worked for a more vigorously anti-Jugurthan policy than the one most favoured in the Senate.[1] The arguments of Frank and Badian to the contrary are without value.[2] The slaughter at Cirta in 112 must have confirmed for all the Romans and Italians in Africa that they depended on the credibility of Rome's power to intervene.[3]

But the question remains whether the economic interests of these Romans (and Italians) outside the Senate had any important effects on Rome's external policies in the second century, or whether, as Hatzfeld argued of the *negotiatores* in the East, they merely took the opportunities provided by expanding imperial power. The latter view is in general much closer to the truth, at least until the last years of our period.

Second-century senators, it should be conceded, were far from being cut off from the rest of the possessing class of Roman society, and indeed recent work has shown how closely intermingled senators and well-to-do non-senators were.[4] Furthermore senators who needed to win elections can never have been immune to the opinions of men in the higher census-classes; and the interest which the second-century Senate sometimes took in the affairs of the *negotiatores* can clearly be seen in public construction that was undertaken mainly for their benefit.[5] Certain actions of the Roman state do become significantly easier to understand if we

---

[1] Their support for Marius' consular candidacy: Sall. *BJ* 64.5–6, 65.3–5. Cf. Vell. ii. 11.2 ('per publicanos aliosque in Africa negotiantis criminatus Metelli lentitudinem' etc.). It is not entirely clear what the alliances of the tribunes C. Memmius (111) and T. Manlius Mancinus (107) were, but the *quaestio Mamiliana* was set up with equestrian jurors (Cic. *Brut.* 128) and may have reflected the feelings of the *negotiatores* (cf. Gabba, o.c. 775). The role which the latter may have played in the popular vote by which the Numidian war was assigned to Marius is not revealed by the sources (for which see *MRR* i. 550).

[2] Frank, *Roman Imperialism*, 267–8, Badian, *RILR*² 26. Both rely heavily on the fact that Numidia was not annexed in 105 (so also P. A. Brunt, *Second International Conference of Economic History* (Paris–The Hague, 1965), i. 131 [→ Bibl.]). In reality annexation would have been very difficult at that time: see below, p. 151. What we have to consider is in any case the attitude of *negotiatores* towards Roman *power*.

[3] Cf. further Gabba, o.c. 776–7

[4] For the closeness of senators to non-senatorial members of the equestrian order see Brunt, o.c. 117–18, and better still C. Nicolet, *L'Ordre équestre*, i. 249–69, 470–1.

[5] On the *basilica Porcia* of 184: Liv. xxxix. 44.7, Plu. *Cat. Mai.* 19 (probably wrong to suggest that the Senate in general opposed it), *De vir. ill.* 47.5. M. Fulvius Nobilior as censor in 179 built harbour-works, a *basilica* (later known as the *basilica Aemilia*), and a

suppose that *negotiatores* exercised some political influence—the continuance of the free harbour at Delos after 165, for example, and perhaps the destruction of Corinth in 146.[1] It should be conceded too that we know very little about how policy was formed at Rome and about who if anyone was listened to by members of the Senate.

Some ill-founded arguments have been used to show that non-senatorial influence was small: for instance, the view that the Senate acquiesced in Carthaginian exclusion of Italian businessmen from Africa in the period prior to the Third Punic War, though it has some ancient authority, is incorrect.[2]

However there were clearly limits to the privileges which even the *publicani*, the most organized interest group outside the Senate, could obtain. *Censoria locatio*, the system by which the censors sold the provincial tax-contracts at Rome, was introduced for the taxes of the province Asia by C. Gracchus, but was not applied to many, if any, other provinces during most of our period;[3] on the whole it would have been advantageous to the *publicani*. The more remunerative of the Macedonian mines were closed for a few years (but only a few) after the battle of Pydna, even though some Romans must have been keen to operate

fish-market 'circumdatis tabernis quas vendidit in privatum', etc. (Liv. xl. 51.4–6). The *basilica Sempronia* of 169: Liv. xlv. 16.10–11; the *basilica Opimia* of 121 (a special case clearly): *MRR* i. 520. For the functions of *basilicae* in this period see E. Welin, *Studien zur Topographie des Forum Romanum* (Lund, 1953), 111–20. For the *emporium* by the Tiber and the *porticus Aemilia*, both vast constructions initiated by the curule aediles (together with another *porticus*) as early as 193, see Liv. xxxv. 10, F. Coarelli in P. Zanker (ed.), *Hellenismus in Mittelitalien* (Göttingen, 1976), 23. See further Liv. xxxv. 41.10, xli. 27.8–10.

[1] For an explicit statement that Delos benefited from this event see Strabo x. 486 (ἐκεῖσε γὰρ μετεχώρησαν οἱ ἔμποροι). For the sources and modern views on the question of Roman motives cf. De Sanctis, *SR* iv. 3.158, R. Feger, *Hermes* lxxx (1952), 440–2, E. Will, *Histoire politique*, ii. 332–3 (the first and last of these writers being strongly opposed to a 'commercial' explanation). Badian, *RILR*[2] 20, wrongly assumes that because the Romans did not settle the site, their motive was not economic, and like H. Hill (*The Roman Middle Class in the Republican Period* (Oxford, 1952), 99) he claims that Corinth was destroyed because it was a centre of opposition to Rome. But many cities had gone much further in that direction without suffering utter annihilation, and it is easy to suppose that businessmen established at Delos were hostile to Corinth.

[2] In spite of T. Frank, *Roman Imperialism*, 283, G. Giannelli, *Trattato di storia romana*, i (Rome, 1953), 330. Fenestella does indeed say (*HRR* fr. 9) that there was no *commercium* between *Italici* and Africa before 146, but Plaut. *Poen.* 79–82, Cato, *ORF*[3] fr. 185 (p. 75), Polyb. xxxvi.7.5, *ILLRP* 1177 show that he was wrong (and cf. App. *Lib.* 92); Frank's attempt to evade the evidence (*ESAR* i. 202–3) fails.

[3] Cic. *II Verr.* iii. 12. It remains uncertain whether the system was also used in certain other provinces (Sicily, the Spains and 'most of the Poeni' are excluded).

them.[1] Ultimately, however, it is not their failure to obtain privileges which is crucial, for no one supposes that the *publicani* were all-powerful. What matters more is that the narrative sources of Roman history in the pre-Gracchan period show the Senate and its leaders in effective control of external policy, and the general character of this policy—regular warfare and the cautious but relentless expansion of power during many generations—and most of its particular manifestations, are readily comprehensible without references to financial or business interests outside the Senate.

When financiers, *publicani*, and other well-to-do *equites* gained a more definite place in the political structure in the 120s, their influence over external policy was bound to increase. The effect which *equites* and sub-equestrian businessmen had on Roman treatment of Jugurtha has already been mentioned; there should not be any doubt that they exercised a significant influence in the years 110–105. The Senate had tolerated piracy in the eastern Mediterranean for a long time, and it is no wild conjecture that when a different policy was put into effect in 102, the increased influence of the *equites* had something to do with it. Some of the financial interests which pushed Nicomedes IV into war against Mithridates VI in 89, and so helped to bring about Rome's war with Mithridates, were presumably equestrian.[2] Whether the Roman state should exert itself on behalf of financial and commercial interests was a question that could be disputed, and it evidently was disputed: in 66 we find Cicero arguing that they should be defended, claiming exaggeratedly that the *maiores* had 'often' gone to war on behalf of merchants and ship-owners.[3] This was not true, but in Cicero's stated view it would have been proper policy for the Roman state. The new power which the *equites* enjoyed as a result of C. Gracchus' jury law really did have some effects on Rome's external policy. The notion that equestrian interests made no use of this power until the case of P. Rutilius Rufus in 92 is disproved, if disproof is needed, by the

---

[1] Above, p. 73.

[2] See above, p. 90. Brunt, o.c. 132, rightly denies that Aquillius was an instrument of equestrian designs; but πολλὰ δ'ἄλλα παρὰ τῶν ἐπομένων Ῥωμαίων δεδανεισμένος καὶ ὀχλούμενος (App. *Mithr.* 11) does imply that equestrian interests played a significant role. The presence of T. Manlius Mancinus (T. J. Luce, *Historia* xix (1970), 188–9), whose apparently pro-equestrian activities in 107 have already been mentioned (p. 98 n. 1), is significant in this respect.

[3] *Man.* 11. The same is asserted in *II Verr.* v. 149.

passion which went into L. Crassus' oration against the Gracchan jury system in 106.[1] External policy, however, was not the main subject of dispute between senators and *equites*. The provinces were the important issue,[2] ever since C. Gracchus had given the latter power to punish unco-operative governors. *Equites*, or at least *publicani*, were far more interested in the fact that Lucullus had harmed their interests in Asia than in his vigorous attempts to extend Roman power.[3]

We should extend our inquiry to consider Roman citizens in general. The willingness of large numbers of citizens to fight wars, and their will to expand Roman power, are essential elements in Roman imperialism. In the second century, as the number of *assidui* declined—and perhaps for other reasons as well—it became difficult to recruit as many legionaries as the leaders of the state wished. This change throws into sharper relief the fact that many Roman citizens regarded many of Rome's wars primarily as economic ventures.

The collective economic benefits which citizens derived from imperialism have already been mentioned, as has the continuing second-century demand for land in Italy and the Po valley. In this same period large numbers of Italians, among them an unknown proportion of Romans, migrated to the provinces to take economic opportunities of various kinds. The difficult question remains whether such opportunities had any significant effect on the readiness of ordinary citizens to support wars and to serve in them. Though evidence is slight, it seems likely that some areas which were known, or believed, to be sources of extraordinary wealth—the mining districts of Spain, for example, and the Kingdom of Pergamum—were regarded by ordinary Romans as especially worth fighting for.[4] But although from the time

---

[1] L. Licinius Crassus, *ORF*[3] fr. 24 ('eripite nos ex miseriis, eripite ex faucibus eorum, quorum crudelitas nostro sanguine non potest expleri . . .'). E. Badian, *Publicans and Sinners*, 86–7, tries to show that the Gracchan juries in the extortion court did not make any 'political' use of their power, even though he thinks that in the *quaestiones extraordinariae* they did so; but poorly documented though the period 119–93 is, apart from the Jugurthine War, it reveals six or seven *repetundae* convictions (for which cf. E. S. Gruen, *Roman Politics and the Criminal Courts*).

[2] Cf. the material collected by Nicolet, *L'Ordre équestre*, i. 348–55.

[3] Cf. Plu. *Luc.* 20.

[4] Diod. v. 36.3 tells of the πλῆθος Ἰταλῶν attracted to Spain by the silver mines. Cf. Strabo iii. 146–7 (part of which = Poseid. *FGrH* 87 F47) for some evidence of the fabulous reputation of Spanish mineral resources.

of C. Gracchus settling overseas colonies became a definitely *popularis* activity, the popular attraction, such as it was, of farming provincial land does not seem to have done anything to hasten Roman expansion.[1]

More significant in determining the attitudes of potential recruits towards war was the prospect of booty. Compulsion and patriotic enthusiasm played their parts, but the prospective legionary must often have weighed hopes of booty against the dangers of campaigning. The sums of money which could be obtained were on occasion large enough to influence poor men who had to toil hard for their livings.[2] Some of the effects of booty are plainly visible in the narrative sources: in 171, we learn, many volunteered because they saw the veterans of the war against Philip and Antiochus were rich.[3] Similar expectations were clearly behind the enthusiasm with which citizens and allies enlisted to fight Carthage in 149.[4] Great care was taken to ensure an equitable division of booty on campaign, and the most common threat to military discipline was conflict over the booty division.[5]

In discussing the recruitment of legionaries in the second century, Brunt emphasizes the uncertainty of obtaining booty and he infers that it was not a sufficient incentive for enlistment.[6] There may have been plenty of uncertainty about the amount of booty that would be won, but there was not much uncertainty that survivors would bring home some. People's expectations are the important factor, and they may not have been entirely rational. It is most striking that Plautus, the only author of our period who offers a view of an authentically non-aristocratic attitude towards war, repeatedly treats it as a means of making

---

[1] C. Gracchus' Iunonia was settled in an established province, and it would be hard to suppose that the colony of Narbo Martius (*popularis*, Cic. *Brut.* 160) was premeditated by ordinary citizens during the war of 125–121. On the murky question of the Marian settlements in Africa, cf. P. A. Brunt, *Italian Manpower*, 577–80.

[2] Brunt, o.c. 394, collects the evidence on money distributed at triumphs between 201 and 167. On the first century: ibid. 412. The booty which was customarily divided on campaign (cf. F. W. Walbank on Polyb. x. 16.5) cannot be measured, nor can plunder retained contrary to the oath.

[3] Liv. xlii. 32.6.

[4] App. *Lib.* 75.

[5] The soldier took an oath to turn over plunder to the tribunes (Polyb. vi. 33.2); on the system for plundering cities: Polyb. x. 16.2–17.5. On conflicts over the division of booty cf. Brunt, o.c. 401 n. 9, 640.

[6] O.c. 412.

money.[1] There is an echo here from the world of the Greek mercenary, and an element of worldly cynicism, but sometimes the Roman concepts and terminology show beyond doubt that we are not simply faced with a translation from Greek. Thus speaks the slave Epidicus when he needs to raise some money quickly:

> ego de re argentaria
> iam senatum convocabo in corde consiliarium,
> quoi potissumum indicatur bellum, unde argentum auferam.[2]

In a heavily Romanized passage it is said that Amphitruo, by his victory over the Teleboae

> praedaque agroque adoriaque adfecit popularis suos
> regique Thebano Creoni regnum stabilivit suom.[3]

On many other occasions Plautine characters treat booty as the main result of successful warfare.[4] Sudden riches gained in this manner are likely to have been a common fantasy among the members of his audiences.

It would be a mistake to regard plunder as the only inspiration of soldiers. The noteworthy discipline the Roman army often showed before the 140s, epitomized by the ideal centurion who under overwhelming attack stays at his post and dies for his country,[5] could hardly be based on such a foundation. Equally, however, it would be a mistake, an anachronism, to suppose that in a relatively primitive society the desire for plunder could not be a most important influence in driving ordinary citizens to war. This was probably the case in Rome in the first half of the second century, and there is evidence that it remained true in the Marian and post-Marian army.[6]

The complex set of historical facts described in this chapter can only be reduced to a simple formula at the cost of some distortion. I have attempted to show that desire for economic gains of various kinds was throughout our period an important motive

---

[1] E. Fraenkel, *Elementi plautini in Plauto*, 231 n. 2, noted the author's fondness for *praeda*.

[2] *Epid.* 158–60. Cf. Fraenkel, o.c. 226, 428, E. J. Bikerman, *REG* lxvi (1953), 482.

[3] *Amph.* 193–4.

[4] E.g. *Bacch.* 1069, *Most.* 312, *Poen.* 802–3, *Pseud.* 583–9, *Truc.* 508.

[5] Cf. Polyb. vi. 24.9. How disciplined the pre-Marian army really was is discussed by J. Harmand, *L'Armée et le soldat à Rome*, 272–4; a decline from the 140s onwards seems probable.

[6] Cf. Harmand, o.c. 283–5, 410–21.

force in sending the Romans to war and causing them to expand their power. From a society in which war served all citizens—in varying degrees—by providing them with land and booty, there evolved a wealthier and more sophisticated one in which economic gains were sometimes held to be of secondary importance, but in which citizens of all classes still strove to exploit their economic opportunities. Such evidence as we have suggests that the Romans who determined policy were thoroughly aware of the economic results, both for the state and for themselves, of successful warfare and the expansion of Roman power. To suppose that because seizure and direct exploitation, rather than investment, were the prevailing modes of behaviour these Romans were not moved by greed is an error disastrous to the understanding of Roman imperialism.

III

EXPANSION AS A ROMAN AIM

1. INTRODUCTION

THE rulers of the Roman state wished to increase the empire, and this was one of the overriding and persistent aims of their external policy. The conclusion should not be startling, but scholars have often denied that it was so, or more commonly they have written accounts of Rome's external relations which simply ignore the fact.

An obstacle to understanding which must be removed at once derives from the modern view that, during much or all of our period, the Senate was reluctant to *annex* territory. As we shall see in the next chapter, this conventional view is mistaken, and the Senate was perfectly willing to annex when it was possible and profitable to do so. But the point here is that even if the conventional view were correct and the rulers of Rome were reluctant to annex, none the less they may well have desired to increase the empire.[1] The paradox in this is merely on the surface, for the Roman conception of the empire, as early as we know anything about it, was a realistic one: they usually thought of it *not* as being the area covered by the formally annexed provinces, but rather as consisting of all the places over which Rome exercised power.[2] The earliest developments in terminology cannot be traced, but it is certain that the Romans had a clear notion of the power they exercised over their Italian allies, and very likely that by the last stage of the Italian wars they regarded all of Italy, in Polybius' phrase, as their private

---

[1] The view that the Senate was reluctant to annex appears to lead some historians into the view that expansion in general was unwanted or opposed. See M. Holleaux, *RGMH* 312, 314, *Etudes*, v. 429–30 (cf. *CAH* viii. 237–8); also M. Gelzer in *Das Reich. Idee und Gestalt. Festschrift für Johannes Haller* (Stuttgart, 1940), 14 = *Vom Römischen Staat* (Leipzig, 1943), i. 42 [→ Bibl.], H. E. Stier, *Roms Aufstieg zur Weltmacht und die griechische Welt* (Cologne–Opladen, 1957), 193 n. 440, and for a recent instance K.-E. Petzold, *Historia* xx (1971), 220. E. Badian's view is not clear: thus while Rome 'rejects opportunities for the extension of power' (*RILR*² 1—a long discussion follows of reluctance to annex; and cf. chapter iii, 'The Senate against Expansion'), Rome is sometimes described as pursuing power, 'hegemonial' power, in spite of its reluctance to annex (e.g. *RILR*² 4).

[2] Mommsen, *R. Staatsrecht* iii. 826, is misleading on this matter.

property.[1] For a long time the *res Romana* grew with relatively little use of annexation, and when provinces began to be created beyond Italy, there were always states outside their boundaries which were more or less under Roman power. Polybius attributes to Scipio Africanus the public claim that he had made the Romans lords of Asia, Libya, and Iberia, and though this was hyperbole, it was surely easy for Romans to understand.[2] In 133 Ti. Gracchus was apparently able to assert that Rome ruled the world.[3] These were rhetorical statements, but even such an official document as the Treaty of Apamea (188) reveals the concept of the empire as extending far beyond the provinces: Antiochus was forbidden to recruit mercenaries or accept fugitives 'from territory subject to the Romans', a description which has nothing to do with annexation.[4] Numidia, to take one example of a vassal state, is explicitly treated by Roman sources as being under Roman power in the pre-Jugurthan period;[5] and when Roman writers begin to appear who are concerned with such matters—in the first century—they regularly write of the empire as the area of Roman power, not limited to the provinces.[6] Thus even if there were some validity in the supposition that the Senate opposed annexation, its members may still have been eager to extend Rome's dominion as far as possible.

[1] Polyb. i. 6.6, quoted below. According to Plu. *Pyrrh.* 19.3, App. *Samn.* 10.2, Ap. Claudius Caecus referred in his famous speech against Pyrrhus to Rome's ἡγεμονία in Italy. This may be authentic (so Badian, *RILR*[2] 6), but it is quite uncertain.

[2] Polyb. xxiii. 14.10, cf. xxi. 4.5. The sentiment is Scipio's beyond reasonable doubt (see below, p. 116, on Polybius' reliability in such matters); Gelzer (o.c. 4 = 32) gave no reason to think otherwise. Polybius' history would have been unintelligible to a reader who found any difficulty in understanding his assertion that Rome held world power from the time of Pydna onwards. According to Liv. xxxiv. 13.7 Cato said in 195 that the Ebro treaty had marked that river as the *finis imperii*, long before any Roman annexation in Spain, but it would be very optimistic to regard this statement as truly Cato's.

[3] Plu. *TG* 9.6; see below, p. 126 n. 4. Cato was already close to this notion in 167 (*ORF*[3] fr. 164, p. 64).

[4] Polyb. xxi. 43.15: ἐκ τῆς ὑπὸ 'Ρωμαίους ταττομένης. Cf. also Liv. (A.) xxxviii. 45.3.

[5] Sall. *BJ* 14, Liv. xlv. 13.15–16, App. *Num.* 4.

[6] For the empire as covering the *orbis terrarum* see *Rhet. ad Her.* iv. 9.13, and below, p. 129. Other evidence: Caes. *BG* i. 33.2, Liv. xxi. 2.7, xxxviii. 48.3–4, Diod. xl. 4, Strabo vi. 288, xvii. 839, Tac. *Ann.* iv. 4–5. Cf. A. N. Sherwin-White, *The Roman Citizenship*[2] (Oxford, 1973), 182–9, and in *Greece and Rome* n.s. iv (1957), 37, T. Liebmann-Frankfort, *La Frontière orientale dans la politique extérieure de la République romaine* (Brussels, 1969), 10 (though there are points to disagree with in these accounts), and (on Augustus' attitude) C. M. Wells, *The German Policy of Augustus* (Oxford, 1972), 248–9.

One other preliminary point is essential. Those who have denied that there was any real drive at Rome to increase the size of the empire have very often claimed to settle the issue by arguing that the Senate did not *plan* the expansion of the empire over long periods,[1] which is true in a sense (though the Senate was capable of adopting long-term policies), but irrelevant. What is in dispute is not whether there was planning of strategy over long periods—for which no ancient state was equipped—but whether there was a strong continuing drive to expand. Little long-term planning lay behind even the most vigorous imperialisms of the nineteenth century. These non-existent Roman plans are an artificial target, an Aunt Sally. We should turn our attention instead to the direct evidence concerning Rome's drive to expand.

2. POLYBIUS

Only one reasonably well-informed ancient historian who wrote a narrative history of Roman expansion in this period showed any inclination to analyse as well as narrate the process—this is true at least of writers who have survived in substantial quantities—namely Polybius. He felt no doubts that the Romans of his own and earlier times wanted to expand their empire, and the theme is presented intelligibly in his work, though not with total consistency. Yet his interpretation has been attacked by some of those most competent to judge, and their arguments need to be assessed.

When the Gauls withdrew from the city of Rome, Polybius tells us, the Romans 'got a sort of beginning of their aggrandizement, and subsequently they warred against the people near the city.'[2] After the conquest of the Latins, they went on to defeat the Etruscans, Gauls, and Samnites, and so when the Tarentines invited the intervention of Pyrrhus, 'for the first time the Romans

[1] Cf. Mommsen, *RG* i[12]. 781, Holleaux, *RGMH* 169–71, *Etudes*, v. 430 (cf. *CAH* viii. 238), M. Gelzer, o.c. (*passim*), and in *Hermes* lxviii (1933), 137 [→ Bibl.], H. Bengtson, *WaG* v (1939), 176, H. E. Stier, *WaG* vii (1941), 10 (also in *Roms Aufstieg*, 192), H. Triepel, *Die Hegemonie*[2] (Stuttgart, 1943), 465–6, G. Giannelli, *Trattato di storia romana*, i (Rome, 1953), 199–200, J. Vogt, *RG* i[4] (Basel etc., 1959), 98–9, K.-E. Petzold, o.c. 199–201, R. Werner in *ANRW* i. 1.542, 548. For a good corrective see F. Cassola, *I gruppi politici romani*, 69–70.

[2] i. 6.3: λαβόντες οἷον ἀρχὴν τῆς συναυξήσεως ἐπολέμουν ἐν τοῖς ἑξῆς χρόνοις πρὸς τοὺς ἀστυγείτονας.

attacked the remainder of Italy, their view being that most of what they were going to fight for was not foreign territory, but already properly belonged to themselves as private property.'[1] The Romans began their first war against Carthage with limited aims, but in the course of the war the capture of Agrigentum 'delighted the Senate, and excited their minds so that they passed beyond their original designs, and in the expectation that they would be able to turn the Carthaginians out of Sicily completely, and that this would lead to a great growth in their country's strength, they turned their minds to these designs and to the necessary preparations.'[2] This is the first occasion when he refers clearly not only to Roman actions, but to intentions. And having been trained in the First Punic War, he says, 'they aimed boldly at universal dominion and power, and furthermore achieved their purpose.'[3] In several passages he treats the Hannibalic War as having been the first step to the acquisition of universal power.[4] This view is implied in the speech which he puts in the mouth of Scipio Africanus before the battle of Zama: Scipio tells his troops that if they win the battle, 'not only will they be securely in control of affairs in Africa, they will obtain for themselves and their country incontestable dominion and power over the rest of the world'[5]—a view of the battle virtually identical with the one expressed just before by Polybius in his own person.[6] Elsewhere, however, he states that the idea of conquering the whole world was conceived by the Romans in general only after they had won the Second Punic War.[7] In any case it is clear that Polybius

---

[1] i. 6.4–6: ... τότε πρῶτον ἐπὶ τὰ λοιπὰ μέρη τῆς Ἰταλίας ὥρμησαν, οὐχ ὡς ὑπὲρ ὀθνείων, ἐπὶ δὲ τὸ πλεῖον ὡς ὑπὲρ ἰδίων ἤδη καὶ καθηκόντων σφίσι πολεμήσοντες.

[2] i. 20.1–2: περιχαρεῖς γενόμενοι καὶ ταῖς διανοίαις ἐπαρθέντες οὐκ ἔμενον ἐπὶ τῶν ἐξ ἀρχῆς λογισμῶν ... ἐλπίσαντες δὲ καθόλου δυνατὸν εἶναι τοὺς Καρχηδονίους ἐκβαλεῖν ἐκ τῆς νήσου, τούτου δὲ γενομένου μεγάλην ἐπίδοσιν αὐτῶν λήψεσθαι τὰ πράγματα, πρὸς τούτοις ἦσαν τοῖς λογισμοῖς καὶ ταῖς περὶ τοῦτο τὸ μέρος ἐπινοίαις. For the extension of Roman ambitions to Sardinia see i. 24.7.

[3] i. 63.9: ἐν τοιούτοις καὶ τηλικούτοις πράγμασιν ἐνασκήσαντες οὐ μόνον ἐπεβάλοντο τῇ τῶν ὅλων ἡγεμονίᾳ καὶ δυναστείᾳ τολμηρῶς ... Cf. K.-E. Petzold, *Studien zur Methode des Polybios und zu ihrer historischen Auswertung* (Munich, 1969), 175 n. 4.

[4] i. 3.6: πρὸς τὴν τῶν ὅλων ἐπιβολήν. Cf. v. 104.3 (Agelaus' speech at Naupactus, on the authenticity of which see below, p. 116 n. 4), ix. 10.11.

[5] xv. 10.2: οὐ μόνον τῶν ἐν Λιβύῃ πραγμάτων ἔσονται κύριοι βεβαίως, ἀλλὰ καὶ τῆς ἄλλης οἰκουμένης τὴν ἡγεμονίαν καὶ δυναστείαν ἀδήριτον αὐτοῖς τε καὶ τῇ πατρίδι περιποιήσουσιν.

[6] xv. 9.2.

[7] iii. 2.6. This passage is somewhat inconsistent with those cited above, n. 4; cf. F. W. Walbank, *JRS* liii (1963), 5–6.

thought that desire for world conquest was the supreme aim of
Rome's external policy in the period after 202.[1]

Attempts have been made by various means to show that
Polybius was mistaken. This was Gelzer's view.[2] One of his
arguments took the extraordinary form of asserting that since
Fabius Pictor offered an interpretation of Roman external policy
as defensive, self-defence and honour (consisting mainly of
respect for *fides*) were in reality the sole concerns of the third-
century Senate when it considered matters of external policy.[3]
This is supported by selective references to some of Cicero's
more idealistic theories about international politics,[4] and to the
ius fetiale,[5] which, however, exercised at most a minor influence
on the course of Roman policy. Some of these matters can only be
dealt with in chapter V.[6] Here the essential point is that even if
we knew that Fabius claimed that the Romans had never
entertained thoughts of foreign conquest—and in reality we have
very little precise information about what Fabius did say
concerning Rome's external policy[7]—it would not be logical to
accept his claim, for his work was propagandistic not only in
effect,[8] but also (whatever other motives he may have had) in
intent.[9] Fabius would have been primitive indeed if in explaining

---

[1] Cf. xxxi. 10.7. It may be that there is a Polybian element in the speech before the
battle of Thermopylae delivered by M'. Acilius Glabrio in Liv. xxxvi. 17 ('. . . Asiam
deinde Syriamque et omnia usque ad ortum solis ditissima regna Romano imperio
aperturos. quid deinde aberit, quin ab Gadibus ad mare rubrum Oceano finis
terminemus, qui orbem terrarum amplexu finit . . .?'). H. Nissen (*Kritische
Untersuchungen*, 180–1) and Gelzer (*Das Reich*, o.c. 4 = i. 32) took the speech to be entirely
un-Polybian, but the narrative context at least is his, and some of the speech may be.

[2] Gelzer, in *Das Reich*, o.c., 1–20 = i. 29–48; developed in part from *Hermes*, o.c. 137,
163–6.

[3] Hence the misleading and hardly defended claim that in Hannibal's time 'ihre [i.e.
senators'] Gedanken kreisten jedoch um die Begriffe Sicherheit und Ehre des Staats'
(*Hermes*, o.c. 163). However even Gelzer refers to Rome's 'defensive *Eroberungspolitik*' (o.c.
137).

[4] O.c. 137–8.   [5] O.c. 165.

[6] On Cicero's views and on the *ius fetiale*, see below, pp. 166–75.

[7] Cf. A. Momigliano, *Rend. Acc. Linc.* ser. 8, xv (1960), 317–19 = *Terzo contributo alla
storia degli studi classici e del mondo antico* (Rome, 1966), 64–7.

[8] Despite Momigliano's caution, the comments on Fabius' chauvinism made by
Polybius (i. 14.1–3, 15.12)—a reader of Fabius essentially friendly to Rome—make this
entirely clear.

[9] As the choice of the Greek language is sufficient to show (on this cf. Gelzer, *KS* iii. 51,
A. Lippold, *Consules*, 19–21, R. Werner, *Der Beginn der römischen Republik* (Munich–
Vienna, 1963), 119 n. 4, E. Badian in T. A. Dorey (ed.), *Latin Historians* (London, 1966),
3–6, D. Musti, *EFH* xx (1974), 120–1).

the outbreak of the First Punic War he had emphasized to his Greek-speaking readers Rome's greed and ambition,[1] rather than the alleged danger from Carthage. Gelzer did not examine the full array of other evidence concerning the attitudes towards war and empire of third-century senators, and indeed his argument would hardly have been taken so seriously had it not lent support to the widespread view of Roman imperialism as fundamentally a result of Rome's defensive measures.[2]

Subsequently Heuss argued that Polybius was being excessively schematic in asserting that the Romans were already struggling for world power in the third century.[3] The point has been taken up in the most searching critique that has been offered of the Polybian view, that of F. W. Walbank.[4] In his view, Polybius' interpretation is factually incorrect, and can be shown to be incorrect from his own text[5]—an assertion to which I return shortly. He further claims that the allegedly over-schematic character of the whole interpretation reveals its falsehood: Polybius believed it not because of evidence but because he assumed that it was in the nature of a sovereign state to expand.

There are certainly some passages in which Polybius seems to write over-schematically about Roman expansion. An outstanding example occurs when he claims that Rome's war against Antiochus in 191 'took its origins from the Second Macedonian War, that the latter took its origins from the Hannibalic War, and this in turn from the war about Sicily, the events between all tending towards the same purpose.'[6] But there is no historiographical crime here: the context requires a brief illustration of the notion that causes are what matter in historical writing, and Polybius provides it. The illustration he offers is a reasonable

[1] But note that he may have been the source for Polybius' statement (i. 11.2) that the commanders persuaded the Roman assembly to go to war partly by describing the booty to be gained; and it seems very possible that his description of the Senate's reaction to the victory at Agrigentum (i. 20.1–2) is also Fabian.

[2] For the insignificance of the withdrawal of the garrisons from Greece in 194, which he cites, see below, p. 142.

[3] A. Heuss, *HZ* clxix (1949–50), 487–8 = *Der erste punische Krieg und das Problem des römischen Imperialismus*[3] (Darmstadt, 1970), 47–8.

[4] F. W. Walbank, *JRS* liii (1963), 1–13, and *Polybius* (Berkeley–Los Angeles–London, 1972), 160–6.

[5] Cf. W. Siegfried, *Studien zur geschichtlichen Anschauung des Polybios* (Leipzig–Berlin, 1928), 100, H. E. Stier, *Roms Aufstieg*, esp. 38–51, G. A. Lehmann, *Untersuchungen zur historischen Glaubwürdigkeit des Polybios* (Münster, 1967), 360.

[6] iii. 32.7.

summary of his complex and indeed—as far as we can see—quite subtle views about the causes of the three wars in question. Another valid criticism of Polybius' view of Roman imperialism is that like some other Hellenistic writers he turned too readily to the phraseology of 'universal rule'.[1] But again the difficulty is a minor one. If we substitute for Polybius' words the slightly modified statement that, after the Second Punic War, the Romans conceived the idea of unlimited conquests throughout the known world, the criticism is defused.

Polybius cannot, in my view, be convicted of *imposing* on the Roman history of the years 262–171 an artificial pattern of Roman ambition. It is supposed to be damaging to his credibility that, having said (in a passage already cited) that the Senate extended its ambitions and plans after the capture of Agrigentum to include the total expulsion of the Carthaginians from Sicily, he also says that because of the defeat of the Gauls at Telamon in 225 the Romans formed the hope of expelling the Gauls completely from the Po valley and set to work to do so.[2] Yet he can hardly be far wrong in either case, and Heuss's attempt to argue that he was wrong about the years 262–261 lacks any solid foundation[3]— though no doubt Roman views about Sicily altered less abruptly than Polybius here implies.[4] More seriously, the allegation that Polybius' interpretation was founded on the simple hypothesis that all states rule wherever they can demonstrably under-estimates his intelligence. The theory was of course well known among Greeks,[5] though there is no evidence that it was generally

[1] For other instances cf. Poseid. fr. 253, line 86 (Edelstein–Kidd) = Athen. 213 b–c, Plu. *Flam.* 9.6 (with the comments below). Cf. further Walbank on Polyb. xv. 15.1.

[2] ii. 31.8. Cf. Heuss, o.c. 488 = 48–9.

[3] According to Heuss (l.c.) there can have been no rejoicing at Rome, as Polybius says (i. 20.1), since the Romans had not defeated the Carthaginians in battle at Agrigentum (this no doubt really was the reason why the consuls celebrated no triumph). But what had happened? The Carthaginians having garrisoned Agrigentum, the second largest city in Sicily and now the focal point of their strategy, the Romans concentrated all their efforts on the siege (Polyb. i. 17.8), and after considerable difficulties (i. 17.10–13, i. 18.10–19.5) and probably the longest siege in living memory, they compelled the Carthaginians to withdraw, and took possession of the city with many prisoners and large quantities of booty of every kind (i. 19.15); thus rejoicing was in order. Diodorus' statement, probably deriving from Philinus (so G. De Sanctis, *SR* iii. 1.122 n. 56), that the Romans lost 30,000 infantry in the siege is merely absurd (xxiii. 9.1, cf. 8.1). For other defects in Heuss' version see below p. 187 n. 2.

[4] Cf. i. 17.3.

[5] Walbank, *JRS* 1963, 7–8 and 11, refers to Hdt. vii. 8–11 (the Persians only), Thuc. v. 105.2 (the Athenians at Melos), vi. 18.3 (Alcibiades speaking).

believed in a rigorous form. Polybius reasonably enough attributes large-scale ambitions to some other states: at least he says
that the young Philip V in 217 had fantasies of a world-wide
empire, an ambition that rather ran in the family.[1] It is claimed
that Polybius was the source of Plutarch's statement that when
Hannibal came to the court of Antiochus III in 195 the latter was
contemplating universal dominion[2]—but in reality Plutarch
probably got this notion somewhere else.[3] Among those to whom
Polybius did *not* attribute such ambitions were the Carthaginians
and the older Philip V (otherwise we should probably have heard
of it from Livy). As for ruling where one can, Polybius makes it
clear that in his opinion some states are ἡγεμονικοί, domineer-
ing, as the Peloponnesians were and the Athenians apparently
were not (in 217).[4] The Romans, Polybius obviously thought,
were in his time surpassingly ἡγεμονικοί.[5] He may have been
wrong, but if so it was not because of a simple-minded general
principle. Indeed such an interpretation of Polybius is fundamentally implausible, for Rome and Roman expansion were
central and vital in the formation of his mature historical thinking,
and while he may have forced a schematic interpretation on the
history of other states and other periods, he really did know, unless
he was far less competent than any scholar has supposed, how the
Roman senators of his own time regarded the expansion of the
empire.

It is similarly implausible to maintain that Polybius took his
view from those numerous contemporary Greeks who saw Rome
as an expanding power with sinister intentions,[6] without examining the evidence for himself. He was of course well aware of the
various currents of Greek opinion about Rome, but with ample
justification he claimed to be in a position by the time he wrote to
be able to explain Rome to his fellow-countrymen.

[1] v. 102.1. There is nothing incredible in Polybius' statement (cf. Walbank, *Philip V of
Macedon* (Cambridge, 1940), 65; Polyb. xv. 24.6).

[2] Plu. *Flam.* 9.6. On the unreality of this cf. H. H. Schmitt, *Untersuchungen zur Geschichte
Antiochos' des Grossen und seiner Zeit* (Wiesbaden, 1964), 93 n. 4.

[3] Tentatively in favour of Polybius as the source: Walbank, *JRS* 1963, 7; but in fact it is
probably Liv. xxxiii. 49.7 that gives Polybius' (very different) account of Antiochus' state
of mind on Hannibal's arrival (see J. Briscoe, *A Commentary on Livy, Books XXXI–XXXIII*
(Oxford, 1973), 335, 341, following H. Nissen and others).

[4] Polyb. v. 106.5; cf. vi. 48.6–8 (it would have been possible for Sparta *not* to be an
expansionist state).

[5] Cf. vi. 50.3–6.   [6] Walbank, *Polybius*, 164.

But the facts allegedly show that Polybius was mistaken in his description of Roman intentions. In part, these are the 'facts' provided by Holleaux's interpretation of Rome's first expansion to the East, and I shall be arguing in chapter V that neither Holleaux nor any of his followers has established any facts about this expansion that are seriously in conflict with Polybius' interpretation. Thus though there is an element of truth in the exaggerated statement that Roman governments were indifferent to the Greek world for most of the third century, that is no reason to doubt that in the late third century or early second century they conceived the aim of establishing Roman supremacy there.[1] Here it will be enough to deal with the internal contradiction that allegedly exists in Polybius' work between his description of Roman aims and his description of how Rome's most important wars began. Polybius does not of course attribute the responsibility for the major wars in this period simply to Roman aggressiveness — he is too good a historian to make such a crude judgement—nor is it in the least necessary to his interpretation that he should do so. On the other hand it is an extraordinary reading of Polybius to say that in his narrative 'the responsibility for the war seems invariably to rest with the other [i.e. non-Roman] side.'[2] He provides a balanced and coherent account of the Roman decision to answer the Mamertine appeal, and so go to war with Carthage, in 264 (whether his account contains mistakes is a separate question): he pays attention to Roman nervousness about the power of Carthage, but he attributes more importance in the actual decision (made by the people, he says) to the collective and individual benefits that the Romans could expect from helping the Mamertines; and in his explanation of the war as a whole (as distinct from the first three

[1] As M. Holleaux claimed, *RGMH* III. When he argued against those who had regarded the Roman Senate as 'presque dès l'origine, des "impérialistes" nourrissant d'immenses ambitions' (171), he is opposing a position essentially different from that of Polybius. One of the reasons why Holleaux' view seems unconvincing is that 'imperialism' has broadened its meaning since his day. But in any case his character sketch of the Roman senator (168–72) is far removed from reality. It is undeniable that the Senate showed caution and (not surprisingly, given the structure of the government) failed to forward its ends with a continuously sustained programme of diplomacy, but the assertion that it showed little desire for expansion (171) is only intelligible against the background of the colonial expansion that took place in the historian's own lifetime, expansion which was of almost unparalleled rapidity in world history, and which was made possible by conditions very different from those of the late third-century Mediterranean world.

[2] Walbank, *Polybius*, 163.

campaigning seasons) his previously quoted description of the
psychological effect of the capture of Agrigentum has a leading
part.[1]

Similarly when he comes to the period of his main narrative,
beginning in 220, and is more concerned to provide full-scale
explanations of the wars he describes, Roman aims are given an
appropriate amount of weight. It is not correct to say that 'the
Second Punic War emerges clearly [from Polybius] as the
handiwork of the Barca family, who left Rome no alternative to
avenging the attack on her ally Saguntum.'[2] 'The second [in
order of appearance] and the most important cause' of the war,
Polybius says, was the settlement that the Romans imposed on
Carthage by blackmail in the aftermath of the Mercenary War,
increasing the 'indemnity' and turning the Carthaginians out of
Sardinia.[3] Once again, Polybius may be in error, but there is
nothing here which contradicts his theory of Roman expansion.
After 216 many of the crucial sections of the text are missing, but
we can assume for example that in his full text he gave some
details about the state of Roman ambitions as the Carthaginian
war effort gradually failed and the Romans extended their power
in Spain and invaded Africa.[4] It is not at all surprising that
Polybius has been criticized with the arguments Walbank uses, for
in the extant sections he *does* fail to explain what the significance of
Rome's aim of achieving world-power was in the vital war-
decisions of 192 and 171. In the former case, however, he certainly
did not exempt the Romans from all responsibility.[5] And the case
of the war against Perseus was one which he evidently found

---

[1] i. 10.3–11.4, 20.1–2. Walbank (ibid.) does not cite any evidence to show that Polybius
put the responsibility for the war on Carthage, *tout court*. Nor does Polybius state that the
First Illyrian War was 'forced on' Rome: he does not explain the war in terms of its
background, and if he had done so he would no doubt have had more to say than he does
in ii. 8.2–3 about the initial Roman decision to pay more attention to complaints against
the Illyrians. This is not to deny that Polybius accepted the Roman (and possibly up to a
point correct) version of the causes of this war, namely that it was provoked by the actions
of Queen Teuta.
[2] Walbank, *Polybius*, 163–4.
[3] Polyb. iii. 10.1–4, cf. 13.1, 30.4.
[4] On Polybius' view of the causes of the Second Macedonian War, cf. below, p. 216.
[5] To be put in the balance against Polybius' statement that the cause of the war against
Antiochus was the anger of the Aetolians against Rome (iii. 7.1) is xxi. 4.5: Scipio
Africanus clearly recognized διότι τὸ τέλος ἐστὶ τοῦ πολέμου καὶ τῆς ὅλης ἐπιβολῆς
οὐκ ἐν τῷ χειρώσασθαι τὸ τῶν Αἰτωλῶν ἔθνος, ἀλλ᾽ ἐν τῷ νικήσαντας τὸν
Ἀντίοχον κρατῆσαι τῆς Ἀσίας. Some account must have been taken of this view in
book XIX.

awkward and embarrassing.[1] How could the pro-Roman political agent in the tragic Greece of the late 140s admit that it was the
Romans who had upset the tolerable equilibrium of the years
before the Third Macedonian War? It would scarcely be
surprising if Polybius' science of causes broke down in this
instance. And if he really contented himself with saying that the
war of 171 resulted from the plans of the long-dead Philip V,[2] it
had indeed broken down. But his full account of the causes of the
war is, as we all too easily forget, missing; and it is perfectly
possible to see how he might in book XXVII have combined his
theory about Philip with his views about Rome's drive to power.[3]
Not even in this case can it be shown that Polybius' detailed
analysis contradicts his general notion of Roman expansion.

By the best modern standards—which are honoured more in
theory than in practice—Polybius did not succeed, in his extant
work, in building up an entirely satisfactory explanation of
Rome's foreign wars.[4] A link is missing between his generaliz-
ations about the Roman attitude and his complex explanations
of particular wars, a link which could have been supplied by a
more detailed analysis of Roman, especially senatorial, attitudes
during the crucial periods. But possessing only one full-scale
Polybian war-explanation, the one concerning the Hannibalic
War, we are hardly in a position to complain. What may he have
had to say, for example, about Roman attitudes towards Philip V
and Macedon before the war of 200? And as far as surviving
evidence is concerned, his theory of Roman expansionism was
expounded in a manner reasonably consistent with his version of
the facts. The consistency may have broken down in some
particularly sensitive cases—the Third Macedonian War above

[1] See below, pp. 227–8.
[2] xxii. 18.10–11.
[3] Notice that Polybius does not in fact say that the plan Philip made before his death in
179 was the sole αἰτία of the war (in spite of P. Pédech, *La Méthode historique de Polybe*, 125,
and many others). No doubt he considered it one of the αἰτίαι. But the growth of Roman
power in the Greek world is likely to have been mentioned as a reason for Philip's attitude
(see Liv. (P.) xxxix. 23.5–29.3), the case appearing to Polybius in some respects parallel to
the Second Punic War, of which Hamilcar's hatred was one cause, while some of Rome's
acts of expansion were the most important cause. It is noteworthy that the προφάσεις for
the Third Macedonian War mentioned by Polybius were προφάσεις for *Roman* action;
see Walbank, *Polybius*, 160.
[4] Cf. the remarks of A. Momigliano, *Acta Congressus Madvigiani* (Copenhagen, 1958), i.
205–7 = *Secondo contributo alla storia degli studi classici* (Rome, 1960) 20–2 = *Studies in
Historiography* (New York, 1966), 118–21.

all—but in general it seems to have survived. In several specific instances we have indications that Polybius described particular acts of policy as manifestations of the Romans' continuing will to expand their power.[1] In short, the grounds for rejecting the historian's description of the dominant Roman attitude are lacking.

A subsidiary Polybian question remains. Was the historian correct to represent Scipio Africanus as saying, in his exhortation before the battle of Zama, that the Romans would there be striving for universal empire?[2] It has often been doubted. But Polybius' theory about the sort of speeches that should appear in historical writing is strict—he repeatedly emphasizes that they must contain only what was actually said, τὰ κατ᾽ ἀλήθειαν λεχθέντα (that is, the opinions expressed, but not necessarily the very words used).[3] It is not to be believed that he always maintained this standard, and the battle of Zama virtually required him to write a speech for Scipio, however poor the available information. On the other hand Polybius' speeches are certainly not easy to fault in those cases where we know that he could without difficulty have found a good authority.[4] Nor is it true that Africanus' speech at Zama was entirely colourless in diction and thought,[5] for the very phrase under discussion is a striking one on the lips of a Roman general in such circumstances—indeed it may be the only authentic element in the speech. Nor is it a good argument against the authenticity of Scipio's remark that it is almost identical with the view that Polybius himself has just expressed about the importance of the battle[6]—that implies too blatant a contravention of his own principles of historical speech-writing. Further, although Scipio's speeches were not preserved as such, and least of all his

---

[1] Cf. xxxi. 10.7, and see chapter V on the Illyrian War of 156 and the Third Punic War.

[2] Polyb. xv. 10.2. The other sources (Liv. xxx. 31.10–32.3, attributing a similar outlook to Hannibal as well; App. *Lib.* 42) do not help us to decide this question.

[3] ii. 56.10, xii. 25b.1, 25i.8, xxxvi. 1.7, cf. xxix. 12.10. See Walbank, *Commentary*, i. 13–14, *Miscellanea di studi alessandrini in memoria di Augusto Rostagni* (Turin, 1963), 211–13, *JRS* liii (1963), 9–10, *Commentary*, ii, on xii. 25 i. 4–9. The words οἰκείως δὲ τῆς ὑποκειμένης περιστάσεως (xv. 10.1) seem to emphasize the claim to authenticity in this case.

[4] Cf. P. Pédech, o.c. 259–76. O. Mørkholm's attack (*C & M* xxviii (1967), 240–53; cf. also *Chiron* iv (1974), 127–32) on the authenticity of Agelaus' speech at Naupactus (v. 104) is to be rejected (see Walbank, *Polybius*, 69 n. 11).

[5] As was claimed by P. La-Roche, *Charakteristik des Polybios* (Leipzig, 1857), 67, followed by Walbank (*Commentary*, on i. 2.7–8 and xv. 10.2, *JRS* 1963, 10) and others.

[6] xv. 9.2; this argument was used by Walbank, *JRS* 1963, 10.

exhortations to armies, Polybius had a good chance of finding out what he said on this occasion and may have done so through the elder Laelius,[1] who was present at the battle. It can be assumed that Polybius wanted to make book XV acceptable to Scipio Aemilianus and his friends and that these people believed that they knew what Africanus' policies had been. Yet an inspection of Polybius' other exhortation speeches[2] strongly suggests that he was at best too trusting towards the available sources. And since he wanted to portray Africanus as a leading, perhaps the leading, exponent of Roman ambitions,[3] he may have sought to 'clarify' what was only implicit in his real speech. None the less Polybius' report is valuable as an indication of Africanus' attitude in 202;[4] and although Africanus was both exceptionally vigorous and exceptionally determined, it is a mistake to think that his ideas were out of harmony with those of the aristocracy in general.[5]

3. ROMAN SOURCES

Roman aims can best be inferred from Roman actions. There is, however, a background of general statements about the expansion of the empire that requires consideration. Naturally enough the Romans did not proclaim in their diplomacy that they aspired to increase their power. In the Senate and in informal discussions among leading aristocrats it is probable that a common view was for long assumed and very seldom debated;[6] in

[1] On Laelius as a source for Polybius' speeches cf. Pédech, o.c. 274–5, and as a source in general, Pédech, 364–5, Walbank, *Commentary*, on x. 3.2. For Laelius as a source for book XV cf. R. Laqueur, *Hermes* lvi (1921), 216 n. 1, M. Gelzer in J. Vogt (ed.), *Rom und Karthago* (Leipzig, 1943), 195–6 = *Vom Römischen Staat* (Leipzig, 1943), i. 69–70, Musti, o.c. 124. On the quality of Polybius' information about Africanus cf. Walbank, *Commentary*, i. 30–1, Pédech, o.c. 364–8, 380–2. T. Frank's comment, *Roman Imperialism*, 134 n. 15, is a characteristic distortion: 'Polybius ... could hardly have had a report of the speech. Scipio's whole career proves him as anti-imperialist. The first treaty he signed with Carthage in 203 recognized that state as independent' (on the insignificance of this fact cf. below, p. 138).

[2] Listed by K. Ziegler, *RE* s.v. Polybios (1952), col. 1526.

[3] Cf. x. 40.7–9, xxi. 4–5, xxiii. 14.

[4] Cf. F. Cassola, *I gruppi politici romani*, 393.

[5] As suggested by (e.g.) J. Vogt, *Orbis Romanus* (Tübingen, 1929), 10 = *Vom Reichsgedanken der Römer* (Leipzig, 1942), 176.

[6] A. E. Astin, *Scipio Aemilianus*, 155–6, was surely right to make this point about Rome's Spanish wars in the mid-second century; but he was not justified in concluding from the fact that the crucial decision in Spain had been made long before that the policy was not 'aggressive imperialism'; part of Rome's aggressiveness was her extraordinary persistence in fighting such wars.

any case debates in the Senate are almost as inaccessible to us as private discussions, and this was to a very large extent already true for Roman annalists.[1] Furthermore, by the time that many of the late-republican annalists and Cicero came to write about Roman imperialism, the empire had grown so large that the appetite for growth diminished, and in the same period heightened moral and pseudo-moral scruples required that the more justifiable aspects of Rome's past behaviour should be emphasized. In the *De republica* Cicero could imaginatively attribute to a Roman consular the view that expanding the empire, while in accord with *sapientia*, was at least in part contrary to justice.[2] As views about the morality and expediency of imperialism changed, so did history; but the changes were incomplete (and it was not until late in Augustus' reign that the first serious attempt was made by the government to bring the traditional policy of expansion to a halt), with the curious result that while in the primary analyses of Roman imperialism offered by Cicero, Livy, and others—which it would not be unkind to call pseudo-historical—the drive to expand scarcely appears, there are certain vestiges of the aristocracy's real outlook scattered in the late-republican and early-imperial evidence. From these vestiges, the significance of which has never been properly considered,[3] this outlook can be reconstructed.

The censor who, at the end of each censorship, performed the *lustratio* and the *suovetaurilia* sacrifice uttered a prayer 'quo di immortales ut populi Romani res meliores amplioresque facerent rogabantur'—'by which the immortal gods were asked to make the possessions of the Roman people better and more extensive.' 'Res ampliores' may originally have included fertility, but in our period the phrase undoubtedly referred to enlargement of the power of the Roman state. The existence of this customary prayer is known to us only because Valerius Maximus recounts the story that Scipio Aemilianus, when he was censor in 142/1 and the moment came for him to say these words, said instead 'Satis bonae et magnae sunt: ita precor ut eas perpetuo incolumis servent'—'they are good and great enough: so I pray that the

---

[1] See Additional Note 1.

[2] *De rep.* iii. 15.24 (quoted below, p. 125 n. 1). Cicero evidently felt the awkwardness of this (iii. 5.8).

[3] J. Vogt, *Ciceros Glaube an Rom* (Stuttgart, 1935), 74, gathered some of the evidence, but it has made no impact on any narrative history, not even his own.

gods may keep them for ever unharmed.' He ordered the prayer
to be emended in this way in the *publicae tabulae*, and this was the
wording used by subsequent censors.[1] The appropriateness of
making this change in 142/1, the first censorship since Scipio
Aemilianus himself had finally destroyed Carthage, is obvious
enough. However, since the authenticity of the story was
attacked by F. Marx,[2] it has been rejected by most of the scholars
who have considered the question in detail.[3] The weightiest
argument is that Cicero seems to have believed that not
Aemilianus, but L. Mummius, the other censor, was the one
selected by lot to carry out the final ceremony of the *lustrum*,[4] and
so was the person who uttered the prayer, whatever it was.[5]

But how much of the story was invented, and who invented it?
That the prayer was changed at some date is very likely,[6] and the
significance of the change is plainly that its author attached less
importance to the growth of the empire than earlier Roman
opinion had. Against the authenticity of the earlier version of the
prayer, it has recently been argued that 'it would have stood in
conflict, at least in spirit, with fetial law', according to which
desire for territorial expansion was not acceptable as an official or
formal reason for war.[7] But this is to see the fetial law with the
eyes of a first-century moralizer such as Cicero. Even when the
fetials retained a significant role in the declaration of war, in the

---

[1] Val. Max. iv. 1.10: 'Qui [Aemilianus] censor cum lustrum conderet inque
solitaurilium sacrificio scriba ex publicis tabulis sollemne ei precationis carmen praeiret,
quo di ... rogabantur, "Satis", inquit, "bonae ... servent", ac protinus in publicis tabulis
ad hunc modum carmen emendari iussit. Quo votorum verecundia deinceps censores in
condendis lustris usi sunt.'

[2] *RhM* xxxix (1884), 65–8.

[3] E.g. F. Münzer, *RE* s.v. Cornelius (1901), no. 335, cols. 1451–2, A. Aymard, *Mélanges
de la Société toulousaine d'études classiques*, ii (1946), 101–20 [→ Bibl.], F. W. Walbank, *GRBS*
v (1964), 253, A. E. Astin, o.c. 325–31. M. Gelzer continued to accept the authenticity of
the story, without discussion, *Philologus* lxxxvi (1931), 293 = *Vom Römischen Staat*, i. 116
[→ Bibl.]. K. Bilz, *Die Politik des P. Cornelius Scipio Aemilianus* (Stuttgart, 1935), 42–4, and
H. H. Scullard, *JRS* l (1960), 68–9, argued for the authenticity of the story; their views
are criticized in turn by Astin, l.c. R. Werner (*ANRW* i. 1.537 n. 119) wrongly implies
that Cicero knew of the supposed change.

[4] *De orat.* ii. 268.

[5] It is also questionable whether a censor, even Aemilianus, could either have got away
with altering the text of an official prayer (on the importance of verbal precision, cf. G.
Appel, *De Romanorum precationibus* (Giessen, 1909), 205–7, Astin, o.c. 327–8), or have
altered it for future censors, in the manner described.

[6] Cf. E. Badian, *RILR*[2] 94 n. 7.

[7] Astin, o.c. 329. Note that an echo of the prayer can be heard in Dion. Hal. iv. 80.4
(εὐδαιμονεστέραν τε καὶ μείζω).

earliest part of our period, the fetial law required no more than formal correctness in making the declaration, and the onus of proof is on any scholar who asserts what the narrative sources never suggest, that the fetial law made a certain general course of external policy morally unacceptable to the Senate.[1] This is not to strip the minds of Roman senators of all moral sensibilities, but simply to reject the anachronistic view that they regarded increasing the empire as morally reprehensible in any way.

The prayer was probably used in the older form in the second century, at least until 141 and probably later. The evidence suggests that for most, and indeed probably all, of his life Aemilianus was completely in sympathy with it. His opinions as well as his career were probably reflected accurately by what the younger Laelius said on this matter in his *laudatio* for Aemilianus' funeral (according to Cicero): 'he thanked the immortal gods that the man had been born in this country rather than any other: for of necessity where he was, there was an empire' ('necesse enim fuisse ibi esse terrarum imperium ubi ille esset.')[2] As for Valerius Maximus' story, there is much to be said for Aymard's suggestion that it was an attempt to support an innovation in policy made by Augustus, namely the abandonment of territorial expansion, by attributing something like it to one of the great empire-builders of the Republic.[3] This will only make sense if the prayer was indeed changed from Valerius' older to his newer form at some date or other.

In harmony with this prayer was another, which though very rarely used, gains importance from the solemnity of its occasion. This was the prayer for the increase of the empire offered at the *ludi saeculares*. When Augustus revived the rite in 17, he prayed to the Moerae 'uti imperium maiestatemque p.R. Quiritium duelli domique auxitis, utique semper Latinus obtemperassit . . .'—'to increase the empire and majesty of the Roman people, the Quirites, in war and at home, and that the Latin may always obey . . .' Augustus and Agrippa repeated the prayer to Jupiter Optimus Maximus, Augustus then repeated it to Ilithyia and to Juno Regina, 110 matrons again repeated it to Juno Regina,

---

[1] See below, pp. 166–71.

[2] Cic. *Mur.* 75 = *ORF*³, no. 20, fr. 23. Astin (o.c. 330–1) very cautiously concludes that 'the balance of probability inclines against an anti-expansionist interpretation of Scipio's policy'.

[3] Aymard, o.c. 119–20.

Augustus once again to Terra Mater, finally Augustus and Agrippa to Apollo and to Diana.[1] The restorations in the epigraphical text are beyond reasonable doubt.[2] What matters here is whether the same prayer was used at the *ludi saeculares* of 249,[3] commonly held by scholars to have been the first,[4] at those which may have taken place in 236,[5] and at those of 149 or 146. No answer can be certain, for Augustus unquestionably made major changes in the rite.[6] However there is no reason why such a prayer should not have been offered to Dis Pater and Proserpina in 249, and the phraseology of the whole prayer may well have been put into its existing form at that date.[7] Indeed the words 'utique semper Latinus obtemperassit' are a strong argument in favour of the view that the games were celebrated in an early form in 348 with a similar prayer.[8] The prayer would then have been preserved as a matter of course by the *decemviri*, later *quindecimviri*, *sacris faciundis*. If this view is correct, the representatives of the Roman state prayed on this extremely solemn

---

[1] *CIL* vi. 32323 = *ILS* 5050, lines 92–146. A more accurate restoration was made possible by the discovery of new fragments of the Severan *acta* in 1930, and the text should be read in G. B. Pighi, *De ludis saecularibus*[2] (Amsterdam, 1965), 107–19. The prayer goes on 'incolumitatem sempiternam victoriam valetudinem p.R. Quiritibus duitis, faveatisque p.R. Quiritibus legionibusque p.R. Quiritium remque p. populi R. Quiritium salvam servetis ⟨maioremque?⟩ faxitis . . .'

[2] The crucial word *imperium* was supplied by Mommsen (*EE* viii (1899), 264–6 [→ Bibl.]) from the parallel wording of the Severan *acta*, *CIL* vi. 32329, line 11 (cf. vi. 32328, line 72, and the line given by Pighi as Va. 50). On the history of the phrase 'imperium maiestasque p.R.', cf. Additional Note xii.

[3] Sources: Varro *ap*. Censorin. *De die natali*, xvii. 8, Censorin. xvii. 10, Verrius Flaccus *ap*. Ps.-Acro *ad* Hor. *Carm. Saec.* 8 (ed. O. Keller, i. 471) (on which cf. L. R. Taylor, *AJPh* lv (1934), 104 n. 14), Liv. *Per.* 49, *Oxy. Per.* 49, Zosimus, ii. 4.

[4] E.g. by M. P. Nilsson, *RE* s.v. saeculares ludi (1920), col. 1704, Pighi, o.c. 6, K. Latte, *Römische Religionsgeschichte*, 246.

[5] On this celebration cf. *MRR* i. 223.

[6] On which cf. Taylor, o.c. 103–7. A. Momigliano, *JRS* xxxi (1941), 165 = *Secondo contributo*, 400, tentatively suggested that 'utique tu imperium . . . obtemperassit' was an 'antiquarian forgery' of the Augustan period. Increasing the *imperium* was for long an official Augustan policy (cf. *RG* pr., 26.1, P. A. Brunt, *JRS* liii (1963), 170–6), but it is of interest that future expansion is referred to somewhat vaguely in such a crucial text as Horace's *Carmen saeculare* (47, 67), which emphasizes rather that Scyth, Mede, and Indian are already subjects (53–6, with E. Fraenkel's suggested interpretation, *Horace* (Oxford, 1957), 376 n. 4). The republican parallels set out in this section make the suggestion of forgery quite unnecessary. (The attempt of P. Weiss, *MDAI-R* lxxx (1973), 205–17, to show that the republican *ludi saeculares* were an annalistic fiction is far-fetched.)

[7] See Additional Note xii.

[8] Cf. Taylor, o.c. 112–5, A. Piganiol, *REA* xxxviii (1936), 220–2, R. E. A. Palmer, *Roman Religion and Roman Empire: Five Essays* (Philadelphia, 1974), 102–5, and Additional Note xii.

occasion not only for the safety of the state, but explicitly for an increase in the empire. And there may well have been other official prayers for the same purpose.

Just as in the official religious rites of the state the Romans asked for increase of the empire, so the officially approved prophets from time to time predicted such increases. In 200, as the decision to declare war against Philip V approached, the Senate instructed the consuls to obtain predictions about the war's outcome. The *haruspices* announced favourable *exta* 'et prolationem finium victoriamque et triumphum portendi'.[1] Similar instructions on the eve of the war against Antiochus elicited from the *haruspices* the reply that 'eo bello terminos populi Romani propagari, victoriam ac triumphum ostendi'.[2] Once again in 172, just before the Third Macedonian War, the *haruspices* interpreted a *prodigium* as favourable, 'prolationemque finium et interitum perduellium portendi', a prediction they repeated in the following year.[3] This evidence is of great importance, all the greater because it is out of harmony with Livy's views as to why these wars were fought. A recent critic's attempt to explain it away by saying that it 'may reflect Augustus' interest in the extension of the boundaries of the empire'[4] ignores most of the other evidence, and invites us to assume that Livy himself inserted these notices into the record, which is not plausible. And while the *haruspices* remained somewhat alien at Rome, there can be no doubt that in general they took care to prophesy what their patrons wanted to hear.[5]

One more religious text can contribute. In his account of the Social War, Diodorus records the oath of loyalty said to have been sworn to Livius Drusus by his Italian supporters.[6] They swore by, among others, 'the demigods who founded Rome and the heroes who increased the empire'.[7] The whole text raises

---

[1] Liv. xxxi. 5.7.

[2] Liv. xxxvi. 1.3.

[3] Liv. xlii. 20.4, 30.9 ('propagationem ⟨imperii⟩ *or* ⟨finium⟩'). Compare the victory prophecy of a *haruspex* in 296 (Zonar. viii. 1, cf. Dio fr. 36.28).

[4] J. Briscoe, *A Commentary on Livy, Books XXXI–XXXIII*, on xxxi. 5.7. In a superficial discussion, P. Frei (*MH* xxxii (1975), 76–8) claims that these notices were invented by annalists—though they run counter to the annalists' view of Roman foreign policy.

[5] On their position at Rome in this period cf. W. V. Harris, *Rome in Etruria and Umbria*, 194–5.

[6] Diod. xxxvii. 11.

[7] τοὺς κτίστας γεγενημένους τῆς Ῥώμης ἡμιθέους καὶ τοὺς συναυξήσαντας τὴν ἡγεμονίαν αὐτῆς ἥρωας.

many interesting problems which deserve a fuller study than they have ever received. For a time scepticism about its authenticity seemed to prevail, but without any overwhelming reason.[1] What we probably possess is a very clumsy rendering from a Latin text (this would be no surprise in Diodorus), a Latin text which probably does go back to the year 91.[2] The Latin form of the pertinent phrases might, for example, have been 'Quirinum et Castorem Pollucemque ceterosque qui imperium maiestatemque p.R. amplificaverunt'. The text may go back to Drusus' enemies rather than his friends, but for our purpose that would not matter. In any case the phrase which mosts interests us receives some support from the texts previously cited; and it adds to the evidence that increasing the empire was an accepted public objective.

These facts fit comfortably into the background of Roman religious beliefs and practices.[3] Believing that their empire had been bestowed by the gods,[4] they naturally turned to the gods when they wished to express their desire for still greater dominion. In this context one should recall the attention which they paid, in various ways, to Victoria—as well as to Mars, Bellona, and Neptunus, and to Jupiter and Hercules with military attributes. Of all the 'abstract' concepts which received attention in the middle Republic, Victoria probably received the most. In 294 a temple which had been begun several years before was dedicated to Victoria herself,[5] and by 296, it seems, there was

[1] H. J. Rose, *HTR* xxx (1937), 165–81 (claiming that Diodorus himself invented it; but his discussion was defective); A. von Premerstein, *Vom Werden und Wesen des Prinzipats* (*Abh. Bay. Ak. Wiss.* no. 15 (1937)), 27–9 (claiming (29) that the second half of this phrase had no place in Roman cult; but he ignored the evidence). R. Syme, *The Roman Revolution* (Oxford, 1939), 285 n. 6, agreed that the phraseology of the oath was not authentic. H. Wagenvoort, *Roman Dynamism* (Oxford, 1947), 90–96, while using the text to explore the early Roman psyche, professed Rose's view of its origin; also somewhat negative is P. Herrmann, *Der römische Kaisereid* (Göttingen, 1968), 55–8.

[2] Accepted as at least authentically Roman by G. Wissowa, *Religion und Kultus*[2], 17, O. Hirschfeld, *KS* (Berlin, 1913), 288–90, C. Koch, *Gestirnverehrung im alten Italien* (Frankfurt-a.-M., 1933), 89–93, L. R. Taylor, *Party Politics in the Age of Caesar* (Berkeley–Los Angeles, 1949), 45–6, S. Weinstock, *Divus Julius* (Oxford, 1971), 224; cf. also E. Gabba, *Athenaeum* xxxii (1954), 111 n. 2 = *Esercito e società*, 280 n. 14.

[3] Note, however, that Valerius Maximus' opinion that a triumph could only be granted 'pro aucto imperio' (ii. 8.4) is definitely mistaken (cf. W. Ehlers in *RE* s.v. triumphus (1939), cols. 498–9).

[4] Among contemporary expressions of this: *RDGE* no. 34 (= *SIG*[3] 601), lines 14–15; cf. *RDGE* no. 38 (= *SIG*[3] 611), lines 24–5.

[5] It had been begun by the consul L. Postumius Megellus during his aedileship (Liv. x. 33.9), which is best dated before his first consulship in 305. *MRR* sets it tentatively in 307.

already a statue of her in the forum;[1] in 295 a temple of Jupiter Victor was promised; and in 193 Cato dedicated another small temple to Victoria Virgo. The didrachm type of the First Punic War period shows Victoria on the reverse.[2] From 225 until about 140 almost all the reverse types of silver coins depict either Victoria or the Dioscuri or both, and Victoria sometimes appears in the bronze coinage as well. She continues to make frequent appearances on coins after 140. In Plautus' time Victoria had recounted her acts of benevolence in a prologue on the tragic stage.[3] Additional evidence could be cited.[4] And at the end of our period, Victoria was extensively exploited by Marius and by Sulla.[5]

The origins of Victoria's prominence are scarcely known.[6] However certain important developments did take place in the period of the Italian wars. The Romans may possibly have had statues of Victoria before that time, but there was no cult. The old cult of Vica Pota may, for all we know, have been quite important, but even if she was in some sense the equivalent of Victoria,[7] she was not herself a personification of victory. The ruthless and ambitious patrician L. Postumius Megellus was apparently responsible for the major innovation, the temple;[8] but he obviously did not act in isolation. As has been suggested before, the new concern with Victoria does not *necessarily* mean that the Romans, or even Roman leaders, were eager to expand the empire. But though Victoria had Greek antecedents, her Roman manifestation is markedly different.[9] There was probably no cult of Nike in the classical Greek world. The Romans— perhaps, more accurately, some Romans—of the early third century were truly devoted to Victory, and aspired to win

---

[1] Zonar. viii. 1, cf. Dio fr. 36.28. The circumstantial detail lends credibility. Liv. xxvi. 23.4 may possibly refer to a fourth-century statue.

[2] M. H. Crawford, *RRC* no. 22/1 (which he dates to 265–242).

[3] Plaut. *Amph.* 41–5.

[4] For the other evidence concerning the middle Republic see S. Weinstock, *HTR* l (1957), 215–23, and in *RE*, s.v. Victoria (1958), cols. 2511–13.

[5] Weinstock, *HTR*, 224–6, and in *RE*, cols. 2513–14, T. Hölscher, *Victoria Romana* (Mainz, 1967), 138–47.

[6] It is clear that Greek ideas were affecting Roman practices in this matter during the 290s (Weinstock, *HTR*, 216). The evidence on non-Roman Victoriae in Italy was gathered by Weinstock, *RE*, cols. 2502–4.

[7] Cf. Weinstock in *RE* s.v. Vica Pota (1958), cols. 2014–15.

[8] On Postumius cf. F. Cassola, *I gruppi politici romani*, 194–8.

[9] Weinstock, *HTR*, 218–9, Hölscher, o.c. 136–7.

Victoria's favour regularly year by year. The attention they paid to her expressed their imperial ambition.

The theme of territorial expansion often recurs in the 'secular' texts. Inscriptions erected in Rome by the great commanders boasted 'finis imperii propagavit'—'he advanced the frontiers of the empire', and it was expected that the public would be impressed. That there were such inscriptions we know from Cicero, who puts the information in the mouth of one of the speakers in the *De republica*, the dramatic date being 129.[1] No such inscriptions survive,[2] but the total number of surviving honorific inscriptions from Rome of the relevant period is so small that this is no evidence against Cicero's accuracy.[3] The views of Scipio Africanus and Scipio Aemilianus about expanding the empire have already been discussed.[4] We know that Africanus boasted about his conquests of new territory,[5] and we must suppose that other third- and second-century commanders did so too, though probably in less extreme terms.[6]

The literature of the middle Republic confirms, as much as we have any right to expect, that extending the boundaries of the empire was a laudable aim in the eyes of the Roman aristocracy. The speaker in Ennius' *Annals* who was given the solemn lines

[1] iii. 24: 'sapientia iubet augere opes, amplificare divitias, proferre fines—unde enim esset illa laus in summorum imperatorum incisa monumentis: "finis imperii propagavit", nisi aliquid de alieno accessisset?—imperare quam plurimis, frui voluptatibus, pollere regnare dominari; iustitia autem praecipit . . .' (Ziegler's text). The speaker is L. Furius Philus, *cos.* 136, the theme that of Carneades (iii. 8).

[2] The first known text of this kind was the inscription set up by Pompey—Diod. xl. 4: . . . καὶ τὰ ὅρια τῆς ἡγεμονίας τοῖς ὅροις τῆς γῆς προσβιβάσας, καὶ τὰς προσόδους Ῥωμαίων φυλάξας, ἅς δὲ προσαυξήσας . . . (cf. Plin. *NH* vii. 97).

[3] In spite of J. Briscoe's implication (l.c.). For Cicero's interest in inscriptions see esp. *Att.* vi. 1.17; for the care taken over historical accuracy in the *De rep.* cf. E. Badian, *Publicans and Sinners*, 56.

[4] As to Cato, obviously a vigorous expansionist, authentic statements of an explicit nature are lacking. In the speech which Livy attributes to him in opposition to the law of 195 that repealed the *Lex Oppia* (xxxiv. 2–4), he approves of expanding the empire, anxious though he is about some of the side-effects (4.3). But the authenticity of the speech is at best very limited (E. Malcovati, *ORF*[3] p. 14, H. Tränkle, *Cato in der vierten und fünften Dekade des Livius* (Abh. Mainz, 1971, no. 4), 9–11). On his views about Macedon in 167 see below, p. 144.

[5] P. 106.

[6] However the supposed tradition that a magistrate who had extended the frontier of the empire was entitled to extend the *pomoerium* (Tac. *Ann.* xii. 23, cf. Gell. *NA* xiii. 14.3) apparently referred only to those who had extended the frontiers of Italy (see Seneca, *De brev.* 13.8). In any case one suspects that the 'tradition' was no older than Sulla.

audire est operae pretium procedere recte
qui rem Romanam Latiumque augescere vultis

must have been addressing the Roman Senate or people, and assuming that his hearers would share this aim.[1]

A certain change seems to be detectable in Roman attitudes in the Gracchan period, but the outlook remains essentially the same. Accius' *fabula praetexta* entitled *Brutus*, which was probably produced at some date in or soon after 136,[2] contained an account of a prophetic dream seen by Tarquinius Superbus. A detailed interpretation is given, ending with the words

pulcherrume
auguratum est rem Romanam publicam summam fore.[3]

Accius must have felt that this was Rome's national aim. Presumably he thought that by his time it had been largely achieved. By 133—if Plutarch's report is accurate—some Romans had accepted the idea that they were 'masters of the whole world', κύριοι τῆς οἰκουμένης. Whether Tiberius Gracchus really said this or not,[4] we should accept Appian's statement that when he dilated on the Italian manpower problem in a speech on behalf of the proposed *lex agraria*, he referred not only to the Romans' past conquests, but also specifically to their hopes that they would conquer and possess

[1] *Ann.* 465–6V (the book is not known). H. E. Stier (*WaG* vii (1941), 14 n. 28) alleged that the second line reflected Ennius' contact with Greece, but the falsity of this should now be clear. For the solemnity of *procedere* in such a context cf. Liv. xxiii. 11.2.

[2] See F. Leo, *Geschichte der römischen Literatur*, i (Berlin, 1913), 398, B. Biliński, *Accio ed i Gracchi* (Accademia Polacca di Scienze e Lettere, Biblioteca di Roma, Conferenze, fasc. 3, Rome, 1958), 45.

[3] Quoted by Cicero, *De div.* i. 45 (= Accius, *Praetext.* 37–8 Ribbeck²). For important background concerning dreams in early Latin literature cf. A. La Penna, *Studi Urbinati* xlix (1975), 49–60. Cf. also *Praetext.* 14: 'quibus rem summam et patriam nostram quondam adauctavit pater' (the speaker is probably Decius Mus at the battle of Sentinum in 295). It is possible, however, that Accius merely meant to say that the dream foretold the power of the *populus* in place of the king.

[4] For earlier Greek statements concerning world-wide Roman power cf. Polyb. xxi. 16.8 (Antiochus' envoys in L. Scipio's *consilium* in 190; cf. Liv. xxxvii. 45.8), xxi. 23.4 (Rhodian envoys); cf. Walbank on Polyb. xv. 15.1. For Ti. Gracchus: Plu. *TG* 9.6 (= *ORF*³ no. 34, fr. 13); and in favour of the basic soundness of Plutarch's quotations from Tiberius' speeches see P. Fraccaro, *Studi storici per l'antichità classica* v (1912), 424–6. I can see no reason whatsoever to date the statement of one Aemilius Sura, interpolated in Vell. i. 6.6, that Rome now dominated the world, to a date in the period 189–171 (so J. W. Swain, *CPh* xxv (1940), 1–21, F. W. Walbank, *JRS* liii (1963), 8; see instead F. Cassola, *I gruppi politici romani*, 65–6).

the rest of of the world.[1] There is no sign, or I think likelihood, that any Romans disagreed with him about this—what was controversial was the means he suggested of obtaining the necessary supply of soldiers. Far from being merely a demagogic phrase,[2] the reference to hoped-for fresh conquests was, like some other elements in his thinking, thoroughly traditional.

It is true—this may be noted in parenthesis—that certain Roman writers describe a theory which might conceivably have led some aristocrats to doubt the wisdom of extending Roman power. This was the idea that decisive victory over foreign states had a corrupting effect on the victorious. It was a quite well-known idea among Greeks,[3] and it is no surprise to find something like it appearing in second-century Rome, particularly in the mind of a man like the elder Cato, who was in any case morbidly preoccupied with moral corruption. The question here is whether anyone of importance at Rome took the further mental step of advocating that hostile powers should be allowed to retain some strength for the sake of maintaining the soundness of the Roman state, and if so whether this view had any real effect on policy. The first and indeed the only political leader who is widely attested as having taken the argument to its logical conclusion in this manner is Scipio Nasica Corculum, in the famous dispute about policy towards Carthage in the years before the Third Punic War.[4] In reality even he may not have used the

---

[1] App. *BC* i. 11.45: ἐπῄει τὰς τῆς πατρίδος ἐλπίδας καὶ φόβους διεξιών, ὅτι πλείστης γῆς ἐκ πολέμου βίᾳ κατέχοντες καὶ τὴν λοιπὴν τῆς οἰκουμένης χώραν ἐν ἐλπίδι ἔχοντες κινδυνεύουσιν ἐν τῷδε περὶ ἁπάντων, ἢ κτήσασθαι καὶ τὰ λοιπὰ δι' εὐανδρίαν ἢ καὶ τάδε δι' ἀσθένειαν καὶ φθόνον ὑπ' ἐχθρῶν ἀφαιρεθῆναι. This has been accepted as Tiberian by Malcovati (on *ORF*[2] no. 34, fr. 15) and E. Gabba (on App. 44). The authenticity of the reference to future conquest has been doubted (e.g. by E. Schwartz, *GGA* clviii (1896), 803; sufficiently answered by P. Fraccaro, *Studi sull' età dei Gracchi* (Città di Castello, 1914), 90–3), but not by any scholar who has considered the other relevant evidence on the second century.

[2] As alleged by T. Frank, *Roman Imperialism*, 250–1, with assorted speculation about the attitudes of aristocrats towards expansion at this time. T. S. Brown asserted (*CJ* xlii (1946–7), 471) that Tiberius' conception of future conquests was Greek, not Roman; this turns out to be false.

[3] Note especially Aristot. *Pol.* vii. 1334ᵃ, Polyb. vi. 18 and 57.5–9, xxxi. 25.5–7 (cf. also Pl. *Laws* iii. 698 b–c).

[4] Sources: Diod. xxxiv/xxxv. 33.3–6 (with gross errors), Plu. *Cat. Mai.* 27 (ὡς ἔοικεν, this was the basis of his policy), Flor. i. 31.5, App. *Lib.* 69.314–5, Augustine, *CD* i. 30, Oros. iv. 23.9, Zonar. ix. 30 (also seriously in error). For some analysis of their differences cf. A. E. Astin, *Scipio Aemilianus*, 276 n. 4. On others supposed to have used this argument see Additional Note XIII.

argument at all.[1] The important argument Nasica and others used for a time against declaring the Third Punic War was the lack of a *iusta causa*.[2] Even if Nasica used the 'counterweight' argument, this need not have dictated the whole character of his foreign policy.[3] The Senate in any case declared war and ordered Carthage destroyed. Later, at least from the time of Sallust, the year 146 became the most favoured of the alleged turning-points at which foreign conquest began to corrupt Rome, and certain historians elaborated on the 'foresight' with which some of the leading figures of the time before 146 had attempted to prevent the corruption.[4] Even early in the second century, it is true, some senators felt anxiety about the harmful effects of imperial expansion on the Romans themselves,[5] and in consequence some of them may well have become, perhaps subconsciously, less eager for expansion. But belief in the beneficial effects of *metus hostilis* never during our period had more than the most marginal influence on Roman external policy.[6]

The belief that the Roman empire already included the whole world, first known to have been expressed by a Roman in 133, must have contributed to the decline in Roman ambitions for further conquests. Many practical considerations led in the same direction. The acquisition of 'Asia' in 133–129 must have been particularly satisfying. In the last two decades of the century military service was losing its appeal, as we have seen. From 105 for many years the main military preoccupations had to be with defence and with Italy itself. And still other impediments to expansion appeared, as we shall see when we consider Rome's failure to take the opportunity to annex Cyrene in 96.

[1] The case is argued by W. Hoffmann, *Historia* ix (1960), 340–4 [→ Bibl.]. But he overstated it: Polybius may possibly have attributed the argument to Nasica in a passage falling between our xxxvi. 1 and xxxvi. 2, in spite of Hoffmann, 341.

[2] Liv. *Per.* 48–9. This was normal in dealings with major enemies (and concerning this occasion cf. Polyb. xxxvi. 2, Diod. xxxii. 5). It is not very likely that Nasica felt any obligation to look after Carthaginian interests because of family connections (as suggested by E. Badian, *Foreign Clientelae*, 132); he was not of course a descendant of Africanus.

[3] Diod. xxxiv/xxxv. 33.5 thought that the ultimate aims of Nasica's policy were the maintenance *and increase* of the empire; but H. Strasburger, *JRS* lv (1965), 49, and others who attribute this passage to Poseidonius are too sanguine.

[4] Cf. Additional Note XIII.

[5] The best sources are Cato, *ORF*³ fr. 163 (= *Orig.* fr. 95a (Peter) = Gell. *NA* vi. 3.14; the Greek background for this (H. Fuchs, *HSCPh* lxiii (1958), 378 n. 47) does not decrease its importance for Roman thought); fr. 122; Plu. *Cat. Mai.* 19.3. Polyb. xxxi. 25–9, and other related passages in the same author, may reflect some Roman feelings.

[6] Cf. Hoffmann, o.c. 342–4, Badian, *RILR*² 4.

Direct evidence on the immediate problem is unfortunately lacking for the period between Tiberius Gracchus and the *Rhetorica ad Herennium*. The latter, usually regarded as a production of the years between 86 and 82, speaks of the *imperium orbis terrae* as an established fact.[1] Then in the 70s certain Roman coin-types which depict globes in association with other symbols of Roman power suggest that Rome's world power was by now a widely accepted idea.[2] Precisely to the last years of this decade belongs the opinion that Sallust reported, probably about Lucullus: 'he was thought outstanding in every respect, except for his extreme desire for extending the empire.'[3] One could now be criticized for excess in this direction (there is no reason to doubt that this was contemporary opinion)—a significant novelty, even though Lucullus was a highly adventurous general by any standards. Pompey in a grandiose inscription set up in 61 boasted that he had extended the frontiers of the empire to the end of the earth,[4] a claim already surpassed on his behalf by Cicero's rhetoric—'finis vestri imperi non terrae sed caeli regionibus terminaret.'[5] Thus it was quite easy for Cicero to argue in the same year, apropos of Egypt—though there were really other more direct reasons for not annexing the kingdom—that 'the Roman people ought not to seem eager to acquire every

[1] *Rhet. ad Her.* iv.9.13: 'nedum illi imperium orbis terrae, cui imperio omnes gentes, reges, nationes partim vi partim voluntate consenserunt ... ad se transferre tantulis viribus conarentur.' A. E. Douglas (*CQ* N.S. x (1960), 65–78) attempted to date the work somewhat later, but for the traditional date see S. Mazzarino, *Il pensiero storico classico*, ii. 1 (Bari, 1966), 178, G. Kennedy, *The Art of Rhetoric in the Roman World* (Princeton, 1972), 112–13. The empire comprises the *orbis terrarum* in Cic. *Rosc. Am.* 131 and frequently in Cicero's late writings (cf. R. Werner in *ANRW* i. 1.531–2, who, however, ignores the evidence concerning Ti. Gracchus).

[2] M. H. Crawford, *RRC* nos. 393 (76–75 B.C.), 397 (74). The former shows on the reverse a globe between (left) a rudder and (right) a sceptre with wreath and fillet. The latter shows on the reverse a figure representing the *genius* of the Roman people, being crowned by Victory and holding a cornucopia and a sceptre, with a foot resting on a globe. Note also the reverse type of *RRC* no. 403 (70). Cf. H. A. Grueber, *Coins of the Roman Republic in the British Museum*, ii (London, 1910), 359 n. 1, A. Schlachter, *Der Globus, seine Entstehung und Verwendung in der Antike* (Leipzig–Berlin, 1927), 76–7, J. Vogt, *Orbis Romanus* (Tübingen, 1929), 14 = *Vom Reichsgedanken der Römer* (Leipzig, 1942), 184, H. Fuhrmann, *MDAI* ii (1949), 38, S. Weinstock, *Divus Julius*, 42–3.

[3] 'imperii prolatandi percupidus habebatur, cetera egregius': Sall. *Hist.* iv. 70 (referred to Lucullus by Maurenbrecher and others; but note the reserve of A. La Penna, *SIFC* N.S. xxxv (1963), 50). Cf. Plu. *Luc.* 24.3.

[4] Diod. xl. 4 (quoted above, p. 125 n. 2).

[5] *Cat.* iii. 26. Cf. the more general statement in *Mur.* 22: 'haec [rei militaris virtus] orbem terrarum parere huic imperio coegit.'

kingdom',[1] advice not about diplomatic tactics, but about the desirability of acquiring new territory.

However even in the late Republic the traditional outlook underwent not fundamental change but only modifications. Both Pompey and Cicero gloried in the expansion of the empire.[2] In the *Lex Gabinia Calpurnia* of 58 an official Roman text did likewise.[3] In the same year began one of the most aggressive of Rome's wars of expansion, Caesar's war in Gaul, which would eventually have been followed, if Caesar had lived, by the most grandiose attempt that had ever been made to expand the empire, the war against Parthia.

What is the significance of all this evidence? Is it perhaps all to be dismissed as mere verbiage, or the ravings of extremists, or grandiloquent sentiments intended to impress the masses? By no means. Those who prayed on behalf of the state for increase in the empire must have echoed the real wishes of the aristocracy. Ennius and Accius could assume that the expansion of power was a Roman aim. Coupled with Polybius, this material makes up a large proportion of the evidence we possess concerning Rome's over-all purposes in foreign affairs. It would be far-fetched to suppose that senators regularly articulated this aim when they discussed practical matters of foreign policy. Rather, it was a question of a shared attitude—shared over a long period (though we cannot trace it back much beyond the mid-third century)— and of a common determination within the aristocracy to add to Rome's power.

[1] Cic. *De leg. agr.* ii. 42: 'non oportere populum Romanum omnium regnorum appetentem videri.'

[2] The full text of Pompey's inscription deserves attention. Cf. Cic. *Rosc. Am.* 50 ('suos enim agros studiose colebant [maiores nostri], non alienos cupide appetebant [this has both public and private reference], quibus rebus et agris et urbibus et nationibus rem publicam atque hoc imperium et populi Romani nomen auxerunt'), *Leg. Man.* 49, *Mur.* 22 ('in propagandis finibus . . .'), *Prov. Cons.* 29, *De rep.* vi. 13 (Scipio's dream: 'omnibus qui patriam conservaverint, adiuverint, auxerint, certum esse in caelo definitum locum, ubi beati aevo sempiterno fruantur'), *Phil.* xiii. 14.

[3] *CIL* i[2]. 2500, line 19: 'imperio am[pli]ficato [p]ace per orbem [terrarum parta]'; cf. lines 5–6.

IV

ANNEXATION

1. INTRODUCTION

FROM the year 202 onwards, Rome chose *not* to annex territory on a number of occasions when it had sufficient military power to do so—so many scholars have believed. Mommsen propounded the theory that this behaviour represented an important principle of Roman policy, and virtually no one has questioned his judgement.[1] It has been accepted even by some who have attributed to Rome a relatively aggressive imperialism.[2] The theory has taken various forms: Mommsen believed that the policy was at an end by 148, but Frank, followed by Badian and others, argued that it lasted longer.[3] According to Badian, the whole of the second century was characterized by a policy of avoiding annexation wherever possible, and down to the 70s at least this policy was still in evidence. Advocates point out that the defeat of Carthage in 202 and the defeat of Macedon in 197 were not immediately followed by annexation, that after the war against Antiochus, and again after the Third Macedonian War, it was still avoided. In 148—

[1] For Mommsen's view of policy in and after 202 see especially *RG* i[12]. 683–4, 699, 747, 780 ('Die Schlacht bei Pydna bezeichnet aber auch zugleich den letzten Moment, wo der Senat noch festhält an der Staatsmaxime wo irgend möglich jenseit der italischen Meere keine Besitzungen und keine Besatzungen zu übernehmen, sondern jene zahllosen Klientelstaaten durch die blosse politische Suprematie in Ordnung zu halten'), 781–2, ii[12]. 20. There was in fact a long delay before Mommsen's view became widespread. Among later scholars it is enough to mention P. C. Sands, *The Client Princes of the Roman Empire under the Republic* (Cambridge, 1908), 143–9; T. Frank, *Roman Imperialism*, 185–6, 196, 237, 265–6, 274; M. Holleaux, *RGMH* esp. 314 ('tant reste forte son [the Senate's] aversion pour la politique d'annexion' (referring to 167)), *Etudes*, v. 429–30 (cf. *CAH* viii. 237–8) (on the period down to Apamea); G. De Sanctis, *SR* iv. 1. 90, 98, 111–12, 235, and iv. 3.20–21; F. Münzer, *Die politische Vernichtung des Griechentums* (Leipzig, 1925), 65; F. B. Marsh, *The Founding of the Roman Empire*[2] (Oxford, 1927), 3–20; G. H. Stevenson, *Roman Provincial Administration till the Age of the Antonines* (Oxford, 1939), 17–18, 21–8; H. H. Scullard, *HRW*[3] 315–21; J. Carcopino in G. Bloch–J. Carcopino, *Histoire romaine*, ii[3] (Paris, 1952), 132; G. Wesenberg in *RE* s.v. provincia (1957), col. 1011; G. Giannelli, *Trattato di storia romana* (Rome, 1953), i. 282–3; U. von Lübtow, *Das römische Volk* (Frankfurt-a.-M., 1955), 662–3; F. Cassola, *I gruppi politici romani*, 64–6; see also below, p. 148 n. 3, p. 151 n. 2.

[2] E.g. M. Rostovtzeff, *SEHHW* 70–1.

[3] Frank, Stevenson, ll.cc., E. Badian, *RILR*[2] esp. 1–15 (cf. his *Foreign Clientelae*, esp. 96–7, 139–40, 287–9).

146, though some annexation was 'forced' on to the Romans in Macedon, Greece, and Africa, the Senate still preferred to support client states. The Senate accepted the bequest of Attalus III only with reluctance. Even in the West annexation of large areas of territory was avoided as much as possible: even the war of 125–121 in Transalpine Gaul did not, in Badian's view, lead to any annexation there until after the Cimbric War, and similarly in Numidia after the capture of Jugurtha annexation 'was never even contemplated'. Whatever happened in Cyrene after it was bequeathed to Rome in 96, it was not organized into a province until 75 or 74, or even later. Egypt was bequeathed to Rome by Ptolemy X Alexander I in 88 or 87, but there was no serious pressure to claim this rich bequest until the 60s. There were some acts of annexation during the period in question, but they took place only when Rome was 'forced' into them.

This supposed policy of avoiding annexation has been explained in various ways. For Mommsen (as for many of his followers) there was little need for explanation, since he regarded Roman foreign policy as fundamentally defensive. Scholars believing that a more specific explanation was necessary have pointed to four factors as the sources of the alleged policy. The Senate (it is argued) held that large increases of territory could not easily be administered within the existing city-state constitution, and it was in particular unwilling to create extra magistracies to provide officials for new provinces.[1] Aristocratic politicians feared the overwhelming prestige and power individuals might obtain by carrying through acts of annexation; the Scipios had threatened the aristocratic system and in consequence great commands were as far as possible avoided.[2] Further, the Senate disapproved of the corrupt behaviour in which provincial governors sometimes indulged, and consequently it sought to minimize the number of provinces.[3] Finally, a certain restraint was placed on Roman policy towards Greek states by respect for the disapproval of their cultural superiors.[4]

[1] See esp. Marsh, o.c. 5–20, Scullard, *HRW*[3] 317, Badian, *RILR*[2] 7–8.
[2] Stevenson, o.c. 59, H. Hill, *The Roman Middle Class in the Republican Period* (Oxford, 1952), 57, Wesenberg, o.c. cols. 1010–11, Von Lübtow, l.c., Badian, *RILR*[2] 8.
[3] Scullard, l.c., Carcopino, l.c., Badian, *RILR*[2] 8–10.
[4] So Giannelli, l.c., Badian, *RILR*[2] 10–12 (therefore the non-annexation principle had more effect in relations with Greek states than in relations with barbarians (11)).

Some unwillingness to annex is often spoken of as a maxim or principle, it is evidently thought to be an established policy with a certain force of regularity behind it in addition to the specific arguments that might be used on a particular occasion.

It is important to assess the validity of the modern theory that Rome was reluctant to annex territory. It has been heavily emphasized in, and is apparently central to, much recent writing on Roman imperialism, and, as we have already seen, it has suggested to many that the Romans were reluctant to expand the empire not merely in this fashion but in any way at all. Furthermore, we might hope that in considering the Senate's attitude towards annexation we shall find out more about what the Romans hoped to gain from imperial power.

In reality there was, I believe, no non-annexation principle, and in this chapter I propose to show that a different interpretation of the events in question is to be preferred. On the one hand, the occasions when annexation was possible but was rejected were very few; on the other, when annexation was rejected, it was not because of any general principle, but because of particular down-to-earth considerations of Roman advantage.

2. TRADITIONAL POLICIES, DOWN TO 101 B.C.

What is meant by annexation in this context? We are not concerned here with the annexations of territory which the Romans carried out in Italy as part of their complex system of control and exploitation. The power acquired in Sicily and the other overseas territories presented problems of a new kind. No one wanted to settle colonies there, so a different form of control was needed. To some extent the other instruments of control already in use in Italy—treaty obligations and ties with the local élites—would serve the purpose. But the maintenance of power and the extraction of revenue required permanent and direct government. The features of an annexed province are, besides taxation, subordination of a defined area to a continuing series of designated magistrates (of consular or praetorian rank) and the presence when necessary of Roman garrison troops.[1]

The procedures by which provinces were annexed at various

[1] For the regular magistrate as a defining feature of a province cf. App. *Sic.* 2.2, *Iber.* 38.152, *Lib.* 135.641.

periods are obscure but do not require lengthy investigation here. Most commonly the Senate sent out a commission of ten *legati* to investigate and organize, having presumably instructed them in advance whether the territory was to be annexed. The earliest known instance is that of Achaea in 146,[1] but since the procedure was undoubtedly modelled on the old practice of sending ten *legati* to arrange matters at the end of a major war, it had probably been used earlier. The number ten was not invariable: we know that the commission sent to 'Asia' in 133 consisted of five *legati*.[2] By contrast the province Africa appears to have been annexed by a law, under which *decemviri* were appointed;[3] and Cilicia too, it now seems probable, was annexed by a law. The arrangements which the *legati* made under the standard procedure were held to be valid without any further vote at Rome; but the Roman magistrate in command issued a decree 'de decem legatorum sententia', which was sometimes known as the *lex provinciae*.[4]

The interesting point, however, is this: since commissions of ten *legati* were commonly appointed at the ends of wars and sometimes to deal with other problems abroad, even when no annexation was intended,[5] there was in a sense no special procedure for annexation. In other words, the same sort of commission was thought appropriate for annexation and for making a settlement that stopped short of annexation. And the abruptness of annexation must not be exaggerated: dominant power could be exercised without it, as happened in northern Italy for a long period before a province was established there; regular revenue could be exacted without it, as from Hiero of

---

[1] The activities of this commission are to some extent known from Polyb. xxxix. 4–5, Pausan. vii. 16.9; for the one that went to Asia in 129 see Strabo xiv. 646 end, and also *RDGE* no. 25 (= *IG* xii suppl. 10), line 15. Cf. F. De Martino, *Storia della costituzione romana*, ii (Naples, 1964 edn.), 284.

[2] Strabo xiv. 646. A commission of five *legati* had been sent to settle the affairs of Illyricum in 167 (Liv. xlv. 17.1).

[3] It is usually believed (L. Lange, *Römische Alterthümer*, ii[3] (Berlin, 1879), 674, Mommsen, *R. Staatsrecht*, ii[3]. 643 n. 2, *MRR* i. 466) that the *Lex Livia* mentioned in the text of the *Lex Agraria* (*FIRA* ed. Riccobono, i no. 8), lines 77 and 81, under which *decemviri* had, among other actions, assigned land to the Uticenses, was a law of 146 and that these *decemviri* were the commissioners who carried out the annexation (cf. App. *Lib.* 135.640 for the land they awarded to Utica). In spite of some difficulties, this appears to be correct.

[4] This seems the most probable reconstruction. See further B. D. Hoyos, *Antichthon* vii (1973), 47–53, esp. 50 n. 32.

[5] E.g. Liv. xxx. 43.4. It was evidently a traditional practice by this period (Liv. xxxiii. 24.7). Other instances: Mommsen, o.c. ii[3]. 692–3.

Syracuse after 263, from the Illyrians after 228, and most clearly of all from Macedon after 167. Annexation was merely one of the steps, neither the first nor usually the last—since rebellions were common in annexed provinces—by which Rome took control. An annexed territory was only one of the forms taken by Roman power, and (as we have already seen) the empire was not, to Roman minds, by any means coextensive with the annexed provinces.[1]

In order to see how little emphasis the Romans placed on annexation we have only to look at the sources. Alliances, national 'friendships', conquests—these matter and receive ample attention; acts of annexation receive very little. The terminology of Roman control points in the same direction. This terminology has been endlessly discussed, but the most important fact of all has been somewhat neglected. There are in fact *no* special words to describe those who were outside the annexed provinces but none the less to some degree or other under Roman power. They were certainly not known as 'clientes' of the Roman state, though this has (thanks largely to Mommsen) become the standard label. Some elaborate houses-of-cards have been built on the supposition that they were perceived as clients, but this is not contemporary usage.[2] The rulers and the cities in question were commonly referred to as 'amici' or 'socii' of the Roman people (or both at once). These terms were also used to refer, respectively, to some or all of the provincials.[3] Thus the

---

[1] Above, p. 105.

[2] The 'client' metaphor is of course pervasive as a description of such people. On the metaphorical character of the term cf. A. N. Sherwin-White, *The Roman Citizenship*[2] (Oxford, 1973), 188 (not refuted by E. Badian, *Foreign Clientelae*, 42 n. 4). It was first used to provide an analogy for Rome's relationship with some of its subjects by Proculus in the first century A.D. (see *Dig.* xlix. 15.7.1), whence it passed, via early modern legal writers such as Grotius and Zouche, to Mommsen. The history and the validity of the idea that republican Romans assimilated their state's relations with other states to the bond of *clientela* deserve further examination, but not here. On the limits of its validity see esp. J. Bleicken, *Gnomon* xxxvi (1964), 180–2. There is no secure evidence that Romans used terminology specifically belonging to *clientela* for their international relationships in the middle Republic (Sherwin-White, o.c. 187–8, somewhat misrepresents the content of Liv. xlv. 18.2); the nearest thing to such evidence is probably Liv. (P.) xxxvii. 54.17. D. Timpe, *Hermes* xc (1962), 357 n. 1, mistakenly cited Cic. *De rep.* i. 43 ('Massilienses nostri clientes'), which is a reference to Scipio Aemilianus' own *patrocinium* (as M. Gelzer saw, *Roman Nobility*, 88 = *KS* i. 90 [→ Bibl.]).

[3] For certain provincials as *amici* cf. Cic. *II Verr.* v. 83, *Lex Agraria* (*FIRA* no. 8), lines 75, 79. For the provincials as *socii* cf. M. Wegner, *Untersuchungen zu den lateinischen Begriffen socius und societas* (Göttingen, 1969), 90–3.

distinction between provincials and non-provincials was, to the Romans, of secondary importance.

The first annexations outside Italy seem to have been undertaken without any detectable reluctance. The sources, admittedly, are extremely sparse,[1] and what arrangements Rome made for controlling Sicily in the years before 227 we do not know. That there was no intention of leaving that part of the island that lay outside Hiero's kingdom to enjoy its independence is plain enough. Sardinia and Corsica, similarly, were meant to remain under Roman control. As for direct rule, the *imperium*-holding magistrates (recently increased from three to four) may have been thought sufficient to handle the situation, with the help of the promagistracy and the junior offices.[2] For the year 227, apparently, two additional praetorships were created to provide governors for the two provinces. The delay (thirteen years in the case of Sicily) need have no significance for the history of annexation. The Senate naturally tried to rule the territories without increasing the magistracies, but agreed to such a step when it became necessary.[3] In Spain, similarly, there is no real sign of any Roman reluctance to retain direct power, even when the treaty of 201 finally eliminated any possible Carthaginian influence there. We do not in fact know when Rome resolved to retain permanent power in Spain or annexed territory there. At first it was ruled by private citizens *cum imperio*, and there was some natural delay before the constitution was altered to provide governors for the new territory. In 198 six praetors instead of four were elected so that praetors could govern the provinces of Hispania Citerior and Ulterior.[4]

---

[1] Polybius (i. 63.4, ii. 1.2; cf. App. *Sic.* 2.6 Viereck–Roos) confirms what should be obvious, that there was no hiatus in Roman control. Solinus 5.1 (pp. 47–8 Mommsen) says that Sicily and Sardinia were both made provinces in a year which can only be 227 (see *MRR* i. 229).

[2] During the Hannibalic War the promagistracy (first devised in 327) was often used as the means of providing enough men to govern these provinces when the praetors were all needed elsewhere. It is possible, but quite uncertain, that a quaestor was regularly stationed at Lilybaeum even before 227 (cf. W. V. Harris, *CQ* N.S. xxvi (1976), 94, 104).

[3] Precisely what brought about the change of policy cannot be determined. Local restiveness is one possibility. The increased involvement of Rome in other regions (Gaul, Illyria) is another. C. Flaminius was the first praetor in Sicily (Solin. 5.1) and he naturally benefited from the opportunity (cf. Liv. xxxiii. 42.8). It seems likely that he was chosen for the position not by the Senate but by the *concilium plebis*, but that is no reason to think that senators opposed direct rule in the three islands.

[4] The six praetorships: Liv. xxxii. 27.6. Neither their creation nor the instructions they

But what of the cases in this same period in which annexation was avoided? Let us first consider the Illyrian situation of 228—though no one has tried to attach great significance to Rome's failure to annex in this instance. How did Illyria differ, in Roman eyes, from the recently acquired islands off the Italian coast? Brief consideration of the campaign of 229/8 will supply the answer. It was a successful campaign in that it swiftly broke up the dominion of Queen Teuta and established the beginning of Roman power and influence to the east of the Adriatic. But the conquests were not extensive. The Ardiaei—probably those of that name who lived in the hinterland of Lissus—were defeated, as were certain cities, not named by our sources, further north along the coast.[1] It was a small area and not one rich in resources. The final stage of the 229 campaign showed that Rome could not establish control even over the whole coast up to the level of Pharos without making sacrifices: at the unidentified city of 'Noutria' the enemy killed many Roman soldiers, some military tribunes and a quaestor.[2] It was an excellent area to give to a deserving ally—Demetrius of Pharos, who had earned consideration by his prompt treachery at Corcyra. A further effort might have been made to capture Teuta's refuge at Rhizon, but there would not have been much point, since her nuisance-making capacities had been destroyed and she was willing to pay tribute. As to the much more attractive territory further south, the area of Rome's so-called protectorate, it was made up of states that had sought Rome's friendship in the first stage of the campaign. These were Corcyra, Apollonia, Epidamnus, the Parthini, and the Atintani.[3] Again, the area was not huge. But more to the point, it would have been the height of political folly, and also an offence against *fides*, to attempt to exploit these states.

The Roman commander L. Postumius Albinus sent representatives to the Aetolian and Achaean Leagues to capitalize on Rome's good behaviour,[4] an action which shows that the Senate received to fix the boundary between the provinces (28.11) shows that 198–7 was the date of the first annexation in Spain. App. *Iber.* 38.152 apparently sets the event in 206 (στρατηγοὺς δὲ Ἰβηρίας ἐτησίους ἐς τὰ ἔθνη τὰ εἰλημμένα ἔπεμπον ἀπὸ τοῦδε ἀρξάμενοι . . .).

[1] Polyb. ii. 11.10, 13. On the Ardiaei see N. G. L. Hammond, *JRS* lviii (1968), 6, with his map (p. 3).

[2] Polyb. ii. 11.13. Dio fr. 49.7 presumably alludes to the same event.

[3] For the topography see Hammond, o.c. 7–8 (convincingly revising earlier views).

[4] Polyb. ii. 12.4.

(which must have authorized it) was very much alive to the propaganda value of timely restraint. Shortly afterwards further Roman embassies were sent to Athens and Corinth.[1] The target of this policy, it must have been clear, was Macedon.[2] The Macedonians, naturally, were not deceived about the real character of Rome's achievement in Illyria, and neither was Polybius.[3] Roman power was established there, and annexation would have been decidedly harmful to Rome's long-term interests. Furthermore it might well have required garrison troops; and whatever was happening in other regions in the winter of 229/8 (events in Sicily, Sardinia, and Gaul are obscure), the Senate was probably beginning to see that increased efforts were about to become necessary in much more vital places.

The next decision which needs examining is the Senate's choice of policy after the defeat of Hannibal in 202. The battle of Zama itself did not create an immediate opportunity to annex territory in north Africa, as is often assumed by modern writers. Further efforts would have been needed. Livy, probably basing his account on Polybius, explains that Scipio Africanus did not persevere with the war once the battle was over both because the task of besieging such a well-defended city as Carthage was so great, and because he was unwilling to lose the fruits of victory to a successor in the command.[4] Even the peace terms that were offered met some real opposition in Carthage,[5] and no doubt an attack on the city would have met a strong spirit of resistance as

[1] Polyb. ii. 12.8: the Corinthians responded by giving Romans the right to participate in the Isthmian games (cf. Zonar. viii. 19). The date was either spring 228 or less probably spring 226. According to F. W. Walbank (ad loc.) the embassy had 'no political background', and the embassies to the Leagues were 'a purely formal exchange of courtesies, without any political sequel'. On the contrary, no Roman convention required such behaviour, and the Senate was obviously making a bid to the Greek states for their *eventual* co-operation.

[2] Cf. Hammond, o.c. 9–10.

[3] Polyb. vii. 9.13 (Philip V's treaty with Hannibal treats the Romans by implication as the 'masters' of the area), iii. 16.3.

[4] Liv. xxx. 36.10–11: 'In consilio quamquam iusta ira omnes ad delendam stimulabat Carthaginem, tamen cum et quanta res esset et quam longi temporis obsidio tam munitae et tam validae urbis reputarent, et ipsum Scipionem exspectatio successoris venturi ad paratum victoriae fructum [?], alterius labore et periculo finiti belli famam, sollicitaret, ad pacem omnium animi versi sunt.' Cf. App. *Lib.* 56, Zonar. ix. 14. That Polybius was Livy's source here is doubted by F. W. Walbank (on Polyb. xv. 17.3–19.9), who regards Livy's account as suspect (but see the text). Livy did use other sources as well as Polybius for the African war in Book XXX; but A. Klotz, *Livius und seine Vorgänger* (Stuttgart, 1940–1), esp. 117, 199, argued convincingly that Polybius was his main source.

[5] Polyb. xv. 19.2, Liv. xxx. 37.7, App. *Lib.* 55–6.

well as strong fortifications. Scipio is indeed supposed ('ferunt')
to have said on many later occasions that he was hindered from
destroying Carthage by the greed of Ti. Claudius Nero and Cn.
Cornelius Lentulus,[1] but if he really said any such thing[2] it was an
optimistic boast; far more than the victory at Zama would have
been necessary.

Nor should we doubt Livy's account of the effects on Africanus
of his personal ambition. Mommsen reacted strongly to
the statement that Scipio was influenced by fear of being replaced,[3] and, taking little notice of the sources, asserted that
Scipio's position at Rome was so strong that he cannot have
feared recall, and that it was his noble and magnanimous
impulses that prevented him from pressing his military advantage. Yet there were strong feelings against Scipio in the Senate in
204–202, and after his prolonged period of command it is
perfectly credible that some wanted to see him superseded. If
Livy is to be believed, his command had been prorogued in 203
'donec debellatum in Africa foret', and early in 202 a popular
vote confirmed his position;[4] but that is no reason to deny that the
consuls of 203 wanted to obtain an African command, or that Ti.
Claudius Nero succeeded in obtaining an anomalous command
in Africa from the Senate, or that Cn. Cornelius Lentulus also
wanted Africa.[5] Livy's account is thus to be accepted.[6]

The decision of 202 is scarcely difficult to understand. The
whole expedition to Africa had met opposition at Rome, and
after the sufferings of the previous fifteen years some respite was

---

[1] *Coss.* in 202 and 201 respectively. The statement is reported in Liv. xxx. 44.3.

[2] Dismissed as unhistorical by W. Hoffmann, *Historia* ix (1960), 315 n. 13 [→ Bibl.] (cf.
F. Münzer in *RE* s.v. Cornelius no. 176 (1900), col. 1358).

[3] *RG* i[12]. 660.

[4] Liv. xxx. 1.10, 27.3–4.

[5] For these points see respectively Liv. xxx. 27.2; 27.5–6; 40.7–16, 43.1 (also Dio fr. 59).
For similar cases see above, p. 34.

[6] Hoffmann's objection (l.c.) that Scipio had already shown himself ready for
negotiation before the meeting of his *consilium*, by receiving a Carthaginian delegation, is
not relevant. He obviously did not have to wait for a formal meeting of the *consilium* to
know his own mind or the general feeling among his councillors. H. H. Scullard, whose
account is the most detailed one, argued (*Scipio Africanus in the Second Punic War*
(Cambridge, 1930), 251–2; cf. *Scipio Africanus: Soldier and Politician* (London, 1970), 155)
that Scipio made peace because (1) Carthage would have been difficult to besiege (Livy);
(2) its destruction would have alienated the other African nations (not in the sources); (3)
he thought that Rome, though no doubt willing to carry out a siege, needed a period of
peace. Scullard once dismissed Scipio's alleged fear of being superseded as a 'ridiculous
charge' (252); but see his *Roman Politics*, 80, 277–8.

needed, as in 240.[1] Appian, however, makes no contribution to understanding when he describes a senatorial debate that allegedly took place after the battle of Zama, a debate in which an anonymous friend of Scipio advocates a continuation of the war.[2] Many arguments are used, including (in favour of peace) the expensiveness of a garrison army, the danger of having the Numidians as neighbours, and finally the fear and jealousy that successful colonists would arouse in Rome. This last point is founded on a bizarre anachronism, and the speeches are merely rhetorical exercises, without value as evidence for what was actually said in the Senate on this subject.[3]

In regard to Macedon after the battle of Cynoscephalae a similar but more complex situation prevailed. The defeat certainly did put Philip V in a very weak position, though the battle did not take place in Macedon itself or immediately deprive Philip of the strategically important cities of Demetrias, Chalcis, and Corinth.[4] Quite apart from its political effects, the battle cost the Macedonians and their allies about 8,000 dead and at least 5,000 prisoners out of a total force of 25,500.[5] Superficially it may seem to have been a fairly straightforward task thereafter to annex Philip's kingdom.[6] As to why Flamininus did not in the event follow up the victory with an attack on Macedon itself, Polybius provides two sets of explanations. The first he puts into Flamininus' own mouth,[7] when the Roman broke the news to his Greek allies, at the meeting at Tempe, that Rome did not intend to pursue the war further. The Romans, he

---

[1] The distaste of Scipio's veterans for more fighting was important in 200/199 (Liv. xxx. 8.6, 14.2, xxxii. 3.3).   [2] App. *Lib.* 57–65; cf. Diod. xxvii. 13–18.

[3] Similarly Hoffmann, o.c. 315–16. Some scholars have tried to defend Appian's account, but in vain. K. Bilz (*Die Politik des P. Cornelius Scipio Aemilianus* (Stuttgart, 1935), 16 n. 30) and Scullard (*Roman Politics*, 277–8) suggested that it might derive from Polybius, but this is most unconvincing, particularly as it seems that neither Appian nor Diodorus made much use of Polybius for the latter part of the Second Punic War (De Sanctis, *SR* iii. 2.660–7 (Appian), 667–70 (Diodorus)), and the debate is not described by Livy. The arguments of H. Volkmann, *Hermes* lxxxii (1954), 466–7 [→ Bibl.], in favour of some authenticity in Diodorus' account are not to the point. F. Cassola, *I gruppi politici romani*, 417–19, apparently intends to defend the authenticity of these speeches on the grounds that rejecting them implies that ancient writers knew nothing of the Senate's activities in 201; but the implication is not there, and if it were it would not be relevant. On sources concerning senatorial proceedings see above, pp. 6–7.

[4] On the question whether he still controlled Oreus and Eretria see Walbank on Polyb. xviii. 45.5.

[5] Casualties: Polyb. xviii. 27.6, Liv. xxxiii. 10.7–10; initial force: Liv. (P.) xxxiii. 4.4–5.

[6] And this is often assumed, e.g. by P. Veyne, *MEFRA* lxxxvii (1975), 815.

[7] Polyb. xviii. 37.2–9; adapted by Liv. xxxiii. 12.7–11, App. *Mac.* 9.2.

said, were accustomed when victorious not to destroy their opponents utterly or to carry on inexpiable war; nor was it in the interest of the Greeks that Macedon should be destroyed, for if it were to be destroyed, they would soon experience once more the lawlessness of the Thracians and Gauls. The diplomatic and partially deceptive character of these remarks is clear and recognized. In fact the principal cause of Flamininus' eagerness to make peace with Philip was, Polybius says,[1] the news that Philip's most powerful ally, Antiochus III, had set out from Syria with an army to come to Europe. Flamininus consequently feared that Philip might prolong the war, and that he might lose his glory to a successor.[2] That such a consideration as this last one should have weighed heavily with Flamininus seems to be entirely consistent with what we know of his character,[3] and Polybius' interpretation should be accepted. M. Claudius Marcellus, *cos.* 196, was eager for a command in Greece,[4] but was evidently not able to arouse enough support for a continuation of the war.[5]

A war involving Antiochus would have been a most imprudent undertaking at this point, and it was much better to conserve the advantages that had been achieved. Flamininus had won his victory with a force that contained only two legions,[6] which indicates that Rome was not exerting itself to the uttermost in this theatre; and further exertions and dangers of some magnitude would have been necessary to provide a real opportunity for annexation. Flamininus' discomfort with the Aetolian allies also discouraged any attempt at further campaigning, and from the Roman point of view Philip's dethronement would have made the Aetolians inconveniently powerful in Greece.[7] While it would

---

[1] xviii. 39.3–4.   [2] Cf. Liv. xxxiii. 13.15. For Appian's explanation cf. *Mac.* 9.1.

[3] Cf. Plu. *Flam.* 1.2. Already at the time of the Locris conference (November 198) Flamininus was anxious about being superseded (Liv. xxxii. 32.5–8; cf. Plu. *Flam.* 7.1); cf. M. Holleaux, *REG* xxxvi (1923), 155–63 [→ Bibl.], Walbank on Polyb. xviii. 9.5. On the character of Flamininus see also E. Badian, *Titus Quinctius Flamininus, Philhellenism and Realpolitik* (Cincinnati, 1970), esp. 23–7; and on the Locris conference, ibid. 40–8.

[4] Polyb. xviii. 42.3; cf. Liv. xxxiii. 25.4–6.

[5] Note esp. Liv. xxxiii. 25.7.

[6] See Walbank on Polyb. xviii. 27.6.

[7] As Flamininus knew: Polyb. xviii. 34.1 (cf. Liv. (P.) xxxiii. 11.9). On the meaning of ἐκβαλὼν ἐκ τῆς ἀρχῆς here cf. M. Holleaux, *RPh* lvii (1931), 203 n. 4 [→ Bibl.], and Walbank ad loc. But this was hardly a major reason for Flamininus' decision to end the war, as J. Briscoe states (n. on Liv. xxxiii. 12.10–11), not taking proper account of Polyb. xviii. 39.3.

have been possible for the Roman people to reject the peace terms agreed to by Flamininus and to insist on a settlement much more unfavourable to Philip, that would clearly have been regarded as an extreme expedient. In any case several months elapsed before the *plebs* came to pass judgement on the agreement, and in the meanwhile news had reached Rome of a major rebellion in Spain. The power over policy that was allowed to a field commander such as Flamininus, power that had not been significant in much earlier times, may in a sense have showed Rome's expansion, but it did not reflect any policy of rejecting annexation.

Since annexation is the topic, a full analysis of the policies of Roman senators towards Macedon and Greece in the three years after Cynoscephalae is not called for. However certain other facts need to be put in their places. The decision to end the war does not mean that Rome wished to avoid further involvement in Greek affairs, for an 'equilibrium' in Greece, with various powers in rivalry, was bound to produce appeals to Rome for assistance. Rome's determination not only to retain influence but to extend its power further and further into the region is made abundantly clear by the *senatus consultum* of 196 which proclaimed the freedom of 'all the other Greeks, both those in Asia and those in Europe'.[1] Then in 194 Rome withdrew all its forces from their bases in Greece, Demetrias, Chalcis, Corinth, and Leucas, an action which is always cited as evidence for Rome's lack of interest in exercising direct control in Greece. From Philip's point of view the first three of these places were 'the fetters of Greece',[2] but for the Romans possessing them was positively harmful, as Flamininus realized and as the ten senatorial commissioners eventually came to believe. Other factors perhaps entered in, such as the presumable hostility of soldiers to garrison duty; but Rome served the cause of its own expansion very well by exchanging useless bases—useless because Rome's military resources were so great that a lightning return to Greek soil was always possible—for the great fame, εὔκλεια, to be obtained by withdrawing.[3]

---

[1] Polyb. xviii. 44.2 ('other' means other than those under Philip's authority); cf. Liv. xxxiii. 30.2.

[2] The phrase was of course Philip's, and taken up by Greeks (Polyb. xviii. 11.5).

[3] On which cf. Polyb. xviii. 45.8–10.

Why did Rome refrain from annexing territory in Asia Minor in the settlements of 189 and 188? The opportunity appeared to be available. Polybius reports that in addressing the Senate in 189, Eumenes of Pergamum mentioned the possibility that Rome might continue to occupy certain areas of Asia that had formerly been subject to Antiochus; he would be very pleased, he claimed.[1] The Rhodian ambassadors followed, asserting that it was open to the Romans to give to anyone they wished Lycaonia, Hellespontic Phrygia, Pisidia, the Chersonese, 'and the parts of Europe near to it'.[2] But for Rome, as for any other state, an attempt to rule the Galatian tribes directly at this time would probably have been unrewarding, and the Galatians lost no territory to anyone.[3] Even the more accessible parts of Asia Minor which had to be redistributed were inconveniently remote and exposed for direct Roman control.[4] Instead of attempting any annexation in Asia Minor, the Senate chose to use the territories more or less at its disposal to strengthen those states, Pergamum and Rhodes, that Rome had been using as counterweights against Philip and Antiochus. Whether other arguments against annexation, such as the difficulties of providing garrison armies, had a significant effect we do not know. On the other hand annexation would have brought only slight advantages. To Scipio Africanus, the war had made the Romans 'masters of Asia';[5] and the wealth of Asia soon arrived in Rome to prove it.

The Roman settlement in Macedon after the Third Macedonian War plays a very important part in all interpretations of Roman foreign policy as non-annexationist. The kingdom was thoroughly reorganized in accordance with Roman wishes, and tribute was exacted. It is not surprising that the Periochist of Livy erroneously stated that Macedon actually did become a Roman province in 167.[6] How are we to explain that it did not? Livy's version of the Senate's policy is that the Macedonians and the Illyrians were to be 'free' as an advertise-

---

[1] Polyb. xxi. 21.7–8, cf. Liv. xxxvii. 53.25–6.

[2] Polyb. xxi. 22.14; sloppily paraphrased by Liv. xxxvii. 54.11. The authenticity of these speeches has sometimes been denied (E. Bikerman, *REG* l (1937), esp. 234, D. Magie, *Roman Rule in Asia Minor*, i. 108).

[3] Liv. xxxviii. 40.2.

[4] Cf. E. Badian, *Foreign Clientelae*, 98.

[5] Above, p. 106.

[6] *Per.* 45.

ment to the outside world of the Roman people's devotion to freedom.[1] Similarly Diodorus, who also says that it was 'contrary to the expectation of all' that the captured cities were set free.[2] Such explanations of the failure to annex Macedon oblige us to search more deeply.

When Hadrian abandoned Roman territorial claims beyond the Euphrates and the Tigris he asserted that he was following the *exemplum* of Cato, 'qui Macedones liberos pronuntiavit, quia tueri non poterant'—who pronounced in favour of the freedom of the Macedonians, because they could not be guarded.[3] The emperor evidently took Cato's meaning to have been that Macedon could not be held without disproportionate military effort. Most historians have believed that Rome's power was quite sufficient to impose annexation, and consequently they have been reluctant to admit that Cato, who must have had some solid reasons for his statement, can have been referring to the military difficulties of the task.[4] But let us ask what the military consequences of annexation would have been. The amount of

---

[1] Liv. xlv. 18.1–2: '. . . ut omnibus gentibus appareret arma populi Romani non liberis servitutem, sed contra servientibus libertatem adferre, ut et, in libertate gentes quae essent, tutam eam sibi perpetuamque sub tutela populi Romani esse, et, quae sub regibus viverent, et in praesens tempus mitiores eos iustioresque respectu populi Romani habere se crederent et, si quando bellum cum populo Romano regibus fuisset suis, exitum eius victoriam Romanis adlaturum, sibi libertatem.'

[2] xxxi. 8. The text of Polyb. xxxvi. 17.12–15 does not in its present state offer any explanation of why Rome bestowed many great so-called φιλανθρωπίαι on the Macedonians.

[3] SHA, *Hadr.* 5.3 = *ORF*[3] fr. 162 (p. 61). H. Jordan, followed by B. Janzer (*Historische Untersuchungen zu den Redenfragmenten des M. Porcius Cato* (diss. Würzburg, 1936), 67–8), unnecessarily changed 'tueri' to 'teneri'; 'tueri' is read by Hohl, Malcovati (see her n.), and others.

[4] Scholars who refer to this passage often pay no effective attention to it (e.g. T. Frank, *Roman Imperialism*, 214, D. Kienast, *Cato der Zensor* (Heidelberg, 1954), 117–18). G. Colin (*Rome et la Grèce de 200 à 146 av. J.-C.* (Paris, 1905), 445–6) did not believe in the fundamentally defensive character of Rome's policy, and so tried to use this piece of evidence to discover Roman motives; he thought that Cato's opposition to annexation of Macedon in 167 arose from his fear that governors would enrich themselves, and that *publicani* would also (cf. Liv. xlv. 18.4), and thus Roman morals would be corrupted; but this goes far beyond 'quia tueri non poterant'. According to Scullard, *Roman Politics*, 212 n. 3, Cato cannot have argued that Rome was unable to hold Macedon, and he was probably arguing that it 'could not be guarded adequately without Roman commitments to the Balkans which he regarded as undesirable.' The meaning of this is unclear. There is no reason to think that Cato regarded such commitments as undesirable for other than military reasons—the word is *poterant*. P. Meloni's interpretation, *Perseo e la fine della monarchia macedone* (Rome, 1953), 413, is that Cato cannot have been referring to military difficulties, but to the political, economic, and social consequences of annexing and garrisoning Macedon; he does not specify what these could be expected to be.

resistance to Rome that might still be expected in Macedon we can partially gauge by the successes of Andriscus and other putative sons of Perseus down to 143.[1] The warlike neighbours of Macedon, the Bastarnae, Dardanians, Odrysae, and other Thracians, could be expected to attempt invasions of Macedon, and it was necessary to allow the three Macedonian republics with external frontiers armed forces with which to protect them,[2] even though the authority of Rome was in the background. How much unpleasantness these peoples caused to the Macedonian republics between 167 and 148 it is impossible to tell in the absence of proper sources, but after the annexation an army of two legions was often, perhaps continuously, considered necessary for the security of the province, until the frontier was pushed northwards under Augustus.[3] Without annexation Rome exacted tribute from Macedon at half the rate of Perseus' taxation, and it can easily be believed that to exact more would have required the presence of a garrison. The necessary garrison would have cost something not much less than 4·8 million sesterces a year if two legions were stationed there, while the additional revenue to be gained was probably not more than 100 talents[4]—the equivalent of half of this sum. As we have seen, there is not the least reason to doubt that such calculations were important at Rome, and they may well have been central.

Furthermore garrison service in a recently annexed province of Macedon would not have been at all attractive, and the Senate was probably alive to the fact, since the war against Perseus had revealed the first serious recruiting difficulties that Rome had experienced in normal times.[5]

Thus it is perfectly credible that Cato calculated that annexation would require disproportionate military effort. It may of

---

[1] On which cf. De Sanctis, *SR* iv. 3.127.

[2] Liv. xlv. 29.14, Diod. xxxi. 8.8.

[3] For a list of the recorded military activity in the province see F. Geyer in *RE* s.v. Makedonia (1928), cols. 765–6; cf. R. E. Smith, *Service in the Post-Marian Roman Army* (Manchester, 1958), 22.

[4] For the strange view that Rome did not want to exact the maximum possible amount of tribute see above, p. 73. On the amount exacted: Plu. *Aem.* 28 sets the figure at 100 talents a year, stating that that was somewhat less than Perseus' rate; Livy (xlv. 18.7 and 29.4) says that the rate was half of Perseus', and this should probably be accepted. The revenues from the Macedonian mines did not come into the matter, since they could be obtained without annexation, as they were from 158.

[5] See above, p. 49.

course have been other arguments that convinced the rest of the
Senate of the same conclusion, but there is certainly no sign in the
sources of the reasons for avoiding annexation usually given by
modern scholars.

Many of those who have argued that the Senate shunned
annexation as much as possible have admitted that this policy
came to an end after the Macedonian settlement of 167, and that
in 148–146 the Senate showed that its views had changed. For
some, however, the annexation of Macedon, of parts of Greece,
and of Africa in those years are aberrations from a fundamentally
unchanged policy. These aberrations were supposedly forced on
to the Senate by the disorders that arose as consequences of the
earlier settlements. As far as Macedon is concerned, Rome was
clearly compelled to act. But with regard to the Achaeans and to
Carthage, senatorial policy in the years immediately before 146
seems to have been aimed quite voluntarily at establishing direct
control, and this almost inevitably meant annexation. Fuller
justification of this view will be presented in the following
chapter; here the annexation settlements themselves will be the
only objects of attention.

In the case of the Achaean League, there is no sign that the
Senate hesitated to annex the territory of the defeated after the
campaign of 146.[1] It has been implied that because some of the
arrangements were left to Polybius, after a ten-legate commission
had spent six months organizing the affairs of Greece, the Senate
lacked interest in the annexation.[2] The fact tells us far more
about Polybius than about the Senate. Even less plausible is the
attempt to play down the amount of annexation in Greece itself.[3]
Half-empty bottles are also half full, and the territory of the
Achaean League, the Peloponnese (except Laconia), Megara,
Boeotia, Chalcis, Phocis, and eastern Locris constituted a
considerable area, comparable to that of Macedon itself.

As for the settlement of Carthaginian territory which Rome

[1] The annexation was of a peculiar kind, the new territory being subjected to the
governor of Macedonia. The extent of the annexed territory was established by S.
Accame, *Il dominio romano in Grecia dalla guerra acaica ad Augusto* (Rome, 1946), esp. 7–15
(generally accepted). The conclusion of T. Schwertfeger, *Der achaiische Bund von 146 bis 27
v. Chr.* (Munich, 1974), esp. 72, that Achaea did not become a province until 27, is based
merely on his artificial insistence that a province had to have a *separate* governor.

[2] E. Badian, *RILR*[2] 21. The commission: Polyb. xxxix. 4.1, cf. Paus. vii. 16.9. Its stay in
Greece: Polyb. xxxix. 5.1. Polybius' own role: xxxix. 5.

[3] Badian, *RILR*[2] 21.

carried out in 146, it too has been forced to give a strange meaning. Allegedly the annexation came from 'political necessity, and not from any desire for gain or expansion'.[1] The frontier established for the new province did not require the sons of Massinissa to forgo any of the territorial gains they had made before 150. 'Liberty' and immunity were given to towns that had been on the Roman side during the war with Carthage, and allies of Rome, notably Utica, gained territory.[2] But these were prudent investments by the Senate in local good will, and there is no justification for reading any other motives into the settlement. If the Romans had not desired gain and expansion—and we have reviewed at length the evidence that they did—they could, after the destruction of Carthage, have left the territory to the Numidians. Of course it never occurred to them to do so.

Once again, it was only with reluctance, allegedly, that the Senate accepted the bequest when Attalus III left the kingdom of Pergamum to Rome in 134 or 133. There is no evidence for this very paradoxical supposition. It is misleading to claim that Tiberius Gracchus 'passed a law in the Assembly accepting the inheritance',[3] and so forced the Senate's hand. What the sources say is that Tiberius got a law passed, or proposed one, or—this is most likely—declared his intention of promulgating one, to distribute Attalus' money to those citizens who received land by the agrarian law.[4] Such a proposal obviously had no chance in

---

[1] Badian, *Foreign Clientelae*, 139.

[2] On these arrangements see R. M. Haywood in *ESAR* iv. 3–5, P. Romanelli, *Storia delle province romane dell'Africa* (Rome, 1959), 46–50.

[3] Badian, *RILR*[2] 21; similarly T. Frank, *Roman Imperialism*, 243, and many others, most recently T. Liebmann-Frankfort, *RIDA* ser. 3, xiii (1966), 83 and n. 33, F. Carrata Thomes, *La rivolta di Aristonico e le origini della provincia romana d'Asia* (Turin, 1968), 35, and (by implication) H. C. Boren, *The Gracchi* (New York, 1968), 71. Nor incidentally do the sources say (though it may be true) that the Pergamene envoy Eudemus lodged with Tiberius Gracchus when he came to Rome (so Badian, *Foreign Clientelae*, 174, followed by D. C. Earl, *Tiberius Gracchus, A Study in Politics* (Brussels, 1963), 93, and others); all we are told is that Q. Pompeius alleged that he had seen Eudemus offer a crown to Tiberius, who was his (Pompeius') next-door neighbour (Plu. *TG* 14), a story which Badian rightly finds hard to believe. The point is not trivial, for exaggerating the importance of Tiberius in Roman–Pergamene relations can lead to exaggerating his influence in getting the bequest accepted.

[4] *De vir. ill.* 64.5: 'dein tulit, ut de ea pecunia quae ex Attali hereditate erat, ageretur et populo divideretur'; Oros. v. 8.4; 'legem tulit, uti pecunia, quae fuisset Attali, populo distribueretur'; Plu. *TG* 14: ἐπεὶ δὲ τοῦ Φιλομήτορος Ἀττάλου τελευτήσαντος Εὔδημος ὁ Περγαμηνὸς ἀνήνεγκε διαθήκην ἐν ᾗ κληρονόμος ἐγέγραπτο τοῦ βασιλέως ὁ Ῥωμαίων δῆμος, εὐθὺς ὁ Τιβέριος δημαγωγῶν εἰσήνεγκε νόμον, ὅπως

the Senate, and if Tiberius chose to take his proposal to the
assembly rather than to the Senate, that shows nothing at all
about the Senate's attitude towards annexing the kingdom of
Attalus. Plutarch adds that as far as the cities in Attalus' kingdom
were concerned, Tiberius said that the Senate should not discuss
them, but that he himself would propose a bill to the people.[1]
This strongly suggests that Tiberius disagreed with the weight of
senatorial opinion as to whether the cities of the kingdom should
be immune from taxation—but not that there was a disagreement about annexation, an entirely different matter.[2] Nor do the
eventual territorial arrangements that were made for the
province Asia, in which considerable areas were given to neighbouring kings who had helped to defeat Aristonicus, provide any
evidence that the Senate was reluctant to annex the kingdom. As
in Africa in 146, the Senate was making a prudent investment in
the future security of the province, and M'. Aquillius (cos. 129)
may in addition have favoured Mithridates V of Pontus in
exchange for a substantial bribe.[3]

The actions taken to annex the kingdom and to resist
Aristonicus reflect a quite vigorous determination to take
possession. Unfortunately the dates of some crucial events are
unclear. However the commission of five legati must have been
sent to organize the territory well before the end of 133.[4] It is

τὰ βασιλικὰ χρήματα κομισθέντα τοῖς τὴν χώραν διαλαγχάνουσι τῶν πολιτῶν
ὑπάρχοι, πρὸς κατασκευὴν καὶ γεωργίας ἀφορμήν, κτλ. Liv. Per. 58: 'legem se
promulgaturum ostendit ut his, qui Sempronia lege agrum accipere deberent, pecunia,
quae regis Attali fuisset, divideretur.' This confusion as to whether the law was passed,
promulgated, or suggested, is most likely to have arisen if the law was only suggested; cf.
P. Fraccaro, Studi sull' età dei Gracchi (Città di Castello, 1914), 133–4, Earl, o.c. 94 n. 2.
   [1] TG 14.
   [2] Attalus' will had apparently specified that the city of Pergamum should remain 'free'
(OGIS 338, lines 1–7), and probably that other cities should also. This seems to have been
accepted by the Senate (see RDGE no. 11 = OGIS 435; cf. also H. B. Mattingly, AJPh xciii
(1972), 412–23, C. P. Jones, Chiron iv (1974), 196). The law of C. Gracchus de provincia Asia
probably ended this privilege: App. BC v. 4.17 (with the interpretation of E. Gabba ad
loc.).
   [3] On these arrangements see D. Magie, Roman Rule in Asia Minor, i. 155–7. R. K. Sherk,
RDGE 75, draws the unjustified conclusion that they were part of the Senate's policy of
annexing as little territory as possible. On the bribing of Aquillius see App. Mithr. 12, 57
(disbelieved by Magie, ii. 1048 n. 41).
   [4] Since Scipio Nasica Serapio was sent on the mission to save him from the unpopularity
he earned for the killing of Ti. Gracchus (Val. Max. v. 3.2 e, Plu. TG 21.2, De vir. ill. 64.9).
Cic. De amic. 37 (cf. Val. Max. iv. 7.1) shows that Plu. TG 20 was wrong to hold that

evident that the Senate knew nothing at this point of any serious local insurrection.[1] But things began to go wrong. The head of the Roman commission, Scipio Nasica Serapio, died at Pergamum in late 133 or in 132, which impeded action. Aristonicus was an unpleasant surprise, and in 132 the forces of Rome's allies in Asia Minor proved insufficient. The required Roman army was duly sent (131). The original bequest also speaks against the alleged reluctance on the part of the Senate, for it would be hard to understand unless there was always a good prospect that it would be accepted. Attalus had sufficient connections at Rome to be able to ascertain what the Senate's attitude would be.[2] Just conceivably he knew that the Senate would be reluctant to accept it, but still considered that the will would be a deterrent to potential assassins who might be less knowledgeable about senatorial policy (this was perhaps the only intention of Ptolemy Physcon when he announced in 155 that if he continued to lack an heir his kingdom of Cyrene would be bequeathed to Rome). Much more probably, while Attalus hoped that the will would act as a deterrent, he also expected to gain credit in Rome and perhaps a relatively untroubled future for his kingdom after his death. In any case there is no serious evidence that the Senate was reluctant to accept the bequest.

Serapio was still in Rome in 132. The senatorial decree recorded in *RDGE* no. 11 = *OGIS* 435 presupposes the decision to annex; the decree probably belongs to 133 (Magie argued for a later date, 1033 n. 1, but see *MRR* i. 496 n. 1, Sherk, o.c. 61), and to a date between 14 August and 11 December (lines 4–5). The political preoccupations of 133 which might have slowed senatorial action are obvious; and there were military preoccupations in Sicily and at Numantia (cf. J. Vogt, *Atti del III Congresso internazionale di epigrafia greca e latina* (publ. Rome, 1959), 49 = *Sklaverei und Humanität* (Wiesbaden, 1965), 64).

[1] The seriousness of his rebellion was perhaps not appreciated at Rome until early 132. App. *BC* i. 18.73 provides only a general synchronism between Tiberius' tribunate and Aristonicus' rebellion (in fact Aristonicus was hardly 'warring against the Romans' before Tiberius' death). If the rebellion lasted four years before its leader's death (App. *Mithr.* 62), it began in 134 or 133. More significant, however, is that the regnal years given on the cistophori which Aristonicus minted under the title of Eumenes III run from two to four, with no sign of the first (E. S. G. Robinson, *NC* ser. 6, xiv (1954), 1–8; cf. L. Robert, *Villes d'Asie Mineure*[2] (Paris, 1962), 252–3), which probably means that the rebellion was not causing wide effects until late 133 at the earliest.

[2] For Attalus' Roman connections see Polyb. xxxiii. 18.3 (in general). For the connection with Aemilianus see Cic. *Reg. Deiot.* 19 (with Σ Ambros. p. 272St) and cf. Lucian, *Macrobioi*, 12. The connection with the Sempronii Gracchi is emphasized by Badian, *Foreign Clientelae*, 173–4; the evidence (besides Plu. *TG* 14) is that the elder Ti. Gracchus reported favourably to the Senate on Eumenes when he led an embassy to the eastern states c. 165 (for the sources see *MRR* i. 438).

We possess no explicit evidence about the exact date of the annexation of Transalpine Gaul. It has been almost universally assumed that it took place at the conclusion of the successful wars of 125–*c.* 121, and this view is a reasonable one unless solid arguments can be found to the contrary. No large-scale local resistance which might explain annexation occurred at any later date. None the less an old theory that the annexation was carried out by Marius after the Cimbric Wars has recently been revived and developed.[1] Summarily stated, the arguments are that the sources make no mention of the ten *legati* who would normally have helped Cn. Domitius Ahenobarbus (*cos.* 122) to establish the province, or of the *lex provinciae*; and that no governors are known until L. Licinius Crassus, *cos.* 95, who governed 'Gallia' in 94 and perhaps already in 95.

But while the very fragmentary sources on the wars of Domitius Ahenobarbus and Fabius Maximus Allobrogicus make no mention of an annexation commission, neither do the sources concerning the aftermath of the Cimbric War make any mention of one; the fact that nothing is known of a *lex provinciae* is equally useless as evidence for the establishment of the province after the Cimbric War rather than *c.* 120. As for governors, no source tells us the precise title or nature of the *provincia* allotted to M. Iunius Silanus (*cos.* 109), L. Cassius Longinus (*cos.* 107), Q. Servilius Caepio (*cos.* 106), or Cn. Mallius Maximus (*cos.* 105). They may merely have been given the war against the Cimbri and their allies, but they may have been given 'Gallia'. If the later charge against Silanus, which is reported by Asconius,[2] that he fought against the Cimbri 'iniussu populi', was to be other than ridiculous, he was surely in Gaul as a regular governor (Silanus was, admittedly, acquitted by a large majority). So sparse are the sources for the period 120–106 that our not knowing of any specific assignment of Transalpine Gaul is insignificant; the *fasti* are at least as fragmentary for most other provinces. The wars of 125–*c.* 121 can probably be said without exaggeration to have broken the resistance of the tribes of Provence, and there is some additional evidence (unfortunately

---

[1] A. W. Zumpt, *Studia Romana* (Berlin, 1859), esp. 23; E. Badian, *Mélanges d'archéologie et d'histoire offerts à André Piganiol* (Paris, 1966), 901–18, following up *Foreign Clientelae*, 140, 264 n. 3, *PACA* i (1958), 11 = *Studies in Greek and Roman History*, 89; cf. *RILR*[2] 23–4. This is accepted by E. Gabba, *Esercito e società*, 550 n. 52.

[2] *In Cornelian.* 80 C.

not conclusive) that Domitius' stay in the region was extended after the war.[1] The balance of probability is heavily in favour of a formal annexation at the earliest possible date, about 120.

In the case of Numidia in 105 there is no reason to think that an opportunity for annexation of territory was voluntarily given up.[2] It is possible, but unproven, that the existing province of Africa was extended westwards.[3] More important, it remains unclear, in spite of Sallust's lengthy narrative, to what extent Numidia had come under Roman control by 105. The war was brought to an end by the capture rather than the defeat of Jugurtha, and if the Senate had wanted to annex a large area of Numidia the Romans would still have had to contend with Numidian tribesmen (and if they had taken too much, also with Bocchus and the Mauretanians). In addition Numidia was an exceptionally unattractive prospect as a province. But in any case the question of a large annexation can hardly have been discussed at any length, because by the time the startling news of Jugurtha's capture arrived at Rome, the news of the overwhelming disaster suffered at Arausio on 6 October 105 had already arrived there, or was very soon to arrive.[4] According to Sallust,

---

[1] This evidence is the Pont-de-Treilles milestone, *ILLRP* 460a, the text of which is 'Cn. Domitius Cn. f. Ahenobarbus imperator XX'. The 20 miles are numbered from Narbo, and so it was suggested that the inscription was later than the foundation of the Roman colony of Narbo (P.-M. Duval, *Gallia* vii (1949), 218, *MRR* ii. 644), which Velleius (i. 15.5, ii. 7.8) and Eutropius (iv. 23) set in 118 with a consular date. Thus Domitius may have remained in the region until 118. Badian, however, pointed out (*Foreign Clientelae*, 313) and A. Degrassi argued in detail (*Hommages à A. Grenier* (Brussels, 1962), i. 513 [→ Bibl.]; accepted by E. Gabba, *RFIC* xcii (1964), 100) that the milestone and its road may in fact be earlier than the colony, since Narbo was already an established centre (cf. Duval, o.c. 218 n. 39, G. Clemente, *I romani nella Gallia meridionale* (Bologna, 1974), 12). None the less one may think that the road preceded the colony only by a few months, if at all. Whether 118 is the true date of Narbo has been discussed at length, but the controversy will not be revived here. In my view 118 is preferable (cf. A. E. Douglas on Cic. *Brut.* 160, Gabba, l.c., B. M. Levick, *CQ* n.s. xxi (1971), 170–9, M. H. Crawford, *RRC* 71–3, who between them have dealt with all the noteworthy arguments advanced by H. B. Mattingly in *Hommages Grenier*, iii. 1159–71, *Revue archéologique de Narbonnaise* v (1972), 1–19); hence there is some reason to think that Domitius stayed in the Transalpine region long after the fighting was over.

[2] Otherwise R. Syme (*Sallust* (Cambridge, 1964), 176, referring to the failure to annex as 'the traditional policy of the Roman Senate'), as well as Frank, Badian, etc.

[3] So T. Frank, *AJPh* xlvii (1926), 55–73 (esp. 64), T. R. S. Broughton, *The Romanization of Africa Proconsularis* (Baltimore, 1929), 31–5, E. Gabba, *Athenaeum* xxix (1951), 16; contra P. Romanelli, *Storia delle province romane dell'Africa* (Rome, 1959), 82–3, P. A. Brunt, *Italian Manpower*, 578.

[4] The Cimbri may have been regarded as a serious problem even before Arausio (cf. M. Holroyd, *JRS* xviii (1928), 3), but tens of thousands of Roman soldiers fell there (on the

'per idem tempus [as the capture of Jugurtha]' the battle of
Arausio took place. 'At this the whole of Italy shuddered with
fear . . . but after it was reported that the war in Numidia had
been completed and that Jugurtha was being brought to Rome in
chains, Marius was made consul in his absence.'[1] This chronology receives some slight confirmation from Eutropius.[2]
Plutarch, on the other hand, says that the news of the capture of
Jugurtha had recently arrived when rumours about the Teutones
and Cimbri began to reach Rome.[3] These are the only indications which we possess of the date of the capture of Jugurtha,[4]
but they are sufficient to exclude Numidia from the non-
annexationist case.

In short, it turns out that in the period from 148 to 105 there is
not the slightest trace of any Roman reluctance to annex territory
or of any basic principle of refraining from annexation.

Finally, we return to Asia Minor. After the suppression of
Aristonicus, Rome made territorial dispositions in favour of the
various rulers who had performed service. Mithridates V of
Pontus received Phrygia. In 121 or 120, however, he was
assassinated, and Rome thereupon added Phrygia to the province of Asia.[5] The fact is well known, and until recently it was
thought by some scholars to be the last of Rome's annexations in
Asia Minor until the campaigns of Lucullus and Pompey fifty
years later. Some on the other hand maintained that a province
named 'Cilicia' was annexed in 102 or shortly afterwards. The

casualty figures cf. P. A. Brunt, o.c. 82, 685), and the battle clearly transformed the
Roman view of the situation in the north. S. Gsell, *Histoire ancienne de l'Afrique du Nord*, vii
(Paris, 1928), 262, also argues that anxiety about events in the north prevented Rome
from considering the annexation of Numidia in 105.

[1] *BJ* 114.

[2] v. 1.1: 'dum bellum in Numidia contra Iugurtham geritur, Romani consules M.
Manlius et Q. Caepio a Cimbris, etc., victi sunt iuxta flumen Rhodanum ingenti
internicione . . .' The chronology of Sallust's *BJ* has often been studied (most exhaust-
ively by H. Chantraine, *Untersuchungen zur römischen Geschichte am Ende des 2. Jahrhunderts v.
Chr.* (Kallmünz, 1959), 29–62); the only result relevant here is that Sallust was not
interested in chronology.

[3] Plu. *Mar.* 11: ἄρτι γὰρ ἀπηγγελμένης αὐτοῖς τῆς Ἰουγούρθα συλλήψεως, αἱ περὶ
Τευτόνων καὶ Κίμβρων φῆμαι προσέπιπτον . . .'.

[4] The text of Vell. ii. 12.1 is too corrupt to be of any help.

[5] The assassination: Strabo x. 477, Justin xxxvii. 1.6 (and for the date Plin. *NH* xxv. 6,
App. *Mithr.* 112). The annexation is inferred from *RDGE* no. 13 = *OGIS* 436 (on which cf.
T. Drew-Bear, *Historia* xxi (1972), 79–87), App. *Mithr.* 11, 12, 15, 56, 57 (αὐτόνομον
μεθῆκεν in 57.232 is probably a rhetorical equivocation), Justin xxxviii. 5.3.

evidence on this problem was simply insufficient.[1] Now a newly published inscription from Cnidos, apparently part of a text of the 'Piracy Law',[2] shows that this picture requires radical alteration. The inscription not only adds further evidence that Cilicia was already a territorial province in 101 or 100,[3] but it also shows—to the surprise of scholars—that Lycaonia too was already a province,[4] and that a section of Thracian territory had recently been annexed to the province of Macedonia.[5] Lycaonia, like Phrygia, had presumably been annexed on the death (*c.* 116) of the vassal who had received it after the revolt of Aristonicus, namely Ariarathes VI of Cappadocia.[6]

The annexation of Phrygia in about 120 was by no means forced on to the Senate. It might have been quite difficult to find a suitable ruler for the territory, but there was as yet no danger in Asia Minor of the kind which Mithridates VI was soon to create. Mithridates himself was eleven years of age. Neither did the murder of Ariarathes VI, though it was probably instigated by this precocious youth, in any way require annexation for the protection of Roman interests. (It may of course have been a few years later that Lycaonia was annexed.) The annexation of

---

[1] For M. Antonius' command against the pirates see *MRR* i. 568, 572, 576. The earliest evidence for a territorial province of Cilicia concerned Sulla's command there: App. *Mithr.* 57, *De vir. ill.* 75 (to be dated in 96/5 rather than 92: E. Badian, *Athenaeum* xxxvii (1959), 279–303 = *Studies in Greek and Roman History*, 157–78). However these might merely be references to a non-territorial 'provincia' (cf. Magie, o.c. 1162–3, who lists previous views on the subject, Badian, o.c. 285 = 161). See further E. Will, *Histoire politique*, ii. 391, T. Liebmann-Frankfort, *Hommages à M. Renard* (Brussels, 1969), ii. 447–57), according to whom there is no trace of annexation in this period.

[2] M. Hassall, M. Crawford, and J. Reynolds, *JRS* lxiv (1974), 195–220.

[3] Col. III, lines 28–37: the senior consul is to write that the Roman people τήν τε Κιλικίαν διὰ τοῦτο τὸ πρᾶγμα κατὰ τοῦτον τὸν νόμον ἐπαρχείαν στρατηγικὴν πεποιηκέναι. The editors suggest (o.c. 211) that this may not necessarily mean territorial annexation, apparently because they think that the praetorian 'provincia' may have been merely the (unannexed) one held by M. Antonius himself. But that 'provincia' had already been created *before* the date of the law (on which see o.c. 216). Since there is, in addition, reason to think that the law defined the territory of Cilicia in a lost section (o.c. 211), the weight of the evidence heavily favours the creation of the territorial province by means of the Cnidos law.

[4] Col. III, lines 22–7: the praetor or proconsul who governs the province of Asia governs Lycaonia, and the province (ἐπαρχεία) of Lycaonia is under his government, just as before the passage of this law. . . . The editors also suggest reading Λυ[καονία] in Piracy Law (*FIRA* ed. Riccobono, i no. 9), A6–7 (o.c. 209).

[5] Col. IV, lines 5–31: the conquests of T. Didius in the Caeneic Chersonese are the subject.

[6] Hassall etc., o.c. 211. See also on Pamphylia o.c. 209.

Cilicia was another matter, but since the annexation was carried out by a law—the earliest clear case of this—one may doubt whether the Senate thought that the menace of pirates required any such action. Phrygia and Lycaonia, at least, and perhaps Cilicia too, show that Rome was perfectly willing to annex territory when the opportunity arose.

The principle of non-annexation is a delusion, as far as the period down to 101 is concerned. When it was possible and profitable to annex a territory, annexation was carried out. The accrued political wisdom of the middle-republican Senate naturally prevented a headlong rush to paint the map red; but neither were there any delays except for the most practical reasons.

3. THE NON-ANNEXATION OF CYRENE AND EGYPT

We come now to a new period and to two cases in which the Senate undoubtedly did show reluctance to annex.

In 96 the kingdom of Cyrene was bequeathed to Rome by Ptolemy Apion, but it was not formed into a province until 75, or conceivably even later.[1] It would have been a fairly simple task to annex Cyrene at any time between 96 and 92, and again under Sulla. The sources provide no explanation of the delay. Historians who believe in a continuing non-annexation policy can of course treat it merely as a part of that policy.[2] Other explanations have been offered, for example the hypothesis that the 'royal land' actually bequeathed to Rome may have been so limited in extent that it was not worth making a province out of it.[3] Alternatively, the Senate may have wanted to avoid giving another opportunity to *publicani*,[4] or it may have found the prospect of defending Cyrene against the desert tribes unattractive.[5] Unfortunately we do not know for certain whether

---

[1] The bequest: for lists of sources see S.I. Oost, *CPh* lviii (1963), 22 n. 3, G. Perl, *Klio* lii (1970), 319 n. 1. On the annexation see Additional Note xiv.

[2] E.g. T. Frank, *Roman Imperialism*, 273, Badian, *RILR*² 22, 29–30.

[3] W. Otto, *Zur Geschichte der Zeit des 6. Ptolemäers* (*Abh. Bay. Ak. Wiss.* N.F. xi (1934)), 109 n. 1. But cf. R. S. Bagnall, *The Administration of the Ptolemaic Possessions outside Egypt* (Leiden, 1976), 32–3.

[4] Oost, o.c. 15. This also seems to have been the view of G. I. Luzzatto, *SDHI* vii (1941), 286.

[5] Oost, l.c. On some fighting against the Libyans in this general period see the new inscription discussed by L. Moretti, *RFIC* civ (1976), 385–98.

Rome drew any tribute from the region before 75;[1] but if it was able to do so, the incentive to establish a province was evidently weaker.

This problem is not going to be cleared up in definitive fashion by means of the existing evidence. However, another factor in the situation requires close attention, a factor that was, as we shall see, important in the case of Egypt, namely the unwillingness of leading senators to let any one of their number gain the wealth and power that was likely to accrue to the man who was first sent out to take command in Cyrene. Least of all will they have been willing to let Marius undertake the task.[2] Such an interpretation will not explain why Sulla did not annex Cyrene, but it is only by a sort of accident that we know why he did not annex the far more important territory of Egypt. It is, however, confirmed by the fact that when the annexation of Cyrene was eventually carried out it was done through a magistrate of the lowest possible rank, the quaestor P. Cornelius Lentulus Marcellinus; the only possible explanation of this odd fact is that a quaestor could not be a threat to any of the leading men.[3]

Egypt was bequeathed to Rome by Ptolemy X Alexander I in 88 or 87. The arguments in favour of thinking that it was Alexander I, not Alexander II, who was responsible for this bequest, now seem decisive.[4] The Senate at least seems to have acted as if a genuine and valid bequest had been made, though in 63 there were some significant people at Rome who maintained that there had been no such will.[5] In any case Alexander I had lost his throne to the former king Ptolemy IX Soter II some time before he died,[6] and so the situation that faced the Senate after Alexander I's death was somewhat awkward. The discussion in the Senate resulted, according to Cicero, in a *senatus auctoritas*, a decree vetoed by a tribune and therefore invalid, to accept the

[1] Oost's thorough discussion (o.c. 12–14) leaves the matter open. Cf. also L. Gasperini, *Quaderni di archeologia della Libia* v (1967), 56 (publishing a relevant new inscription, *AE* 1967 no. 532), Perl, o.c. 320, Bagnall, o.c. 33 n. 26.

[2] See below, p. 158.

[3] E. Badian, *JRS* lv (1965), 120.

[4] E. Badian, *RhM* cx (1967), 178–92; cf. W. Drumann—P. Groebe, *Geschichte Roms*, iv² (Leipzig, 1908–10), 97, A. Afzelius, *C & M* iii (1940), 230.

[5] Cic. *De leg. agr.* ii. 42 (quoted later in the text); cf. ii. 41 'video qui testamentum factum esse confirmet.'

[6] Justin, xxxix. 5.1; Porphyr. Tyr., *FGrH* 260 F2.8; Euseb. *Hieron. Chron.* p. 150, 15–18 Helm. Cf. Badian, o.c. 183–4.

bequest.[1] We do not know what arguments were used for and against acceptance, or for and against the immediate establishment of a province. There may have been doubts of various kinds about the validity of the will. The political reality was that Soter II was in power and the war with Mithridates needed all of Rome's attention in the East. In the period 86–82 the government at Rome was hardly in a position to mount an expedition to Egypt, and it was obviously in Sulla's interest during that period to allow Soter II to remain in power. Soter died in the year 80 and was succeeded by his daughter Berenice. Sulla now attempted to stabilize the situation, and make a large profit for himself, by installing Ptolemy XI Alexander II as her husband and co-ruler.[2] This arrangement lasted only for some eighteen days before Alexander, who had murdered Berenice, was himself murdered by the Alexandrians. It was evidently more difficult to impose a government in Egypt than had been thought. Ptolemy Auletes seized power quickly, it seems, after the death of Alexander II, and though it was denied later by those who wanted to establish the legitimacy of Auletes' tenure of power, some said that he had actually been responsible for his predecessor's death.[3]

In failing to take further action in Egypt after Alexander II's death, Sulla, it has been argued, 'stood in the line of Senate tradition, opposed to the expansion of administrative responsibilities.'[4] But the chronology of these events needs further attention. According to the most probable chronology of 81/0, Alexander II was killed not earlier than August 80; Auletes, who was regarded a few months later as having become king by 1 Thoth, i.e. by (Julian) 12 September, thus came to power only shortly before that date.[5] Therefore the news of Alexander's

---

[1] Cic. *De leg. agr.* ii. 41–2. On this cf. Badian, o.c. 180–1.

[2] App. *BC* i. 102.476–7 (ἐλπίσας χρηματιεῖσθαι πολλὰ ἐκ βασιλείας πολυχρύσου).

[3] The charge is referred to and naturally denied by Cicero, *De Rege Alex.* p. 93St, who appears to say that Auletes was in Syria at the time of Alexander II's death.

[4] Badian, o.c. 189–90. In addition he points out the danger that a proconsul in Egypt would have been to the regime at Rome.

[5] For the chronology of the dynastic history in the crucial period between December 81 and September 80 we are mainly dependent on the self-contradictory evidence of Eusebius' excerpts from Porphyry, preserved in an Armenian translation (given in German in *FGrH* 260 F2.7–11). For the solution preferred in the text see T. C. Skeat, *The Reigns of the Ptolemies* (Munich, 1954), 36–7, A. E. Samuel, *Ptolemaic Chronology* (Munich, 1962), 152–5), and in *Chronique d'Égypte* xl (1965), 376–400. Less likely seems the

death, accompanied or soon followed by the news of Auletes' accession, is most unlikely to have reached Rome much before the end of (Julian) October.[1] Sulla may then have spent some time considering whether there was still some way in which the situation could be used for his private advantage. The question of annexation must also have been discussed. It is obvious that the leading men in the state, steadily gaining power in the last months of 80,[2] will have felt strong rivalry about the possible Egyptian command. There thus seems to be nothing remarkable about Sulla's failure to convert Egypt into a province, and there is no need to summon the aid of a supposed senatorial tradition opposed to such actions.

It is worth tracing this topic somewhat further, to see why Egypt was not annexed in the thirty years after Sulla's dictatorship. While Pompey was in Spain he must have done his best to make sure that no one else succeeded in obtaining an Egyptian command. Meanwhile Auletes will have been trying to get his claim to the throne recognized in Rome. By 65, when Crassus as censor attempted to obtain the privilege of turning Egypt into a province, the opposition to such a move was strong; Catulus, the other censor, and no doubt all his immediate allies, were against it,[3] and it was probably at this time that Cicero, in his speech *De rege Alexandrino*, sought to establish that Auletes should be left in power.[4] Two years later in *De lege agraria II* he voiced objections that were felt at Rome to annexing Egypt: 'It is said on the other side that there is no will, that the Roman people ought not to seem eager to acquire every kingdom, that our population will settle over there because of the quality of the land and the general

reconstruction of E. Bloedow, *Beiträge zur Geschichte des Ptolemaios XII.* (diss. Würzburg, 1963), 11–20 (which has the effect of setting the death of Alexander II, and the accession of Auletes, about the end of June in 80).

[1] On the slowness of the Alexandria–Puteoli route see L. Casson, *TAPhA* lxxxii (1951), esp. 145. It is also likely that the date by the actual Roman calendar was even later.

[2] The date when Sulla laid down the dictatorship is much debated; see especially G. V. Sumner, *JRS* liv (1964), 45 n. 44 (suggesting that he may have done so immediately after the elections for 79); cf. also E. Badian, *Athenaeum* xlviii (1970), 8–14, B. L. Twyman, *Athenaeum* liv (1976), 77–97, 271–95. There is apparently no evidence about the date of the consular elections in 80, but it is probable that in such a well-ordered year they were over by late October.

[3] Plu. *Crass.* 13.2; cf. Cic. *De leg. agr.* ii. 44.

[4] For the fragments see Stangl, *Ciceronis Orationum Scholiastae*, pp. 91–3, as well as the standard collections of Cicero's fragments. On the date: Mommsen, *RG* iii[12]. 177 n., H. Strasburger, *Caesars Eintritt in die Geschichte* (Munich, 1938), 112.

abundance there.'[1] We can hardly doubt that what really mattered were arguments that Cicero could not parade in public: while there was a certain balance of power between the *principes viri* none of them could be allowed by the others to steal a march by annexing Egypt. When individuals seized power, as Pompey and Caesar effectively did in 60/59, there was an immense private profit to be made, some 6,000 talents according to Suetonius,[2] not by annexation but by securing the recognition of the reigning king.

4. THE DETERMINING FACTORS

The Senate's policy concerning annexation turns out to be less mysterious than in the conventional interpretation. In the instance which most requires explaining, Rome's failure to annex Macedon in 167, it is impossible to know the precise weight which senators attached to the various disadvantages; but major disadvantages there certainly were.

The mutual rivalry of leading senators did not inhibit Roman annexation as such until the last years of our period (though the rivalry had sometimes slowed down the extension of Roman power). Marius was the first to reach a position in the Roman state that seriously threatened to destroy the oligarchical equilibrium. His military successes and fame, his veterans loyal to his own person, his imperfect respect for the constitution, and finally his alliance with Saturninus, alarmed and antagonized the *nobilitas*. He chose not to subvert the system, but he had had the choice. Four years after the crisis of 100 the Senate elected not to annex Cyrene, when it could have done so. Marius' career may have been one of the inhibiting factors. He had travelled to Cappadocia and Galatia (in 99 or 98) in the hope of stirring up a war with Mithridates and being chosen for the resulting command, so Plutarch says;[3] even if this is not the true explanation of his journey, it is likely that the story is a contemporary one. His election to the augurate during his

---

[1] ii. 41–2.

[2] Suet. *DJ* 54.3 (the figure might be suspected); cf. Dio xxxix. 12.1, Plu. *Caes.* 48.8. On the recognition of Auletes cf. also Caes. *BC* iii. 107, Cic. *Att.* ii. 16.2.

[3] Plu. *Mar.* 31. Hassall etc., o.c. (p. 153 n. 2), 218 n. 29, are too sceptical about Marius' intention. See T. J. Luce, *Historia* xix (1970), 161–8.

absence shows that he still had plenty of popular support,[1] and there was a possibility that a tribune would, in the event of a decision to annex Cyrene, propose and get passed a law in Marius' favour like the Sulpician law of 88. Sulla afterwards showed what a successful and ruthless commander might do on his return from the East, and Egypt was a much richer prize than Cyrene. It is natural therefore that in 80–78 the Senate was unwilling to try to resolve the Egyptian situation by annexation, and remained so after 66 when it again became a relatively easy military task.

The first-century Senate tended to oppose commands of unusual extent or duration. It even showed itself more cautious than formerly in allowing individuals advantageous civilian opportunities of performing public services. Thus from the last decade of the second century there was an otherwise un-explained halt in major road-construction,[2] and similarly no more major aqueducts were built at Rome between the Aqua Tepula (125) and Agrippa's Aqua Iulia (33).[3] These activities had previously permitted leading senators to bestow numerous useful *beneficia*, and in the generally stable atmosphere of pre-Marian politics that was acceptable. After the crisis of the year 100 the leaders of the state intensified their mutual precautions; one of the results was that the Senate became more reluctant to allow individuals the privilege of carrying out annexations.

The argument that annexation was inhibited by senatorial disapproval of the corrupt behaviour of provincial governors[4] is most unconvincing. It is certainly important for the understanding of the aristocracy's attitude towards the empire that as early as 171 the Senate was prepared to listen to, and to some extent even to act on, the complaints of mistreated provincials. In that year an embassy from *socii* in Spain pleaded before the Senate that they had been exploited by Roman officials, and the praetor appointed senatorial *recuperatores* to hear the case.[5] What happened more often before 149 was that the grievances of provincials (and foreigners) were taken up at Rome by tribunes

---

[1] Cic. *Ad Brut.* i. 5.3. On the election cf. E. S. Gruen, *Roman Politics and the Criminal Courts, 149–78 B.C.* (Cambridge, Mass., 1968), 192, Luce, o.c. 164–6.

[2] Cf. T. P. Wiseman, *PBSR* xxxviii (1970), 150.

[3] Cf. Frontin. *De aq.* 8–9.

[4] See above, p. 132.

[5] See above, p. 78.

and brought before the people. This is what happened in the case
of C. Lucretius Gallus and the Chalcidians in 170, which resulted
in Lucretius being fined 1 million *asses*.[1] L. Cornelius Lentulus
Lupus, *cos.* 156, was apparently convicted *c.* 153 under a
tribunician *Lex Caecilia*, and in 149 Ser. Sulpicius Galba narrowly
overcame the effort of a tribune, L. Scribonius, who proposed to
set up a special court to try him.[2] Some provincial governors were
actually convicted of 'avaritia' during the 150s,[3] and this was
probably also through tribunician activity. As has already been
argued, the *Lex Calpurnia* of 149 stemmed not from an increased
sensitivity on the part of the Senate concerning the grievances of
the provincials, but from a desire to take the whole matter into
sympathetic senatorial hands. The notion that the leaders of the
Senate were so dismayed by extreme cases of official greed that
they not only had the offenders punished, but even deprived the
state (or tried to deprive it) of new provinces deserves no further
consideration.

It is commonly claimed that annexation was inhibited by the
Senate's unwillingness to add to the state's administrative
capacity, and to adapt the city-state constitution to imperial
government, any more than was absolutely necessary. This is a
reasonable argument. However the precise senatorial view of the
matter is more difficult to discover than one might gather from
modern assertions. Obviously enough, aristocrats were not
willing to make governmental changes that might endanger their
own political and social position, and the addition of excessive
magistracies would for this reason have been unwelcome. The
long interval between 197 and 81 during which neither the
praetorships nor probably the quaestorships were multiplied—in
spite of the creation of seven new provinces—supports this
interpretation. So perhaps does the *Lex Baebia* of 181, which
reduced the number of praetors from six to four in alternate
years,[4] though this provision did not last beyond 177. Yet these

---

[1] Liv. xliii. 7.5–8.10. The case did not concern provincials, as Gruen says, o.c. 11.
[2] On these cases see above, p. 78.
[3] Liv. *Per.* 47 end.
[4] Liv. xl. 44.2. Livy offers no explanation of the law, but since it should probably be
associated closely with the *Lex Cornelia Baebia* of 181, and may indeed have been part of the
same law (cf. H. H. Scullard, *Roman Politics*, 172–3), it was probably intended to decrease
the fierceness of competition for the consulship by decreasing the number of those who
were eligible to run for the office (cf. Mommsen, *R. Staatsrecht*, ii³. 198–9). A. Afzelius

facts are only part of the truth, and one should also remember that the crucial innovation, the promagistracy, was available throughout the period of overseas conquest and was readily used at least from the Hannibalic War onwards. It did in fact enable Rome to annex new provinces in the period from 148 without adding to the curule offices. Rome did not in any case wish to impose on the provinces any extensive bureaucracy of officials. If the Senate had been willing to multiply magistracies in the period after 197, there is scarcely any act of expansion, and there is no specific act of annexation, which would have been made significantly easier.

Were the Senate's decisions not to annex territory affected by fear of the disapproval of, and unfavourable publicity among, the culturally superior Greeks? This is not the place for an investigation of the large and important subject of Roman attitudes towards Greek culture during the middle Republic. It is plain that from 228 onwards Roman conduct was often influenced by the wish to make a favourable impression on a Greek audience. But whether the substance of Roman policy was affected, and whether the expansion of Roman power was seriously delayed, are largely matters for speculation. It certainly seems likely that Roman policy towards the old Greek states would have been even more ruthless between 197 and 147, had it not been for dawning Roman respect for Greek civilization.[1] The only annexation issue that may have been affected was the one that arose after the battle of Pydna—whether to annex Macedon. But

---

objected (*C & M* vii (1945), 198) that 'je weniger Aemter, desto grösserer ambitus', and he suggested that the purpose of the law was to diminish the number of new families entering the *nobilitas* (for which, in his view, election to the praetorship was at this time sufficient); this may be right. The *Lex Baebia* on the number of the praetorships would, however, have tended to reduce *ambitus* at *consular* elections, and that may have been regarded as much the most objectionable form of *ambitus*. Some were probably eager to restrain *ambitus*, not that there is much evidence for legislation before Sulla (there was a law in 159, Liv. *Per.* 47, and much of the sumptuary legislation was probably intended to reduce this practice), still less for prosecutions (Marius is the first known defendant in 116). Others have argued that the purpose of reducing the number of praetors was to prolong the period of provincial commands (Mommsen, l.c., Scullard, o.c. 173). On the brief duration of this system see Scullard, l.c.

[1] But the practical effects of this can be exaggerated. In Badian's view (*RILR*[2] 11) 'a hegemonial policy was pursued [in the Greek world] in a cautious and, on the whole, fairly civilised way, at least without violence and open treachery and certainly (as long as it proved possible) without direct control and major wars.' On the contrary: violence and the threat of it were the foundation of Roman policy.

the Senate did not decline to annex this territory so that it could boast to the Greeks of Rome's services to freedom. (Having decided not to annex, the Romans naturally did boast about it.) If respect for the Greeks and their freedom could not prevent Rome from subjecting Greek cities to Eumenes after the war against Antiochus, and could not prevent the exile of 1,000 leading Achaeans, it was not a very powerful political force. Practical considerations determined the decision to leave Macedon unannexed.

The theory of the non-annexation principle is closely connected with some undoubted truths—the lack of Roman machinery for direct government of new territories and the Senate's willingness to use indirect methods of control. None the less it is unsound. It would probably never have gained such wide acceptance if scholars had not striven so hard to find justifications for Roman expansion. Merely 'hegemonial' imperialism did not seem so deplorable. We shall meet a similar case of scholarly distortion in the next chapter.

V

IMPERIALISM AND SELF-DEFENCE

I. THE PROBLEM

THE interpretation which more than any other has coloured modern writing on Roman imperialism can conveniently be called 'defensive imperialism'. This is the view that, for much of our period at least, contemporary Romans generally saw the wars they decided on and fought as acts of self-defence. When they made their war-decisions, so it is often assumed and sometimes argued, they felt themselves to be more the subjects of pressure from others than the source of an expansionist drive.[1] These decisions resulted primarily from the belief that Rome or Rome's vital interests were in danger. All that the Romans wanted, it has often been said, was to rid themselves of 'frightening neighbours'.[2]

The Roman aristocracy had ample reasons to favour aggressive foreign policies, and the mass of citizens had reasons to support such policies. Having set forth these reasons in the first three chapters of this book, I shall now assess the real significance of defensive thinking in Roman foreign policy. Almost inexplicably, no such analysis has been offered before, the 'defensive imperialism' notion having grown up without plan or architecture at the hands of narrative historians.

[1] References to Mommsen, T. Frank, Holleaux, and other more recent writers who have adopted such views are given in later notes. The views Mommsen expressed in *RG* i[12]. 781–2 are fundamental. On the third century see M. Gelzer, *Hermes* lxviii (1933), 137 [→ Bibl.] (the Romans 'fühlten sich gewiss tatsächlich mehr als Getriebene denn als Treibende'), 165, G. Giannelli, *Trattato di storia romana*, i (Rome, 1953), 276. Research on the second century, according to H. Volkmann (*Hermes* lxxxii (1954), 465 [→ Bibl.], 'hat . . . das Sicherheitsbedürfnis als ein entscheidendes Motiv erkannt, das die Römer jeweils nach den Umständen zum Eingreifen oder zum Abwarten veranlasste.' Cf. C. Meier, *Res Publica Amissa* (Wiesbaden, 1966), 47–8. The essay of P. Veyne, *MEFRA* lxxxvii (1975), 793–855, belongs to this school. A. Heuss (*Römische Geschichte*[3] (Braunschweig, 1971), 552) usefully emphasized the compatibility of a defensive psychological outlook with an actually 'dynamic' policy; to what extent the Roman outlook really was defensive in this sense is the question discussed in this chapter. In practice the Roman state of mind may on any given occasion have been extremely complex.

[2] Cf. Polyb. i. 10.6: λίαν βαρεῖς καὶ φοβεροὶ γείτονες. The phrase φοβεροὶ γείτονες was made into a general principle by Mommsen, *RG* i[12]. 699, 781, Gelzer in *Das Reich. Idee und Gestalt. Festschrift für Johannes Haller* (Stuttgart, 1940), 19 [→ Bibl.], E. J. Bickerman, *CPh* xl (1945), 148.

Excluded from direct discussion in this chapter will be the question whether Rome's wars in the middle Republic were in some *objective* sense defensive. This question amounts to asking what the real interests of the Romans were. It is often said that the Second Macedonian War and the Third Punic War, for example, resulted from unwarranted anxiety on the part of the Senate: it insisted on a defence against dangers which were not really there. On the other hand it could be argued that Rome's dynamic expansion was truly defensive in that it tended to make the empire, though not its frontier areas, stronger and stronger; and this improvement in security continued at least until Augustus, in the last years of his power, brought expansion to a halt. One of the results of this expansion was that Italy and several other regions of the empire were untroubled by major invasions for some 500 or 600 years. Whether the Romans paid too heavily—in political, moral, or any other terms—for the security their empire gave them, and whether their ultimate security would have been better served by the conquest of the Parthians and the Germans—these are questions worth discussing, but they will not be answered here. What is to be investigated is the mentality and behaviour-patterns of the Romans who constructed the empire in the middle Republic.

In their diplomacy and historiography the Romans of this and later times often claimed that they had undertaken particular wars in self-defence, and the theory is found in a generalized form in Cicero's philosophical writings. The exact content of his claims deserves attention. In *De republica* the younger C. Laelius is made to claim that Rome had acquired its empire (before the dramatic date, 129) by defending its allies. According to the famous phrase, 'noster autem populus sociis defendendis terrarum iam omnium potitus est'—'our people has now gained power over the whole world by defending its allies.'[1] In the same context Laelius was apparently made to claim that Rome had always fought its wars either *pro fide* or *pro salute*.[2] However the context prevents us

---

[1] *De rep.* iii. 35, from Non. Marc. 800L. Cf. *Leg. Man.* 14 beginning. As we shall see, the allies defended were often of suspiciously recent vintage, so that the alliances look like excuses for intervention (cf. J. H. Thiel, *Het Probleem van de natuurlijke Vijandschap in het romeinsche Oorlogsrecht* (Amsterdam, 1946), 13).

[2] Augustine, *CD* xxii. 6; 'scio in libro Ciceronis tertio, nisi fallor, de re publica disputari: nullum bellum suscipi a civitate optima nisi pro fide aut pro salute' = *De rep.* iii. 34. Cf. Isid. *Etymol.* xviii. 1.2–3 '. . . in Republica Cicero dicit: illa iniusta bella sunt

from simply transferring these opinions to the author, since Laelius is arguing the case, in response to L. Furius Philus, that Rome has indeed acted according to *iustitia*.

In the *De officiis*, by contrast, Cicero admits that Roman motives had been less pure. The exact import of the following is unclear: 'ex quo [the fetial law] intellegi potest nullum bellum esse iustum, nisi quod aut rebus repetitis geratur aut denuntiatum ante sit et indictum.'[1] It seems, however, to mean that declaration of war is enough, even without a *rerum repetitio* or any other conditions.[2] Elsewhere in the work it is said that many Roman wars had been fought not as matters of life and death but 'de imperio', for the sake of empire, and for the sake of *honos* and *dignitas*.[3] Though his examples are oddly chosen, Cicero seems to recognize that the defence of Rome and its allies was not an adequate explanation of many of the wars of the middle Republic. Similarly he speaks of the time, well before that of Sulla, when 'bella aut pro sociis aut de imperio gerebantur', and though he goes on to say that magistrates then 'ex hac una re maximam laudem capere studebant, si provincias, si socios aequitate et fide defendissent',[4] he does not in fact claim that Rome had always fought its wars in order to defend itself, its

---

quae sunt sine causa suscepta. nam extra ⟨quam⟩ ulciscendi aut propulsandorum hostium causa bellum geri iustum nullum potest. et hoc idem Tullius parvis interiectis subdidit: nullum bellum iustum habetur nisi denuntiatum, nisi ⟨in⟩dictum, nisi de repetitis rebus' = *De rep.* iii. 35. The addition of revenge as an admitted motive is an important exception, though revenge was morally quite acceptable to most Romans.

[1] *De off.* i. 36.

[2] The 'aut . . . aut . . .' can be paraphrased as 'either . . . or at least . . .'. Cf. *OLD* s.v. 2b. It does not mean 'et . . . et . . .'. Cicero knew that Rome had in fact often fought without a *rerum repetitio*. Whether he admits the same point in *De rep.* ii. 31 is not clear (Tullus Hostilius 'sanxit fetiali religione, ut omne bellum quod denuntiatum indictumque non esset, id iniustum esse atque impium iudicaretur'). As to the *De officiis* passage, F. Hampl (*HZ* clxxxiv (1957), 250 n. 2 [→ Bibl.]) asserts that Cicero cannot have meant what he said, without offering any other explanation. Others have insisted on distorting the meaning of the text (G. Gandolfi, *Archivio Giuridico*, ser. 6, xvi (1954), 44, H. Hausmaninger, *Österreichische Zeitschrift für öffentliches Recht*, N.S. xi (1961), 343 n. 43, F. H. Russell, *The Just War in the Middle Ages* (Cambridge, 1975), 5).

[3] *De off.* i. 38: 'sed ea bella, quibus imperii proposita gloria est, minime acerbe gerenda sunt. ut enim cum cive aliter contendimus, si est inimicus, aliter si competitor—cum altero certamen honoris et dignitatis est, cum altero capitis et famae—sic cum Celtiberis, cum Cimbris bellum ut cum inimicis gerebatur, uter esset, non uter imperaret, cum Latinis, Sabinis, Samnitibus, Poenis, Pyrrho de imperio dimicabatur.'

[4] *De off.* ii. 26 ('. . . wars were fought either for the allies or for the sake of empire . . . [the magistrates] sought to gain outstanding fame from this one thing, the just and honest defence of the provinces and the allies').

provinces or its allies. Even the patriotic idealist refused to go quite so far. 'Maiores quidem nostri non modo ut liberi essent sed etiam ut imperarent, arma capiebant . . .'[1]

2. THE FETIAL LAW AND THE JUST WAR

What was the meaning, for the Romans of our period, of the *ius fetiale*, in so far as it concerned the procedures for declaring war? The question is an essential preliminary. Few scholars perhaps would now claim that the fetial law represented, even in the late fourth century, a Roman resolve to fight only defensive wars. However the view has been widely held that the fetial law did to some extent inhibit Roman aggressiveness, or at least that the fetial law shows that the Romans were unwilling to fight wars unless they perceived them as defensive.[2] Either fact would be most remarkable and important, if fact it were.

The *fetiales*[3] carried out a form of their war-declaring procedure on a number of occasions during the Italian wars of the late fourth and early third centuries, visiting the potential enemy *ad res repetendas* before a formal war-decision was made at Rome. Particular notices in Livy may be suspect, since the annalists obviously regarded the fetial law as characteristic of old Rome, but extreme scepticism would be out of place, and indeed the procedure was probably used more often than Livy tells us.[4] At some point—281/0 seems to be the most likely time—war-declarations were simplified and transferred to senatorial *legati*. The reason was presumably the increasing remoteness of Rome's enemies, which made the three journeys prescribed for the fetials

---

[1] *Phil.* viii. 12. ('Our ancestors took up arms not only for their freedom, but also to have an empire . . .'). See H. Roloff, *Maiores bei Cicero* (diss. Göttingen, 1938), 120.

[2] Cf. Frank, *Roman Imperialism*, 9 (the fetial law shows that 'the Roman *mos maiorum* did not recognize the right of aggression or a desire for more territory as just causes for war. *That the institution was observed in good faith for centuries there can be little doubt*' [my italics]), Gelzer, *Hermes* lxviii (1933), 165, J. Vogt, *Vom Reichsgedanken der Römer* (Leipzig, 1942), 130–1, H. H. Scullard, *HRW*³ 43. Twenty years ago views of this kind could be said to be dominant (Hampl, o.c. 262).

[3] On the *fetiales* in general see most recently W. Dahlheim, *Struktur und Entwicklung*, 171–80. For parallels in primitive societies cf. M. R. Davie, *The Evolution of War* (New Haven, 1929), 292–3.

[4] Known cases: Liv. viii. 22.8 (Palaeopolis in 327), ix. 45.5–8 (the Aequi in 304), x. 12.1–3 (the Samnites in 298), x. 45.6–8 (the Faliscans in 293); on all these occasions, but as far as we know never again, the *fetiales* were sent *ad res repetendas* before the formal war-decision. Cf. also Dion. Hal. xv. 7–10, Liv. viii. 23.3–10.

too burdensome, but the change also decreased the control over war-decisions available to the Senate and people (since it was no longer in their power to decide whether the *rerum repetitio* had been satisfied or not). Later war-declarations followed the fetial procedure only in the limited sense that they were, nominally at least, conditional: the relevant *legatus* 'res repetivit', and if satisfaction was not given, a state of war came into existence. Such a procedure is only known to have been used on a few highly important occasions, to declare war against Carthage (probably in 264 and 238, certainly in 218), against Philip V and against Perseus; otherwise it was probably used little, if at all.[1] It was not used against Antiochus III in 191, and no war-declaration of any kind was carried out against the Aetolians.[2] After 171 the fetial procedure for declaring war seems to have disappeared entirely,[3] until Octavian revived it for his personal advantage.

Even in the third century it was probably permissible to fight wars without the benefit of the fetial procedure if the enemy was not especially daunting. When Cicero was looking back idealistically into the past, he could not claim that the fetial law had really required more than the declaration of war, for he well knew that in the middle Republic the *rerum repetitio*, not to speak of the older fetial procedure, had often been omitted.[4]

If Rome was actually attacked in serious fashion by an enemy, there was no opportunity to bring the fetial procedure into play. It was therefore essentially a mechanism for setting an attack in motion. The question is only whether the procedure, in its older form or its later one, somehow prevented Roman attacks that were not felt to be defensive in purpose.

Though the *rerum repetitio* had formal similarities to legal procedures, it was closely akin to blackmail. This is the case at least when reliable details are known. The *rerum repetitiones* were in a precise sense non-negotiable demands, and they were usually set at an unacceptable level. In fact it must normally have been

[1] On war-declaration procedures between 281 and 171 see Additional Note xv.
[2] Liv. xxxvi. 3.7–12.
[3] S.I. Oost (*AJPh* lxxv (1954), 147–9) failed, in spite of some good observations, to show that fetial procedure was used against Jugurtha.
[4] *De off.* i. 36: 'ac belli quidem aequitas sanctissime fetiali populi Romani iure perscripta est. ex quo intellegi potest' etc. (quoted above), *De rep.* ii. 31 (quoted above). It is uncertain whether Isid. *Etymol.* xviii. 1.3 was repeating the structure of Cicero's sentence precisely when he quoted him as writing 'nullum bellum iustum habetur, nisi denuntiatum, nisi ⟨in⟩dictum, nisi de rebus repetitis' (= *De rep.* iii. 35).

expected that the demands would be refused.[1] We know of only
one historical occasion when the *res repetitae* were handed over—
in 238, when Carthage's severe internal difficulties compelled it
to surrender Sardinia and promise Rome 1,200 extra talents. It is
relevant to note that the old term *clarigatio*, which lasted long
enough as the name of the *rerum repetitio* for the elder Pliny to be
able to discover it[2] (therefore probably at least into the third
century), may have lacked the implication, present in the words
rerum repetitio, that redress was being sought for an injury. After
the fetial procedure was revised in the early third century, the
possibility that in any particular case Rome would consider that
its demands had been met probably decreased still further. The
fetiales themselves confessed the utter irrelevance of the procedure
to international affairs by telling a consul in 200 that there was no
need to deliver the declaration to Philip V in person, a ruling
which was repeated in 191 with regard to Antiochus III.[3]

The fetial procedure for declaring war apparently did have
something to do with *ius*. Some scholars have treated Livy's
detailed account of the early procedure, in which *ius* is repeatedly
invoked,[4] as solidly historical. Since there was no practical reason
to preserve the old formulae after 281, the date at which they
probably went out of use, this is perilous; and the Livian version

[1] According to Liv. x. 12.1–3, the Samnites were told to leave Lucania, Rome having
just made an alliance with the Lucanians in order to provoke war; but the source cannot
be relied on to have reported the *rerum repetitio* correctly or in full. The demands made to
Tarentum in 281 are given in App. *Samn.* 7.2 (cf. 7.3)—hardly λόγους ἐπιτηδείους, as
Zonar. viii. 2 claims, for they included the surrender of political leaders. This latter kind of
demand may have been common (cf. Plaut. *Amph.* 207). The demand of 218 (Polyb. iii.
20.6–10, which is to be preferred to Liv. xxi. 18.2) was to surrender Hannibal and his
σύνεδροι. In 200 Rome demanded that Philip V should not make war on any Greek state
or intervene in the Ptolemaic possessions, and that he should submit to arbitration with
respect to his ἀδικήματα against Attalus and Rhodes (Polyb. xvi. 34.3); for some analysis
of the implications see below, p. 217. Rome had decided on war and had not the slightest
expectation that these demands would be met.
[2] Plin. *NH* xxii. 5; cf. G. Wissowa, *Religion und Kultus der Römer*[2], 553 n. 4.
[3] Liv. xxxi. 8.3–4, xxxvi. 3.7–9.
[4] Liv. i. 32.4–14. 'Audi Iuppiter,' says the 'legatus' on his first visit, 'audite
fines . . . audiat *fas* . . . *iuste* pieque legatus venio . . . si ego *iniuste* impieque illos homines
illasque res dedier mihi exposco...' On his second visit, 'Audi Iuppiter, et tu Iane Quirine,
dique omnes caelestes, vosque terrestres vosque inferni, audite; ego vos testor populum
illum . . . *iniustum* esse neque *ius persolvere*; . . . consulemus, quo pacto *ius* nostrum
adipiscamur.' Cf. Dion. Hal. ii. 72.6–8 (where, however, nothing is said about justice on
the second visit). I doubt whether the differences between these two accounts are
significant. The version in Gell. *NA* xvi. 4.1 needs no attention here (it is a forgery of
Augustan date or later).

is betrayed by certain anachronisms.[1] However the tradition did preserve some convincing details of the actions performed by the *fetiales*, and Livy and Dionysius are likely to have been right in believing that the *fetiales* used the words *ius* and *iuste* in their *rerum repetitio*. To some extent this is confirmed by Cicero's and Varro's comments on the fetial law,[2] though, as we shall see, the justice of the fetial law had very little similarity to abstract *iustitia* or to Ciceronian *aequitas*. It is clear from the remains of Fabius Pictor that the third-century Romans believed that their war-declarations established the justice of Roman wars.[3] This is further confirmed by a somewhat unexpected source, Sosia's war-narrative in the *Amphitruo* of Plautus. Here is the decisive intervention of the cavalry in the battle against the Teloboae:

> ab dextera maxumo
> cum clamore involant impetu alacri
> foedant et proterunt hostium copias
> iure iniustas.[4]

The surprising addition of the last two words recalls Sosia's detailed description of the *rerum repetitio* and probably reflects the contemporary Roman belief that such a procedure made the enemy into *iure iniusti*.

Insincerity is not the main question. No doubt many Romans believed that their foreign enemies were *iniusti*. But the justice at issue was of a technical kind, as the known *rerum repetitiones* demonstrate. It had nothing to do with any philosophically

---

[1] The problem of transmission is often evaded (e.g. by P. Catalano, *Linee del sistema sovrannazionale romano*, i (Turin, 1965), 37 n. 76). 'Modernization' of language might not matter, and there has been mistaken criticism (K. Latte argued (*ZSS* lxvii (1950), 56 [→ Bibl.], *Römische Religionsgeschichte*, 5 n. 1, 37–8, 121 n. 2) that 'audiat fas' is an impossible phrase for the early period, since *fas* is always a predicate until Livy, and E. Fraenkel accepted this argument (*Horace* (Oxford, 1957), 289 n. 1; cf. *Elementi plautini*, 426, for a severe judgement on the authenticity of the fetial formulae), as did R. M. Ogilvie; but it rests in large part on the arbitrary exclusion of Accius, *trag.* 585R ('ibi fas, ibi cunctam antiquam castitudinem'). However the phrase 'puro pioque duello quaerendas censeo, itaque consentio consciscoque' (i. 32.12) is highly suspect (see Ogilvie's n.). The question of the authenticity of the *foedus*-making formula in Liv. i. 24 is separate, as is the question of the secular prayer (above p. 120), since in those cases there were reasons to preserve the old wording. There was every reason to refurbish the war-declaring procedure in Livy's time (Dio l.4.4–5). Ogilvie, however, argues (128) that it was put into its present form in the second century.

[2] Cic. *De off.* i. 36 (quoted p. 165); cf. *De leg.* iii. 9, Varro, *LL* v. 86.

[3] Below, p. 171.

[4] *Amph.* 244–7.

conceived system of impartial equity.[1] In its earliest phase the war-declaring procedure was devised to gain the support of the gods. Since Rome's enemies were generally familiar neighbours whose gods either were identical with Rome's or were at least felt to be powerful, elaborate arrangements had to be undertaken to make sure that Rome, and not the enemy, received divine favour. Rome had to compete before a sort of divine tribunal,[2] and the form which the preliminaries of the war assumed was, not surprisingly, similar to those of the *legis actiones*, the contemporary form of civil procedure. As has been noticed, the fetial war-declaration resembles in particular the *legis actio per condictionem*.[3] According to the *legis actiones*, the defendant had to react to the plaintiff's claim by an unambiguous admission or denial,[4] just as the enemy of Rome was supposed to answer the *rerum repetitio*. But in international disputes there was no *iudex* to resort to—only the divine *iudices* who decided who was to be victorious in war. For the Romans therefore a war was finally proved just in the event itself, by a Roman victory; this is why Sosia chooses precisely the turning-point of the battle to say that the enemy were *iure iniusti*—their defeat showed that they were. Prior to the war itself, all that the Romans thought was required was the proper procedure, the formally correct actions and words. This religious obligation was treated in the apparently pedantic and formalistic manner in which the Romans (among others) commonly treated such obligations[5]—an outlook which also allowed them to substitute a patch of ground in the city of Rome for the enemy territory into which the *fetialis* had to throw the magical spear. Naturally they had to decide on something to ask for if they were going to 'res repetere', but that is no evidence that they always or usually felt they were being forced to defend themselves.

[1] Cf. Dahlheim, o.c. 172–3. Gelzer (*Hermes* lxviii (1933), 165) was quite wrong to suppose that a war declared by fetial procedure could only be a *Verteidigungskrieg*, even in a subjective sense.

[2] On the first visit the spokesman of the fetials nominally admitted that the justice of Rome's cause was not yet settled, according to Liv. i. 32.7: '*si ego iniuste impieque . . . exposco, tum patriae compotem me numquam siris esse.*'

[3] M. Voigt, *Das ius naturale, aequum et bonum und ius gentium der Römer*, ii (Leipzig, 1858), 186–8, A.-E. Giffard, *RHDFE* ser. 4, xv (1936), 771 n. 2, Ogilvie, *Commentary*, 127; further bibliography in Hausmaninger, o.c. 340 n. 27.

[4] Cf. A. Watson, *Roman Private Law around 200 B.C.* (Edinburgh, 1971), 162–3.

[5] Cf. H. Drexler, *RhM* cii (1959), 103–5, Dahlheim, o.c. 173, and more generally P. De Francisci, *RPAA* xxvii (1952–4), 200–1, K. Latte, *Römische Religionsgeschichte*, 211. Liv. x. 40 offers an excellent example.

The significance of the fetial procedure for declaring war was solely psychological.[1] The magical elements in the procedure have been duly noticed,[2] and they are quite at home in a society in which certain other obviously magical practices long continued to appeal even to some aristocrats. The procedure was one of a set of religious precautions which were thought necessary when a major war was initiated. 'The Romans', as Polybius observed, 'are very effective in moments of crisis at propitiating both gods and men, and in such situations they regard no rite that has this purpose as unbecoming or undignified.'[3] The fetial procedure was one such means of self-reassurance.

Emerging into a more complicated world in which public opinion in other states not only mattered but could be influenced, certain leading Romans attempted to present a positive interpretation of Rome's policies and particularly of Roman wars. The process began in the second quarter of the third century, at the latest.[4] The first explicitly attested propaganda about justice is the speech attributed by Polybius to one of the Roman ambassadors who visited Queen Teuta the Illyrian in 230—'The Romans have the fine custom of joining together to punish the injustices done to individuals and of helping the victims of injustice.'[5] These words may be a fiction invented or transmitted by Fabius Pictor, but Polybius' report of the Roman embassies sent to Greece after the First Illyrian War should be accepted; they were sent to defend Rome's reasons for fighting.[6] The ruthlessness of the proconsuls who commanded Roman forces in Greece during the Hannibalic War shows that a section of the aristocracy was still insensitive to the value of Greek opinion, but Fabius Pictor in the historiographical sphere and T. Flamininus in the diplomatic sphere strove, above all others, to improve Rome's reputation. In Fabius' history there was to be found the argument that Rome's wars were just in a sense much wider than that of the fetial law. Justification, according to Fabius, was

[1] Cf. A. Nussbaum, *Michigan Law Review* xlii (1943–4), 454.

[2] On the woollen headgear of the spokesman *fetialis* cf. Ogilvie on i. 32.6, and concerning the iron-tipped or cornel-wood spear his n. on 32.12. The latter is discussed at length by J. Bayet, *MEFR* lii (1935), 29–76.

[3] iii. 112.9.

[4] On early claims to be respecters of *fides* see Gelzer, o.c. 146 (supplemented in *KS* iii. 70).

[5] Polyb. ii. 8.10.

[6] ii. 12.4–8. Cf. Gelzer, o.c. 132 (supplemented in *KS* iii. 54–5).

provided by the fact that Rome had fought its wars to defend itself and its allies.[1] The theory had Roman roots, but it was also well calculated to appeal to the Greeks.[2] It became a part of the Roman technique of handling international relations,[3] together with advertisements of Rome's benevolence and *fides*.[4]

In the judgement of Polybius—by far our best informant about the second-century Senate—the Romans were always careful to offer a *pretext* for going to war; they took care not to appear to be the aggressors, but always to seem to be defending themselves and entering war under compulsion.[5] In fact they propitiated mankind as well as the gods. Polybius cannot be dismissed as unduly sceptical about Roman motives; indeed he was partially willing to accept Roman claims of goodwill towards foreigners.[6] He ought to have been more sceptical about Fabius Pictor's account of the defensive preoccupations of the Senate at the beginning of the First Punic War.[7] The Third Punic War is a specifically attested case in which the Senate sought for a pretext with which to disguise the real reasons for its policy, and other cases in which this may have happened are plentiful. This is not to deny *a priori* that the Senate sometimes decided to begin a war for what it perceived as defensive reasons. And the Senate did take heed of certain ethical standards in international affairs.[8] However these standards demanded no more than adherence to Roman constitutional procedures and to some very rudimentary

---

[1] On the First Punic War see Polyb. i. 10.3–11.1; on the First Illyrian War, ii. 8.3–12: on the Gallic wars of the 220s, ii. 21.3 and 6, ii. 22; on the Hannibalic War, iii. 8.1–7 (= *FGrH* 809 F21). For analysis of Fabius' views see Gelzer's article, o.c. 129–166, *KS* iii. 51–92.

[2] On the Greek belief in the justice of wars fought in defence of oneself or one's allies see V. Martin, *La Vie internationale dans la Grèce des cités* (Paris, 1940), 394–5, D. Loenen, *Polemos* (*Med. Nederl. Akad.* 16 no. 3 (1953)), 72.

[3] For such claims see Additional Note XVI.

[4] These qualities are involved in the claim that Rome fights only defensive wars. On the theme of benevolence in second-century propaganda see Gelzer, o.c. 145–7, *KS* iii. 68–70, H. Volkmann, *Hermes* lxxxii (1954), 474–5 [→ Bibl.]. For second century claims to respect for *fides* see Gelzer, *KS* iii. 70 n. 72 end (Plu. *Flam.* 16 is particularly striking) and Liv. (P.) xlv. 8.4.

[5] Fr. 99B-W, cf. xxxii. 13.8, xxxvi. 2. For Polybius' belief in the desirability of pretexts cf. xv. 20.3.

[6] xxiv. 10.11–12; cf. §§ 4–5 (to be weighed against xxxi. 10.7, 11.12). However we lack evidence that Polybius endorsed the Roman claim to have fought just wars (S. Weinstock, *Divus Julius*, 244, notwithstanding).

[7] Below, p. 186.

[8] As is said by Gelzer, o.c. 138 (somewhat vaguely), Volkmann, o.c. 475 (not denying that the Senate made many decisions for reasons of power politics).

rules of international behaviour, such as the inviolability of ambassadors.[1] When a pretext was found, the second-century Senate no doubt believed that the ensuing war was a *bellum iustum*, but that does not mean that such wars—not to speak of the cases where pretexts were neglected—were felt to be primarily defensive. And the fact that some second-century Romans proclaimed to the outside world that the Romans fought only defensive wars establishes nothing about the confidential proceedings in the Senate or the private thoughts of leading senators. We know that Roman diplomats could lie patriotically as well as any others: witness, for example, the history of Roman foreign policy offered by L. Furius Purpurio to the meeting of the Aetolian League in 199.[2] We cannot assume that in any given case the Senate's real concern was with defence.

There was apparently a change of emphasis in senatorial thinking about war-policy between the period of the Italian wars and the first half of the second century. It was a change from formal correctness in an elaborate procedure of declaring war (though in Polybius' time Rome continued to make some kind of formal declaration of war)[3] to a concern for the appearance of virtuous behaviour towards other states. However neither policy dictated that Rome should fight only defensive wars.

A further slow and very partial change began in the mid-second century, in the same period, paradoxically, as some of the most brutal acts of Roman imperialism. Panaetius was probably the first philosopher whose arguments in favour of restraint in war-making became known to any significant number of Romans.[4] The short-term effect, as far as we know, was nil.

---

[1] Volkmann gives as examples of senators' high-mindedness Scipio Africanus' refusal to retaliate against Carthaginian envoys after the Carthaginian attack on Roman *legati* in the winter of 203/2 (Polyb. xv. 4.5–12; cf. Liv. xxx. 25.10, Diod. xxvii. 12, App. *Lib.* 35)— but the alleged provocation is quite suspect (G. De Sanctis, *SR* iii. 2.548 n. 161, M. Treu, *Aegyptus* xxxiii (1953), 50–1)—and the disapproval felt by some senators of the deceit practised by Q. Marcius Philippus against Perseus in 172. The weakness of the evidence disproves the case.

[2] Liv. xxxi. 31. See J. Briscoe's commentary. I follow P. Pédech (*La Méthode historique de Polybe*, 266) and others in referring the main lines of the speech to Polybius' account.

[3] Polyb. xiii. 3.7. This passage continues to be misinterpreted by some (e.g. J. Heurgon in J.-P. Brisson (ed.), *Problèmes de la guerre à Rome*, 29). It does not say that βραχύ τι ἴχνος of the fetial procedure lasted into Polybius' time (see Walbank, *CPh* xliv (1949), 17).

[4] On Panaetius at Rome cf. G. Garbarino, *Roma e la filosofia greca* (Turin, 1973), 380–412. Though it cannot be formally proved, it seems very likely that the argument in Cic. *De off.* i. 35 ('quare suscipienda quidem bella sunt ob eam causam, ut sine iniuria in pace

Poseidonius presumably propounded similar arguments, and in his generation a handful of senators probably felt a serious philosophical aversion to wars that were not genuinely defensive. Rome's overwhelming power, as well as intellectual sophistication, made it easier and easier to take a detached view of foreign politics.

In Cicero's generation we come to the full confusion of traditional and modern viewpoints. On the one hand, as we have seen, the drive to expansion retained a good deal of its old force. Indeed its chief exponents, Pompey and Caesar, showed—among other qualities—far greater greed and ambition than most of the old magistrates had done. Much of the time they could carry with them, at least in public, some of those, conspicuously Cicero, who were most deeply attracted by Greek philosophy.[1] The philosopher himself attacked the Cilician town of Pindenissum on behalf of the *existimatio* of the empire and in a slightly hesitant spirit of personal ambition.[2] Yet Cicero meant it seriously when he wrote at the end of his life that the justification for war is that one may live in peace 'sine iniuria', a phrase, this, which he would perhaps have interpreted in a quite philosophical and liberal way. It is wrong to discount the Stoic contribution to Cicero's thinking on this subject by referring to the Roman tradition,[3] since it was he and his contemporaries who first gave some real philosophical meaning to the term 'bellum iustum'. In a Ciceronian speech it almost became possible for barbarians to wage a just war against Rome.[4] And a few people took the *bellum iustum* even more seriously. In a traditional sense Caesar's Gallic War was sufficiently *iustum*—he explained in some detail the hostile behaviour and disobedience which 'justified' it. But to the serious Stoic, Cato Uticensis, the plea was (or would have been—we do not know whether any of *De Bello Gallico* had yet been published) quite insufficient. He declared in the Senate in 55 that

vivatur . . .'; cf. i. 80, Sall. *Ep. ad Caes.* i. 6.2) is Panaetian (cf. M. Rostovtzeff, *SEHHW* iii. 1458 n. 6, Hampl, *HZ* clxxxiv (1957), 249–50 [→ Bibl.]). For the pre-Stoic philosophical background see H. Fuchs, *Augustin und der antike Friedensgedanke* (Berlin, 1926), 136–7. There is no surviving Roman precedent for this view of Cicero's (cf. A. Otto, *Die Sprichwörter und sprichwörtlichen Redensarten der Römer* (Leipzig, 1890), 54), certainly not in the remains of Ennius, in spite of Fuchs, *MH* xii (1955), 204.

[1] Cicero expresses his admiration for an aggressive war in *Prov. Cons.* 32–5.

[2] *Fam.* xv. 4.10 (to Cato), ii. 10.3, *Att.* v. 20.5.

[3] So Gelzer, *Hermes* lxviii (1933), 138 [→ Bibl.].

[4] *Prov. Cons.* 4.

the war was *iniustum*, apparently because it was not defensive. Caesar should be handed over to the Germans to prevent divine punishment from falling on Rome.[1]

Neither the fetial law nor the concept of the just war significs, during our period, any resolve to fight only those wars which were felt necessary for the defence of Rome or its allies. Particular grievances had to be sought out, however, and this may sometimes have been a limitation. To what extent the grievances convinced the Senate that the wars in question were just is sometimes an obscure question, especially because of the secrecy surrounding the Senate's decisions. A detailed investigation is necessary.

Modern historians have often concluded in many cases that the grievances alleged were *not* the reasons why Rome went to war (for example, against Philip V in 200 and against the Achaean League in 146), and they have devised for Rome another kind of 'defensive' war which is to be found relatively seldom in the sources. This kind of war is defensive in a wider and more strategic sense. It is a war intended, for example, to prevent the power of Philip V from growing more dangerous to Rome, or to re-establish in the minds of the Greeks the conviction that Rome's wishes must be obeyed. Here again the validity of the interpretation must be investigated case by case.

3. THE WARS OF 327–220 B.C.[2]

THE ITALIAN WARS

Contemporary Roman perceptions of the Italian wars fought in the years 327–264 cannot be recovered. Some of the most fundamental facts about the wars of this period, even the identity of Rome's opponents in certain years, are uncertain. In most cases the conflicts began in circumstances that are virtually unknown to us. As for the reasons or motives which actuated leaders or citizens in any particular case, we cannot go beyond speculative inferences. The second-century Senate is hard to penetrate, but at least we have some texts deriving from its members and from people who were acquainted with senators.

---

[1] Suet. *DJ* 24.3, Plu. *Caes.* 22.4, *Cat. Min.* 51, *Crass.* 37.3, App. *Celt.* 18. Cf. S. Weinstock, o.c. 245 n. 3. [2] On this periodization see above, p. 58 n. 7.

The period of the Italian wars on the other hand is an almost complete blank, which writers from Livy to the present have filled with their own more or less informed imaginings.[1]

Much of this warfare may perhaps have been undertaken by Rome in a defensive spirit. It was a period of extraordinarily vigorous action against other states, of almost annual warfare, but conceivably Roman senators saw this as a result of external pressure.[2] Some of the Italian peoples were, potentially at least, very dangerous to Rome during the Second and Third Samnite Wars, until the battle of Sentinum in 295. Even by themselves the Samnites were sufficiently numerous and warlike to deserve attentive precautions; and their mutual hostility with Rome was already deeply rooted. Had the Etruscan cities been able, by a political miracle, to mobilize their joint resources against Rome at an opportune moment, catastrophe for the Romans might have resulted. International combinations could obviously be sources of great danger, as when the Samnites and Etruscans co-operated in fighting against Rome in 296/5[3] and certain Etruscans co-operated successively with the Senones and Boii in 284–282.[4]

Some of the Italian peoples did act vigorously and perhaps aggressively against Rome. There is no single campaign in this period which can confidently be attributed simply to the aggression of one of Rome's Italian enemies, but the Samnites at least invaded the territory of Rome or its allies on some occasions.

---

[1] Livy often refers to the anxiety, fear, and terror engendered in the Senate or in the Romans generally by external events (e.g. viii. 29.1,3, 38.1, ix. 29.2, 38.9, 41.11). These statements are valueless, since his ultimate sources are most unlikely to have recorded such facts. Livy probably did not add much of this pseudo-psychologizing himself, since he was somewhat puzzled by the fears which the early Romans are supposed to have felt (cf. vi. 22.1, vii. 21.19, x. 4.1); some of it at least was probably the invention of writers who believed that *metus hostilis* was an important factor in keeping the old Romans united (cf. Harris, *Rome in Etruria and Umbria*, 94 n. 6).

[2] Thus, e.g., De Sanctis (*SR* ii. 429) concluded that the Romans were compelled by the struggle for existence to undertake a series of wars, but they did not have imperialistic aspirations to power. General histories often describe the Samnite wars as largely the result of Samnite pressure on Rome (cf. F. E. Adcock, *CAH* vii. 594–9, 604, H. H. Scullard, *HRW*³ 108). According to A. Afzelius (*Die römische Eroberung Italiens (340–264 v. Chr.)* (Copenhagen, 1942), 194), Rome's whole policy in Etruria from the 380s to the end of the 290s was defensive—otherwise they would have annexed more territory.

[3] But it is very doubtful whether Etruscans and Samnites, not the most natural of allies, joined forces on any previous occasion.

[4] I gave my view of the latter events in o.c. 79–83.

Whatever the ultimate origins of the Roman–Samnite conflict were, such behaviour had to be resisted. The Samnites attempted to use the opportunity of their victory at the Caudine Forks to establish peace. However, not only were they probably willing to seize by force the Latin colony of Fregellae (theoretically conceded by Rome in the Caudine treaty),[1] but when the peace irrevocably broke down they attacked various Roman-controlled areas (316–313). After they had defeated Rome at the battle of Lautulae, near Tarracina, in 315, they even seem to have penetrated the southern part of Latium as far as Ardea.[2] In 306 and 305 they again attacked Roman possessions.

Such campaigns were only a small part of the Samnite wars. Not even Livy claimed that the Samnites attacked Roman or allied territory in the first seven years of the Second Samnite War (327–321), though he did try to put some responsibility on to their shoulders.[3] To a surprising extent (in view of the aggressiveness which ancient and modern writers attribute to them) the Samnites restricted their military activities to their own territory. Concerning the actual beginning of the Second Samnite War, one can only say that while Rome must already have regarded the Samnites with hostility, the sources preserve no record of any event which can have impelled the Romans to undertake a prolonged war for their own defence.

Other Italian states and peoples are occasionally said to have attacked the Romans or their allies (I omit cases in which new colonies or garrisons were attacked by locals). Livy makes a vague charge of this kind against Palaeopolis (Naples) in 327,[4]

---

[1] Liv. ix. 12.6–8. The fact that Rome had agreed to withdraw colonies from Samnite territory (ix. 4.4, App. *Samn.* 4.5), meaning presumably Fregellae and Cales (even though neither was on Samnite territory), does not show that Rome actually did withdraw; therefore the Samnite attack of 320 may be historical; but it is quite uncertain.

[2] Lautulae: Liv. ix. 23.4–6, Diod. xix. 72.7. The site must be somewhere just north-east of Tarracina (cf. H. Nissen, *Italische Landeskunde*, ii (Berlin, 1902), 642; not at Itri, in spite of E. T. Salmon, *Samnium and the Samnites* (Cambridge, 1967), 234 n. 3). Ardea: Strabo v. 232, 249 (can hardly refer to any other occasion: cf. A. Boethius, *Atti del V Congresso Nazionale di Studi Romani*, ii (Rome, 1940), 231–8).

[3] However App. *Samn.* 4.1, a passage replete with suspect statements, says that the Samnites invaded the territory of Fregellae at some date before the battle of the Caudine Forks. Attempts to blame them: Liv. viii. 22.9–10, 23.1–10. According to Salmon (o.c. 221), the Samnites carried out 'border raids' in 324; a gratuitous assumption.

[4] Liv. viii. 22.7 ('multa hostilia adversus Romanos agrum Campanum Falernumque incolentes fecit'), Dion. Hal. xv. 5.1. De Sanctis (*SR* ii. 297) was probably right to reject these claims.

and claims that Etruscans besieged Sutrium, though without success, in 311 and 310. If the latter claim is true, the Etruscan war of 311–308 may indeed have been regarded by Rome as a necessary defensive operation.[1] But the whole story of the siege of Sutrium may have been a propagandistic invention or distortion.

Defensive campaigns need not have been restricted to repelling outright attacks on Rome and allied territory. It has been asserted that the Romans' purpose in attacking Naples was to resist the spread of Samnite power.[2] This is possible, though entirely unproved. On a larger scale, Rome is said to have conquered central Italy in order to protect itself from military co-operation by the Etruscans and Samnites.[3] It may have been one of their intentions, but the danger of Etruscan–Samnite co-operation was probably not at all clear when the first central Italian campaigns were fought, and Rome continued to expand in this region even after the danger had passed.[4]

One reason to doubt that defensive thinking was the dominant reason for Rome's Italian wars is simply that most of the campaigns were fought outside the territory of Rome and its allies. The sources cannot be relied on to have transmitted purely reliable details about the topography of these wars, and they

---

[1] *Rome in Etruria and Umbria*, 48–9, 58. However the brief duration of the Etruscan war (three campaigns) might suggest that the Romans did not freely choose to begin the war in 311.

[2] De Sanctis, *SR* ii. 297. Naples was already allied with the Samnites (Dion. Hal. xv. 5.1 end, with the notes of K.-H. Schwarte, *Historia* xx (1971), 375; cf. Liv. viii. 22.7), and perhaps had been for several years. The Roman tradition apparently tried to obscure this fact (hence perhaps the claim that the war was fought against Palaeopolis) (cf. Schwarte, l.c.). Salmon, however, is probably wrong to claim (o.c. 218) that it was the occupation of Naples by Samnite troops that caused the Roman attack, since the occupation is said to have occurred *after* the Roman declaration of war (Liv. viii. 22.8, 23.1).

[3] A. J. Toynbee, *Hannibal's Legacy*, i. 144, 151.

[4] Apprehension of this danger is not likely to have been felt at Rome before 311, since Etruria had been quiet for so long. The alleged Samnite plan of an expedition to Etruria in 310 (Liv. ix. 38.7) is entirely fictional. Until 296 the way for the Romans to defeat the Samnites was to fight them in Samnium. Campaigns against the central Italian peoples apparently began with the Vestini in 325, the latter having supposedly allied themselves with the Samnites (Liv. viii. 29.1, 6–7, 11–14) (there is absolutely no sound reason to treat D. Iunius Brutus Scaeva's campaign as a doublet of C. Iunius Bubulcus' campaign in Apulia in 317, as do K. J. Beloch, *Römische Geschichte*, 404, Salmon, o.c. 220; distinct individuals are involved, specific topography is given, and no military incongruity is raised by the 325 campaign). The Marrucini were attacked by Rome in 312 (according to Diod. xix. 105.5), the Umbrians first in 310 or 308 (Liv. ix. 37.1–2, 39.4, 41.8), the Paeligni and Marsi perhaps in 308 (ix. 41.4), more probably in 305 and 302 respectively (305: Diod. xx. 90.3; 302: Liv. x. 3.2–5; a treaty had been made with the Marsi in 303).

undoubtedly exaggerated Roman success from time to time. Yet the outline of Livy's narrative of the Etruscan wars is, as I have argued elsewhere,[1] to be accepted, and the same applies to the Italian wars after 327 in general.[2] Early historians such as Fabius Pictor can be expected to have preserved information about any serious enemy attacks against Roman territory because of their justificatory value. Many, though certainly not all, of the obscure place-names in Livy and the other sources are authentic traces of campaigns fought in enemy territory.[3] If these judgements are correct, the following facts seem secure. Having colonized Fregellae in 328, Rome campaigned annually in Samnite territory, with no major counter-invasion until after the Caudine Forks. Having decisively strengthened their position with four new anti-Samnite Latin colonies in the years 314–312, the Romans for the rest of the war (until 304) did most of their fighting against the Samnites on enemy soil. The Third Samnite War (298–290) was fought at first in Samnium, later in Etruria and Umbria, from 294 (apart from a Samnite raid on Interamna Lirenas in that year) entirely in Samnium again. The Etruscan wars of 311–308, 302–292, and 284–280 were fought, after the supposed siege of Sutrium, entirely in Etruscan territory. No credible source even claims that any Umbrian, Sabine, Praetuttian, or any of the Marsi, Paeligni, Vestini, Marrucini, or Frentani, or for that matter any Apulian, Sallentine, Lucanian, or Bruttian, at any time attacked the lands of Rome or its allies.[4] All the fighting against these peoples took place outside Roman and allied territory.

A very revealing phase of the Italian wars is that of the earliest interventions against the Vestini and Marrucini on the east coast, since it is implausible to suppose that in 325 or 312 the Romans

[1] *Rome in Etruria and Umbria*, 49–78.

[2] On the Samnite wars see M. W. Frederiksen, *JRS* lviii (1968), 226–7.

[3] Rufrium (Liv. viii. 25.4), Cutina, Cingilia (29.13), Imbrinium (30.4), Materina (ix. 41.15), Milionia, Plestina, Fresilia (x. 3.5).

[4] However some Umbrians participated in the rather suspect siege of Sutrium in 310 according to Liv. ix. 37.1–2. Of the Sabines Front. *Strat.* i. 8.4 does say that they had invaded 'our' territory in 290, but the passage is vague and exaggerated, and the act would have been one of desperation. In the cases of the Sabines and Praetuttians it is interesting to see how historians concoct 'justifications' for the Roman conquest (e.g. De Sanctis, *SR* ii. 349, Salmon, o.c. 265, 276—neither makes use of the Frontinus passage). The notice about the Marsi and the colony of Carseoli in Liv. x. 3.2 is muddled, since the colony was not in their territory but that of the Aequicoli and was probably not set up until four years later (x. 13.1, Vell. i. 14.5).

were led in that direction by a wish to resist their own major enemies. Also very revealing is the campaign of 290, when with the Samnites and Etruscans at last unmistakably beaten, a Roman army attacked the Sabines and Praetuttii. The opposition was so slight that part of one season's campaigning by one consular army was enough to establish Roman power. It is no use supposing that M'. Curius Dentatus' invasion of those territories was opposed by the Senate.[1] There is no evidence whatsoever in favour of this hypothesis,[2] and since the Senate specifically voted him a Sabine triumph, in addition to his Samnite one, it is highly improbable. M'. Curius' behaviour that year was unusual in only one respect—he was even more vigorous and efficient in warfare than most other consuls. As generally happens, the attempt to attach a distinctive foreign policy to one of the individual politicians of the early period leads almost nowhere.[3] Some such divisions may have existed from time to time, but modern attempts to reconstruct them are usually fantasies.

Rome's conquest of Italy resulted from an almost uninterrupted succession of annual campaigns. It is the regularity of the Romans' warfare which distinguishes them from other Italians, even from the Samnites and much more so from the Etruscans. This belligerence was, as we have seen in detail, far from being aimless. It was normal, and it was thought to be advantageous, for a sizable section of the community to spend part of the year at war. The aristocracy, patrician and plebeian, seems to have been virtually united behind this policy.[4] More or less rational considerations determined which direction each expedition should take. Sometimes the choice was fixed by

[1] Toynbee, o.c. i. 144–5 (and others).

[2] It rests on the assumption that the Senate was hostile to the subsequent land grants in Sabine territory. Of course it is very likely that many senators resented the influence Curius gained by these activities and that the distribution of land caused bitter disputes. The hostility between him and (some) senators alluded to by App. *Samn.* 5 should probably be referred to his tribunate (cf. Beloch, o.c. 484; G. Forni, *Athenaeum* xxxi (1953), 200, fails to show that it belongs to his first consulship), when he succeeded in preventing a patrician *interrex* from barring plebeians from the consulship (cf. Forni, 187–191), an important constitutional victory which he evidently won by some unusual pressure (cf. Cic. *Brut.* 55: 'coegerit'—this coincides with the squad of 800 supporters mentioned by Appian).

[3] Now even a historian who claims to reconstruct the aristocratic political groupings of the late fourth century detects no foreign-policy disagreements among them: E. J. Phillips, *Athenaeum* l (1972), 337–56.

[4] On the competition between patricians and plebeians as a cause of this policy, see above, p. 28.

external dangers, but very often the choice was between opportunities, though risky opportunities.

As to the motives which settled the matter in any given year, they can only be imagined. In 327 Q. Publilius Philo set out to seize Naples:[1] the action would weaken and displease the Samnites; it would bring a wealthy trading city within Roman power; it would be a glorious and profitable success for Publilius and his associates.[2] The motives for beginning and continuing the Second Samnite War were no doubt complex, but it was not simply a forced response to Samnite pressure. After the Caudine Forks the Samnites necessarily continued to be the main enemy, but by 312 Rome evidently felt strong enough to move forward simultaneously on other fronts.[3] Neither the alleged external pressure of the years from 327 nor the serious defeats of 321 and 315 had caused the regular number of legions to rise above two, but from 311 the total was doubled.[4] An aggressive spirit brought about the change. Part of the enlarged army fought the Etruscan–Umbrian war of 311–308, penetrating far to the north, enriching itself considerably, and earning triumphs over the Etruscans for Q. Aemilius Barbula and Fabius Rullianus. In 308 the Etruscans bought themselves a year of peace (in the shape of *indutiae*), and in the following campaigning season one of the consuls, L. Volumnius Flamma Violens, led an expedition to the far south-east, against the Sallentines. In 306 the Senate had little choice about where to send the armies, since there was a rebellion among the Hernici and a Samnite force entered Campania.

The temporary peace with the Samnites established two years later permitted a further advance in central Italy and the resumption of the Etruscan and Umbrian wars. The central

---

[1] For speculation about the motives for this decision cf. F. Cassola, *I gruppi politici romani*, 121–4.

[2] And bring corresponding chagrin to his enemies. By 314 he was 'invisus nobilitati' according to Liv. ix. 26.21 (probably a crude inference from his reforms of 339), but the *nobilitas* cannot in general have been opposed to the foreign policy he carried out in 327–6.

[3] The notion that in and after 314 certain leaders succeeded in discrediting the previous forward policy against the Samnites (elaborated by Salmon, *Samnium and the Samnites*, 240) is a fiction. It also makes the colonization of 314–312 and the Roman campaigns against the Samnites between 313 and 304 unintelligible.

[4] Liv. ix. 30.3 (311 B.C.) strictly speaking only gives the latest possible date for this change (and the new legions cannot have been instituted by the tribunician law which is the subject of Livy's notice); Salmon, o.c. 232, may be right to date it back to the years 320–316, but it is also possible that the censorship of 312/11 made it clear that more men were available.

Italian peoples were all under Roman control by 302, and the
desirable and commanding site of Nequinum (Narnia) in
southern Umbria was settled with a Latin colony in 299. In the
following year Rome took the initiative in starting a new Samnite
war. Perhaps to Roman surprise, this became for two or three
years (from 296) an essential defensive operation, as a result of the
Samnite alliances in the north. The wave of temple vows by the
consuls of these years may be a symptom of unusual anxiety
among the leaders of the state.[1] In any case, with the Etruscans
and Samnites apparently near to final defeat in 290, the opportunity was taken to reduce the Sabines and Praetuttians. By this
time, if not earlier, Rome had clearly resolved to control the entire
peninsula from the Etruscans, Umbrians, and Picentes southwards.

From 289 until 264 Roman armies were almost annually taken
up with achieving this purpose. The process was of course very
much slowed by the political crisis of 287 at Rome and the
invasions by the Gauls and by Pyrrhus. In so far as there were any
extensions of Rome's enmities within Italy itself, they concerned
only the peoples in the far south, the Bruttians (also Locri and
Croton) and the Messapians. However the Senate must have
regarded most of the fighting carried out in this period as
unavoidable work to suppress the disobedient and to repel
invaders. Not only were there Gauls and Pyrrhus to deal with;
even after the latter's final Italian defeat in 275, there were still
rebels among the Samnites, Lucanians, Bruttians, and even
among the Etruscans and Picentines. None the less, in the late
270s, the Senate's thoughts were, as we shall soon see, turning to
possible wars beyond the peninsula.

THE FIRST PUNIC WAR

All historical periodization raises difficulties, but the common
and natural decision to begin a narrative of Roman expansion (a
book or a chapter) in 264 creates special risks. The Roman

---

[1] The following vows made during the Italian wars can be dated: in 311, that of C.
Iunius Bubulcus (unless it belongs to 317 or 313) in the Samnite War (Liv. ix. 31.10–11,
43.25, x. 1.9); in 296, that of Ap. Claudius Caecus (Liv. x. 19.17, etc.); in 295, that of
Fabius Rullianus (Liv. x. 29.14 etc.); in 294, that of M. Atilius Regulus (Liv. x. 36.11 etc.).
We are not specifically told of the vow of Sp. Carvilius Maximus (*cos.* 293), but one can be
assumed (cf. Liv. x. 46.14). Those made by P. Sempronius Sophus (*cos.* 268) during the
Picentine rebellion (Flor. i. 14.1–2 etc.), and by M. Atilius Regulus (*cos.* 267) during the
war against the Sallentines (Flor. i. 15) do not fit this theory well.

decision to accept the appeal of the Mamertini, and so to undertake war with Carthage and Syracuse, was clearly of the utmost importance; but to understand this decision it is essential to keep in mind previous Roman actions. There was much continuity. Rome was not suddenly presented with the problems of the world outside Italy. The straits of Messina were less of a psychological barrier than they have usually been in subsequent times, since the concept of the whole mainland as Italy was relatively new and cities on both sides of the straits were peopled by Greeks. In fact the Senate had had plenty of time to think about extra-Italian politics. Pyrrhus' invasion of Italy had compelled them to do so. One of Rome's reactions was to make a new and up-to-date treaty with Carthage.[1] Among the contingencies envisaged by the treaty-makers was Roman help to Carthage against Pyrrhus, help which might be needed in Sicily.[2] Once Pyrrhus had been defeated in Italy (275), the possibility of conflict with Carthage probably became clear. In all likelihood the Latin colonies of Paestum and Cosa (273) were founded in part to strengthen Rome's position in such a conflict.[3]

In the same year Rome exchanged ambassadors and established friendship with Ptolemy II Philadelphus, which shows at least that the Senate was actively interested in obtaining the king's goodwill.[4] Historians are sometimes naïve enough to suppose that this exchange had no political content,[5] but blunt practical Roman senators are unlikely to have omitted Carthage from their conversation with the Ptolemaic representatives. Carthage was in effect their mutual neighbour.[6] This Roman–Ptolemaic relationship was, Badian vaguely asserts, 'not taken very seriously by anyone', but inconvenient facts cannot be

---

[1] See H. H. Schmitt, *Die Staatsverträge des Altertums*, iii. 101–6. The date is (in my view) late 279 or early 278.

[2] Polyb. iii. 25.3–4 (transport ships to be provided by Carthage). However the only help given went no further than Rhegium (Diod. xxii. 7.5).

[3] On Cosa cf. Harris, *Rome in Etruria and Umbria*, 155.

[4] Sources in *MRR* i. 197; add Eutrop. ii. 15 and cf. App. *Sic.* 1. The initiative was taken by Ptolemy (Dio fr. 41, Zonar. viii. 6), but the Roman ambassadors were not sent to Alexandria merely because of diplomatic convention; neither Hellenistic nor Roman practice required such a thing (E. Badian, *Foreign Clientelae*, 33 n. 1, is misleading). On the resulting *amicitia* cf. W. Dahlheim, *Struktur und Entwicklung*, 142–5.

[5] E.g. E. Will, *Histoire politique*, i. 174. None the less he believes that there was a monetary agreement—for which there is no real evidence (cf. M. H. Crawford, *RRC* 39–40).

[6] We do not know how Carthage had behaved during Philadelphus' troubles with Magas of Cyrene *c.* 275.

disposed of so easily; and if it is true, as it probably is, that Philadelphus in consequence refused to lend Carthage 2,000 talents at a crucial moment in the war with Rome, it was serious enough.[1] The year after the friendship was established a Carthaginian flotilla appeared at Tarentum while the Romans were still besieging it. The Carthaginians seem, despite later Roman libels, to have behaved correctly,[2] but the incident necessarily turned Roman attention once more to the possibility of a Carthaginian war. Soon afterwards Rome apparently expropriated from the defeated Bruttians half of the Sila forest; Dionysius comments at length on its outstanding value for ship-construction.[3] In 267 we find a Roman fleet being manned under *duumviri navales* for the purpose of the war against the Sallentines,[4] and in a state whose naval expeditions had been small and infrequent, the development may have been connected with senatorial thoughts about Carthage. It is in any case clear that the Senate had not excluded Carthage from its thoughts before 264.

What is even more essential to the understanding of the Roman war-decision of 264 is the role of war in Roman society. The fixed pattern of annual warfare fulfilled such essential functions that it was not likely to be given up. In default of good contemporary sources, it would be wrong to dogmatize about senatorial attitudes. But in the years after 272, and much more so from 266 onwards, the imminent completion of the Italian empire must have made many Romans think about what would happen next. Some perhaps looked forward to peace, but it would be peace without glory or plunder or the discipline and distraction of military service. Consuls could be expected to be particularly belligerent. In 264, because of the Senate's indecision, the consuls played an even more critical role than usual. Ap. Claudius Caudex, and apparently his colleague too,[5] wanted war with

---

[1] *Foreign Clientelae*, 44. See App. *Sic*. 1. Curiously Holleaux ends his long discussion (one of the weaker parts of his book) by suggesting that the Senate's Egyptian interest was in possible emergency supplies of grain (*RGMH* 81–2).

[2] Zonar. viii. 6 is by far the most credible source; the others are Liv. *Per.* 14, Oros. iv. 3.1, Dio fr. 43.1.

[3] Dion. Hal. xx. 15. Toynbee (*Hannibal's Legacy*, ii. 120 n. 7) gratuitously redates this event to the end of the Hannibalic War.

[4] Sources in *MRR* i. 200, except that the most important is omitted—Ioannes Lydus, *De mag.* i. 27 (on which see W. V. Harris, *CQ* xxvi (1976), 92–106).

[5] Polyb. i. 11.2: καὶ κατ᾽ ἰδίαν ἑκάστοις ὠφελείας προδήλους καὶ μεγάλας ὑποδεικνυόντων τῶν στρατηγῶν.

Carthage and persuaded the assembly to support their policy. We can assume that the arguments heard on the subject in any *contio* were predominantly those in favour of the war and that the consuls, influenced presumably by personal ambition, thus guided Rome into the decision.

War in northern Italy was another possibility which must have entered senatorial minds in the years before the Punic War. A Roman army had defeated the Gauls at Sentinum, beyond the Appennine watershed, in 295; another had taken land from the Senones in 284 and founded the citizen colony of Sena Gallica; Ariminum was colonized in 268, the last year of Picentine rebellion; and in 266 the Sarsinates on the north-eastern slopes of the Appennines were subjugated. Rome was ready to advance in this direction. The alternative was Carthage.

Was it then with defensive purposes that Rome accepted the appeal of the Mamertini at Messene in 264, thereby involving themselves, as they expected, in war against Syracuse and Carthage? Was it, on the Roman side, a 'preventive' war? Polybius says that two motives were important. One was anxiety about the growing power of Carthage, anxiety which influenced the Senate but did not prevent it from leaving the question unsettled.[1] When the consuls came to persuade the assembly to vote for war, they used, in addition to this argument, the prospect of booty to be won.[2] What had hindered the Senate from deciding in favour of war was, he says, the illogicality of helping the Mamertines, who had behaved as badly at Messene as the Campanian troops had at Rhegium a few years earlier.[3] However desire for plunder and anxiety about Carthaginian power were not, in Polybius' view, the only forces at work on the Roman side. There was also the will to expand Roman power.[4] And this, in his version, became an even more important part of the Roman purpose as the war progressed. After the original aim of preventing Carthage from obtaining (or retaining) control over Messene had been achieved, Roman aims expanded. Self-

[1] i. 10.5–9: θεωροῦντες δὲ τοὺς Καρχηδονίους οὐ μόνον τὰ κατὰ τὴν Λιβύην, ἀλλὰ καὶ τῆς Ἰβηρίας ὑπήκοα πολλὰ μέρη πεποιημένους, ἔτι δὲ τῶν νήσων ἁπασῶν ἐγκρατεῖς ὑπάρχοντας τῶν κατὰ τὸ Σαρδόνιον καὶ Τυρρηνικὸν πέλαγος ἠγωνίων, εἰ Σικελίας ἔτι κυριεύσαιεν, μὴ λίαν βαρεῖς καὶ φοβεροὶ γείτονες αὐτοῖς ὑπάρχοιεν κτλ.
[2] See p. 63 n. 2.
[3] i. 10.4, 11.1.
[4] Cf. i. 6.3, 12.7, with K. F. Eisen, *Polybiosinterpretationen* (Heidelberg, 1966), 153–4.

confidence was generated in the Senate by the capture of Agrigentum in 262 and by the naval victory at Mylae in 260; from 262 onwards they aimed to expel the Carthaginians entirely from Sicily.[1] Because of their φιλοτιμία the Romans persevered.[2]

Of the two special factors Polybius mentions as active in 264, modern historians have generally brushed aside the more credible one, while inflating the other into the dominant force in Roman policy. That the consuls dangled the possibility of plunder before the citizens is entirely credible.[3] On the other hand the claim that Roman anxiety about Carthaginian power was one of the determining factors presumably derives from Fabius Pictor, Polybius' main source, perhaps in effect his only source, concerning the contemporary Roman outlook.[4] Since, as we have already seen, Fabius Pictor made propaganda for a 'defensive' interpretation of Rome's past wars,[5] it is very likely that he exaggerated the defensive element in the 264 decision. And he somewhat deceived Polybius, partly because the latter did not look into the question as thoroughly as he would have done for part of his main subject,[6] partly because of the lack of other sources of information.

The 'defensive' explanation is not quite as cogent as it is normally held to be.[7] Of course it seems entirely reasonable that Romans should have been apprehensive about Punic power:

---

[1] i. 20.1–2, 24.1.

[2] i. 39.7, 52.4 (cf. 57.2, 59.6).

[3] De Sanctis (*SR* iii. 1.99) attempted to show that it could not be so by the somewhat inconsistent arguments, (a) that not much booty was to be expected in Sicily (this is plainly incorrect), and (b) that Fabius Pictor invented the explanation *ex eventu*, because of the large quantity of booty the war actually produced. Cf. also J. H. Thiel, *A History of Roman Sea-Power before the Second Punic War* (Amsterdam, 1954), 139. W. Hoffmann's objection that Fabius Pictor cannot have recorded such a fact (*Historia* xviii (1969), 171 n. 41) was not altogether without force, but Hoffmann failed to realize the role of booty in Roman society. It is likely that many of the references to booty in Polybius' narrative of the war go back to Fabius (cf. i. 19.11, 19.15, 20.1, 29.6–7, 29.10, 30.4, etc., for explicit references).

[4] See F. W. Walbank on Polyb. i. 14.1 and F. Hampl, *ANRW* i. 1.413, for the most significant items in the bloated bibliography of this topic. I do not suppose that Polybius' account slavishly reproduced that of Fabius.

[5] This will have been especially desirable in the case of the First Punic War, since Philinus' anti-Roman account was already in circulation (cf. G. De Sanctis, *Ricerche sulla storiografia siceliota* (Palermo, 1958), 71–2, Hoffmann, o.c. 161–2).

[6] See Polyb. i. 5.3.

[7] For views of this kind cf. Frank, *Roman Imperialism*, 90–1, M. Gelzer in J. Vogt (ed.), *Rom und Karthago* (Leipzig, 1943), 186, H. Bengtson, *Grundriss*², 75, R. M. Errington, *The Dawn of Empire* (London, 1972), 16. For some valuable remarks about the underlying presuppositions see Hampl, *ANRW* i. 1.425–6.

Carthage may recently have been increasing its power in Sicily, and in any case it constituted a far more formidable enemy than Rome had encountered for several generations. The Carthaginians' presence in Sardinia, as well as in Sicily, put them within easy striking distance of Roman possessions. The coast of southern Italy was raided on several occasions during the war,[1] and indeed was obviously vulnerable while Carthage retained naval superiority. However Carthage took no overt action against Rome before the Roman war-decision, and, more significantly, appears not to have raided the Italian coast until the Romans had already laid siege to the main Carthaginian base in Sicily, Agrigentum.[2] If Rome's interest had been mainly defensive in 264, the sensible policy was to make an alliance with, not against, the strongest independent state in Sicily, the Syracuse of Hiero II.[3] Such an alliance could have stabilized eastern Sicily for very many years to come. The extension of Roman aims after the capture of Agrigentum and Rome's subsequent conduct of the war might, in theory, be put down to over-reaction against a supposed Carthaginian danger. Unquestionably the Senate wanted to make it impossible for Carthaginians to raid the coast of Italy, but the Romans also wanted, and this was probably the greater part of their desires, to gain the prizes that could be won from an enemy as rich as Carthage. Rome's refusals to make peace even on terms which would have looked very advantageous in 264 are significant.[4] A new theatre of war was certain to be created in or soon after 264: the dangerous strength of Rome's Carthaginian neighbours was

[1] In chronological order: Zonar. viii. 10 (an unsuccessful expedition in 261, a more successful one in 260), Polyb. i. 20.7 (πολλάκις—but probably just referring to the same events), Oros. iv. 7.7, Zonar. viii. 15, viii. 16, Polyb. i. 56.10.

[2] A. Heuss (see above, p. 110 n. 3) usefully pointed out the Carthaginian raids but overestimated their importance in determining Rome's over-all policy after 262. Polybius (i. 20.1–8) is much better balanced: the Senate did not merely decide to build ships, but to conduct a forward policy aimed (he says) at expelling the Carthaginians from Sicily; they needed ships to dominate the Sicilian coast, and also (ἔτι, § 7) to turn the balance so that Libya, not Italy, would be raided. Heuss neglects most of this, and to support his case gratuitously postpones the siege of Agrigentum by a year (beginning it in June 261 instead of June 262; the theory was thought up by K. J. Beloch and demolished by De Sanctis; cf. Walbank on Polyb. i. 17.9), with the intention of destroying Polybius' explanation of the policy change of 261.

[3] Heuss, o.c. 473 = 27–28.

[4] Polyb. i. 31.4–8, Diod. xxiii. 12, Dio fr. 43.22–3, Eutrop. ii. 21.3–4, Oros. iv. 9.1, Zonar. viii. 13 (256/5 B.C.), Dio fr. 43.26, Zonar. viii. 15 (during Regulus' captivity—but this peace-offer may be fictitious—see Walbank on Polyb. i. 35); cf. also Zonar. viii. 15.14.

one of the reasons why they, and not the Boii or the Ligurians, were the new enemy.

Certain elements in Polybius' account of the origins of the war have sometimes been rejected. Apparently Livy contradicted his report that the Senate failed to accept the Mamertine appeal.[1] If Polybius was in error on this point, the 'defensive' interpretation might be stronger, since we would have better reason to think that the Senate really felt a Carthaginian threat; but in fact Polybius was almost certainly correct to say that the Senate left the issue open.[2] Other anti-Polybian theories, such as that he was wrong to deny the existence of the famous treaty which the pro-Carthaginian Philinus said bound Rome to keep out of Sicily, make little difference to the present argument. It is possible (the problem is unanswerable) that Philinus was right; even if he was, we are left with the problem of reconstructing the Roman motives of 264.[3]

It is important to ask what caused the Senate to hesitate. Polybius' explanation is that 'the illogicality of the help [asked by the Mamertines] seemed so obvious',[4] since Rome had punished its own citizens for the treachery at Rhegium and would now be helping men who had committed the same crime at Messene and also at Rhegium; this would be a 'crime hard to excuse'.[5] But past events in Messene are not likely to have affected the Senate's

---

[1] Liv. *Per.* 16: 'auxilium Mamertinis ferendum senatus censuit.' Polybius' statement has been doubted by some scholars (most recently, but with weak arguments, by Hoffmann, o.c. 171–4).

[2] His version cannot simply have been invented by Fabius to exculpate the Senate in the eyes of foreigners (as implied by De Sanctis, *SR* iii. 1.99 n. 14, Gelzer, *Hermes* lxviii (1933), 137 [→ Bibl.]), since Fabius had a Roman audience as well, and since he undoubtedly thought that he could justify the war as a 'defensive' operation. Add to this the fact that some late republican annalists will have wanted to 'rectify' a story in which the people had made a war-decision without senatorial approval—hence the different version in Livy—and the question is virtually settled.

[3] The 'Philinus treaty' is known from Polyb. iii. 26. In support of Polybius' negative judgement cf. P. Pédech, *La Méthode historique de Polybe*, 188–91 etc. In Philinus' favour: R. E. Mitchell, *Historia* xx (1971), 633–55, Hampl, *ANRW* i. 1.422–3 etc. It may well be that Polybius made a mistake, in implying that the Carthaginians had not already occupied Messene before 264 (i. 10.1, 6–9); they may have done so shortly after the battle of Longanus (cf. 9.7–10.1), which is perhaps best dated *c.* 269 (cf. Hoffmann, o.c. 158–61, K.-E. Petzold, *Studien zur Methode des Polybius und zu ihrer historischen Auswertung* (Munich, 1969), 129–74). In that case the Roman decision of 264 did not result from a sudden alarm.

[4] i. 10.3: διὰ τὸ δοκεῖν ἐξόφθαλμον εἶναι τὴν ἀλογίαν τῆς βοηθείας.

[5] i. 10.4: δυσαπολόγητον . . . τὴν ἁμαρτίαν.

decision greatly,[1] and Polybius' explanation is deeply tinged with Roman propaganda.[2] The enemies of Rome presumably made much of the gratuitous nature of Roman intervention in Sicily and of the undeserving character of the Mamertines, and the Romans in turn emphasized the *fides* which supposedly brought them to the help of the Campanian invaders[3] and the moral punctiliousness with which the Senate had behaved. What probably caused many senators to baulk was not a desire for years of peace,[4] or a preference (which some may really have felt) for northward expansion, but the fact that sufficient preparations had not been made for a Punic war, above all with regard to naval forces. In fact it was foolhardy to go to war against Carthage without a sizable navy, and the more cautious senators must have realized this. But arguments about naval preparedness are not likely to have been publicized at the time or preserved afterwards. In any case a propagandistic explanation was eventually provided.

The events of 264 provide one of the earliest clear instances of what became a standard Roman technique. Rome accepted the Mamertines into alliance quite freely,[5] and in full knowledge that war with new enemies would result. It was an intentional step into a new area. In a quite similar way Rome had made an alliance with the Lucanians and gone to war with the Samnites in 298 (though in that case the enmity of the Samnites was a given fact). Later the technique becomes such a normal part of the armoury that the burden lies on any historian who wishes to suggest that Saguntum, for example, was accepted into alliance before the Second Punic War without the Senate's full awareness of the probable consequences. The technique could provide an

[1] Cf. Frank, *Roman Imperialism*, 89, Badian, *Foreign Clientelae*, 35, Hoffmann, o.c. 168–71. Yet the Mamertines may have had a reputation as offenders against *fides* and aroused some real hostility in consequence.

[2] Perhaps contemporary propaganda, since the passages quoted above emphasize the bad *appearance* of helping the Mamertines.

[3] See the evidence referred to above, p. 35 n. 2.

[4] Frank argued (*Roman Imperialism*, 91, 107 n. 6) that Ap. Claudius Caudex's failure to win a triumph showed that the Senate still disapproved of the campaign. A more probable explanation is that his conduct of the war was not very successful, as is sufficiently shown by the fact that M'. Valerius Maximus (*cos.* 263) won the *cognomen* Messala by rescuing Messene (that is to say, Polyb. i. 11.14–12.4 is based on excessive faith in Fabius Pictor, and Polybius should have accepted more of the Philinus narrative which he criticizes in i. 15). Cf. H. H. Scullard, *HRW*[3] 146 n. 2, F. W. Walbank on i. 15.1–11.

[5] A *deditio* such as the Mamertines made (Polyb. i. 10.2) could of course be rejected, as in the case of Utica *c*. 240.

excuse for an advance in almost any direction under the sanctifying banner of *fides*.[1]

It was not simply to defend existing Roman possessions that Rome decided on war in 264. Still less was that the limit of the new aims that were formed after the fall of Agrigentum. The traditional incentives to war had their usual effects. How soon the leaders of the Senate formed the idea of seizing the whole of Sicily cannot be known. As I have already argued, we should probably accept Polybius' account of the growth of Roman ambitions after the fall of Agrigentum. In 259 they began to contest Sardinia and seized Aleria, the most important city in Corsica.[2] Naturally we have no evidence of grandiose plans concerning these three islands, but normal Roman behaviour was to follow up such new ventures until some permanent form of power was established. Not that any clear strategy evolved for obtaining this result. Some campaigns were probably intended as little more than booty-gathering expeditions, most notably the one led by the consuls of 253 to the island of Meninx.[3]

The final phase of the war is also instructive here. Catastrophic losses in 250 and 249 must have reduced Roman enthusiasm. Yet they held on to their position in Sicily. Their resolution, and the final efforts of 242/1, can best be explained by their desire to take the whole island into their possession.

SARDINIA, CORSICA, NORTHERN ITALY: THE FIRST STAGES

Once we discard the notion that the First Punic War resulted merely from a Roman wish to be rid of 'frightening neighbours', their subsequent seizure of Sardinia, which many historians have been compelled to treat as an aberration, becomes easy to understand. Through two years, it is true, the Romans remained passive, exhausted by their great efforts.[4] It was probably in 241 (and not in 235) that they ceremonially closed the doors of the

---

[1] Cf. above, pp. 34–5.

[2] Polybius' statement that Corsica was possessed by Carthage in 264 (i. 10.5) is open to some doubt (cf. F. W. Walbank ad loc.); in support of Polybius cf. J. and L. Jehasse, *La Nécropole préromaine d'Aléria (1960–8)*, *Gallia*, Suppl. xxv (1973), 111–12.

[3] Sources in *MRR* i. 211. Walbank (on Polyb. i. 39.1), following Thiel (o.c. (p. 186 n. 3) 248–9), assumes that the aim was not to plunder but 'to stimulate native revolts and to hinder the Punic naval programme', an unlikely tale.

[4] See above, p. 10.

temple of Janus, thereby indicating that no war was being contemplated.[1] When the mercenaries in Sardinia, in rebellion against their Carthaginian employers, invited the Romans to seize the island (at some point in 240 or 239), they refused. Similarly they refused an offer of submission by the city of Utica, after that city had joined the mercenaries. This would certainly have been contrary to the treaty of 241. Acceptance of either arrangement would have made a war with Carthage quite probable. And there should be no difficulty in accepting Polybius' explanation that Rome was all the more inclined to observe the treaty because of the obliging behaviour of Carthage with regard to the Italian traders captured during the Mercenary War.[2] But inevitably normal ambitions began to return. Sardinia presented an obvious opportunity: not only had the mercenaries there rebelled, they had subsequently been driven out by the indigenous people of the island.[3] One of the consuls of 238, Ti. Sempronius Gracchus, led an expedition there, probably in violation of the treaty with Carthage.[4] Carthage protested. But this was no exploratory probe on the Roman side, it was a determined act of policy. A conditional declaration of war was sent to Carthage: cede Sardinia and pay 1,200 talents, in addition to the 2,000 already agreed, or we are at war. There was a strong possibility that war with Carthage would result from this set of demands; war with the Sardinians was in any case an absolute certainty.

---

[1] 241 is a far more likely context than 235, and the latter date (sources in *MRR* i. 223) probably arose from a confusion between the consuls A. Manlius Torquatus (241) and T. Manlius Torquatus (235) (cf. K. Latte, *Römische Religionsgeschichte*, 132 n. 3, *Der Historiker L. Calpurnius Frugi* (*SB Berlin* no. 7 (1960)), 14–16 [→ Bibl.]). (However Oros. iv. 12.7 provides no help for this view, in spite of A. Lippold, *Consules*, 126 n. 202.) De Sanctis' claim (*SR* iv. 2.1.206) that the doors were often closed under the Republic is unconvincing; evidently no other closing in historical times was known to the second-century annalist L. Piso (Varro, *LL* v. 165). Some have suspected, following G. Wissowa (*Religion und Kultus*[2], 104–5), that the closing only became a symbol of peace under Augustus; but Piso's testimony is against this, and it is pointless to argue that there would otherwise have been other closings (Latte, ll. cc.)—how many years were there when Rome firmly intended to avoid war? 241 was a truly exceptional time.

[2] On all this see Polyb. i. 83.5–11. Other sources (listed by Walbank ad loc.) add nothing of value, except the number of Punic prisoners exchanged for these Italians (above, p. 65 n. 2).   [3] Polyb. i. 79.4–5.

[4] Cf. Polyb. iii. 27.3–4. The role of the rebellious mercenaries in 238 is unclear from i. 88.8. It looks as if a pro-Roman source of his (almost certainly Fabius Pictor) tried to justify the Roman expedition as a response to the expelled mercenaries' appeal for help. On the chronology of the first Sardinian expedition cf. Walbank on i. 88.8.

There was no defensive theory behind this apparently aggressive behaviour, as far as we can see. The Romans claimed in justification of their Sardinian expedition that the preparations Carthage was making against Sardinia were really directed against themselves.[1] This was obviously nothing more than camouflage, the only matter of doubt being whether the excuse was contemporary. Later Roman writers devised for the Romans such pretexts as they could.[2] De Sanctis argued that the Roman case had some appearance of justice in that Rome was seeking satisfaction for Carthaginian attacks on Italian merchants during the Mercenary War; but they had already been set free well before Rome invaded Sardinia.[3] No doubt the Senate saw the advantage of any action that weakened Carthage, but the unmistakable advantages of extending Roman power are likely to have weighed more heavily than the distant possibility of improved defence (the possession of Sardinia had done very little for Carthage during the First Punic War). Thus historians have been faced with the virtual impossibility of explaining the seizure of Sardinia as a subjectively defensive act on the part of the Romans; their response has been to fall back on the argument that the act was exceptional[4]—what was exceptional, however, was the preceding two-year period of peace.[5]

The campaign of Ti. Gracchus, and the five successive years (235–231) in which one at least of the consuls campaigned in Sardinia—three consuls earning triumphs over the inhabitants—effectively established Roman control over part of the island. Corsica too was invaded in 238, and another new series of colonial

---

[1] Polyb. i. 88.10.

[2] See Walbank, l.c. An important index of Livy's unreliability on the Punic wars is provided by the fact that he apparently said that Carthage had ceded Sardinia in 241 (cf. De Sanctis, *SR* iii. 1.280 n. 34).

[3] De Sanctis, *SR* iii. 1.399–401. He tried to evade Polybius' explicit evidence that the prisoners had been restored (i. 83.8, iii. 28.3) by saying that in any case renewed differences were inevitable!

[4] Thus, e.g., Badian, *Foreign Clientelae*, 43, H. Bengtson, *Grundriss*[2], 84. The claim of R. M. Errington (*The Dawn of Empire*, 32–3) that Rome's policy was merely 'strategic' nicely illustrates the difficulties which the proponents of defensive imperialism get into; he has to suppose that the Senate suddenly realized the strategic importance of Sardinia when the expelled mercenaries reached Italy. This is plainly absurd.

[5] Attempts to explain this as a result of the ascendancy of a particular group or party (cf. Frank, *Roman Imperialism*, 113, Lippold, *Consules*, 119 n. 176, etc.) are unnecessary (see the text) and unsupported by evidence.

campaigns began.[1] Such actions are wholly unintelligible as a defensive strategy;[2] they were simply aimed at increasing Roman power and possessions.

That external pressure was not the reason for these Sardinian and Corsican wars is also demonstrated by other events of 238 and 237. Far from concentrating on Sardinia and Corsica, Rome entered into entirely separate and equally unprovoked campaigns in Liguria and Gaul. In the Ligurian case the sources consist of a few phrases only.[3] The initiative was an obvious one for Rome to take, particularly after the invasion of Corsica. It had nothing detectable to do with defence,[4] yet the Ligurian wars went on spasmodically until the late 220s, yielding three triumphs and an uncounted quantity of plunder.

The Gallic wars are a somewhat more complicated question. Polybius and the annalistic sources give different versions of the first phase, Polybius describing a single campaign, which he dates to 237, Zonaras three campaigns (238–236), the last of which seems to correspond with that of Polybius. The significance of this disagreement is that Polybius describes the war as a Gallic invasion (which collapsed when it got 'as far as Ariminum'), thus providing by implication a respectable motive for Roman behaviour.[5] The non-Polybian sources leave the impression of an unprovoked Roman invasion of Gallic territory.

Can it be that Zonaras is for once to be preferred to Polybius? On general principles, it is not very likely. Yet Polybius' account is somewhat suspect: he offers some imaginary psychologizing

---

[1] On 238: Festus 430L, citing the Augustan Sinnius Capito; on 236: Zonar. viii. 18. Almost nothing of significance is known about these or later raids; they produced one triumph (in 231) and brought the island to annexation by 227 at the latest.

[2] According to Mommsen (*RG* ii[12]. 544) the aim was the security of Italy, but he does not explain why this, rather than the other advantages he enumerates, should be considered the essential reason for seizing Sardinia and Corsica.

[3] On the first three years: Eutrop. iii. 2 (237), Zonar. viii. 18 (238, 236), *Acta Tr.* (on 236), Liv. *Per.* 20, Flor. i. 19.2.

[4] De Sanctis (*SR* iii. 1.289) suggested that Ligurian piracy was one reason for the Roman attack, and in F. Cassola, *I gruppi politici romani*, 221, this leads to the hypothesis that in 236 the Senate was 'under the influence of groups more interested in maritime than in territorial problems'. All that is lacking is evidence. However Rome did already count the Massiliots as friends (W. Dahlheim, *Struktur und Entwicklung*, 138–9), and that may have encouraged Rome to operate against Massilia's natural enemies.

[5] Polyb. ii. 21.1–6, Zonar. viii. 18 (dating the Ariminum incident to 236); cf. Oros. iv. 12.1 (starts the war in 238), Flor. i. 19.2, Liv. *Per.* 20.

about the Gallic state of mind, and in a curious phrase, which seems designed to disguise Roman aggression, he says that the Gauls became 'exasperated with the Romans over any chance event'.[1] Ariminum, on the other hand—Rome's outpost in Gallic territory since 268—remains apparently untouched by any serious attack. There are of course other factors in the background—past Gallic invasions and their continuing ability to penetrate deeply into Roman territory. But perhaps the most likely reconstruction of the events of 238/7 is that P. Valerius Falto, the consul of 238, intruded into Gallic territory, which provoked a feeble Gallic move against Ariminum in 237.[2] Fabius Pictor would have passed lightly over the first event and perhaps misled Polybius, who saw no reason to investigate the matter; Polybius in any case regarded the Gauls as virulent enemies whom it would be natural to attack on any occasion. For the present argument any conclusion must be tentative, but we hardly have sufficient reason to think that the new Roman war with the Gauls was perceived by the Senate as primarily a defensive operation. Indeed, since the first conflict with the Gauls for some forty-five years took place at a singularly convenient moment for the Romans, it was probably they who took the initiative.

The Sardinians, Corsicans, and Ligurians, however, were the chosen enemies for several years after 237. Since both the consuls of 230 served in Liguria, the Senate was presumably satisfied with the pacification of the islands. The Ligurian war was probably neither very pressing nor very attractive. Q. Fabius Maximus, as consul in 233, seems to have inflicted a severe defeat.[3] In these circumstances the Senate decided on Rome's first military expedition across the Adriatic.

---

[1] ii. 21.3: τραχύνεσθαι μὲν ἐκ τῶν τυχόντων πρὸς Ῥωμαίους . . .

[2] The campaign of 236 described by Zonaras may have resulted from a confusion between the consuls of 237 and 236, L. and P. Cornelius Lentulus Caudinus (cf. Walbank on Polyb. ii. 21.5). Valerius Antias is more likely to have exaggerated P. Valerius Falto's achievements in 238 than to have invented his whole campaign (cf. De Sanctis, *SR* iii. 1.287).

[3] Not only did he celebrate a triumph, Plutarch claims (*Fab.* 2.1) that the Ligurians retreated 'into the Alps' and gave up plundering the nearby parts of Italy; 'frasi ampollose' admittedly (De Sanctis, *SR* iii. 1.290), but it is possible that there is an authentic tradition here.

THE FIRST ILLYRIAN WAR

In the spring of 229 both consuls of the year set out to make war against Queen Teuta and the Illyrians, one in command of 200 warships, the other of some 20,000 infantry and 2,000 cavalry.[1] What gave rise to this expedition, overwhelming in relation to the object of the attack? The war-decision was apparently made after the failure of a Roman embassy sent to Teuta in the previous year (the embassy of the Coruncanii) and the murder of one of the Roman representatives.[2] This murder seems to be a fact, and even the leaders of the Senate may have believed the somewhat implausible claim, afterwards put about by Romans, that Teuta herself was responsible.[3] In any case historians have naturally looked for some further explanation of a Roman expedition of such size; and the embassy of 230 itself needs explaining—for even without the murder its rejection was likely to lead to war. Polybius briefly tells us why it was sent: in previous times the Illyrians had been in the habit of attacking trading vessels that sailed from Italy, but the Romans ignored the resulting complaints; in 230, however, Illyrian pirates robbed or killed Italian traders and also took a considerable number of them prisoner. The Senate sent an embassy to investigate. This is an entirely credible account, as far as it goes.[4]

---

[1] Polyb. ii. 11.1, 7.

[2] Sources: *MRR* i. 227. Holleaux's view (*RGMH* 99–100) that the embassy had delivered a *rerum repetitio* has some attractions, but in this period that would have meant a conditional declaration of war. Polybius (ii. 8) clearly held that the war-decision was made after the mission of the Coruncanii, and no source contradicts this. E. Badian's view is obscure (*PBSR* xx (1952), 75 = *Studies in Greek and Roman History*, 3–4: the Coruncanii 'in effect' declared war, having themselves decided that it was necessary).

[3] For the death itself Plin. *NH* xxxiv. 24 is important confirmation. Teuta's responsibility is another matter: it was highly convenient for Rome to blame her, yet there can hardly have been much evidence; and to make the charge plausible, after her reasonable reply to the Roman mission, Polybius has to rely on the sexist comment that she reacted γυναικοθύμως καὶ ἀλογίστως (ii. 8.12) and gave way to rage (on this aspect of Polybius' account, cf. K.-E. Petzold, *Historia* xx (1971), 204). For what his evidence is worth, Dio fr. 49.5 (cf. Zonar. viii. 19) said that she claimed innocence.

[4] ii. 8.1–3. Certain recent writers have attempted to revive Appian's story that the occasion of Roman involvement was an appeal by the island city of Issa (Vis) (*Ill.* 7; cf. Dio fr. 49, Zonar. viii. 19): Lippold, *Consules*, 131 n. 220, Petzold, o.c. 218–23. This, however, involves rejection of most of Polybius' account without reason (Petzold's arguments on this point (222–3) are too feeble to require fresh refutation). Appian's aberration, on the other hand, is easy to explain as an annalistic tale designed to strengthen Rome's retrospective case for intervention (see Holleaux, *RGMH* 23 n. 6; Walbank on Polyb. ii. 8.3). P. S. Derow (*Phoenix* xxvii (1973), 118–34) interestingly shows

One explanation of the Illyrian war which must be rejected is that the Senate of 230 or 229 saw the Illyrian state as a serious threat to Roman power. The theory is not needed unless we burden ourselves with the presuppositions that the Senate cannot really have been much interested in protecting Italian merchants[1] or at all eager for a new theatre of warfare. In what sense can the Coruncanii, or any of their fellow-citizens, have become convinced that the Illyrians were 'a danger to Rome'?[2] Teuta's military power was by Roman standards slight, and no one would suppose that she was fatuous enough to plan an attack on Italy. We must return to piracy and the Senate's desire to protect Italian merchants. The growth of Illyrian power had evidently made life more dangerous for them,[3] and the Senate's war-decision was indeed subjectively defensive in the sense that it was designed to protect this interest.

More needs to be said. The Senate could probably have avoided responding strongly to the merchants' appeals, and it could perhaps have absolved Teuta from the suspicion of murder. The massive expedition of 229 was not inevitable, and the way in which the expedition was conducted suggests that the aim was to establish Roman power in Illyria, not just to humiliate or weaken Queen Teuta.[4] We must put the war against the background of

that Appian gave the authentic name (Kleemporos) of an Issian ambassador, but his conclusion that Appian's over-all account is to be preferred does not follow. He understates the difficulties in Appian's story, and (crucially) he fails to explain what reason Fabius Pictor can have had for concocting the supposedly misleading version he passed on to Polybius. Appian's version is a clumsy abbreviation, probably at second hand, of a reasonably good source that was probably more detailed, but more pro-Roman, than Polybius.

[1] Badian, o.c. 75 = 3; yet Polybius gives a clear account of the intensification of Illyrian piracy. There is no reason whatsoever to suppose that the merchants in question were 'blockade runners'; even if they were, the Senate may have thought them worthy of protection. Cf. in general above, p. 65. Even Holleaux, normally opposed to 'economic' interpretations, admitted that the attacks on merchants were the reason for Roman intervention (*RGMH* 99–100)

[2] Badian, o.c. 76 = 4. Petzold, o.c. 220, is equally vague. Holleaux's view (*RGMH* 102 n. 3) that the size of the Roman expedition resulted from fear of Macedonian intervention is unconvincing, since there was no reason to expect Macedon to join Teuta against Rome (her late husband Agron had perhaps *not* been an ally of King Demetrius II—the latter had simply bought Agron's services against the Aetolians, Polyb. ii. 2.5; H. J. Dell, *CPh* lxii (1967), 95, otherwise Holleaux, 22 n. 2). Demetrius died early in 229 apparently, but we do not know when this fact was appreciated at Rome (on the chronological problem cf. E. Will, *Histoire politique*, i. 321). [3] Cf. esp. Polyb. ii. 2.4, 4.8, 5.2, 6.8.
[4] See the useful article of N. G. L. Hammond (*JRS* lviii (1968), 1–21). He overstates his

Rome's recent policies. The Latin colony founded at Brundisium in 244 accords badly with the view that the Senate was uninterested in Italy's south-eastern coastal waters. More important still is the habit of annual warfare. In 230 both consuls campaigned in Liguria, in 229 in Illyria. The attractions of the recent scenes of war had diminished, as we have seen, and in 230 the Illyrians attracted unfavourable attention to themselves. In the absence of pressing enmities elsewhere, the result was almost inevitably war.[1] Far from showing 'astonishing patience'[2] in the Adriatic, Rome took almost the first opportunity to intervene there once the acquisitions of the First Punic War had been put in order.

NORTHERN ITALY, 225-221

It seems unquestionable that the Gallic wars that began in 225 were felt at Rome to be a necessary response to the Gallic attack. An enemy force invaded allied territory. The essentially passive part played by the Romans is emphasized by Polybius, according to whom they were constantly, in the years before the war, 'falling into alarms and disturbances' at the prospect of a Gallic invasion.[3] Yet the war resulted at least as much from Roman as from Gallic pressure. Behind it lay the colony of Ariminum and the campaign of 237. Then in 232 the tribune C. Flaminius carried a law to distribute the *ager Gallicus* among Roman citizens.[4] Polybius claims that this popular policy was the cause of

case, however, in implying (20) that a punitive expedition would not have begun with the move against Demetrius of Pharos at Corcyra, but further north; no such expedition could afford to leave Demetrius' force in its rear.

[1] Senators' possible thoughts about future policy east of the Adriatic have some relevance here. The issue is not whether the Senate was making *plans* (see above, p. 107) for expansion in the East (those are the terms of the problem as it is set by F. Cassola, *I gruppi politici romani*, 230, Petzold, o.c. 201), but whether, when the expedition had been put into effect, the Senate showed interest in expanding Rome's power and influence. The correct answer to the latter question is affirmative, since Rome held on to a degree of power in Illyria after the war and exploited the expedition's success to gain influence among the Greeks (Polyb. ii. 12.4). The assertion that 'for a generation after the Illyrian War nothing was further from the minds of the *Patres* than schemes for Eastern expansion' (Badian, o.c. 75 = 3) is false or exaggerated (exaggerated if 'expansion' is meant in the specialized sense of 'provincial annexation').

[2] Holleaux, *RGMH* 100; cf. 27-8.

[3] ii. 22.7 (the date is somewhat vague), cf. Plu. *Marc.* 3, Dio fr. 50.

[4] Sources: *MRR* i. 225. The date and the region affected are likely to be those given by Polybius, in spite of Cicero's variants (see Walbank on ii. 21.7).

the war of 225–222, since many Gauls, especially the Boii, went to war in the belief that Rome was no longer satisfied with seeking to control them but wanted to annihilate them.[1] This obviously echoes the hostility of Flaminius' contemporary Roman enemies, but it may none the less be largely true that Flaminius' legislation was the cause of the invasion.[2] Further Roman pressure on the Boii seems to be attested by Zonaras' somewhat obscure narrative of the events of 230.[3] The burial alive at Rome in 228 of Gauls and Greeks, a man and a woman of each nation, was understandably interpreted by Plutarch as a result of public alarm about the Gauls; but the involvement of Greeks obstructs this interpretation, and a better alternative was found by Cichorius.[4]

Even Polybius' claim that the Gallic invasion in 225 had been greatly feared for several years might be thought slightly exaggerated, both because of his loathing for the Gauls and because his Roman source (or sources) probably overstated the northern peril as a justification for the ruthless policy in the Gallic lands. By 225 Roman power had been extended by means of alliances with two of the four strongest peoples in the plain of the Po, the Cenomani and the Veneti.[5] It would be interesting to know what Roman armies were doing in the year before the invasion.[6] In any case the consular expedition to Sardinia early in 225 argues strongly against a severe state of alarm at Rome.[7] The

---

[1] ii. 21.8–9.

[2] Cf. Walbank on ii. 21.8.

[3] viii. 19. The virtual trade embargo on the Gauls (Rome forbade anyone to buy from them with gold or silver) is so unusual that it is probably historical. The meaning of the consuls' contacts with the Gauls (who ἀπήντησαν αὐτοῖς ὡς φίλιοι) can only be guessed.

[4] Plu. *Marc.* 3, Dio fr. 47, Oros. iv. 13.3, Zonar. viii. 19, C. Cichorius, *Römische Studien* (Berlin–Leipzig, 1922), 17–20 (see further K. Latte, *Römische Religionsgeschichte*, 256–7, Lippold, *Consules*, 255–6). Cichorius associated each of the known Gallic-Greek sacrifices with preceding condemnations of errant Vestal Virgins, and suggested that the two nationalities of the victims meant that the sacrifices were advised by Etruscans.

[5] Polyb. ii. 23.2, 24.7. The date of the alliances is not clear.

[6] The Sardinian rebellion occasioned by the tightening of Roman control in 227 (Zonar. viii. 19—ἀεί should not be pressed) may have begun in 227 or (perhaps better) 226, though it was going on in early 225 (cf. Polyb. ii. 23.5). Troops may have been needed in Sicily in 227/6 for the same reason (cf. ii. 24.13). Since Roman armies marched ἐπὶ τοὺς ὅρους (of the Gauls) in these years (ii. 22.8), they may also have entered Gallic territory.

[7] This expedition has caused great puzzlement, since historians have believed that Rome was in such extreme terror. For their attempts to evade the difficulty cf. Walbank on ii. 23.5–6. His view (taken over from De Sanctis, *SR* iii. 1.307) that the Sardinian expedition was intended 'to guard against a possible Punic attack' is not convincing (a consul would not have been sent for such a purpose). The answer is simple: a major Gallic invasion was a surprise (Holleaux, *RGMH* 123 n. 3).

Gallic invasion of 225, whether its purpose was plundering or something more complex, should not be treated as the beginning of the war; it was the culmination of a series of hostile acts, many of them Roman. We must not assume that the Senate's view was so distorted that it saw Rome as the mere victim of these events.

When the invasion had been repelled, the Romans not surprisingly pursued the war with determination. They formed the hope, says Polybius, of completely expelling the Gauls 'from the places round the River Po'.[1] They crossed the river for the first time in 223. They refused an offer to negotiate peace in 222, though some senators wished to do so,[2] and they brought the war to a definite conclusion by capturing Mediolanum, capital of the Insubres, and forcing them to surrender.

In 221 a new theatre was found in Istria. Eutropius' reference to the piracy of the Istrians against the Roman grain ships as the explanation of the Roman campaign, if it is correct, suggests a case similar to that of the First Illyrian War.[3] But in this instance the violence of the Roman reaction is even more striking, since the Roman grain trade in Istrian waters cannot have been very great and in any case no Roman emissary had been killed.[4] Once again, the Istrians may have attracted Roman attention, but more than defensive thinking is needed to explain the Roman reaction.

For the whole period from 327 to 220 Roman thinking about

[1] ii. 31.8 (cf. above, p. 111).

[2] Polyb. ii. 34.1, Plu. *Marc.* 6, Zonar. viii. 20. The consuls naturally led the opposition to granting peace (Polyb.). The contrary senatorial view will have come partly from the consuls' personal enemies (like the attempt to hinder Flaminius and his colleague in the campaign of 223); some senators may have been moved by jealousy, some perhaps by a wish to attend to Carthage. In Flaminius' case, at least, it seems eminently plausible to detect the intention of conquering new territory for distribution to Roman citizens (cf. F. Cassola, *I gruppi politici romani*, 228). The theory that the campaign of 222 was designed to provide Rome with a good frontier with which to resist Carthage (F. R. Kramer, *AJPh* lxix (1948), 1–26) has been dealt with by Cassola, 220.

[3] Eutrop. iii. 7 ('quia latrocinati navibus Romanorum fuerant, quae frumenta exhibebant'); cf. App. *Ill.* 8 (blaming Demetrius of Pharos for the Istrian piracy). On early Istrian piracy cf. Liv. x. 2.4.

[4] Cassola, o.c. 222–3, expounds the view that piracy really was the main Roman concern, and he is right to reject the older notion that the aim was to establish a frontier at the Alps (cf. also H. J. Dell, *Historia* xix (1970), 34–6, who, however, invents a whole story about Roman grain-shipments in order to explain the piracy). Fighting continued in 220, to judge from App. *Ill.* 8.23 (ἐς νέωτα), whether under promagistrates or under the consuls (who, according to Zonar. viii. 20, led an expedition to the Alps 'without a battle').

foreign affairs is hard to recover. There were, obviously, external threats that were seen as such. There may sometimes have been irrational fears, about the Gauls above all. Yet Roman behaviour towards foreign peoples can be explained convincingly without much recourse to defensive thinking. Often the hostile or disobedient actions of other states seem to have had the effect of attracting Roman attention. The Romans, for their part, would have found someone to march against in any case. Contrary to Gelzer's view, it was in general Rome that exerted the pressure on others. And as Roman power expanded during the Italian wars, the First Punic War and the years from 241 to 220, the Senate probably tended to feel less and less anxiety about Roman security.

4. THE WARS OF 219–70 B.C.

THE SECOND PUNIC WAR

The problem of delineating the defensive element in Roman thinking about external policy ought to become easier to answer in the period which Polybius attempted to describe in all necessary detail. Unfortunately there is only a single case in which a full-scale Polybian analysis of the origins of a Roman war survives complete, the Second Punic War. It is a case of great importance for those who contend that the external policy of the Roman aristocracy was fundamentally defensive, since the Carthaginian enemy was more powerful in relation to Rome than any that was encountered in the second century, and since some Carthaginians did at times unquestionably give Rome cause for anxiety about certain of its interests; and we have some explicit evidence that in the mid-220s the growth of the Carthaginian empire in Spain caused worry at Rome.[1] Here, if anywhere, is a war which Rome undertook in a defensive spirit.[2] Yet it turns out that even in this case such an interpretation is badly lop-sided.

---

[1] Polyb. ii. 13.3: ὃν [Hasdrubal] καὶ θεωροῦντες Ῥωμαῖοι μείζω καὶ φοβερωτέραν ἤδη συνιστάμενον δυναστείαν, ὥρμησαν ἐπὶ τὸ πολυπραγμονεῖν τὰ κατὰ τὴν Ἰβηρίαν.

[2] And it is so interpreted, with variations, by many historians: see, e.g., Holleaux, *RGMH* 136–7, and H. Bengtson, *Grundriss*², 94.

In Polybius' view, the war's most important cause was the Roman seizure of Sardinia and the extra indemnity imposed on Carthage in 238. The other causes were the anger of Hamilcar at the Romans, and the success of the Carthaginians in creating an empire in Spain.[1] This is a coherent account, as far as it goes. Polybius strove to write without regard for national prejudice; but just as on some other occasions (as we have seen) he accepted a version of events too favourable to Rome, so here he underestimated the importance of certain Roman initiatives.

He was probably right to skip over some Roman threats against Carthage reported from the 230s; their exact significance is unknown, even if they are historical.[2] He may have been justified in ignoring the start—in 231—of Rome's direct interest in Carthaginian activities in Spain.[3] This interest is visible only intermittently during the 220s, as one would expect. It did, however, result in two Roman agreements, one with the Iberian city of Saguntum—probably a formal alliance, but in any case a serious commitment—the other the understanding with Hasdrubal concerning the Ebro River line.[4] The Saguntum alliance clearly represented a forward policy with respect to Carthage, and Polybius should have given it greater emphasis. The event is never explained credibly by those who believe that Rome's policy was in the main defensive. Such an alliance cannot have been intended to serve any defensive function, since Rome had nothing, or virtually nothing, to defend in Spain, and Saguntum could obviously do nothing to defend Roman pos-

---

[1] iii. 9.6–12.6. On the second of these causes, a point on which Polybius has sometimes been over-criticized, cf. G. V. Sumner, *Latomus* xxxi (1972), 470–3.

[2] Reported by Zonar. viii. 18 for 236 (cf. Dio fr. 46.1) and 233 (cf. Gell. *NA* x. 27.3–5).

[3] Dio fr. 48 is the source. Neither Holleaux (*RGMH* 123 n. 4) nor Badian (*Foreign Clientelae*, 48) nor R. M. Errington (*Latomus* xxix (1970), 32–4) succeeded in producing any serious reason to reject this notice, which conflicts with their interpretation; cf. Sumner, o.c. 474–5.

[4] Sources and bibliography in De Sanctis, *SR* iii. 1.417–8, H. H. Schmitt, *Die Staatsverträge des Altertums*, iii. 201–7, F. Hampl, *ANRW* i. 1.428–30. Badian, o.c. 51, 293, argued that the connection between Rome and Saguntum was informal, but Polybius' failure to mention a formal document in iii. 30.1–2 does not show this (he had not 'looked up the documents bearing on Rome's relations with Carthage', but only the treaties between Rome and Carthage). See now Hampl, o.c. 430; Polyb. iii. 21.5 strongly suggests that Carthage admitted that there was a formal treaty. A. E. Astin's view (*Latomus* xxvi (1967), 594) that Rome made no 'long-term commitment' to Saguntum hardly merits discussion.

sessions elsewhere.[1] Rather the action fell into the tradition of establishing connections with friendly lesser states, a tradition which had tended to cause or hasten wars, not to prevent them. The Senate was more interested in pretexts than in bases. If the alliance was made *after* the understanding concerning the Ebro— the less likely alternative, in my view, but the one preferred by some scholars[2]—it looks even less like a defensive act.

In addition, Polybius should probably have given somewhat greater importance to the 'injustices' perpetrated by the Saguntines against the neighbouring Torboletae (Carthaginian subjects) in 221 or 220.[3] Rome may in fact have encouraged the Saguntines to behave aggressively.[4]

The 'defensive' interpretation of Roman thinking rests in large part on certain interpretations of Roman conduct in 219 and 218, especially of Rome's failure to take decisive action to help Saguntum while the eight-month siege was still going on, and of a hypothetical delay which some suppose to have intervened between the arrival at Rome of the news of the city's capture by Hannibal and the decision to declare war against Carthage. The first of these delays does at least seem to be historical, and Livy's method of accounting for it—a Roman embassy sent to Hannibal during the siege to protest—is admittedly dubious.[5] But since the consuls and their armies were engaged in a war in Illyria, it is not surprising that during the summer and autumn of 219 the Senate put off declaring war against Carthage.[6] New wars were not normally initiated until the consuls of a new year entered office.[7]

---

[1] Cf. De Sanctis, *SR* iii. 1.419–20. By itself the Saguntine alliance could do nothing important to restrict Carthaginian power south of the Ebro, as Mommsen (*RG* i[12]. 569) and Holleaux (*RGMH* 136) seem to imply. That the alliance seemed threatening to the Carthaginian command in Spain is clear from Polyb. iii. 15.8–11 (cf. 17.5).

[2] The essential on this problem is in F. W. Walbank, *A Commentary on Polybius*, i. 170–1; the latest is in Hampl, o.c. 428–30, Sumner, o.c. 475–7.

[3] Polyb. iii. 15.8, App. *Iber.* 10.

[4] Cf. B. L. Hallward, *CAH* viii. 28.

[5] Liv. xxi. 6, 9.3–10.3, 11.3, 16.1 (similarly App. *Iber.* 11, Zonar. viii. 21); cf. De Sanctis, *SR* iii. 1.430. The problem presented by this delay is reviewed by Hampl, o.c. 430–4. According to Holleaux (*RGMH* 144 n. 3) and Bengtson (*Grundriss*[2], 94–5), it shows that the Senate was divided about what to do.

[6] L. Aemilius Paullus, and presumably his colleague, returned from Illyria ληγούσης ἤδη τῆς θερείας (Polyb. iii. 19.12). Sumner (*PACA* ix (1966), 9–10) argues that Aemilius is not likely to have triumphed until late in the winter. For a certain senatorial reluctance to take important decisions in the absence of the consuls cf. Liv. xxxi. 2.2.

[7] See J. W. Rich, *Declaring War in the Roman Republic in the Period of Transmarine Expansion* (Brussels, 1976), esp. 39–44.

Many senators, perhaps all of them, saw that war with Carthage was fast approaching; however a new campaign could only be mounted during the same consular year (i.e. before the Ides of March 218) if there were a real emergency, for we are still in a world of seasonal campaigns and militia armies. The way to fight the war was to mount an elaborate double campaign against the Carthaginians in Africa and in Spain, and that could not be done until 218. Senatorial unanimity is of course unlikely, and presumably some members would have preferred to concentrate on expansion in the Po valley; this may have contributed to the delay. Moreover the Senate may well have hesitated for a while in the face of such a decision, for the senior men could remember the exceptional hardships of the first war, and the new Spanish empire had, at least in appearance, strengthened Carthage since 238. On the other hand, Carthage lacked a major fleet of warships and the Senate did not expect Hannibal's astounding march to Italy.[1] However, when the time came to settle policy for the campaigning season of 218, the Senate declared war against Carthage.

The war declaration was sent as soon as the fall of Saguntum became known at Rome, and certainly before Hannibal was known to have taken any further aggressive steps. Polybius' clear statement about this ($\pi\alpha\rho\alpha\chi\rho\hat{\eta}\mu\alpha$) is not to be rejected in favour of any of the fragile chronological hypotheses of modern scholars.[2] The provocation could hardly have been overlooked, and both contemporary Roman diplomacy[3] and much of the later Roman historiography concentrated on the taking of Saguntum as the alleged reason for the war. Fabius Pictor already attributed the war to the attack on Saguntum, as well as to the

---

[1] Hannibal disposed of fifty-seven vessels in Spain (Polyb. iii. 33.14, Liv. xxi. 22.4), Rome put 220 heavy vessels to sea in 218 (Polyb. iii. 41.2, Liv. xxi. 17.3); cf. Holleaux, *RGMH* 154–6. On the unexpectedness of a Carthaginian army's crossing the Alps cf. Polyb. iii. 15.13, 40.2, 49.2, 61.5–9.

[2] Polyb. iii. 20.6–8. There is no agreement as to the month when Saguntum fell; news of the event may have reached Rome quite late in the winter of 219/18 (cf. Astin, o.c. 590–5). It is probable that the war declaration was sent to Carthage after the Ides of March, but even this is not certain (the question turning on whether the Roman ambassadors included the consuls of 219; cf. Sumner, o.c. 24 n. 63, Hampl, o.c. 436). The view of W. Hoffmann (*RhM* xciv (1951), 69–88) and others that the Romans did not declare war until they learned of Hannibal's Ebro-crossing is adequately disposed of by Hampl, o.c. 435–7 (cf. also D. Proctor, *Hannibal's March in History* (Oxford, 1971), 50).

[3] Polyb. iii. 20.6–8, 21.6–8, 29.1.

πλεονεξία and φιλαρχία of Hasdrubal,[1] a version which was obviously intended to serve propagandistic purposes. What these interpretations failed to account for was the very action which gave meaning to the capture of Saguntum, namely Rome's original decision to take the city into alliance.

Polybius asserts roundly that there was no διαβούλιον, debate, in the Senate once the news had arrived.[2] There was probably no lengthy exchange of arguments, and in any case the debate described by Cassius Dio, who purports to recount arguments against the war offered by Fabius Maximus as well as arguments in favour of war, is a palpable fiction. It is betrayed as such both by its content and by the fact that it must have been missing from the only plausible source of an authentic report of such a debate, Fabius Pictor—for otherwise Polybius' statement would have been an absurdity.[3]

We have no reason therefore to think that the Senate was dragged reluctantly into war. By itself the attack on Saguntum does not account for the character or scale of Rome's initial plan of campaign, as represented by the Senate's decision to assign to the consuls the *provinciae* of Africa, with Sicily, and Spain.[4] In particular the large force gathered at Lilybaeum in the summer of 218 for the purpose of invading Africa,[5] while it may have served the needs of defence, certainly had a vigorously aggressive appearance. The Senate's intentions were abruptly upset by Hannibal's success in reaching Italy, and the subsequent course of the war does not give us much help in answering our question. Yet some of Rome's later strategy is suggestive, not only Scipio Africanus' invasion of Africa (which received only weak support from the Senate), but even more the continuous presence of a Roman army in Spain throughout the most difficult period of the war. We do not know what the justifications for this strategy were in the minds of senators, but it serves as some indication that Roman aims were not limited to the mere defence of Italy and the islands.

---

[1] Polyb. iii. 8.1.   [2] iii. 20.1–5.

[3] On the inauthenticity of this debate see Additional Note XVII.

[4] According to Livy (xxi. 17.1) the two *provinciae* which were to be assigned by lot to the consuls of 218 had already been chosen before the news came of Saguntum's fall; Polyb. iii. 40.2 does not contradict this.

[5] Liv. xxi. 17.5 (8,000 legionaries, 600 citizen cavalry, 16,000 allied infantry, 1,800 allied cavalry, 160 *naves longae*); cf. Polyb. iii. 41.2–3.

Modern writers who favour a defensive interpretation of Roman policy usually prefer in this case, as in others, to attribute a wide strategic vision to the Roman Senate, arguing that it must have been impelled to action not by indignation at the fall of Saguntum but by alarm at the growth of the Carthaginian empire in Spain. It is true that when Polybius seeks to explain what he treats as Rome's first positive involvement in Spain (at the time of the understanding with Hasdrubal in 226 or 225), he claims that the Romans saw that Hasdrubal had already established μείζω καὶ φοβερωτέραν . . . δυναστείαν, a greater and more frightening empire.[1] This may accurately describe the thinking which then prevailed in the Senate, or it may merely be a Polybian inference or the justificatory plea of Fabius Pictor. In any case it is not put forward as a full explanation of Rome's conduct towards Carthage between the wars, but only to explain a particular action taken at an unusually dangerous moment in Rome's affairs; and this kind of defensive explanation fails to cover the two most important initiatives of the inter-war years, the seizure of Sardinia and the alliance with Saguntum. A full explanation must include the usual advantages which were expected from successful warfare and the aggressiveness with which these from time to time informed Roman conduct. Spain in particular was probably regarded by Roman senators as a rich prize that could be won in a war against Carthage.[2] Hopes of glory, power, and wealth, together with the habit of armed reaction to foreign opponents, mingled with what were seen as the needs of defence.

THE FIRST MACEDONIAN WAR

It was the necessity of defending themselves, Mommsen, Holleaux, and many others have claimed,[3] which led the Romans to fight the First Macedonian War. In this there is much obvious truth and also some falsehood. In 216 it was in response to a report from the Illyrian Scerdilaidas of Philip V's intention of sailing into Illyrian waters that Rome detached ten ships from the Lilybaeum fleet.[4] The result was that Philip and his 100 little

---

[1] ii. 13.3.   [2] Cf. De Sanctis, *SR* iii. 1.425.
[3] Mommsen, *RG* i[12]. 618, Holleaux, *RGMH* 173.
[4] The background is best described by N. G. L. Hammond, *JRS* lviii (1968), 16–17.

ships precipitously fled[1]—behaviour which can hardly have struck terror into Roman hearts. The hostile intentions with which Philip made his secret treaty with Hannibal in 215 rapidly became known at Rome, and at this point the Romans may well, as Polybius informs us in a chronologically vague statement,[2] have felt fear of Philip's boldness. Philip and Hannibal specified it as one of their aims that Rome would lose its subjects in Illyria.[3] In 215 the Senate might have been apprehensive about possible Macedonian landings in southern Italy; however M. Valerius Laevinus, who was instructed that summer 'non tueri modo Italiae oram sed explorare de Macedonico bello',[4] soon discovered what a negligible naval power Macedon was. Hearing of Philip's aggressions during the summer of 214, he crossed over from Italy. The Macedonian king, defeated, burnt his 120 little *lemboi*, and once again fled.[5] Never throughout the rest of the war did he possess a considerable fleet,[6] and Roman anxiety about his invading Italy presumably declined as this weakness became familiar.[7]

Once Philip had been chased out of Illyrian waters the Senate avoided taking energetic measures beyond the Adriatic, and it could not have behaved otherwise while the war with Carthage remained dangerous. The king turned to a landward strategy. In 213 or 212 he won control over the town of Dimallum, the Parthini, and the Atintani (all within the Roman 'protectorate') and regained access to the Adriatic by capturing Lissus. Even under this provocation Laevinus' forces remained quite passive. From 210 to 206 Rome no longer kept a legion of citizen troops in Greece.[8] By the terms of the Peace of Phoenice (205) Philip was allowed to retain control of the Atintani,[9] for the Senate was of course quite willing to surrender territory temporarily when occasion demanded.

---

[1] Polyb. v. 110.8–11.
[2] v. 105.8.
[3] Polyb. vii. 9.13.
[4] Liv. xxiii. 38.9.
[5] On the Illyrian campaign of 214: Liv. xxiv. 40, Plu. *Arat.* 51, Zonar. ix. 4.
[6] Cf. Holleaux, *RGMH* 159 n. 2.
[7] Philip's attempt to build a sizable fleet in 207 (Liv. xxviii. 8.14) does not seem to have had much result (Holleaux, *RGMH* 246 n. 2).
[8] Liv. xxvi. 28.9, cf. xxvii. 22.10, 36.12–13, xxviii. 10.10–16. Liv. xxvii. 7.15 is evidently mistaken. A somewhat different view was taken by De Sanctis, *SR* iii. 2.429.
[9] Liv. xxix. 12.13.

But there is another side to Roman policy. It was the Romans who took the initiative in making the famous alliance with the Aetolian League in 212 or 211.[1] A Roman fleet, apparently of fifty ships, was kept in Greece throughout the war.[2] An opportunity to make peace with Philip in 208 was refused.[3] After two years of inactivity (207–206), the Senate dispatched considerable reinforcements, undoubtedly intending, until it learned that the Aetolians had already made peace with Philip, to resume the fighting.[4]

The main purpose of Roman policy may have been to keep Philip occupied with difficulties in Greece, or simply to cause harm to an obviously hostile power; another purpose may have been to establish the beginning of Roman power in Greece, though this was done in an inept and intermittent fashion. In the years 211–208, however, at least five Greek cities were sacked by Roman forces,[5] and such political clumsiness suggests that the Roman commanders and their armies were strongly interested in booty. The provision concerning booty in the treaty with the Aetolians shows that this aspect of the war was explicitly brought to the attention of the Senate. The conclusion must be that defensive thinking fails to account for all of Rome's conduct in the war.

The Peace of Phoenice is in one respect hard to reconcile with the theory of a defensive Roman foreign policy. The *adscripti* of the treaty on the Roman side may include some apocryphal additions,[6] but if—as seems likely—not only Attalus and the Illyrian Pleuratus (son of Scerdilaidas), but Nabis, King of Sparta, and the peoples of Elis and Messenia were included and thus implicitly recognized by both sides as friends of Rome, we have yet another case where Rome created conditions which led

---

[1] Roman initiative: Holleaux, *RGMH* 201 n. 5, confirmed by certain Latinisms in the epigraphical text (on which see R. G. Hopital, *RHDFE* ser. 4, xlii (1964), 29, J. and L. Robert, *REG* lxxviii (1965), 114–15).

[2] The size of this fleet is reduced without adequate reason by P. A. Brunt, *Italian Manpower*, 666.

[3] App. *Mac.* 3; cf. Dio fr. 57.58–9. Not in Livy.

[4] On the sequence of events: Liv. xxix. 12.1–4. P. Sempronius Tuditanus was sent with a force of 10,000 infantry, 1,000 cavalry, and thirty-five ships.

[5] Holleaux, *RGMH* 231–2. Cf. Liv. xxvii. 31.1: 'P. Sulpicius . . . adpulit inter Sicyonem et Corinthum agrumque nobilissimae fertilitatis effuse vastavit.'

[6] Liv. xxix. 12.14: Ilium, Attalus, Pleuratus, Nabis, Elis, Messenia, Athens. For bibliography of the debate on the authenticity of this list: W. Dahlheim, *Struktur und Entwicklung*, 210 n. 75, H. H. Schmitt, *Die Staatsverträge des Altertums*, iii. 283–4.

almost inevitably to an appeal for military help. Here, though Holleaux denied it, there is the sketch (*ébauche*) of a forward policy in the Greek world.[1]

SPAIN: BEGINNINGS

A larger enterprise than the First Macedonian War was the Roman occupation of Spain, which employed two legions throughout the Hannibalic War and four in the years 210–206.[2] We have virtually no information about the rationale behind this policy,[3] and even the important decision made in 211, after the defeat and death of the Scipios, to send major reinforcements to Spain,[4] provokes little useful comment in the sources.[5] Whatever the motives were which led to the sending of the expeditionary force in 218, it could be argued after Hannibal's invasion of Italy that the destruction of the Carthaginian empire in Spain would be a good defensive strategy. Yet this empire was a valuable possession and may well have been regarded as worth fighting for. Some Romans at least, above all Scipio Africanus, probably had notions about Spain that went beyond defence.[6] After 201, with the naval power of Carthage broken forever and its other military potential severely curbed, there was no danger that it would once again use Spain as a means to make war against Rome, and the Senate cannot have thought otherwise.[7] If the Romans had

---

[1] Cf. J. P. V. D. Balsdon, *JRS* xliv (1954), 33, E. Will, *Histoire politique*, ii. 82.

[2] De Sanctis, *SR* iii. 2.633.

[3] Polybius appears to offer an informative comment in iii. 97.1–3, where the Senate is said to regard it as essential to keep up the war in Spain: ... πάνυ γὰρ ἠγωνίων μὴ κρατήσαντες Καρχηδόνιοι τῶν τόπων ἐκείνων καὶ περιποιησάμενοι χορηγίας ἀφθόνους καὶ χεῖρας ἀντιποιήσωνται μὲν τῆς θαλάττης ὁλοσχερέστερον, συνεπιθῶνται δὲ τοῖς κατὰ τὴν Ἰταλίαν, στρατόπεδα πέμποντες καὶ χρήματα τοῖς περὶ τὸν Ἀννίβαν. But this analysis seems to be only an anachronistic reconstruction, since Carthage already had a substantial province in Spain. It seems that once having conceived the intention of contesting Carthaginian power in Spain, the Senate was reluctant to change its mind. Yet it may well be true that in 217 the Senate saw the Spanish campaign mainly as a way of defending Italy (this naturally is the interpretation offered by Frank, *Roman Imperialism*, 129; cf. Mommsen, *RG* i¹². 618).

[4] Liv. xxvi. 17.1, 19.10, App. *Iber.* 17,18.

[5] Appian does say (*Iber.* 17–18) that at this point the Romans feared a further invasion from Spain into Italy, but this is probably nothing more than a plausible inference. Scipio Africanus' speech in Liv. xxvi. 41.3–25 is mainly inauthentic (contrast Polyb. x. 6.1–6).

[6] As is recognized by H. H. Scullard (*HRW*³ 212), a proponent of 'defensive imperialism'.

[7] Mommsen (*RG* i¹². 684) and some others notwithstanding.

wanted nothing from Spain but security for their pre-existing possessions, they could have relied on their vast military superiority over Carthage, on the treaty of 201 and on the vigilance of their allies. And if security had been the only benefit of continued Roman occupation, legionary service would soon have become extremely unpopular. What made Spain worth holding on to and securing was above all—to the Romans as to the Carthaginians—its wealth.

The Spanish wars that began in 197, though conducted on the Roman side with varying degrees of energy, took the Romans into one new territory after another. In 195, with reinforcements made easier by successes in other theatres,[1] they entered the land of the Celtiberians (the sustained attack, however, did not begin until more than a decade later).[2] In 193 the conflict with the Lusitanians began, and in the same year we find one praetor fighting the Oretani, well to the north of the River Baetis, and another defeating peoples from the centre (Carpetani, Vettones) and the north (Vaccaei) at Toletum.[3] After an unadventurous period during the eastern wars of 191–188 (there may have been no campaigning at all in the last of these years), Roman armies settled down to the conquest of the Celtiberians, Lusitanians, and Vaccaei. The Senate and the armies persevered with the task year by year, in spite of some occasional reluctance among the soldiers,[4] until a formal peace could be made with the Celtiberians (178) and their final attempt at rebellion defeated (175).

Livy does not attempt to explain why Rome fought in Spain, though by implication he attempts to put some of the responsibility on the Spaniards.[5] There is very little evidence about the views contemporary Romans took of these wars.[6] Perhaps

---

[1] Cf. De Sanctis, *SR* iv. 1.447.

[2] Liv. xxxiv. 19. That Cato also campaigned at Numantia is known from Gell. *NA* xvi. 1.3 (cf. De Sanctis, iv. 1.452) and confirmed by excavation (A. Schulten, *Numantia*, iv (Munich, 1929), 33–40).

[3] Oretani: Liv. xxxv. 7.7. Vettones, Vaccaei: Liv. xxxv. 7.8; Toletum was the capital of the Carpetani. Further campaigns were fought in 192 against Oretani, Carpetani, Vettones (Liv. xxxv. 22.5–8). These significant events are dealt with very briefly by Livy.

[4] Cf. Liv. xxxix. 38.9, Brunt, *Italian Manpower*, 662 n. 2.

[5] On the Celtiberians cf. Liv. xxxiv. 10.1, 17.4, 19.1–7. On the Lusitanians: Liv. xxxv. 1.5. All these allegations may be true.

[6] If Plu. *Cat. Mai.* 10.3–5 derives from a speech of Cato's (as conjectured by Malcovati, *ORF*³ p. 25), he emphasized the extent of his conquests and the quantity of booty the soldiers had obtained.

they regarded them as essential for the strengthening of Rome's hold on its existing possessions in Spain.[1] However the free Spaniards are never claimed, even by the Roman sources, to have invaded Roman territory (as it was in 197) after the defeat of the Lusitanians in 193 and another Lusitanian incursion in far western Ulterior in 186.[2] There is no reason to leave out of the explanation the normal advantages of successful warfare. In the years 195–175 at least eight triumphs were celebrated from Spain and booty was accumulated in enormous quantities.[3] No major dispute arose at Rome about the continuation of the fighting in Spain (though there were disputes about fighting the Second Macedonian War); virtually everyone agreed that a war to conquer a large new segment of Spain was worthwhile.

NORTHERN ITALY FROM 201

In the year in which they effectively revealed their intention of holding on to their Spanish possessions in spite of the peace with Carthage, the Romans began their new onslaught on the Gallic peoples of the Po valley. The Boii and Insubres, traditional enemies of Rome, had supported Hannibal, as had some Ligurians, and in the Roman view deserved to suffer revenge. A certain Hamilcar maintained an insignificant but annoying

---

[1] So De Sanctis, SR iv. 1.408. But on this A. Schulten, CAH viii. 307, is better: the Carthaginians had shown (before Hamilcar's time) that it was possible to maintain a Spanish empire without advancing further and further inland.

[2] The town of Lyco in Bastetanis where L. Aemilius Paullus was defeated by the Lusitanians in 190 (Liv. xxxvii. 46.7) was probably outside Rome's established possessions (in spite of De Sanctis, SR iv. 1.456–7), for otherwise Livy would probably have referred to the provocation committed by the Lusitanians (and note that the Roman survivors returned 'magnis itineribus in agrum pacatum', § 8). In early 186 Celtiberians and Lusitanians were reported to have pillaged what are vaguely described as sociorum agri (Liv. xxxix. 7.7), and later in the year the army of C. Atinius, governor of Ulterior, defeated Lusitanians in agro Hastensi and captured Hasta itself from them; the town lay only a few kilometres to the east of the mouth of the river Baetis. We know from ILLRP 514 that Aemilius Paullus had freed some slaves of the Hastenses, presumably as a reward for their loyalty during a rebellion of the latter; and the 186 incident may in reality have been another rebellion within the province. Another exception to the general statement in the text may perhaps be the fighting with the Celtiberians in agro Ausetano in 184 (Liv. xxxix. 56.1), but it is unclear precisely where the territory of the Ausetani lay (near the Ebro, ibid.; cf. xxi. 6.8, xxvi. 17.2–4) and when they first came under Roman power (perhaps only in 195, cf. xxxiv. 20.1).

[3] Cf. Schulten, CAH viii. 306–14.

Carthaginian presence in the region until 200 or perhaps even 197. Furthermore, the security of the colonies of Placentia and Cremona, resettled in 206, required a serious demonstration of military strength, a need which was confirmed by the sack of Placentia and the attack on Cremona in 200. However what followed was not a demonstration, but a sustained attack, which was carried out in annual campaigns down to 190; and in the case of the Boii the conquest was one of unusual harshness. A recent writer assures us that in these wars the Romans had no policy of conquest.[1] Was it then felt by the Romans to be merely a policy of self-defence? The campaign against the Boii is represented by Livy as a response to 'incursiones in agros sociorum', a questionable claim since the fighting began in Boian territory.[2] Very little progress was made before 197, and Polybius may perhaps offer a genuine insight into the Roman attitude when he attributes the assignments given to the consuls of that year to τὸν ἀπὸ τῶν Κελτῶν φόβον.[3] Yet in that year the war was fought entirely on Gallic soil, as it was in the following years. The ejection of the Boii from their country, or at least from the most valuable part of it, in 190,[4] may have been partly defensive in intent, but its wholesale character suggests that expropriation itself was part of the aim. As in the Spanish wars of 196–175, the essence of the Gallic wars is that Rome, in the face of some real but not very formidable dangers to its outlying possessions, reacted with such force that not only were these possessions secured but extensive and valuable new ones were acquired.

---

[1] U. Schlag, *Regnum in Senatu* (Stuttgart, 1968), 51. Cf. De Sanctis, *SR* iv. 1.407, who declares correctly that in the long term Italy could only be safe if it controlled the Po valley, but thereby implies without sufficient justification that we know that this was the thinking that led Rome to the wars of 201–190 (similarly H. H. Scullard, *Roman Politics*, 89–90).

[2] Liv. xxxi. 2.5–6. The *socii* are not specified, but an incursion is perfectly possible (and the *tumultus* is a circumstantial detail). On the topography see J. Briscoe's n. on § 6.

[3] xviii. 11.2.

[4] Liv. xxxvi. 39.3 ('P. Cornelius consul . . . agri parte fere dimidia eos multavit, quo si vellet populus Romanus colonias mittere posset'), xxxvii. 2.5. Strabo (v. 213, 216) refers briefly to their expulsion as if it had been complete (cf. Polyb. ii. 35.4, Plin. *NH* iii. 116). That is probably too sweeping, but this part of Cisalpine Gaul, unlike others, shows no Celtic traces in its Latin nomenclature. See further E. A. Arslan, *Notizie dal Chiostro del Monastero Maggiore* vii–x (1971–4), 47. Scullard is egregious: the Boii 'ceded half their territory and gradually withdrew to Bohemia or else were absorbed by the spread of Roman civilization' (*HRW*³ 283).

THE SECOND MACEDONIAN WAR

Between the summers of 201 and 200, with the hostilities in Africa over, the Senate made and put into effect the decision to begin a new war against Philip V. Here we are concerned only with contemporary Roman perceptions and motives, so that many of the historical problems concerning the start of the Second Macedonian War can be left aside. The analysis of Roman behaviour that has been most influential is that of Holleaux, according to whom the Senate conceived such a fear of the new threat offered by the alliance between Philip and Antiochus III that it resolved to make preventive war against the former.[1] Absent from senatorial minds was any freely formed notion of seizing the benefits of military success. So just have interpretations of this kind seemed that some have even invoked the opening of the war against Philip as evidence that Roman foreign policy *in general* was defensive in the middle Republic.[2]

The attraction of Holleaux's theory is that it offers a specific explanation for a war-decision that is supposed to be at variance with Rome's past policies east of the Adriatic. Rome had allegedly fought the first war against Philip in a purely defensive spirit, and the Senate showed its continued lack of concern in 202 by refusing the Aetolian offer of a new alliance. But in 201 Philip became a more imposing figure because of his naval successes in the Aegean, and during the summer his (originally secret) alliance with Antiochus of the winter 203/2, an alliance with menacing implications for Rome, was reported and made much of to the Senate by the envoys of Attalus and Rhodes. The news drastically reversed senatorial policy, producing a resolve to make war against Philip as soon as it could be arranged. This fear of the alliance was deluded, as most would admit, since the kings showed no interest at this time in opening hostilities against Rome. None the less, fear moved the Senate to act. When the war was over, it can be added, Rome retained no extra territory east

---

[1] *RGMH*, esp. 276–331; cf. also *REA* xxii (1920), 77–96 [→Bibl.], *CAH* viii. 149–66 [→ Bibl.]. The thesis was developed further by G. T. Griffith, *CHJ* v (1935), 1–14, A. H. McDonald–F. W. Walbank, *JRS* xxvii (1937), 180–207. Other followers of Holleaux' line are referred to by Dahlheim, *Struktur und Entwicklung*, 240. Add Scullard, *Roman Politics*, 90–2.

[2] E.g. among recent scholars R. Schottlaender, *Römisches Gesellschaftsdenken* (Weimar, 1969), 98–9, R. Werner in *ANRW* i. 1.542.

of the Adriatic, satisfying itself with the destruction of Philip's Greek empire and his navy (except for six vessels).

The weaknesses of this theory are by now familiar to scholars.[1] No source has anything to say about Roman fear of Antiochus or of Philip's alliance with him, even though the Roman tradition might have been expected to emphasize any threats that the two kings offered.[2] Nor is there really any evidence of an abrupt alteration in Roman policy, since the Senate's blunt refusal of the Aetolian offer of alliance in 202[3] is easy to understand after the Aetolians' behaviour in 206,[4] and thus fails to show that the Senate had set itself against fighting in Greece. It is not even certain that it was the Pergamene Rhodian envoys who informed the Senate of the kings' alliance.[5] More important, Rome took no defensive measures in the Adriatic of the kind that might suggest some perception of immediate danger.[6]

Livy and some other sources do attribute the war in part to Rome's fear of Philip, and this view has been developed by some recent writers. But Livy's account is weak. The interpretation appears in sections drawn from an annalistic source. On both occasions it is stated somewhat indirectly: first, when M. Valerius Laevinus was sent to Greek waters late in 201, the legate M. Aurelius gave him a disturbing report of Philip's activities, and

---

[1] For important critiques by scholars of various persuasions cf. J. Balsdon, *JRS* xliv (1954), 30–42, E. Will, *Histoire politique*, ii. 103–28, J. Briscoe, *A Commentary on Livy, Books XXXI–XXXIII*, 36–47.

[2] In App. *Mac.* 4 (τήνδε τὴν δόξαν [concerning the alliance] ἐκταράσσουσαν ἅπαντας Ῥόδιοι μὲν Ῥωμαίοις ἐμήνυσαν . . .) ἅπαντας obviously refers to the Greeks. D. Magie (*JRS* xxix (1939), 32–44) argued that the alliance was actually a contemporary fabrication by the Rhodians (and for further bibliography on this question see H. H. Schmitt, *Die Staatsverträge des Altertums*, iii. 290–1). R. M. Errington's theory (*Athenaeum* xlix (1971), 336–54) that the fabrication was not even contemporary seems to depart too far from the evidence.

[3] App. *Mac.* 4 sets the Aetolian embassy to Rome *after* the Pergamene–Rhodian embassy; this is usually rejected, but could be correct. Some have denied that the Aetolians sent an embassy at all (see Briscoe on Liv. xxxi. 29.4, the other piece of evidence).

[4] Liv. (P.) xxxi. 29.4, 31.18–20 (cf. xxxi. 1.8) show Roman feelings; cf. E. Bickermann, *RPh* lxi (1935), 161–2, Balsdon, o.c. 37. A. H. McDonald exaggerates in claiming (o.c. 185) that in 200 Rome 'made most urgent attempts to repair the breach with the Aetolians.' First they sought Aetolian assistance indirectly, it seems (Liv. (P.) xxxi. 28.3), then at the Panaetolicum in a most disdainful speech (31.18–20). Polyb. xvi. 27.4 tells us little (Holleaux, *RGMH* 294 n. 1, notwithstanding).

[5] So App. *Mac.* 4 (not Polybian: F. W. Walbank on Polyb. xv. 20); but Justin xxx. 2.8 has a different story, which Holleaux, *RGMH* 72 n. 2, failed to discredit.

[6] E. Badian, *Foreign Clientelae*, 58.

allegedly asserted that the latter might turn into another Pyrrhus, a report which he was told to send to Rome.[1] Soon after it arrived, it seems, the Senate decided definitely for war.[2] Yet the analysis attributed to M. Aurelius is both vague and manifestly exaggerated, and the comparison with Pyrrhus would have been far-fetched; nor can there have been any documentary basis for this part of the annalistic account. Livy or a source of his is attempting to justify Rome's actions by making Philip into a serious threat, and in the absence of any circumstantial evidence that this was the Roman feeling in 201/0, we must reject the attempt. The interpretation recurs in the speech which the consul P. Sulpicius Galba made in order to persuade the *comitia* to reverse its initial vote against the war, a speech which occupies the central position in Livy's account of the outbreak of the war. It consists entirely of elaborations of the argument that Rome must choose between fighting Philip in Macedon or in Italy.[3] This oration has no claim whatsoever to authenticity,[4] though it may of course accidentally happen to reproduce the arguments Sulpicius really used. The later sources which attribute the war to Rome's fear of Philip add nothing helpful.[5]

Restless and aggressive, Philip had indeed extended his power in the Propontis and the Aegean during 202 and 201;[6] but the battle of Chios, in which the Rhodian and Pergamene fleets deprived him of twenty-six of his fifty-three cataphracts and nearly half his light vessels, a battle perversely described by some historians as a 'strategic' victory for the king, put an end to any temporary possibility there had been that he might become a naval power outside the Aegean.[7] In terms of casualties, it was the

---

[1] Liv. xxxi. 3.4–6, cf. 5.5.

[2] xxxi. 5.7–9.

[3] xxxi. 7.

[4] As is recognized even by H. E. Stier, *Roms Aufstieg zur Weltmacht und die griechische Welt* (Cologne–Opladen, 1957), 103.

[5] Justin xxx. 30.2, Zonar. ix. 15 (also mentioning Roman annoyance ἐφ'οἷς ἐδεδράκει).

[6] Cf. Will, *Histoire politique*, ii. 103–8.

[7] The battle of Chios: Polyb. xvi. 2–9, xviii. 2.2. Philip's losses: xvi. 2.9, xvi. 7 (Attalus lost five decked ships, Rhodes three). Polybius' source(s) may well have been Rhodian (cf. Walbank on xvi. 2–9), but he roundly criticizes the patriotic distortions of the Rhodian historians (xvi. 14–20), and it is very improbable that his verdict on the battle is seriously incorrect (Walbank, l.c., unfortunately fails to specify which of Polybius' details he finds inconsistent with this verdict). *OGIS* 283 (with M. Holleaux, *REG* xi (1898), 251–8 [→ Bibl.]) shows that Attalus claimed victory; cf. M. Segre in L. Robert, *Hellenica* v

worst defeat he had suffered in his twenty years' reign.[1] Not long afterwards, during the early winter of 201/0, the king succeeded in getting himself shut into Bargylia on the Carian coast, whence he was unable to escape for several months.[2] It is not likely that he terrified, or even worried, the Roman Senate from that position. Its information may admittedly have been defective. Senatorial opinion may have hardened to an important extent after the Pergamene–Rhodian embassies, if members lacked reliable news about the Aegean situation that resulted from the battle of Chios. But as an over-all explanation of the Roman decision to go to war, fear of Philip is utterly inadequate (and it was because of this that Holleaux devised his own more subtle and even more erroneous—theory[3]). Nor is this interpretation helped by the claim that Illyria was really the centre of Rome's anxieties about Philip.[4] For this the evidence is altogether insufficient.[5] Still less convincing is the claim that only certain leading senators were frightened by Philip and so believed that a pre-emptive war against him was necessary.[6] Indeed few people are less likely to have overestimated Philip's power than Sulpicius and Valerius.

What then do we know about Roman feelings toward Philip V in 201 and 200? Was it an 'unreasonable panic' that determined Rome's actions?[7] The lack of Polybius severely handicaps us. His

(Paris, 1948), 116–20. 'Strategic': Griffith, o.c. 8 etc. The battle of Chios seems less decisive to those who date it *before* the battle of Lade; but to me it seems clear that the order was Lade–Chios, above all because Polybius wrote in xvi. 10.1 that Attalus 'had not yet arrived on the scene' (μηδέπω συμμεμιχέναι) after the battle of Lade (cf. Briscoe, o.c. 37 n. 4; and in favour of this chronology see also R. M. Berthold, *Historia* xxiv (1975), 150–63).

[1] Polyb. xvi. 8.6.

[2] Polyb. xvi. 24 (Philip shut up in Bargylia from November or December onwards—on the chronology see Walbank ad loc.—and extremely worried in consequence). Precisely when he got out is hard to determine, but probably not until the spring (cf. Walbank, *Philip V of Macedon* (Cambridge, 1940), 309).

[3] *RGMH* 297–303.

[4] This theory is advocated by E. Badian, *Foreign Clientelae*, 61–6 (cf. R. M. Errington, *The Dawn of Empire* (London, 1972), 131–2).

[5] Philip had apparently acquired some additional territory in Illyria soon after the Peace of Phoenice (Polyb. xviii. 1.14), but the territory in question was probably small and outside Roman possessions (cf. Walbank on xviii. 1.14 and 47.12). It is fatal to the 'Illyrian' theory that no Roman complaints were uttered concerning this region in 200 (Will, *Histoire politique*, ii. 120).

[6] So Briscoe, o.c. 45.

[7] Cf. Walbank, *Philip V of Macedon*, 127.

analysis probably gave due prominence to the Roman ἔννοια of world-conquest,[1] a view which Livy naturally rejected. Most modern historians have paid as little attention as Livy did to the real emotions and opinions of senators in 201/0. Bitter resentment resulted from Philip's alliance with Hannibal, and it will have been all the stronger if it was believed, as it probably was, that the king had sent mercenary troops to Carthage in the last months of the Hannibalic War.[2] Philip's retention of power over the Atintani under the Phoenice treaty will have made a minor contribution to this hostility. The senators' hatred must have been known to Philip, and it was for this reason that he expected that he might be attacked as soon as the war with Carthage was finished.[3]

Senators also undoubtedly felt obligations to the allies who asked them for help. When Polybius wrote (in the context of 196) that the Romans had undertaken the war 'for the sake of the freedom of the Greeks', that is to say their independence from Philip, he was presumably alluding to these appeals.[4] To add yet another investigation of the number of Greek embassies and the exact status of their appeals is not my purpose. It is enough to say, first, that the embassies from Attalus and Rhodes certainly contributed largely to the Senate's warlike attitude towards Philip in 201,[5] so that the Senate's mission to the East went with

---

[1] P. Pédech, *La Méthode historique de Polybe*, 118–19; cf. the interesting speculations of E. J. Bickerman, *CPh* xl (1945), 147. But in seeking Polybius' views neither of these scholars gives enough weight to xviii. 46.14 (quoted below).

[2] Liv. xxx. 26.1–4, 40.6, 42.1–10. This has long been regarded as an annalistic fiction, but like Balsdon (*JRS* xliv (1954), 34) I find the details of the story too circumstantial to suppose that these troops were never in Africa at all.

[3] As Polyb. xvi. 24.2–3 implies (the sense is plain in spite of the textual problem; Walbank rather underestimates the force of φοβούμενος . . : τοὺς Ῥωμαίους). Roman hatred: this, rather than personal uncouthness, may have caused the rudeness M. Aemilius Lepidus showed towards Philip at Abydos (xvi. 34.5–6).

[4] xviii. 46.14: θαυμαστὸν γὰρ ἦν καὶ τὸ Ῥωμαίους ἐπὶ ταύτης γενέσθαι τῆς προαιρέσεως καὶ τὸν ἡγούμενον αὐτῶν Τίτον, ὥστε πᾶσαν ὑπομεῖναι δαπάνην καὶ πάντα κίνδυνον χάριν τῆς τῶν Ἑλλήνων ἐλευθερίας. This distorted judgement and indeed the whole chapter reflect the profound emotions that the Isthmian declaration of 196 could raise among pro-Roman Greeks some fifty years after the event, when it looked—somewhat deceptively—like *the* great lost opportunity.

[5] Liv. xxxi. 2.2–4: 'his legationibus responsum est curae eam rem senatui fore; consultatio de Macedonico bello integra ad consules, qui tunc in provinciis erant, reiecta est [standard procedure in the circumstances].' Envoys were sent to the king of Egypt 'ut . . . peterent ut, si coacti iniuriis bellum adversus Philippum suscepissent . . .' When the consul P. Aelius returned, the Senate voted that he should appoint an officer with

the intention of preparing the way for war;[1] and, second, that the Athenian embassy at the beginning of the new consular year may have added something to senatorial resolve.[2] Sulpicius' proposal to the assembly was to declare war 'ob iniurias armaque inlata sociis populi Romani'.[3] The wrongs allegedly suffered by Attalus underlay one of the Roman embassy's two demands to Philip's general Nicanor outside Athens; and both Attalus and Rhodes were cited to Philip himself at Abydos;[4] Roman *fides* was at stake, particularly in the case of Attalus.

But where did these obligations come from? Rome had freely assumed them, even though they were almost certain to lead to new hostilities. This was the Roman tradition. For Rome the time had come to intrude into the affairs of the Greek world, as is vividly shown by the Roman envoys' telling Nicanor, and later Philip himself, that Rome forbade the latter to make war on 'any Greek'.[5] This made war between Rome and Philip entirely inevitable. In the background we should see the imperialistic spirit which caused Scipio Africanus and others in 202 to think of further conquests.[6] The resounding defeat of Carthage made war with Philip possible, and indeed a new outlet was now needed, for a certain section of the aristocracy, including the consul

imperium to take the Sicilian fleet across to Macedonia (3.1–3). The election as consul for 200 of P. Sulpicius, a man highly qualified to fight against Macedon, followed late in the year; at the start of the new year (shortly after Id. Mart. in Roman terms) religious preparations for the war were carried out. On Attalus and Rhodes as Roman allies cf. Dahlheim, *Struktur und Entwicklung*, 244–6, 254–5. I agree with him that the intervention on behalf of allies without *foedera* represents a significant extension of Roman policy (o.c. 252–4).

[1] Certainly not, as T. Frank claimed (*Roman Imperialism*, 147), 'to work for peace in the Aegean' (similarly Badian, *Foreign Clientelae*, 67, Werner, o.c. 545–7). Here is a fundamental misunderstanding.

[2] Liv. xxxi. 5.5–9 (in my view this was the first Athenian embassy, in spite of 1.10; it was also quite probably the embassy of Cephisodorus referred to by Paus. i. 36.6 and evidently regarded by the Athenians as successful). On the status of the Athenians at Rome cf. Briscoe's n. on 5.8.

[3] Liv. xxxi. 6.1.

[4] Polyb. xvi. 27.2–3, 34.3–4. The exact character of the arbitration proposed is unclear (cf. Walbank on xvi. 27.2), but the demand for arbitration rather than definite compensation suggests that the Senate privately took quite a detached view of Attalus' claims.

[5] Polyb. xvi. 27.2, 34.3–5. It is remarkable that Walbank (on xvi. 27.2–3) can call this demand 'not excessive'; as he wrote in *Philip V of Macedon* (131–2), the Senate was by this time intent not on concessions, but on war.

[6] Above, pp. 108, 116. On the aristocratic desire for glory as a reason for the war of 200 cf. T. A. Dorey, *AJPh* lxxx (1959), 289–91.

Sulpicius, was entitled to the opportunities of war.[1] No doubt there were divergent opinions in the Senate, but beyond the obvious fact that Sulpicius was a vigorous militant over the issue, we cannot hope to discover much. There is in any case no sign of a major dispute. In the *comitia* war was initially rejected,[2] and subsidiary though the comitial vote was, it is important to know why it was reversed. Livy supplies only a fictional speech as explanation. Perhaps it was a matter of lobbying. Most likely it was a timely concession to Scipio's veterans (and thus to the man himself) : none of them need serve in Sulpicius' campaign except as a volunteer.[3]

THE WAR AGAINST NABIS

We should briefly consider Rome's war against King Nabis of Sparta in 195. Livy says at one point that the Senate allowed Flamininus to determine what to do about Nabis, at another that it decreed war against the king.[4] Though the latter was probably the Polybian version, the former is on balance more likely to be correct.[5] But what were the thoughts which led the Senate to permit (or instigate) this war and Flamininus to fight it? A Greek 'tyrant' with radical, left-wing policies, who had changed sides twice since the Peace of Phoenice, was not likely to be popular in the Senate. The ten-man commission which had supervised the settlement in Greece, returning to Rome early in 195, allegedly reported to the Senate that Nabis was going to become the dominant power in Greece and would put an end to Greek freedom; thus Livy in an 'annalistic' passage.[6] In analysing the

---

[1] Cf. Briscoe, *Commentary*, 46, arguing that Sulpicius and his friends 'wanted a command to counterbalance [Scipio's] influence'; also Will, *Histoire politique*, ii. 124 (though 'existence *naissante* d'un milieu militaire' is wrong).

[2] Liv. xxxi. 6.3–6 (it would be very interesting to know how much truth there is in 'ab omnibus ferme centuriis'; not complete truth anyway—cf. Briscoe's n. on § 3). The war was never popular: xxxi. 13.2–4, xxxiii. 25.6.

[3] Liv. xxxi. 8.5–6, 14.2 (cf. xxxii. 3.3). Livy will naturally not have been willing to make this the determining factor in the war-decision.

[4] Liv. xxxiii. 45.3–4 ('cum diu disceptatum esset utrum satis iam causae videretur cur decerneretur bellum, an permitterent T. Quinctio, quod ad Nabim Lacedaemonium attineret, faceret quod e republica censeret esse, permiserunt . . .'), xxxiv. 22.5. The former version is in Justin xxxi. 1.6.

[5] It is the more complicated and less expectable version. Cf. H. Nissen, *Kritische Untersuchungen*, 151, 157, A. Aymard, *Les Premiers Rapports de Rome et de la confédération achaïenne* (Bordeaux, 1938), 198–202.

[6] xxxiii. 44.8–9 (on the exaggeration see Aymard, o.c. 198). Cf. also Zonar. ix. 18.

Senate's thinking, most modern scholars simply adapt this passage, which has no claim to derive from a real report of what was said to the Senate, to their own presuppositions.[1] The argument that it was really for the sake of Argive freedom (and perhaps of Spartan freedom) that Rome fought the war (thus it was merely a consequence of the Isthmian declaration of 196) was naturally offered by Flamininus himself to Greek audiences. For the new Achaean allies this had particular appeal.[3] But the Roman commander did not tell the whole story. The war was probably Flamininus' decision (thus the ten *legati* reported nothing which made the Senate think war was necessary). He was certainly committed to Greek freedom as a policy, but when he found that it might take a long siege to defeat Nabis, he settled for a peace which freed Argos but left the king in power at Sparta. Polybius accounts for this by saying that Flamininus feared that during the siege Greece might be assigned to a successor, so that he would lose the credit for the victory.[4] An element missing from modern explanations of the war is here: Flamininus' desire to gain yet greater *gloria*.[5] It must be added that financially the campaign was eminently satisfactory from the Roman point of view: Nabis' domain was thoroughly plundered,[6] and an 'indemnity' of 500 talents (100 to be paid immediately) was imposed on him.

THE SYRIAN–AETOLIAN WAR

A complex diplomatic history precedes the Roman war against Antiochus III and the Aetolians which began in 191. My sole

[1] Thus, e.g., Scullard, *Roman Politics*, 114: 'In Greece also there were troubles, arising from the ambitious designs of Nabis, tyrant of Sparta [not all the ambition was in Nabis]. If he was allowed free play . . . he might even look towards Antiochus [this is derived from xxxi. 43.6, but goes beyond Livy]. To check him would increase stability in Greece [assumed to be the Roman aim] and also afford a legitimate reason for maintaining Roman troops there for another year, which some considered desirable on account of Antiochus . . .' Some of this is probably correct, but all of it is speculation.

[2] Liv. (P.) xxxiv. 22.7–13, 32.1–13. There were some subordinate accusations against Nabis: 32.14–20.

[3] Cf. Walbank, *Philip V of Macedon*, 187.

[4] Liv. (P.) xxxiv. 33.14; cf. Plu. *Flam.* 13. The fear was rational, for he had just learned from the envoy P. Villius Tappulus that Antiochus had returned to Europe with greater forces than before (33.12), which was likely to stir the Senate to action. Aymard, o.c. 235–7, attempts to evade Polybius' explanation, and then substitutes his own (238–47).

[5] Cf. A. Passerini, *Athenaeum* x (1932), 329–30.

[6] Liv. (P.) xxxiv. 28.12, 34.6.

purpose is, once again, to determine the significance of defensive thinking in Rome's war-decision. Defence was beyond doubt primary, though it was a new accretion to the empire that needed defending. The Senate finally decided to make war against Antiochus and his allies when the king invaded a part of Greece, Demetrias, which it had directly regulated.[1] Previously the Senate had expected and prepared for war, but had not resolved to wage it.[2] In name Demetrias was free, but according to the Roman view it was expected to show gratitude and obedience; and clearly any landing by Antiochus in continental European Greece, Thrace apart, would have been held to be an incursion into an area of Roman hegemony.[3] No doubt the Senate felt the war to be in defence of Roman interests, in spite of the fact that Roman troops had returned to Greece before Antiochus landed there.[4]

Already in 196 the Senate gave some thought to the precautions that might be taken against Antiochus on the Greek mainland.[5] His successes in western Asia Minor in 197, his crossing into Thrace in 196, and his further campaigns there in 195 and (probably) 194 presumably added to Roman concern. His empire and military resources were quite formidable, much greater than Philip V's had been. Whenever Antiochus' attitude was tested, it appeared to be unyielding. He persistently rejected the Roman claim to protect certain Greek cities. The demands made in 196 to his envoys Hegesianax and Lysias by the ten-member commission in Greece—that the king must not go to war with any autonomous city in Asia, that he must evacuate

---

[1] But the indifference of the Senate to the freedom of Demetrias is established if, as is probable, it had intended to restore the city to Philip (cf. Liv. (P.) xxxv. 31.7).

[2] This is implicit in Polyb. iii. 11.2. Cf. also Liv. (A.) xxxv. 22.2, (P.) xxxv. 33.3, 50.2, 51.5.

[3] Liv. (P.) xxxv. 39.7 (gratitude); also (P.) xxxv. 31.8 (Flamininus tells the council of the Magnesians that 'cum totam Graeciam beneficio libertatis obnoxiam Romanis esse, tum eam civitatem praecipue'; the Magnesian assertion that Demetrias was really under Roman power provoked Flamininus to wrath, at which the pro-Roman Zeno promised that the Magnesians would not violate Roman *amicitia*, §§ 12–16).

[4] The praetor A. Atilius Serranus was sent to Greece with a fleet and the *provincia* 'classis et Macedonia' (the latter is overlooked in *MRR* i. 350) early in the consular year 192 (about December 193 Julian): Liv. xxxv. 20.10, 22.2, 23.4, 37.3, Zonar. ix. 19. Later in the year M. Baebius Tamphilus, also a praetor, was sent to Apollonia with a large force (Liv. xxxv. 24.7 (cf. 20.11), etc.); this was probably decided before Antiochus' landing was known at Rome (Walbank, *Philip V of Macedon*, 328).

[5] Polyb. xviii. 45.10–11.

those which had been subject to Ptolemy or Philip, that he must not cross with an army to Europe (where he had already arrived months before)—these demands went unheeded. So too at the conference at Lysimacheia a few months later.[1] Menippus' embassy to Rome in 194–193 made no concessions, nor did Antiochus himself do so when P. Sulpicius Galba led an embassy to Asia Minor in 193. Yet it was not because Antiochus refused to abandon Thrace or his claims to Lampsacus, Smyrna, and Alexandria Troas that the Senate decided on war.[2] If the king thought that the three Asiatic cities were the 'beginnings' of the war,[3] he may have been right—but they had little to do with its most profound causes. However Antiochus' refusal of the Isthmian demands did make him seem a more serious potential enemy.

Livy exaggerated Roman anxiety that the Syrian king might invade Italy, and modern writers[4] have done so too. There is no evidence that the Senate expected anything of the sort before 192, since the Italian coastal colonies of 194 require no such explanation.[5] At the beginning of the consular year 192 the Senate left its major decision unsettled by assigning to the consul

[1] L. Cornelius Lentulus' comment to Antiochus is instructive: he was at a loss to know what the king's reason was for bringing such a force to Europe; unless he had it in mind to attack the Romans, there was no explanation any rational person could accept (Polyb. xviii. 50.8–9; cf. Liv. xxxiii. 39.7, Diod. xxviii. 12, App. *Syr.* 3). A well-authenticated early instance of the rhetorical use of the defensive argument; and Livy adorns it from his own imagination with a hypothetical invasion of Italy ('illum quidem, etiam si in Italiam traiciat, negaturum; Romanos autem non expectaturos ut id posset facere').

[2] Even though he may well have invaded Thrace again early in 192 (cf. Walbank, *Philip V of Macedon*, 197). The three Asiatic cities were under attack that year: Liv. (P.) xxxv. 42.2.

[3] Polyb. xxi. 13.3.

[4] For Livy cf. n. 1; T. Frank, *Roman Imperialism*, 170.

[5] This was Frank's view of these colonies (followed by H. H. Scullard, *Roman Politics*, 117, who wrongly attributes them to Scipio Africanus). Of Frank's eight instances (o.c. 188 n. 13), five at least were planned in 197 (Liv. xxxii. 29.3; this was probably in the first part of the consular year, cf. J. Briscoe's n.), and it would be most remarkable if Rome anticipated a Syrian invasion at this date. It is much more probable that the colonies were mainly intended to secure and take advantage of land confiscated from the Italian supporters of Hannibal (cf. p. 61)—this indeed is what Livy implies, xxxiv. 45.2–4; and there is likely to have been some intention of discouraging pirates (for whose presence at Liternum in this period cf. Val. Max. ii. 10.2, Sen. *Ep.* 86.5). Scattered 300-man colonies would have been singularly useless for hindering a large invasion. Briscoe (on xxxii. 29.3) struggles against Frank's view but surrenders to it. The fact that a tribune proposed the five colonies of 197 (no precedent is known) also suggests, without proving, that this view is mistaken. For another discussion too favourable to the Frank view cf. E. T. Salmon, *Roman Colonization under the Republic* (London, 1969), 96–99.

Cn. Domitius Ahenobarbus a *provincia* 'extra Italiam quo senatus censuisset',[1] but when P. Sulpicius Galba's embassy returned from the court of Antiochus, Domitius, like his colleague, went off to invade the Boii. At this time, we are supposed to believe, the Senate was anxious about an invasion in the south. However two of the praetors were directed to prepare for the war, and later in the year (in seems) rumours at Rome 'multa falsa veris miscebant': as soon as the king reached Aetolia he would send a fleet to Sicily. That some believed this is clear from the fact that the Senate—'ad tenendos sociorum animos' according to Livy— made some corresponding defensive dispositions in Sicily and southern Italy.[2]

Too much importance has been attributed to Roman fear[3] and to defensive thinking. It is misleading to assume that Rome's attitude was essentially pacific.[4] By declaring the 'freedom' of certain Greek cities that were subject to Antiochus,[5] Rome had in 196 intruded quite vigorously into his affairs. This was a response to the king's campaign of 197 in western Asia Minor, but it was a provocative response. He had not yet impinged upon the territory of a Roman ally, except briefly in 198, when the intervention of a Roman embassy had been enough to expel a Seleucid force from the kingdom of Pergamum.[6] Having declared the 'freedom of the Greeks in Asia', Rome showed little sign of going to war on the issue—or of significantly relaxing its demands.[7] Meanwhile there were plenty of things for consuls and armies to do in the west.

---

[1] Liv. xxxv. 20.3–4, 7, 14.

[2] Liv. xxxv. 23, xxxvi. 2.7 and 10–11, App. *Syr.* 15, Zonar. ix. 19.

[3] Walbank, e.g., writes that the war was caused by 'the Senate's nervousness' and Antiochus' persistence in his claimed rights (*Philip V of Macedon*, 187). According to Badian (*CPh* liv (1959), 85 = *Studies in Greek and Roman History*, 117), the Romans were 'thoroughly frightened' of Antiochus in 196. Cf. also Magie, *Roman Rule in Asia Minor*, i. 104. In the view of Will, *Histoire politique*, ii. 172, 'qu'il y ait eu très tôt une psychose antiochique à Rome est certain.'

[4] For such a view cf. Will, *Histoire politique*, ii. 160, 165, 168.

[5] Polyb. xviii. 44.2, 46.15, 47, etc.

[6] In spite of Holleaux, this actually took place: H. H. Schmitt, *Untersuchungen zur Geschichte Antiochus' des Grossen und seiner Zeit* (Wiesbaden, 1964), 269–70, Will, *Histoire politique*, ii. 153–5.

[7] Flamininus' policy-statement to the Menippus embassy (Liv. xxxiv. 58.1–3, Diod. xxviii. 15.3) is often so interpreted (thus the Senate, or at least Flamininus, appears more moderate): E. Bickermann, *Hermes* lxvii (1932), 73, Will, *Histoire politique*, ii. 167, etc. In reality, Flamininus, with characteristic ingenuity, was raising the stakes over the Thracian issue.

Underlying Roman policy was not only the Senate's concern for security, but a desire for the positive benefits of a successful war against Antiochus. This undoubtedly affected some more than others. Scipio Africanus unsuccessfully tried to get the *provincia* of Macedon for his second consulship in 194, in anticipation, and presumably eager anticipation, of a war with Antiochus.[1] Polybius tells us that Africanus was willing to compromise temporarily with the Aetolians in 191 because he knew that the purpose of the war was to gain power over Asia by defeating Antiochus.[2] He had long been eager to get on with matters in Asia.[3] The majority of the Senate had opposed him in 194. We do not know why—envy, preoccupation with other wars, the wish to repatriate the legions in Greece? But the ardour of some other Romans for the war reveals itself in due course. The *haruspices* and their prediction of *termini propagati*, of victory and triumph have already been discussed.[4] Admittedly it was to be expected, once war against Antiochus was decided on, that a Roman army would cross to Asia and attempt to defeat him in a major land engagement. Naturally they refused to negotiate in 190 at Elaea (where L. Aemilius Regillus even needed some encouragement from Eumenes) and at the Hellespont.[5] Nor is it remarkable that the Aetolians felt the force of Roman anger in 189.[6] But the Romans not only defeated Antiochus decisively at Magnesia, they ejected him from Asia Minor this side of the Taurus mountains, they forbade him ever again to own a navy, and they imposed a vast levy, hardly to be called an 'indemnity', of 15,000 talents. The war established Rome as the decisive power in the affairs of Asia Minor. All these results were desirable in themselves as well as being guarantees of imperial security.

THE GALATIANS

There follows Cn. Manlius Vulso's campaign of 189 against the Carians, Pisidians, Pamphylians, and above all Galatians.

[1] Cf. Liv. xxxiv. 43.3–9.
[2] xxi. 4.5.
[3] xxi. 5.12. These two passages are often—inexcusably—ignored in modern accounts, e.g. those of Frank (*Roman Imperialism*, 186) and Will.
[4] P. 122.
[5] Polyb. xxi. 10 (cf. Liv. xxxvii. 18.11–19.6); xxi. 13–15 (cf. Liv. xxxvii. 34–36).
[6] ὀργή: Polyb. xxi. 25.10, 29.9, 31.7.

Kindly historians have tried to make it respectable to our moral sense.[1] They have claimed that its purpose was to impress on the Galatians the solidity of the power Rome intended to exercise in Asia Minor—which may well be true. And since detachments from these regions had been on the wrong side at Magnesia,[2] the inhabitants were probably felt to deserve revenge. None the less if the Senate had been interested solely in the security of Rome's existing possessions, it could easily have left the Galatian problem in the hands of the Pergamenes. Manlius did perhaps incur some criticism in the Senate when he requested his triumph—but a triumph was granted.[3] It is hard, and unnecessary, to resist the view that Manlius' main aim was plunder, and that few in the Senate disapproved. Polybius perceived him as having been very energetic in the pursuit of booty, in spite of the fact that the historian, as a Greek, was fully in favour of harsh treatment for the Galatians. Manlius bargained with Moagetes of Cibyra over the sum to be paid for 'friendship', which meant mainly immunity from attack, settling for 100 talents; Termessus and Aspendus received the same privilege for 50 talents each. Having thoroughly plundered Pisidian Cyrmasa and Sagalassus, he sold Roman friendship to the latter for 50 talents and a large donation of grain.[4] Following Polybius, Livy records the levy of 225 talents and large quantities of grain from communities in Pisidia and Galatia and the capture of a number of other towns. Many of these the inhabitants deserted as the Roman army, already

---

[1] See especially Frank, o.c. 177–9; cf. H. H. Scullard, *HRW*[3] 261 ('a necessary piece of police work'), A. H. McDonald, *JRS* lvii (1967), 3 (he 'led his army through central Anatolia in order to display the extent of Roman influence'). To others (e.g. A. Heuss, *RG*[3] 110) it was simply a plundering expedition.

[2] Liv. (P.) xxxvii. 40, cf. xxxviii. 18.1. Florus' doubt concerning the Galatians (i. 27.2) was unfounded.

[3] Opposition to his triumph: Liv. (A.) xxxviii. 44.9–50.3, xxxix. 7.3. One of the grounds was that he had made war on the Gallograeci (Galatians) 'nòn ex senatus auctoritate, non populi iussu' (45.5), a charge which was extended to Pisidia, Lycaonia and Phrygia (45.9). But the opposition was perhaps only a matter of *inimicitiae* and the constitutional and moral arguments in which Livy clothed it may have been manufactured by historians (the speech in the Senate (45.7–46.15)—given by two senators!—is of course pure fabrication), partly at least because of the belief that it was Manlius' booty which first introduced *luxuria* to Rome (xxxix. 6.6–9, cf. Plin. *NH* xxxiv. 14, xxxvii. 12). Cf. De Sanctis, *SR* iv. 1.225 n. 182, and on some of the inaccuracies in Livy's account, H. Nissen, *Kritische Untersuchungen*, 211–12. Manlius may well have come under suspicion concerning the disappearance of the 3,000 talents which was blamed on the Scipios (cf. Liv. xxxix. 6.4–5).

[4] Polyb. xxi. 34, 35.4, 36.

heavily laden with plunder, came near. 40,000 prisoners were taken from the Galatians at Mount Olympus.[1] On a reasonable view, plundering was the main purpose of the war.

THE LIGURIANS

We return briefly to the west. From 197 until 172 Roman armies campaigned annually against the Ligurians, with an intermission during the Syrian–Aetolian war; and in the years 167–154 there were several more campaigns. In spite of Cicero's somewhat prejudiced sneer against those 'qui Ligurum castella expugnaverunt',[2] this was often a very serious business. Modern writers sometimes reduce the Ligurian wars to 'triumph-hunting', and triumphs were obviously one of the advantages that Roman commanders gained. Some twelve were celebrated over the Ligurians in this period, and though some of them may have been spurious and none of them bestowed the glory of an African or Asian victory, their value was real.

The contribution of defensive thinking at Rome is hard to discern. The Ligurians were long-established enemies, at least since 238, and some of them had not unreasonably sided with Carthage during the Hannibalic War.[3] It may also be significant, but does not settle the question, that Polybius probably ascribed great importance to piracy in explaining L. Aemilius Paullus' Ligurian campaign of 182/1.[4] Pirates are not often mentioned, and Roman transport to Spain (which generally went by sea), though it would benefit from Roman political control of the whole Ligurian coast, could certainly function without it.[5] Much more importantly, once the colony at Placentia had been founded, it had to be protected and made safely accessible from the Ligurian sea. Later the colony of Bononia (189) had to be made accessible from Arretium, and the Via Flaminia (187) had

---

[1] Liv. (P.) xxxviii. 12–27. 40,000 is of course an approximate figure.

[2] *Brut.* 255 (with A. E. Douglas's n.). There appears to have been a special monument on the Capitol commemorating a victory or victories over the Ligurians (*AE* 1948 no. 56).

[3] See esp. Polyb. iii. 33.16 (cf. Liv. xxi. 22.2), vii. 9.6, xi. 19.4, xv. 11.1 (cf. Liv. xxx. 33.4), Liv. xxi. 38.3, xxvii. 39.2, 48.7, 49.8, xxviii. 36.2, 46.8–11, xxix. 5.8.

[4] Plu. *Aem.* 6.2–3, probably Polybian (H. Nissen, *Kritische Untersuchungen*, 95, 299); cf. Liv. xl. 18.4, 28.7.

[5] Genua had been under Roman control again since 203 (Liv. xxx. 1.10). A praetor and his entourage on their way to Spain in 189 were attacked with fatal results (xxxvii. 57.1–2).

to be protected from the Ligurian Friniates who lived on or near its course. Hence the campaign of 187.[1] Similarly it may well have been thought necessary for the protection of the Via Aemilia and its settlements to fight decisive campaigns in the region of the River Scultenna (Panaro) and around the Ligurian strongholds near Castelnovo ne' Monti (some 40 kilometres south of Regium Lepidum).[2] Even in 177 the colony of Mutina was captured by the Ligurians, not to be recaptured until the following year.[3] And on the coastal side a number of campaigns were fought in or near the territory of Pisae and perhaps in its defence.[4] It is likely that some at least of the Ligurian campaigns were thought to be necessary for the protection of existing possessions.

The last mentioned of these existing possessions, Pisae, had been taken from the Ligurians themselves.[5] The date (probably in the 270s or 230s) and the circumstances are obscure. At a later stage Rome seized certain desirable tracts of territory, in order to found the colonies of Luca (180) and Luna (177). Shortly afterwards, apparently in 173, the Romans began to take direct control of the fine farming land of southern Piedmont. This campaign against the Ligurian Statellates looks like the most blatant land-grabbing, and though there was a dispute at Rome about how the Statellates should be treated, as a result of which some of them were freed from the slavery M. Popillius Laenas (*cos.* 173) had inflicted upon them, they were forced to move northwards across the Po.[6] Other thoughts of gain probably contributed to the Ligurian wars. Plundering and enslavement

---

[1] Liv. xxxix. 2. The name of the Friniates survives in the Frignano region on the northeastern slope of the Appennines between the R. Secchia and the Pistoia–Bologna road (but this may not correspond exactly with their original territory).

[2] The latter area is that of the three adjacent mountains, Ballista, Suismontium, and Letum, to give them their traditional Latin forms. They are to be identified with Monte Valestra, Pietra Bismantova, and (perhaps) M. Fósola. The campaigns: Liv. xxxix. 2.7–8 (187), xl. 41.1–2 (180), xl. 53.1–4 (179), xli. 12.8–9 (177), 18 (176). In my view Regium Lepidum was probably founded as a *forum* in 187. Mutina and Parma were founded in 183.   [3] Liv. xli. 14.2, 16.7–8.

[4] Liv. xxxiii. 43.5 and 9 (195), xxxv. 3.2 (193; cf. xxxiv. 56.2—allegedly the Ligurians had invaded Pisan territory), xxxv. 21.7 (192), xxxix. 2.5 (187), xli. 19.1 (175).

[5] Erroneous statements that it was Etruscan in the third century (e.g. E. T. Salmon, *Roman Colonization under the Republic*, 109) put the Ligurian wars in the wrong light. For its predominantly Ligurian character see Harris, *Rome in Etruria and Umbria*, 2. Liv. xxxv. 21.11 is misleading over this.

[6] See Additional Note xviii.

went on as usual, the latter relatively more important against poor opponents. Livy's notices sometimes give the impression that plundering was the main objective,[1] and this can be accepted without difficulty.

THE THIRD MACEDONIAN WAR

Wars in Liguria and Spain and occasionally in other regions occupied Rome's military energies from 186 to 172, with ten legions sometimes under arms and never fewer than seven until 172.[2] In the following year, after twenty-five years of peace with Macedon, Rome initiated war against King Perseus. Even in this case some historians have supposed that the Senate decided on war for defensive reasons, though these turn out to be hard to formulate convincingly.

Polybius' explanation of the war is that Philip had intended and prepared it before his death in 179, and Perseus became Philip's agent ($\chi\epsilon\iota\rho\iota\sigma\tau\dot{\eta}s$) in the matter.[3] Some allowances must be made for the historian since his main discussion is lost; presumably we should understand his statement within the context of the drive towards power which he attributes to Rome. None the less his theory is most inadequate. It simply does not explain what needs explaining—namely the *Roman* decision to begin the war. It was the Senate that decided on war, after many years of contenting itself with at most diplomatic manoeuvres against Perseus' attempts to strengthen his position.[4] The main reason why Polybius failed to apply his science of causes adequately to a war whose history he knew intimately was his personal involvement in political events. He deeply regretted the war and the end of the precarious political equilibrium in which the Greeks had lived since 189.[5] He found himself with the

---

[1] Esp. xxxiv. 48.1 (194), xxxv. 40.4 (192), xxxix. 32.4 (185), xlv. 44.1 (167). His statement that the Ligurian wars did not provide much plunder (xxxix. 1.6) is merely part of a sermon on their beneficial effect on the Roman army and is in any case entirely relative (P. A. Brunt, *Italian Manpower*, 187, over-values this passage). In the same passage he attributes all the Ligurian wars to their attacks on neighbouring territory (1.8).

[2] Brunt, o.c. 424.

[3] xxii. 18.10–11; cf. Liv. (P.) xlii. 52.3, Diod. xxix. 30. P. Pédech (*La Méthode historique de Polybe*, esp. 139) is alone among recent scholars in approving this account; he ignores its difficulties.   [4] Cf. E. Will, *Histoire politique*, ii. 218–19.

[5] Liv. (P.) xlii. 30.6–7 is the most important evidence; cf. the fine paper of E. Bikerman, *REG* lxvi (1953), 485–6.

impossible choice of blaming Perseus or the Senate. Perseus had not behaved at all belligerently towards Rome, as Polybius knew; yet the historian could not write, by the late 140s could probably not even allow himself to think, that the Senate had purposefully destroyed the equilibrium. Hence it had to be a Macedonian, and since Perseus was an implausible culprit, it had to be his father, who was widely believed to have been planning a Roman war in the last years of his reign.[1] Some tortured logic resulted: 'the causes of the war must have existed before the death of the man who decided on it.'[2]

No historian believes that the Senate voted for war because Perseus had attacked the Dolopians and Abrupolis, king of the Sapaeans. These were presumably the events referred to when the senatorial and comitial motions spoke of Perseus' having, contrary to his treaty, made war on allies of the Roman people.[3] The charge was factitious,[4] and suggests a shortage of avowable reasons for going to war. Nor does anyone suppose that the Senate's decision resulted simply from the other events, besides these, which Polybius refers to as pretexts or beginnings of the war: Perseus' march to Delphi in 174 (a pretext), the assassination attempt against Eumenes II which was ascribed to Perseus, and the alleged murder—which was probably an accidental shipwreck—of the Theban envoys to Rome ('beginnings').[5]

The motions passed at Rome also mentioned, in addition to attacks on allies, preparations that Perseus was supposed to have made to direct war against Rome;[6] that is to say, the Senate claimed not quite that the war was defensive, but at least that it was preventive. Did the Senate then believe that Perseus

---

[1] F. W. Walbank, *Philip V of Macedon*, esp. 235–254.

[2] Polyb. xxii. 18.11.

[3] Liv. (A.) xlii. 30.10–11.

[4] Rome renewed its treaty with the king of Macedon after his war with Abrupolis (App. *Mac.* 11.6, cf. P. Meloni, *Perseo e la fine della monarchia macedone* (Rome, 1953), 64 n. 2), thus implicitly forgiving anything there was to forgive. The case of the Dolopians is more complex. They were detached from Macedon by Rome in 196 (Polyb. xviii. 47.6), and this was perhaps theoretically confirmed in 185 (cf. Liv. xxxix. 26.14); but Perseus claimed that Rome had recognized Philip's authority (Liv. (P.) xlii. 41.13), and it was probably in Macedonian hands when the treaty was renewed. For a different view see Bikerman, o.c. 489–90.

[5] Polyb. xxii. 18.2–5.

[6] Liv. (A.) xlii. 30.11.

intended an attack of some kind on Rome or its allies? The investigating mission of A. Postumius Albinus does not seem to have reported anything definite of this kind in 175.[1] A Roman embassy which supposedly reported in early 173 that Perseus was preparing imminent war is probably an annalistic fiction.[2] When Eumenes II visited Rome in 172 to urge the Senate to make war, his extensive denunciation of Perseus included not only the claim that he was planning war against Rome but the insinuation that he would invade Italy.[3] Scholars sometimes assert that the alarm caused by these representations decided the Senate on war.[4] This is far from clear. An invasion of Italy was a logistic absurdity, since Perseus had no navy. More significantly still, Livy says no more than that Eumenes' speech 'moved' the senators; according to Appian many senators saw through the Pergamene king and used his charges as a pretext, which implies perhaps correctly that they had in effect already decided on war.[5] The speech probably brought war nearer, but more by demonstrating the grievances that could be exploited than by sounding an alarm. Some time later there returned the mission of C. Valerius Laevinus, bringing with it Praxo, the Delphian woman whose house had been used by the assailants of Eumenes, and a tall story—which may none the less have been believed—about another assassination plot, this time directed against Roman officials. The mission had been sent to spy out affairs in Macedonia, but if it brought back significant information about preparations for war on Perseus' part, Livy does not mention the

---

[1] Cf. Liv. (P.) xli. 19.4–6, App. *Mac.* 11.1.

[2] Liv. (A.) xlii. 2.1–2. Cf. Bikerman, o.c. 506; the alleged ambassadors (Liv. (A.) xli. 22.3) may in reality have been those who were sent to Carthage (cf. H. H. Scullard, *Roman Politics*, 191 n. 3).

[3] On the latter point, Liv. (P.) xlii. 13.10–11: 'cum . . . concessam sibi Graeciam a vobis videat, pro certo habet neminem sibi, antequam in Italiam traiecerit, armatum occursurum . . . ego certe mihi turpe esse duxi, prius Persea ad bellum inferendum, quam me socium ad praedicendum ut caveretis, venire in Italiam.' It is doubtful whether this is purely Polybian.

[4] E.g. Meloni, o.c. 158–9.

[5] Liv. xlii. 14.1 (according to A. Klotz, *Livius und seine Vorgänger* (Stuttgart, 1940–1), 19, 'haec oratio movit patres conscriptos' is Polybian; perhaps so—but Polybius must have said more about senators' reactions to the speech); cf. 15.1, App. *Mac.* 11.3. After a speech by Eumenes Cato said that kings were carnivorous animals, Plu. *Cat. Mai.* 8, and this reaction probably belongs to 172 rather than 189. There may be here the beginnings of the attitude that after the war led the Senate to prevent any kings from coming to Rome (Polyb. xxx. 19, etc.).

fact. However the Senate's decision now became definite, even if it had not been before.[1]

In truth there is no sign that Perseus had been making any immediate preparations for war,[2] and even when his last embassy to Rome reported that there was no hope of peace, some members of the king's council still advocated appeasement.[3] Nor should we doubt that after his victory at Callinicus (171) Perseus offered peace-terms quite humiliating to himself (the Roman consul inevitably refused them).[4] Although Perseus' army was larger than Philip V's had ever been, he lacked any significant allies, and the war could have only one eventual result.[5] According to Appian, the Senate decided on war 'not wanting to have in its flanks' an energetic enemy who had suddenly become so powerful;[6] but correctly assessed, this is merely an exaggeration of part of the truth. Historians have sometimes attempted to make a defensive explanation of the war more credible by widening the supposed oriental menace: it was not Perseus, but a Macedonian coalition with the king of Syria which, so it is once again argued, stirred Rome to fight.[7] Antiochus IV was threatening Egypt. Perhaps the Senate was alarmed by the prospect of a combination between Pella and Antioch. There is, however, no evidence of this, nor the least likelihood of it, since Perseus' marriage to Laodice, daughter of Seleucus IV, did him no good now that Antiochus IV was king, and the latter had made an alliance with Perseus' bitter enemy Eumenes.[8] In any case the

---

[1] Liv. xlii. 17 (the original mission: 6.4). The reaction is described in 18.1: 'Haec ad ea quae ab Eumene delata erant accessere, quo maturius hostis Perseus iudicaretur, quippe quem non iustum modo apparare bellum regio animo, sed per omnia clandestina grassari scelera latrociniorum ac veneficiorum cernebant. belli administratio ad novos consules reiecta est; in praesentia tamen . . .'

[2] Even the later notice in Liv. (A.) xlii. 25.2 is suspect.

[3] Liv. (P.) xlii. 50.1–4. Meloni, o.c. 216–17, does not justify his scepticism.

[4] Polyb. xxvii. 8.1–10 etc.; cf. A. Giovannini, *BCH* xciii (1969), 857 n. 3.

[5] Cf. De Sanctis, *SR* iv. 1.273: for Rome it was the opportune moment.

[6] *Mac.* 11.3.

[7] Bikerman, o.c. 502–4; cf. Will, *Histoire politique*, ii. 227.

[8] The alliance: App. *Syr.* 45, O. Mørkholm, *Antiochus IV of Syria* (Copenhagen, 1966), 42, 51–4. Hence Eumenes lied to the Senate, Liv. (P.) xlii. 12.3. Bikerman's thesis is not proved by Polyb. xxviii. 17.5, which only shows that in 169 Q. Marcius Philippus *may* (Polybius took another view) have hoped to prevent Antiochus from capturing Alexandria and thus becoming a βαρὺς ἔφεδρος; nor by xxix. 2 (in 168 the Senate decided to prevent Antiochus from holding power in Egypt). Of course any extension of Roman power in the eastern Mediterranean would weaken Antiochus, but if the Senate had merely wanted to maintain a balance of power it would have permitted Perseus to

Roman war preparations of 172, which the praetor Cn. Sicinius seems to have carried out in an unhurried fashion, hardly suggest alarm.[1]

A politically energetic king of Macedon such as Perseus was inevitably an enemy in the eyes of the Senate. Up to a point— until the march to Delphi in 174—he had shown some skill in not offering pretexts for war, as the feebleness of Roman complaints against him shows. On the other hand his growing influence in Greece, his *auctoritas* in Livy's word, was no doubt a real irritant, and certainly contributed to the Senate's deciding on war when it did.[2] Particularly tiresome was his appeal to the anti-Roman left in the Greek states. This created the possibility that these states might abruptly change their policies in directions unfavourable to Rome.[3] However Perseus' behaviour merely served to attract Roman hostility and aggressiveness, which were seeking a new target in the years about 175–172.

It is as well to remember how little information we have about the Senate's state of mind. A scholar writes that it was haunted by the fear of an invasion of Italy—an implausible hypothesis.[4] On the other hand it is clear that the consuls of 172, who sought the province Macedonia even before Eumenes came to deliver his slanders,[5] regarded it as a great opportunity. By 175 the Spanish

exist as a balance against Eumenes, and seen that some help was sent to Ptolemy Philometor. In 169 Callicrates and his pro-Roman friends in the Achaean League, who were presumably well informed about the Senate's wishes, *opposed* Philometor's request for aid (Polyb. xxix. 23 25).

[1] Liv. (A.) xlii. 27.6 ('inpigre') notwithstanding. After he received his commission (xlii. 18.2–3) quite early in the consular year (July (Roman)?), Sicinius was given other tasks, one of them a time-consuming mission to do with the Statellates (see *MRR* i. 411), and his forces collected at Brundisium only by Id. Febr. 171 (xlii. 27.5). But there are unresolved problems here (cf. *MRR* i. 415 n. 2).

[2] His influence in Greece: Meloni, o.c. 94–115, 145–50, Bikerman, o.c. 492–3. *Auctoritas*: Liv. (P.) xlii. 11.9. By 173 the Romans hated him, according to the impression M. Claudius Marcellus gave to the Achaean assembly, Liv. (P.) xlii. 6.2.

[3] The Senate held him to blame for the political strife in the Greek cities, Diod. xxix. 33. Giovannini, o.c. 859–61, makes this the main cause of Rome's war-decision. The Senate did send diplomatic missions to intervene in Aetolia in 174 (Liv. xli. 25.5–6, xlii. 2.1–2), also to Crete (xli. 25.7); and in 173 to Thessaly, Perrhaebia, and Aetolia (xlii. 5.8–12). But if these matters had been of central importance, they would have formed a greater part of the complaints against Perseus in 172 (the reference in Liv. (P.) xlii. 40.7 merely lists interference in Aetolia among many other charges).

[4] Bikerman, o.c. 481. For other speculations about the Senate's state of mind cf. Meloni, o.c. 148–9 (alarm after Perseus' aid to Byzantium in 173), 158–9 (alarm and fear in 172).

[5] Liv. xlii. 10.11.

war had visibly reached a natural end, and in the case of Liguria the end was probably thought to be within sight in 174. A new theatre was in a sense needed, and Perseus made Macedonia the obvious choice. The Dardanians and Thessalians complained about him to the Senate in 175, and the resulting mission of A. Postumius, whatever it reported (and as usual we do not have definite and trustworthy information),[1] clearly turned senatoriai thoughts to a Macedonian war. It was probably during 173 that the Senate raked up the issue of King Abrupolis,[2] which resulted from the Senate's having quite gratuitously—but in traditional fashion—accepted a potentially trouble-making alliance.[3] On the eve of the war, the *haruspices* were consulted, and they announced not that Rome would be successful in reducing Perseus' *auctoritas* or in averting danger, but that there would be a victory, a triumph and *propagatio imperii*.[4] The consul of that year who failed to receive Macedonia as his province, C. Cassius Longinus, felt so frustrated that he started a war of his own in Illyria and was suspected of trying to invade Macedonia by an overland route.[5] Some of the consuls of 172 and following years energetically sought personal glory. This has sometimes been attributed to their relative *novitas*, but their *novitas* has been exaggerated, and for the most part they behaved as members of the aristocracy had behaved for centuries.[6] The results were in one respect disappointing—no triumph was celebrated until 167—but expectations were undoubtedly felt.

[1] Polyb. xxv. 6.5–6, Liv. xli. 19.4, App. *Mac.* 11.1.
[2] Diod. xxix. 33; on the date cf. Meloni, o.c. 149 n. 2, Bikerman, o.c. 506.
[3] De Sanctis, *SR* iv. 1.273.
[4] Liv. xlii. 30.9.
[5] Liv. xliii. 1.4–12, 5.1–9.
[6] According to H. H. Scullard (*Roman Politics*, 198), a 'more violent plebeian clique' precipitated war; but even if this is true, there is no sign that it was more than an accident, and in reality war was not precipitated by the plebeian consuls of 172 (they were absent during a crucial period) or by those of 171. It was 'precipitated' by a large body of senatorial opinion. On the *novitas* of the consuls of 172 and its relationship to their desire for *gloria* (suggested also by Meloni, o.c. 150) cf. Additional Note xviii. Of the consuls of 171, C. Cassius Longinus was a *novus homo* whose father probably did not reach the praetorship, but to call P. Licinius Crassus, whose uncle P. Crassus Dives (F. Münzer's hesitation over this relationship, *Römische Adelsparteien*, 220, was misplaced) held the censorship and was *pontifex maximus* for twenty-nine years an 'arriviste' (Bikerman, o.c. 501) is misleading, even though he was not strictly a *nobilis*. Nor were the plebeian consuls of 173–171 a harmonious group: among the *decemviri* of 173 who were probably in competition with the consul M. Popillius Laenas was C. Cassius, *cos.* 171; the latter competed with his fellow-consul Crassus for the province of Macedonia, and he in turn was opposed, in the case of the twenty-three recusant centurions, by M. Popillius (Liv. xlii. 32.7–33.6).

Non-senatorial views also deserve some notice.[1] If we are to believe Livy, such popular appeal as the war possessed derived to an exceptional degree from the expectation of booty (which was not fully satisfied), and later in the war recruits were hard to find in sufficient numbers.[2] It is evident that Perseus was not easily recognizable as a serious danger to the Roman state.

THE YEARS FROM 166 TO 154

In the years between 166 and 157 fighting was restricted to Liguria, the Alps, Corsica, and Spain. Most at least of these years were peaceful only in a relative sense, but no major military opportunities or problems presented themselves to the leaders of the state. A consul occupied himself with the Pomptine marshes;[3] it is impossible to tell how pleased he was to have a *provincia* which needed draining instead of one which needed subduing by war. Senate and citizens, especially the latter, may have been content with a lesser degree of effort after the Macedonian and Illyrian wars. By 157 steps were being taken to find a new sphere of activity, in Dalmatia. As Polybius writes, the Senate was vexed with the Dalmatians for their disobedience and rudeness, but in the main they thought that the moment was right for a Dalmatian war for two reasons: they had paid no attention to the Dalmatian coast since 219, and 'they did not wish the men of Italy to be in any way made effeminate by the long peace.' Thus the purpose of the war was to reduce the Dalmatians to obedience and to renew the eagerness and enthusiasm (ὁρμὰς καὶ προ-θυμίας) of their own people. These were the real reasons for the war decision, but the reason they gave to outsiders was the insult to their ambassadors.[4] Despite a certain vagueness (does he mean that the war was intended in part as a plundering expedition?), this is an invaluable description, since it is one of few instances in which the whole of Polybius' explanation of a Roman war survives. Appian explains the war, as Livy seems to have done,

---

[1] Bikerman, o.c. 494, suggested that Italian businessmen in Greece and Roman financiers had the ear of the Senate, but they are not likely to have been a strong influence; see pp. 99–100.

[2] On 171: xlii. 32.6. Later difficulties: xliii. 14.2–15.1.

[3] M. Cornelius Cethegus, *cos.* 160 (Liv. *Per.* 46).

[4] Polyb. xxxii. 13.4–9. The appeals of the Issians and Daorsi (xxxii. 9.1–2) are not mentioned again. Impoliteness and horse-stealing were the substance of the Roman ambassadors' complaints (13.1–3).

simply as a response to Dalmatian attacks on Roman allies;[1] but this was not even the main pretext offered at the time. Polybius' account is an entirely credible reflection of the Senate's attitudes concerning war, foreign peoples, propaganda, and international law.[2] This campaign being completed in 155, a similar request for help came from Massilia, which was experiencing difficulties with the Ligurians known as the Oxybii and the Deceatae. This case was somewhat different from the Dalmatian one: two seasons of campaigning had just exercised and rewarded the legions, and the Ligurians were unwise enough to give a rough reception to the Roman legates who came 'to correct their ignorance'.[3] None the less we must suspect here the same readiness to satisfy the need for war when a suitable pretext could be found.

THE THIRD PUNIC WAR

The Carthaginian war of 149–146 was a ruthless attack by an overwhelmingly more powerful state on one of its neighbours. Carthage was still one of the richest of the states on the immediate fringes of the empire, perhaps the richest, and it had completed its fifty years of 'indemnity' payments (in effect taxation) to Rome in 152. During these fifty years there had been virtually no occasion when Carthage had behaved in such a way as to cause anxiety at Rome, as is generally agreed;[4] and when the new war came, Roman pretexts were extraordinarily thin. Later Roman writers, attracted to the dramatic story of the destruction of Carthage and the parts played in it by Cato and Scipio Aemilianus, found these facts about the preliminaries of the war unsuitable for general audiences. In consequence they introduced a remarkable number of misrepresentations.[5] The Carthaginians had raised an army contrary to the treaty of 201— which did not forbid it. They had allegedly constructed a navy—

[1] App. *Ill.* 11, Liv. *Per.* 47 (cf. Strabo vii. 315, Zonar. ix. 25).

[2] J. J. Wilkes (*Dalmatia* (London, 1969), 30) claims to know that the Senate cannot have thought as Polybius says.

[3] Polyb. xxxiii. 7–8.

[4] Cf. E. Badian, *Foreign Clientelae*, 125, W. Hoffmann, *Historia* ix (1960), 323–4 [→Bibl.].

[5] To judge from the *Periochae* (47–49), these made up a large part of Livy's account. It may well have been the most misleading part of his whole history (apart from the first decade).

but the allegation was substantially untrue. Gisgo, son of Hamilcar, had roused the people of Carthage against Rome to such an extent that Roman envoys had to flee 'quo minus violarentur'—which is vague and probably false. And 'Arcobarzanes', a Numidian with whom Carthage is supposed to have made a military alliance, probably never existed. Most of these falsehoods are not even likely to have been contemporary.[1] What really happened? We lack certain portions of Polybius' account, but the surviving text does indicate both that the Senate made its war-decision (it is not clear whether he means formally or informally) long before 149 (πάλαι), and that the real reasons for the decision were not such as the Senate wanted to advertise.[2] Polybius was of course in a position to know the views of at least some leading senators,[3] and given his political acumen he is unlikely to have been seriously wrong on these points. Modern attempts to discredit his statement that the war was decided on long in advance have nothing to recommend them.[4] And it may well have been in this context that Polybius said of the Romans

[1] The army is several times referred to in *Per.* 48; for the military clauses of the treaty see Polyb. xv. 18.3–4. It might be suggested that the Senate was capable of making this complaint even though it lacked all legal substance. Perhaps so, but it is against the historicity of the complaint that Appian shows no knowledge of it (e.g. in *Lib.* 79 or 83). Naval material and later actual warships: *Per.* 47 (end), 48 (several times). Ten triremes were permitted by the treaty (Polyb. xv. 18.3; cf. H. H. Schmitt, *Die Staatsverträge des Altertums*, iii. 305), but Rome did not bother to demand any at the disarmament in 149 (Polyb. xxxvi. 6.5–7; cf. App. *Lib.* 79, 80, 83. Florus i. 31.7, Oros. iv. 22.2, Zonar. ix. 26 carry no weight against this evidence). Strabo xvii. 833 says that they had had twelve ships since 201, which is probably an exaggeration, like the preceding statement about armaments (cf. below, p. 236 n. 5). The near-violation of ambassadors in 152: Liv. *Per.* 48; it is never mentioned again. Arcobarzanes: Liv. Per. 48 (beginning), but never mentioned elsewhere. His quasi-Cappadocian name helps to betray him. Cf. P. Pédech, *La Méthode historique de Polybe*, 197.

[2] xxxvi. 2.1: πάλαι δὲ τούτου κεκυρωμένου βεβαίως ἐν ταῖς ἑκάστων γνώμαις καιρὸν ἐζήτουν ἐπιτήδειον καὶ πρόφασιν εὐσχήμονα πρὸς τοὺς ἐκτός. The decision referred to is clearly the decision to make war, not a decision to make the Carthaginians emigrate, as L. Zancan claimed, *AIV* xcv (1935–6), 530–1, 597; that would make the rest of the excerpt unintelligible. Cf. F. W. Walbank, *JRS* lv (1965), 6. πάλαι is admittedly quite a vague word in Polybius (cf. xxxvi. 3.1), but πρὸς ἀλλήλους διαφερόμενοι παρ᾽ ὀλίγον ἀπέστησαν τοῦ πολέμου (2.4) suggests that they had been searching for a pretext for an unusually long period by 149.

[3] In addition to his well-known connections, he was clearly on close terms with M'. Manilius, *cos.* 149 (xxxvi. 11).

[4] Walbank has argued (o.c. 7) that Polybius (and Appian) 'may well be exaggerating the firmness of the Senate's decision in the late 150s to make war', claiming that Polybius seems to have erred in a similar way in describing the Senate's attitude towards war with Carthage in the winter of 219/18, but though in that case he perhaps exaggerated the agreement in the Senate, he did not antedate the war-decision. Walbank also refers to

that they took care not to *appear* to be responsible for unjust acts or aggression, but always to *seem* to be acting in self-defence.[1]

Many historians hold that Rome was driven into war in 149 by anxiety about the growing strength of Carthage.[2] To a certain extent the sources appear to justify this view. Appian tells how, when Cato and other envoys visited Carthage in 153, they observed its growing prosperity and population; on their return to Rome they asserted that Carthage caused them fear rather than envy. To Cato is attributed the statement that the Romans would never even have their freedom secure until Carthage was destroyed.[3] Plutarch gives a similar account.[4] Scholars have tried to show that the Senate may genuinely have feared Carthage by pointing out evidence of the city's resurgence: it surrendered 200,000 ὅπλα and 2,000 catapults in 149, and was none the less able to resist three years of Roman attack. Evidently many Carthaginians were still animated by an independent spirit, and perhaps they gave some evidence of the fact in 150 by making war against King Massinissa without receiving treaty-stipulated permission from Rome.[5]

It is hard to perceive the Senate's thinking through the smokescreen of the ill-informed, melodramatic, and chauvinist non-Polybian sources, but the account summarized in the last

---

Polybius' description of the various judgements that the Greeks made on Rome's behaviour towards Carthage in this period (xxxvi. 9) as evidence that Roman motivation was a controversial subject among contemporaries. But none of the four opinions reported by Polybius contains or implies a denial of Polybius' assertion that the Romans had decided on war 'long before', and in any case these are merely opinions attributed to ordinary Greeks, not those of the close observer of the Senate. H. H. Scullard also argued (*Roman Politics*, 288; similarly D. Kienast, *Cato der Zensor*, 128) that the Senate can have made no definite decision for war as early as 153, since Cato persisted in advocating it. The most likely (though not the only possible) explanation of this is that the Senate had decided to make war as soon as a suitable opportunity presented itself; when Cato came to the conclusion that such an opportunity had arrived, the majority of senators were not yet convinced. By 150, if Liv. *Per.* 48 is to be trusted at this point, other *principes senatus* besides Cato wanted to send an army to Africa, but Scipio Nasica 'dicebat nondum sibi iustam causam belli videri', and presumably had a majority for this view; but the war between Carthage and Massinissa settled the question.

[1] Fr. 99B–W, attributed to this context by H. Nissen, *RhM* xxvi (1871), 275.
[2] E.g. T. Frank, *Roman Imperialism*, 234–5, M. Gelzer, *Philologus* lxxxvi (1931), 296–9 [→ Bibl.], and the most recent scholarly account, A. E. Astin, *Scipio Aemilianus*, esp. 272–6.
[3] App. *Lib.* 69.
[4] *Cat. Mai.* 26.
[5] Arms: Polyb. xxxvi. 6.7 (cf. Diod. xxxii. 6.2). Strabo (xvii. 833) and Appian (*Lib.* 80) exaggerate.

paragraph is definitely misleading. One may begin with certain points emphasized by modern commentators. Carthage possessed weapons, as it must always have done, but surrendered them with extraordinary submissiveness in 149. There is no evidence that the store had been recently increased, nor is it likely that any Roman mission discovered enough about the Carthaginian armouries to be able to alarm the Senate. Carthage did indeed show a will to resist, but only after Rome's murderous demand that they should transfer their maritime city ten miles inland. There is no evidence here that Carthage had long been displaying a mood of militant revanchism. As for the war against Massinissa, which (as both Polybius and Appian admit) came when the Senate had already made its war-decision, it resulted from the intense provocation of an attack on Carthaginian territory by the Senate's friend Massinissa. This attack was at least partially encouraged by the Romans, and—a factor which made it even more dangerous than most Numidian raids—it was supported by the exiled anti-democratic leaders of Carthage itself.[1]

What then of Cato's mission and the fear which it supposedly generated? It may be doubted whether Cato really went to Africa at all,[2] and even if he did little trust can be placed in either Plutarch's or Appian's description of the mission's report and the senatorial reaction. Polybius was by far the best source about these matters readily accessible to them, but probably neither of them chose to rely on him directly.[3] Both accounts betray their

---

[1] This conflict came only in 150 (Liv. *Per.* 48). The topography of the campaign is unknown, but it certainly began with a Numidian raid on Carthaginian territory (App. *Lib.* 70.319). Massinissa's claims had already penetrated as far as 'Tusca', perhaps Thugga (*Lib.* 68). Rome's encouragement of Massinissa: *Lib.* 72.331–2 (as earlier, e.g. in 161: Polyb. xxxi. 21.8). The exiles: App. *Lib.* 70.316, 318. After being defeated Carthage promptly executed those who had led the campaign (*Lib.* 74).

[2] It is perhaps unlikely that Livy sent Cato to Africa either in 157 (*Per.* 47: 'missi a senatu . . .') or in 153 ('legati ad disceptandum . . .') or in 152 (*Per.* 48: 'legatos mitti Carthaginem . . .'), since the Periochist omits from his fairly full summary any mention of the famous man. Consulars of this age (he was born in 234) were not usually sent on such missions, even if mentally vigorous. And on the several occasions in *Cato Maior de senectute* where Cicero (by this time very knowledgeable about the prosopographical history of the period) makes Cato assert his continuing vigour at the dramatic date (150), he noticeably fails to bring in the African mission (cf. 15–18, 32, 38). The story could have been invented for any of several reasons; it was certainly useful in 'proving' that the author of Rome's policy knew what he was talking about. The rest of my argument does not depend on this theory.

[3] See Additional Note xix.

authors' blurred historical vision,[1] and it was an obvious way of justifying Roman behaviour to say that Carthage still, or once again, posed a real threat.[2]

Carthage was a traditional enemy and to the preceding generation had truly been an enemy to fear.[3] Senators may have been short of both information and rationality when they considered whether to begin this war. Their possible lack of rationality is sometimes emphasized.[4] Some of the events of 149–146 suggest intense Roman hatred, especially the order to destroy the city of Carthage in 149. Yet the portrait of a Senate overcome by exaggerated fears leaves out some important facts. Aristocrats in general believed that it was desirable to expand Roman power, and the ending of the indemnity period suggested that some fresh intervention against Carthage would be beneficial. Many leading senators must almost of necessity have been considering, in the mid-150s, where Rome could find a new theatre of war which would provide better opportunities than Alpine or Dalmatian tribes. Fighting against the Spanish rebels, fierce and impoverished, was unrewarding work by comparison with a Carthaginian war. It would be even harder to find sufficient excuse for fighting east of the Adriatic than for fighting against Carthage (Andriscus' Macedonian rebellion had not yet begun). And whereas recruiting for Spain caused serious difficulties in 151, there were plenty of volunteers for plundering Carthage.[5] Thus normal, and in a sense rational, motives carried Rome towards war.

When Polybius says that the Senate had decided on war 'long before', he should be believed. Only a suitable occasion was—in the view of a senatorial majority—still lacking. It was desirable to satisfy foreign opinion,[6] in spite of Cato, who had undergone his

---

[1] Appian (*Lib.* 69) refers to Carthage's having been 'destroyed' by Scipio Africanus 'not long before' 153. Plu. *Cat. Mai.* 26–7 is inept at various points (Cato supposedly said that Carthage's former defeats were in danger of making the Carthaginians 'more skilled' in war etc.); yet perhaps Plutarch was capable of reducing Polybius to this level.

[2] Note that according to Polyb. xxxi. 21.3 (161) Carthage had been softened by prolonged peace. Pédech (*La Méthode historique*, 196 n. 485) oddly says that *even* the partisans of Rome invoked fear as an explanation of the war (xxxvi. 9.4)—but naturally they did so more than anyone else.

[3] Old men liked to harp on the horrors of the Hannibalic war: Cato, *ORF*[3], fr. 187 (p. 76).

[4] E.g. by Astin, *Scipio Aemilianus*, 52.

[5] Above, p. 50.

[6] πρὸς τοὺς ἐκτός, Polyb. xxxvi. 2.1; cf. xxxii. 13.9 (the Dalmatian war).

formative experiences before Greek opinion mattered and scorned the modern Greeks. For his part he tried to stir up senators' feelings against Carthage,[1] presumably with some success. In addition many senators would feel slightly uneasy unless the war had a certain appearance of being technically *iustum*. Massinissa, suitably encouraged, solved this difficulty. Finally, the aim of the Senate majority in 149 was either war and its consequent benefits or the total self-humiliation of Carthage; assured security for Rome was not enough. Carthage was already disarmed and could without difficulty have been forced into an agreement far more exigent than the treaty of 201,[2] but the Senate showed no interest in such a solution.

An informed scholar has claimed that the order to remove the city of Carthage at least ten miles inland was not intended to drive the citizens to resistance (although the Senate is supposed to have detected a resurgence in Carthaginian spirit!).[3] If the Carthaginians agreed even to destroy their own city, there would be a military advantage for Rome and perhaps an even greater commercial advantage—and it may be that the more enterprising large landowners among the Roman aristocracy looked forward to the end of Carthaginian exports.[4] More probably, war was anticipated: Rome had nowhere, as far as is known, made a

[1] For his arguments (including atrocity stories): *ORF*[3] frr. 191–5 (pp. 78–9) (cf. E. Malcovati, *Athenaeum* liii (1975), 205–11).

[2] Even to Massinissa they had recently been prepared to offer 100 talents a year for fifty years (App. *Lib.* 73).

[3] Astin, o.c. 274. The sources: Liv. *Per.* 49, Diod. xxxii. 6.3, App. *Lib.* 81; cf. Polyb. xxxvi. 7.

[4] Some Italian business interests probably lost from the destruction of the city (cf. above, p. 99). The bankers and merchants to whom Mommsen attributed the war policy (*RG* ii[12]. 50) are probably not relevant. But the advantage to large landowners of the ending of Carthage's ability to export is often brushed aside too summarily (e.g. by H. H. Scullard, *Roman Politics*, 243). M. Rostovtzeff's argument (*The Social and Economic History of the Roman Empire*[2] (Oxford, 1957), 21, 547) deserves consideration, though the evidence of the Senate's interest in the wine and olive markets in this period (above, p. 85) and on the geographical range of Carthaginian activities in the second century (cf. Rostovtzeff, *SEHHW* iii. 1462 n. 20) is much more significant than the Carthaginian fig Cato brandished in the Senate. (By the time he wrote *SEHHW* ii. 787, Rostovtzeff had apparently changed his opinion.) W. Hoffmann remarked (in R. Klein (ed.), *Das Staatsdenken der Römer* (Darmstadt, 1966), 230) that the ten miles which the Carthaginians were supposed to move inland correspond precisely with the 80 stades by which, according to Plato, *Laws* 704b–5b, a city must be separated from the coast if it is to avoid being full of trade and the moral consequences of trade. This can hardly be a coincidence; thus the Senate aimed quite specifically at destroying Punic commerce.

demand of comparable severity before, and whatever else the Senate knew about Carthage it presumably knew that the inhabitants were numerous enough to defend the city; moreover everything on the Roman side had been prepared for immediate military action.[1] To many Romans of senatorial and non-senatorial rank this seemed an attractive prospect. In short, while it is possible that defensive thinking played a significant part in making up the minds of the leaders of the Roman state, Roman behaviour must also on a balanced assessment be regarded as an instance of extreme φιλαρχία (power-hunger). Did the leaders of the state then deceive themselves and suppose that the war was defensive? There is no strong reason to think so: rather they will first have made a rather cold-blooded war-decision which was however conditional, as Polybius implies, on the appearance of technical justification; this they duly found in 150.

THE ACHAEAN WAR

The last war against Carthage and the Achaean War of 146 throw light on each other. The physical destruction of the city of Corinth confirms that the destruction of Carthage was not caused by manic enmity such as only a threatening neighbour could produce. The preliminaries of the Punic war show in turn the rude cunning of senatorial policy which most historians have been unwilling to see in the preliminaries of the Achaean War.

These preliminaries are hard to disentangle for reasons of the standard kind: the most crucial section of Polybius is missing, and all the important sources are partisan, including Polybius himself, who more or less confesses that he wrote φιλαπεχθῶς,[2] as he obviously did. It is precisely the thinking of leading senators which is, as usual, the most elusive part of the whole history; and such guidance as Polybius has to offer about this is

---

[1] Cf. Liv. *Per.* 49: 'indignitate rei ad bellandum Carthaginienses compulerunt.' It is true that when Polybius heard at Corcyra that Carthage had delivered the hostages and made a *deditio* he thought that the war was over (xxxvi. 11.3–4), but he may well not have appreciated that the Romans would demand destruction of the city (iii. 5.5 does not prove otherwise). Rome had only destroyed cities before or deported people *en masse* when there had been armed resistance (Volsinii, Falerii, Ligurians)—so T. Frank's admonition to Carthage (*Roman Imperialism*, 235) is out of place.

[2] xxxviii. 4.2.

hopelessly marred by his loyalty to the official Roman case.[1]
The most crucial decision of all was to send the embassy under
L. Aurelius Orestes to the Achaean League in 147 to demand the
detachment from the League of Sparta, Corinth, Argos, Oetaean
Heraclea, and Arcadian Orchomenos. Of these cities only Sparta
and perhaps Heraclea had any wish to secede. The Roman
envoys gave the impression that the whole League was to be
dismembered,[2] and in order to justify their demands they seem to
have relied on the claim that the cities in question had once been
ruled by Philip V.[3] No wonder that some ancient writers thought
that Orestes' mission was intended as a provocation that would
lead to a pretext for making war against the Achaeans.[4] A strong
reaction was inevitable, and there is no reason to doubt that the
senior members of the Senate, many of whom had had plenty of
experience with Greeks, expected such a reaction.[5] War was not
absolutely certain, any more than it had been when Rome
demanded the demolition of Carthage; there were Achaeans
who strove to maintain peace even in these circumstances; but a

[1] At the Achaean treatment of L. Aurelius Orestes' embassy the Senate
ἠγανάκτησεν ... ὡς οὐδέποτε (xxxviii. 9.3). A little later the Romans by no means
wanted to undertake a war or a serious quarrel with the Achaeans (9.8). Polybius was now
of course no longer at Rome. The first claim reflects what seems to have rapidly become
the official Roman explanation of the destruction of Corinth (the envoys were violated; cf.
Cic. *Leg. Man.* 11, Liv. *Per.* 52). Cicero did not believe this explanation (*De off.* i. 35) and
neither should we. Polybius' second claim (9.8) is somewhat inconsistent with the Senate's
unprecedented vexation, but it too must be rejected. There may well have been some
senators who were opposed to war, particularly since Carthage had not yet fallen; but it
made no sense for Polybius to say that the Senate wanted to avoid a serious quarrel with
the Achaean League at the time when it was actually destroying it. That this should be by
far the least objective part of Polybius' history is unsurprising (on his own role after the
war see esp. xxxix. 4–5).
[2] The last point is implied even by Polybius' account, since he says that the next Roman
mission (that led by Sex. Iulius Caesar) was instructed to emphasize that Rome did not
want to dismember the League; see xxxviii. 9.3–8, and for less pro-Roman views of the
Orestes' message Justin xxxiv. 1.5–7, Dio fr. 72.2. Cf. A. Fuks, *JHS* xc (1970), 86–7.
[3] Cf. Liv. *Per.* 51 (end), Dio fr. 72.1. Badian mildly calls this a 'thin excuse' (*Foreign
Clientelae*, 113 n. 2).
[4] Cf. Justin xxxiv. 1.3.
[5] According to M. G. Morgan, *Historia* xviii (1969), 437, 'individual nobles may have
hoped that [Aurelius Orestes' mission] would precipitate a war ... But the Romans as a
whole were obviously caught flat-footed by the violence of the Achaean reaction. Had it
not been so, they would scarcely have allowed themselves to be driven to conciliatory
measures' (i.e. Sex. Caesar's mission). Quite apart from the fact that we are dealing with a
small group of leading senators and not 'the Romans as a whole', Sex. Caesar's mission
was conciliatory in a purely superficial sense (see the text).

good chance of war had been created. After Orestes delivered his message, some Achaeans apparently tried to extract from the envoys' residence the Spartans who had taken refuge there. The attempt failed.[1] It was not the gravest offence imaginable, and when the Romans returned home, as Polybius admits, they exaggerated the ill treatment which they had received.[2] A new mission was sent under the leadership of Sex. Iulius Caesar. According to Polybius, it was a conciliatory mission, but that is an obviously partisan interpretation. Sex. Caesar adopted a moderate tone and claimed that Rome did not wish to dismember the League. However he did not retract the demand L. Orestes had made,[3] and that was what mattered. Some people, Polybius admits, interpreted the new mission as a device to gain time while the siege of Carthage was being finished;[4] it was a reasonable interpretation. Far from making 'strenuous efforts to avoid going to war with the Achaean League',[5] Rome demanded the partial dissolution of the League and stood by this demand in face of Achaean resistance.

What then lay behind the Senate's instructions to L. Aurelius Orestes? It is usual to claim that the Achaean League had gradually succeeded in exasperating the Senate, even in provoking its hatred,[6] by showing less than the required degree of obedience. Loyal observance of Rome's wishes was indeed expected,[7] and a feeling that the Achaeans had in fact rebelled against Rome may have contributed to the brutal treatment of Corinth in 146. But let us concentrate on the period before Aurelius' embassy. That Sparta was a member of the League had been explicitly and formally recognized by the Senate, which in effect confirmed this in the winter of 150/49 when Sparta appealed to it over a territorial dispute.[8] In 150 the surviving members of the group of Achaeans detained in 167 were at last allowed to return home, which suggests that the Senate was not

---

[1] ἐβιάζοντο, Paus. vii. 14.2 (otherwise De Sanctis, *SR* iv. 3.139, Will, *Histoire politique*, ii. 330).

[2] xxxviii. 9.1–3.

[3] This is evident from Polybius' silence and from Paus. vii. 15.2.

[4] xxxviii. 9.7.

[5] J. Briscoe, *Past and Present* xxxvi (1967), 17 (similarly G. A. Lehmann, *Untersuchungen zur historischen Glaubwürdigkeit des Polybios* (Münster, 1967), 325).

[6] Will, *Histoire politique*, ii. 329.

[7] Cf. Polyb. xxxviii. 9.8.

[8] Cf. De Sanctis, *SR* iv. 3.130; Paus. vii. 12.4.

worried about possible disturbances in the League cities. Under
the leadership of Diaeus, the League showed its helpfulness in 149
by resisting Andriscus' invasion of Thessaly.[1] At this point,
however, the Achaeans may have made a serious mistake. Late in
149 Diaeus and the Spartan Menalcidas appeared before the
Senate to debate the exile of twenty-four Spartans which had
been imposed by the League. The Senate's response is, and
perhaps was then, obscure. In Pausanias' version, the Senate
said that it would send envoys to judge 'the mutual differences of
the Lacedaemonians and Achaeans'. Diaeus, he says, misled the
Achaeans into thinking that the Senate had declared the
complete subordination of Sparta to the League, and Menalcidas
misled the Spartans into thinking that they had been completely
freed from it.[2] The Senate's response seems to have been
somewhat ambiguous—perhaps by accident, perhaps because
of a division of opinion, but perhaps intentionally. Sparta in
any case defiantly took back the twenty-four exiles, and the
Achaean League fought a brief campaign (we are now in the
summer of 148) against the rebellious state. While the campaign
was going on, Q. Caecilius Metellus, in command against the
Macedonians, sent a message instructing the Achaeans to desist
from war until the senatorial envoys arrived.[3] The Achaeans
under their *strategos* disobeyed, but then the war was broken off
for other reasons; when Metellus sent further representatives
with the same instructions, Diaeus, who had once again been
elected *strategos*, agreed to keep the peace.

All this was probably known to the Senate when L. Orestes was
given his instructions. The detachment of Sparta from the
League was a natural step, and it would have been easy to enforce
obedience over this. But the order to detach Corinth, Argos, and
Orchomenos, like the order to move the city of Carthage, was a
challenge and was probably meant as such. In truth the League
could cause the Roman Senate no more anxiety than a wasp on a
warm afternoon, but the opportunity for an extension of power

[1] Liv. *Per.* 50 beginning. On the other hand if Pausanias is correct (which is not beyond
doubt since he is a hostile witness), Diaeus had artfully circumvented the Senate's
stipulation (made in the winter of 150/49) that capital charges against Spartans should
not be under the jurisdiction of the League (vii. 12.2–8); presumably this damaged
Diaeus' reputation among senators.

[2] Paus. vii. 12.8–9.

[3] Paus. vii. 13.2–3. This rather vague notice might be doubted, but it fits in reasonably
well with contemporary events in Asia Minor (cf. App. *Mithr.* 7).

was easy to perceive.[1] Nothing was done throughout 148 or until well into the year 147, but during the same period the Senate realized, if it had not done so before, that direct rule was now required in Macedonia. Each new upheaval in Rome's relations with the Greek states had brought a new advance in Roman influence, and the new arrangements in Macedonia invited a different arrangement in Greece proper. Let the most powerful Greek state either reduce itself to political triviality or suffer war and be permanently subordinated in a new, more decisive, and more profitable manner. No need now for much worry about arranging pretexts based on treaties or on allies attacked; failure to obey an order to commit political suicide was pretext enough for Mummius' campaign. When the moment for Roman military intervention came, Metellus showed the normal enthusiasm to annex the victor's glory for himself and might have settled for capitulation.[2] The new commander L. Mummius needed an authentic campaign of his own; and among his legates should be registered A. Postumius Albinus, one of the most passionate Roman lovers of Greek culture in this age, who by his conduct suggests the irrelevance of such proclivities to politics.[3]

RESISTING REBELLIONS AND INVASIONS

Because the empire rapidly increased in size during the second century, the proportion of Rome's military efforts that had to be expended on suppressing provincial rebellions, repelling attacks on the frontiers and simply on garrisoning provinces also increased. In some regions rebellions were frequent, as even our meagre sources show. In Spain, after some fighting in the late 160s, a major rebellion required three or four legions for most of the time from 154 until 133. The war was chiefly concerned with peoples or territory that were already thought to be subject to Rome. This did not of course exclude the operation of the normal

---

[1] Dio wrote (fr. 72.1) that the real reason for Orestes' instructions was to make the Greeks weaker, a reasonable conjecture which fails to get to the root of the subject. Cf. also Justin xxxiv. 1.1,5.

[2] Paus. vii. 15.1, 11.

[3] Polyb. xxxix. 1.11 seems to show that he was a legate of L. Mummius (not in *MRR* as such; 'the battle in Phocis' is the battle Paus. vii. 15.6 sets 'near Chaeronea'—see Oros. v. 3.2). Polybius detested the man, perhaps because of the events described in xxxiii. 1.5–8, and gives an acid account of his cultural philhellenism in xxxix. 1.1–10. On the economic aspects of the destruction of Corinth see above, pp. 95, 99.

ambitions of Roman aristocrats, or some aggressive strokes on the Roman side.[1] However the 'fiery war', as it soon seems to have been called,[2] was relatively unattractive both to aristocrats and to legionaries.[3] From the beginning the Senate presumably regarded it simply as an operation essential to the defence of Roman possessions in Spain. Even after the Numantine war ended in 133, the Spanish provinces were the most troubled, though Sardinians too from time to time resisted Roman authority, and in Sicily slave uprisings caused two major wars.

After the Macedonian rebellion of Andriscus, the Romans stationed in that province fought repeated wars against its northern neighbours. The circumstances are usually hard to discern. In effect Rome was often extending its authority. The first known wars with the Scordistae (to give them their contemporary name) seem to have been fought outside the province in 141 and 135.[4] Later we hear both of Thracian invasions of Macedonia and of Roman campaigning in Thrace. In 119 Gauls and Maedi intruded into the province of Macedonia. Rome responded with a series of invasions of Thracian territory, invasions which eventually added to the Roman province.[5] As to how the Senate regarded these campaigns, we have no direct evidence at all. The sources give the impression that if the frontier of the Macedonian province was fluid,[6] it was partly the Romans who made it so.

THE CIMBRI

Some other wars of the late second and early first centuries were undoubtedly felt by contemporary Romans to be defensive operations, but had been originally provoked by Rome, or at least by individual Roman generals. The first conflict with the

---

[1] Cf. Liv. *Per.* 48: 'Lucullus consul . . . Vaccaeos et Cantabros et *alias incognitas adhuc in Hispania gentes* subegit' (dubious evidence). See also App. *Iber.* 80.349: the determination and ambition of an individual Roman governor (M. Aemilius Lepidus Porcina, *cos.* 137) had the effect of making Roman policy more aggressive; but on his return to Rome he was fined (App. 83), presumably for disobeying the Senate's instructions. Finally, see above, p. 77.

[2] Polyb. xxxv. 1.6.

[3] See above, pp. 36, 49. At one time, in 137/6, the Senate seems to have been willing to accept, at least temporarily, a smaller degree of Roman control (App. *Iber.* 81; cf. H. Simon, *Roms Kriege in Spanien, 154–133 v. Chr.* (Frankfurt-a.-M., 1962), 165–6).

[4] Liv. *Oxy. Per.* 54, *Per.* 56.

[5] See Additional Note xx.   [6] Cic. *Prov. Cons.* 4, *Pis.* 38.

Cimbri was near Noreia in 113, a site which the consul Cn. Papirius Carbo reached by a lengthy route through the mountains beyond the remotest territory, that of the Carni, where Rome had previously made war in this quarter.[1] A claim was apparently made that the Norici had been attacked and that they were friends of the Roman people,[2] but the claim illustrates a Roman technique better than it explains the campaign. A victorious campaign was the main aim, and presumably there were hopes of profiting from the gold-workings of the Norici Taurisci, from which Italians had been expelled in Polybius' time.[3] But the campaign was a disaster.[4] The next consul to lead an army against the Cimbri was M. Iunius Silanus in 109, but the topography and circumstances are even more obscure than in 113.[5] Like Carbo, he was indicted for losing, the charge being that he had engaged with the Cimbri 'iniussu populi'.[6] Strictly speaking, the charge may have been true, but nothing would have been heard of it had the Cimbri not defeated Silanus and gone on in 105 to inflict a horrendous slaughter at Arausio. The following year, five years after the fact, Silanus was indicted, but won acquittal. Coming after the trial of Carbo this charge may suggest, in spite of its result, that the *concilium plebis* was becoming less tolerant of the marauding expeditions of ambitious consuls.

[1] Noreia: Strabo v. 214. The location has most recently been discussed by G. Alföldy, *Noricum* (London, 1974), 47–51, but his identification with the Magdelensberg is unconvincing; St. Margarethen is a better candidate. It is not plausible to say (o.c. 37) that Strabo only 'means . . . somewhere in the mountain country north of Aquileia and north of the southern ridge of the Alps'. The war with the Carni in 115: *MRR* i. 531.

[2] App. *Celt.* 13. According to Liv. *Per.* 63 the Cimbri had invaded Illyricum. The Roman tradition eventually even claimed that they had invaded Italy (Eutrop. iv. 25; cf. Obsequens 38, App. *Celt.* 1.2). According to De Sanctis (*Problemi di storia antica* (Bari, 1932), 194), 'battevano alle porte d'Italia'. Similarly Alföldy claims (o.c. 36) that 'Rome was nervous at the time that there might be a threat to Italy'—for which he refers to Eutropius and Obsequens! A precise understanding of the events of 113 is impossible to recover: note that Rome had been on bad terms with the Taurisci (in 129: *ILLRP* 335; in 115: *De vir. ill.* 72.7, where the Ligurians are a mistake; cf. Polyb. xxxiv. 10.14), who were probably themselves Norici (cf. Alföldy, 25–7).

[3] Strabo iv. 208 = Polyb. xxxiv. 10.10–14.

[4] The ex-consul escaped conviction only by suicide (E. S. Gruen, *Roman Politics and the Criminal Courts, 149–78 B.C.* (Cambridge, Mass., 1968), 131). This does not show beyond doubt that he had lacked the Senate's approval for his campaign.

[5] Flor. i. 38.4 (a muddled passage) claims that the Cimbri had by now migrated into Italy, but the tradition is plain that this did not happen until 102. The campaign is set in 'Gallia' by Vell. ii. 12.2, Eutrop. iv. 27.5; and it is clear from Cic. *Div. in Caec.* 67, *II Verr.* ii. 118, that Silanus was based in the Transalpine province. Cf. above, p. 150.

[6] Ascon. 80 C.

Silanus' campaign may have been undertaken in part to avenge the battle of Noreia, but evidence is lacking.

When the Cimbri next appear, they are definitely encroaching on established Roman interests, but the exact circumstances are once more obscure. L. Cassius Longinus (*cos.* 107) fought an unsuccessful campaign against the Tigurini, a migrating Helvetian people whom he encountered 'in finibus Nitiobrogum', therefore probably outside the Roman province.[1] This Roman defeat led to a rebellion of the Volcae at Tolosa, in which the Cimbri appear to have participated.[2] The defensive character of the succeeding campaigns against the Cimbri (105–101) needs no comment.[3] But it deserves to be emphasized in conclusion that the Cimbrian war, usually treated by historians as resistance to an invasion—an accurate interpretation of the latter part of the war—began with Roman expeditions outside the established areas of Roman control.

AGGRESSIVE WARS FROM 156 ONWARDS

Carbo's campaign in Noricum fits comfortably into a series of expeditions beyond the frontiers in this period. It is possible that these were seen by the Senate as defensive activities, but not at all likely. The tradition goes back of course to the Dalmatian war of 156/5 and indeed far beyond. When Ap. Claudius Pulcher (*cos.* 143) made war against the Salassi in the Val d'Aosta, Dio states explicitly that no charges were made against them, which may well, even though it is drawn from a source which emphasized the arrogance of the Claudii, be true. The consul wished for a creditable campaign, and knew about the Salassian gold-workings.[4] Similarly, when C. Sempronius Tuditanus (*cos.* 129)

---

[1] Liv. *Per.* 65 (but 'Nitiobrogum' is conjectural). Caes. *BG* vii. 7.2 shows that this was outside the province (cf. Strabo iv. 190, E. Linckenheld in *RE* s.v. Nitiobriges (1937), cols. 770–1). [2] Dio fr. 90.

[3] But note Gran. Licin. 12 F (before the battle of Arausio): 'Cimbrorum . . . legatos pacem volentes et agros petentes frumentumque quod sererent'; cf. Dio fr. 91.3.

[4] Dio fr. 74.1: . . . πρός τε τὸ γένος ὠκγωμένος καὶ τῷ Μετέλλῳ φθονῶν . . . ἐπεθύμησε πάντως τινὰ ἐπινικίων πρόφασιν λαβεῖν, καὶ Σαλάσσους Γαλάτας μὴ ἐγκαλουμένους τι ἐξεπολέμωσε τοῖς Ῥωμαίοις. ἐπέμφθη γὰρ ὡς συμβιβάσων αὐτοὺς τοῖς ὁμοχώροις περὶ τοῦ ὕδατος τοῦ ἐς τὰ χρυσεῖα ἀναγκαίου διαφερομένοις αὐτοῖς, καὶ τήν τε χώραν αὐτῶν πᾶσαν κατέδραμεν. I. Beretta, *La romanizzazione della Valle d'Aosta* (Milan–Varese, 1954), esp. 53–66, attempted to show that the purpose of the war was to secure control over the St. Bernard passes, but this is anachronistic.

found himself lacking military duties and opportunities, now that the Spanish and Sicilian wars were over and Aristonicus was dead, he turned to the north-eastern frontier of Italy, which had been quiet, as far as we know, since the 170s (when the Istrians had been conquered). There is a slight hint in the consul's fragmentary *elogium* from near Aquileia that the cult places of Timavus, some 20 kilometres east of Aquileia, had been disturbed.[1] However in Appian's view the campaign was simply a pretext to allow Tuditanus to avoid the political embarrassments of Rome.[2] It is likely that the expedition was also designed to harvest a triumph and some plunder. The Iapydes were logical victims to choose.[3]

In the succeeding twenty years Rome continued to seek military opportunities in the traditional way. The years 128 and 127 may have been peaceful, though troops were still kept in Asia until 126.[4] In 126 a serious disturbance began in Sardinia, but a new theatre was evidently needed. Transalpine Gaul was chosen, in circumstances which are, as so often, unrecorded. One of the consuls of 125, M. Fulvius Flaccus, had the dangerous idea of extending the citizenship to the Italians, and in consequence, Appian claims, he was sent off on a military expedition.[5] The Livian tradition explains the first intervention in more standard terms as being assistance to Massilia, whose territory was being plundered by the Salluvii.[6] The Vocontii were drawn in during 125 or 124, and so eventually, in 122–120, were the Allobroges, Arverni, and Ruteni. In the case of the Allobroges we know what explanations were being offered by Livy's time, but the sources do not permit a close investigation of the whole war.[7] Its duration

---

[1] *ILLRP* 335, lines 5–6 ('[statuamque?] dedit Timavo, [?sacra pat]ria ei restitu[it . . .]'). On the text see M. G. Morgan, *Philologus* cxvii (1973), 40–8.

[2] App. *BC* i. 19.80.

[3] Liv. *Per.* 59, *Fasti Tr.* (A. Degrassi, *Inscr. It.* xiii. 1. pp. 82–3) and App. *Ill.* 10 agree in making the Iapydes the opponents. The expedition was brief, since Tuditanus celebrated his triumph on 1 October. The inscription recorded by Plin. *NH* iii. 129 strongly suggests that he sailed as far as the River Titus (Krka), which he reckoned as 1,000 stades from Aquileia (see Morgan, o.c. 29–40). However his main activities were further north: he conquered the Istrians (Plin., App. *Ill.* 10; cf. Morgan, 33), and the Iapydes he defeated were probably the most north-western ones. As usually restored, *ILLRP* 335 also refers to a short campaign against the Taurisci and Carni (line 1).

[4] But probably not thereafter (P. A. Brunt, *Italian Manpower*, 429).

[5] *BC* i. 34.152.

[6] Liv. *Per.* 60, Flor. i. 37.3. Cf. also Strabo iv. 180.

[7] According to Liv. *Per.* 61, the charges against the Allobroges were that they had received the fugitive Salluvian king Toutomotulus (cf. App. *Celt.* 12), aided the Salluvii

and even more its geographical extension show that Rome went
far beyond providing protection for Massilia. The opportunity
was taken to extend Roman power over a large and desirable new
territory.[1] However contemporary Roman views of the matter
can hardly be recovered.

As soon as the war was over, Roman attention turned again to
northern Dalmatia. One of the consuls of 119, L. Caecilius
Metellus, made war on the Dalmatians although, Appian sa'ys,
'they were doing no wrong'; he aimed to celebrate a triumph,[2]
and did so late in 117. In 118 it was the turn of the Alpine Stoeni
or Styni, who apparently dwelt somewhere between Lake Como
and Lake Garda; they were attacked—the precise circumstances
are of course unknown—by the consul Q. Marcius Rex, and
virtually annihilated in that year and the next.[3] In 115 the Carni
provided the consul M. Aemilius Scaurus with a triumph, and
two years later, as already recounted, Cn. Carbo ventured into
Noricum.

THE JUGURTHINE WAR

Finally certain comments should be added on the war Rome
fought with Jugurtha (111 to 105). The Senate undoubtedly
regarded its partition of the Numidian kingdom between
Adherbal and Jugurtha as requiring the obedience of both
parties.[4] Jugurtha showed himself determined to undermine this

'omni ope' and plundered the territory of Roman allies, the Aedui. If the Aedui were
allies, it was clearly an obligation recently undertaken. Flor. i. 37.4 attributes the war to
Aeduan complaints against both the Allobroges and the Arverni; these may have had
substance (see further Strabo iv. 185, 191, Eutrop. iv. 22, Oros. v. 13.2).

[1] On the likelihood that Roman and Italian *negotiatores* supported this policy, see above,
pp. 95–8.

[2] App. *Ill*. 11. The Dalmatians allegedly welcomed him as a friend and he spent the
winter (which one?) at Salona (ibid.). But he also fought a real war: Cic. *Scaur*. 46, Ascon.
28 C, Ps.-Ascon. p. 254 St, Liv. *Per*. 62, App. *Ill*. 10.30 (the defeat of the Γεσταανοὶ or
Γετανοί, usually identified with the Segestani, i.e. inhabitants of Siscia (cf. *Ill*. 22)). The
campaign is discussed by M. G. Morgan, *Athenaeum* xlix (1971), 271–301.

[3] Their location: Strabo iv. 204. The war: Liv. *Per*. 62, Oros. v. 14.5–6, *Fasti Tr*. under
117 ('de *Liguribus* Stoenis' is a misunderstanding).

[4] The settlement: Sall. *BJ* 16.2–5, Liv. *Per*. 62. The view that Rome had the
sovereignty, the kings only *usus* or something similar, appears in Sall. *BJ* 14.1 (attributed
to Micipsa by Adherbal), Liv. xlv. 13.15 (attributed to Massinissa by one of his sons), App.
Num. 4 (where it is put in the mouth of A. Manlius, a legate of Marius). There is no
absolute proof that this is a pre-111 view, but it seems likely. Cf. Flor. i. 36.3 ('senatum
populumque Romanum, quorum in fide et in clientela regnum erat'). D. Timpe's
contrary assertion (*Hermes* xc (1962), 340–3) is based on nothing.

settlement, by besieging Adherbal in Cirta and ignoring instructions from two Roman missions to disarm. After he had treacherously murdered both his rival and the Italian *negotiatores* who had shared the defence of the city, the Senate as a matter of course decided on war. To Sallust the event needed no explanation, and the only point of interest was that Jugurtha's bribery of senators had protected him for so long and still provided him with some accomplices—*ministri*, as he calls them.[1] The king's provocations had certainly been numerous and grave, starting with the assassination of Hiempsal and the expulsion of Adherbal in about 117. No doubt the Senate voted for war in order to restore obedience in a territory which was thought to belong to Rome, and in order to punish Jugurtha.[2]

The relative tardiness of the Senate in resorting to war invites further discussion. Even when war came, the decision was made under pressure from a tribune and from non-senators.[3] And the Senate apparently did nothing to overturn the lenient peace settlement which L. Calpurnius Bestia, the consul of 111, agreed to after a single campaign.[4] These signs of softness towards Jugurtha have led scholars to suppose that the Senate was averse on principle to making war against him. Traditionally, however, the Senate had not been so hesitant; and those who hold that it was fundamentally reluctant to fight the Numidian king[5] cannot have paid much attention to the train of more or less voluntary wars which Rome had fought in the preceding years.

Sallust's explanation of the Senate's hesitation was simple: bribery.[6] Academic historians recoil from such allegations.[7] In this case, however, the charge should probably be believed. We

[1] The war-decision is referred to in Sall. *BJ* 27. Those who represented Jugurtha's interests 'interpellando ac saepe gratia, interdum iurgiis trahundo tempus atrocitatem facti leniebant'; this is the only line of argument reported.

[2] The short notice in Liv. *Per.* 64 makes the killing of Adherbal the reason for the war (cf. Flor. i. 36.6, Eutrop. iv. 26.1). When H. Bengtson (*Grundriss*², 168) implies that the aim was to prevent a strong unified Numidian state, he perhaps puts the matter in too strategic terms.

[3] On C. Memmius' role see Sall. *BJ* 27.2 (cf. Liv. *Per.* 64).   [4] Sall. *BJ* 30.1–3.

[5] E.g. T. Frank, *Roman Imperialism*, 266, S.I. Oost, *AJPh* lxxv (1954), 148. Knowing more about Numidian topography than Frank (264, 266), senators are not likely to have been fearful of sand dunes.

[6] *BJ* 13.5–8, 15.1, 15.3, 15.5–16.1, 16.3–4, 20.1, 29.

[7] See, e.g., G. De Sanctis, *Problemi di storia antica* (Bari, 1932), 189–95, D. C. Earl, *The Political Thought of Sallust* (Cambridge, 1961), 66–8, C. Meier, *Res Publica Amissa* (Wiesbaden, 1966), 79. W. Steidle discusses Sallust's allegations more sensibly (*Sallusts historische Monographien* (Wiesbaden, 1958), 47–51).

no longer treat Sallust as a simple propagandist for one 'party' against another. The charges of accepting bribes from Jugurtha were contemporary, and more significantly Sallust showed some discrimination in reporting them.[1] He does not suppose that all *nobiles* were venal. That some of them were is a supposition supported by Polybius' comments about bribery in the previous generation.[2] No doubt Jugurtha was also helped by the friendships and esteem he had gained long before while fighting for Rome at Numantia.[3] But though it is inherently impossible to prove that bribery was his most important source of leverage, it should be judged likely.

Whether the Senate sold itself to Jugurtha or not, the period of the Jugurthine War was one of changed attitudes towards war.[4] But warfare still offered valuable opportunities, and for some Romans, both aristocrats and ordinary citizens, retained its appeal. From the standpoint of L. Bestia, it was better to bring the Numidian campaign to a profitable conclusion while he remained in office, in spite of Jugurtha's continuing freedom.[5] The fathers, seeing no necessity of fighting Jugurtha to the death, seem to have acquiesced. However they chose Numidia again as a consular province for 110. One of the new consuls, Sp. Postumius Albinus—greedy, as Sallust says, for war[6]— persuaded the Numidian Massiva to claim Jugurtha's throne from the Senate. Jugurtha with characteristic rashness arranged Massiva's assassination; he was detected, and the war was renewed. The ignominious surrender of the consul's brother A. Albinus, whom he had left in command while he returned to Rome for the elections, was inevitably repudiated by the Senate.

From the beginning a harsh policy concerning Jugurtha had had wide 'popular' appeal, in spite of the fact that it strained citizen manpower and must have led to compulsory recruiting.[7] Sallust is far from specific in explaining this anti-Jugurthine

---

[1] See *BJ* 40.   [2] Above, p. 90.

[3] Note especially *BJ* 7.7, 13.6 ('veteres amicos')–7. Fear of the Cimbri is an improbable explanation of the Senate's tardiness (see above and Steidle, o.c. 43–5; A. La Penna's contrary opinion, *Sallustio e la 'rivoluzione' romana* (Milan, 1968), 174–5, is based largely on an indefensible view of Diod. xxxiv/xxxv. 37, which refers to the effect of Arausio, not Noreia).

[4] Cf. above, p. 38.

[5] Cf. A. La Penna, *Ann. Sc. Norm. Pisa*, xxviii (1959), 68.   [6] *BJ* 35.3.

[7] This is evident not only from Marius' change in recruiting practice (107) but from Ascon. 68 C (referring to 109).

sentiment, but it seems reasonable to suppose that a major part of it came from the *negotiatores* in Africa and their connections and sympathizers at Rome.[1] This sentiment outside the Senate had a vital effect in getting Marius elected on a platform of completing the war, and thus in directing Rome's policy.

Rome fought the Jugurthine War partly with the purpose of defending an outlying part of the empire. The defensive need, as usual in the second century, went no further than that.[2] And a heavily contributing factor was the expectation of certain Romans that the war would reward them in various ways. To Sp. Albinus and to Marius, in particular, the war cannot have appeared as simply a matter of necessary defence.

The outlook of the aristocracy, like much else at Rome, was changing relatively fast in the last years of the second century. The need for personal involvement in warfare was weakening, and interests and beliefs scarcely compatible with the old belligerent style of Roman behaviour were gaining strength. Many of the foreign wars of the late Republic were imposed by the defensive needs of the existing empire. But some, such as the first war with Mithridates, were hastened by Roman actions.[3] The driving force now tended, more than in previous periods, to come from individuals rather than from Rome as a whole. This applied to some unimportant campaigns, or non-campaigns, such as the one which the great orator L. Licinius Crassus (*cos.* 95) tried to fight: according to Cicero, who is speaking of the praiseworthy desire which certain magistrates had shown for triumphs, he 'virtually examined the Alps with surgical probes' in an attempt, apparently unsuccessful, to find enemies who could be taken seriously.[4] And it applied to some major wars, most conspicuously—in spite of the defensive reasons Caesar put

---

[1] Above, pp. 97–8.

[2] A. Albinus' defeat caused some fearfulness among citizens ignorant of military affairs, according to *BJ* 39.1 ('metus atque maeror civitatem invasere: pars dolere pro gloria imperi, pars insolita rerum bellicarum timere libertati'). Metellus' campaign quickly dispelled these feelings: 55.1–2. The earlier report may have been exaggerated to provide justification for the Senate's rejection of Albinus' surrender agreement (39.3). La Penna (o.c. 73) oddly seems to suppose that Sallust shared the conviction of those he called ignorant.   [3] See Additional Note XXI.

[4] Cic. *Pis.* 62. A fuller account: *De inv.* ii. 111. Cf. Ascon. 15 C. Similarly and in the same region, C. Aurelius Cotta (*cos.* 75) (Cic. *Pis.* 62, Ascon. 14 C).

4. The Wars of 219-70 B.C.

forward (among others) for his beginning the war—to the *bellum Gallicum*.

It is plain that on some occasions when Rome went to war, leading senators felt that their country was the victim of external forces. They sometimes believed that threatening neighbours compelled Rome to fight. It should now be equally plain that this is merely a fragment of the senatorial outlook on the new wars Rome undertook during the middle Republic.

The fetial law provides no evidence that the leaders of the state, or anyone else, normally felt that Rome's wars were defensive in intention, even in the period before the ritual became obsolete. Nor, as far as the middle Republic is concerned, does the concept of the just war attest such a Roman attitude. As to what leading senators did think and feel during the making of particular war-decisions, it is very hard to find out. At certain stages of the Italian wars, it can be presumed, the external threat to Rome was the predominant impulse to war—though even then, other needs helped to drive the Romans on. Later, the city itself and its citizens were sometimes threatened in the most direct fashion, for example by the Gauls in 284/3 and in 225. Far more often, as we have seen, the threat was to some imperial interest on the fringe of Roman possessions: such was the case, for example, in 264, in 229, in 218, in 215 (with regard to Philip V), in 201 (Gaul), in 192 (Antiochus III). Such peripheral dangers could sometimes look like growing into grave threats to Roman power—as was probably the case in 218. However we have encountered little evidence of wars which the Romans fought primarily to ward off a long-range strategic danger to their empire as a whole. Italian and Gallic wars aside, the only war which might fit easily into this category is the war against Hannibal.

The power of irrational fears is certainly not to be under-estimated. Historians have often relied on this factor to explain the decision to make war against Philip V in 200 and against Carthage in the 150s. The renewed investigation undertaken in this chapter suggests, however, that such views are incorrect, particularly with regard to the Second Macedonian War.

Many Roman wars have been diagnosed without adequate reasons as subjectively defensive. From the Italian campaigns of the 320s to the conflict with the Cimbri in and after 113, the defensive element in Roman thinking has been greatly exaggerated. This is in part the result of Roman propaganda, in which the Second Punic War, for example, was attributed to the Carthaginian attack on Saguntum, with no explanation of Rome's original commitment to that city. In part it is a result of the more or less naïve preference for the *victrix causa* which has characterized the bulk of modern historiography about Roman imperialism. And it is true that Rome very commonly did begin new wars (though not new campaigns) in response to some external development. Sometimes it was truly threatening development, more often an annoyance. The function of such a development—such as the Illyrian piracy preceding the war of 229 or the Carthaginian war against Massinissa in 150—was often to rivet Roman attention in the new area, and more often still to provide 'justification' for the new war. For a war against some enemy or other, with some 'justification' or other, the Romans expected and intended almost every year.

ADDITIONAL NOTES

I. THE PARTIAL CONFIDENTIALITY OF SENATORIAL PROCEEDINGS (see pp. 6–7)

This quite obscure question is not dealt with satisfactorily in the constitutional handbooks. According to P. Willems, *Le Sénat de la république romaine*, ii (Louvain, 1883), 163–4, the public could normally, if it wanted to, follow what was said in sessions of the Senate, and that body went into secret session 'fort rarement'. However none of the evidence he cites establishes that there was real public access until the last period of the Republic (neither Liv. ii. 48.10 nor xxii. 59 shows anything of the kind). Mommsen (*R. Staatsrecht*, iii. 931) was probably correct to think that citizens in general were not allowed to stay in the *vestibulum*. The most obscure problems are whether the known instances in which the public was excluded and some secrecy was imposed are of general significance or are merely exceptions, and whether the confidentiality was ever meant to be more than temporary. Polyb. iii. 20.3 suggests, but certainly does not prove, that the Senate meeting which took place in 218 on the arrival of the news that Saguntum had fallen, was conducted in secret; but the instance might be exceptional in any case. Liv. xxii. 60.2 ('summotis arbitris') might also refer to an exception, since the issue to be discussed was extremely delicate. It appears from xxiii. 22.9 that in Livy's view the proceedings were not normally secret in 216, but that a senior senator could impose secrecy on part of what had been said. When Eumenes II spoke in the Senate in 172, nothing became known (according to Liv. xlii. 14.1) except that he had been present; when the Third Macedonian War was over, however, the views exchanged 'emanavere'. It seems certain that the decision to fight the Third Punic War and therefore the relevant senatorial proceedings were kept secret for a time (Val. Max. ii. 2.1, App. *Lib.* 74, cf. Polyb. xxxvi. 2.1). The Senate proceedings of the year 100 described by App. *BC* i. 30.135–6 (cf. Plu. *Mar.* 29) appear to have been confidential. All these are historical incidents. The story told by Cato, *ORF*[3] fr. 172, is probably not (and our source, Gellius, *NA* i. 23, has added some confusion; Macrob. *Sat.* i. 6.19–25 has the story from Gellius; cf. Plu. *Mor.* 507 for a similar tale). However there would have been no point to Cato's story if it had not been possible to impose secrecy on a senatorial debate; on the other hand the story assumes also that senatorial proceedings were not *normally* secret (see Gell. *NA* i. 23.5–6).

The secrecy preceding the three wars strongly suggests that it will have been applied to other debates on questions of peace and war. These of course are precisely the debates we are most concerned with. And while secrecy was probably sometimes imposed for very short periods (as apparently in Cato's story), in others (cf. Eumenes' interview) it lasted for several years; in cases such as the latter the confidentiality of the Senate's proceedings probably seriously hindered the writing of accurate history on the subject.

11. YEARS OF PEACE BETWEEN 327 AND 241 (see p. 10).

In favour of the reliability of the annalistic catalogue of Rome's campaigns in the period of the Etruscan wars (from 311) cf. W. V. Harris, *Rome in Etruria and Umbria*, 49–78. The two periods which need some comment here are 320–316 and 289–285. (1) 320–316. As is well known, the Roman tradition distorted the history of Roman–Samnite relations after 321 in order to wipe out the disgrace incurred at the Caudine Forks. It is not necessary here to contest the view that the Romans and Samnites were at peace with each other from the Caudine Forks until 316 or 315 (such views can be traced back from E. T. Salmon, *Samnium and the Samnites* (Cambridge, 1967), 228–33, through G. De Sanctis, *SR* ii. 313–19, to B. G. Niebuhr), but the following points deserve to be made. From the agreed fact that the Roman tradition invented successes against the Samnites in this period, it does *not* follow that the Romans and Samnites were really at peace (and Liv. ix. 21.2 does not, as Salmon claims, o.c. 228, admit that there was no new fighting after 321 until 316). De Sanctis (313–14) rested weight on the *a priori* argument that Romans of this time would have kept the humiliating promises they had been forced to make at the Caudine Forks; and it is assumed that the Samnites made no further attempt to follow up their success. What fighting, if any, the Romans undertook in 320 remains obscure; there seems to be nothing sound in the accounts of Liv. ix. 12–15, Dio fr. 36.21–2, Zonar. vii. 26, and peace is probably the explanation. But the assertion that Rome fought in 319 with the Ferentani, the Satricani, and the Samnites who had occupied Satricum (Liv. ix. 16.1–3; a triumph allegedly resulted, 16.11) is modest enough to be accepted (other sources are *Acta Tr.—de Samnitibus*—and the Oxyrhynchus Chronicle, *P. Oxy.* 12 = *FGrH* 255 § 11; on the question of the date to which the latter refers see De Sanctis, o.c. ii. 311 n. 55); on the topographical questions involved in this campaign see Salmon, o.c. 230, who, however, transfers it somewhat arbitrarily to 315. As for 318, it seems pointless to expunge the campaigns against Teanum and Canusium recorded by Diod. xix. 10.2 and alluded to by Liv. ix. 20.4. The campaign of 317 seems guaranteed by its very modesty, Liv. ix. 20.9 (Nerulum at least is so obscure that it is probably authentic); see further M. W. Frederiksen, *JRS* lviii (1968), 226. The Roman–Samnite war of 316 (Liv. ix. 21, Diod. xix. 65.7) does not deserve serious doubts. Running through modern criticism there seems to be the view that Livy was unwilling to let any year pass without recording a war, even if none took place; but an examination of his narrative in Books XXXI to XLV suggests rather that he sometimes missed authentic wars recorded by other sources (cf. Additional Note IV). (2) 289–285. This is an obscure period, with no Livy and no *Acta Triumphalia*. According to De Sanctis (o.c. ii. 365), from 289 there were four or five years of peace. The *graves et longae seditiones* leading to the *Lex Hortensia* of 287 (Liv. *Per.* 11) would make this easy to understand. However certain wars have to be fitted in. The campaigns against Volsinii and against the Lucanians mentioned at the end of Liv. *Per.* 11 appear where they do because of the Periochist's custom of gathering minor war notices at the end of an entry; they might belong to any year from 292 to 285. Between triumphs recorded in the *Acta Tr.* for the years 291 and 282 we are faced with a large gap, estimated by A. Degrassi at nineteen lines (*Inscr. It.* xiii. 1.544). Not enough triumphs are known from the literary sources to fill this gap: that of L. Postumius Megellus in 291 will have taken two lines, that of P. Cornelius Rufinus in 290 another two, the double triumph of M'. Curius Dentatus in the same year probably three, the third triumph of M'. Curius (actually an *ovatio* over the Lucanians) probably took two in 289 (cf. *De vir. ill.* 33.3, Degrassi, o.c. 545), and the triumph of P. Cornelius Dolabella probably took two. If Cn. Domitius Calvinus (*cos.* 283) took two lines and Q. Aemilius Papus (*cos.* 282) took two or three (but neither of these triumphs is attested), three or four lines still remain. A lost triumph over the Volsinienses, to be dated somewhere in the years 289–285, is probably part of the answer. In addition, C. Aelius Paetus (*cos.* 286) is quite likely to have been responsible for a campaign against the Lucanians (in spite of disparities; cf. Salmon, o.c. 282 n. 1). However 288, 287, and 285 may well have been years without warfare.

III. THE EARLIEST MAGISTRATES WITHOUT TEN YEARS' MILITARY SERVICE (see p. 12).

T. P. Wiseman, *New Men*, 143, cites the cases of M. Brutus (*RE* Iunius no. 50) and L. Crassus. Brutus did no military service, so it was claimed in invective (Cic. *De orat.* ii. 226)—but neither did he seek office (*Brut.* 130). Crassus (b. 140) made at least one major forensic speech when he was of an age to be serving in the army, his accusation of Carbo in 119 (*Brut.* 159, *De orat.* iii. 74); but twelve months on duty can never have been a strict requirement (cf. *Tab. Her.*, ll.cc.), and court pleading had long been common for young aristocrats (see above, p. 19). Probably as early as 118 he took part as a triumvir in the founding of Narbo—an extraordinary appointment for a man of his age. He evidently spent as much time as possible in the forum and his quaestorship was his longest absence (Cic. *De orat.* ii. 365). He may have broken the rule and may have been one of the first to do so. Sallust's remark about Sulla (b. 138) that he was 'rudis ... et ignarus belli' before 107 (*BJ* 96.1; cf. Val. Max. vi. 9.6, which may suggest how the story grew up) is an exaggeration at least, in view of the responsibilities Marius gave him; throughout the passage Sallust is obviously contrasting Sulla with Marius as much as possible. M. Gelzer (*Roman Nobility*, 82 n. 177=*KS* i. 86 n. 177) mentions as evidence of the lack of military experience among politicians Sall. *BJ* 85.12 ('ego scio ... qui postquam consules facti sunt et acta maiorum et Graecorum militaria praecepta legere coeperint: praeposteri homines ...'), but this is merely rhetoric appropriate to the speaker Marius, who was certainly more of a soldier than most *nobiles*. Of Lucullus Cicero says (*Luc.* 2) that before his quaestorship in 87 'adulescentiam in forensi opera ... consumpserat', and he was 'rei militaris rudis' when he went to make war against Mithridates. According to Plutarch (*Luc.* 2), he had served as an officer under Sulla in the Social War, and to say that he was 'rei militaris rudis' after his activities in the 80s was quite misleading (cf. Gelzer, *RE* s.v. Licinius no. 104 (1926), col. 384, J. Van Ooteghem, *Lucius Licinius Lucullus* (Brussels, 1959), 61). However Lucullus' consular colleague, M. Cotta, may have lacked military experience (App. *Mithr.* 71). On the changing situation see also Cic. *Font.* 42–3 ('studiis militaribus apud iuventutem obsoletis' etc.), Caes. *BG* i. 39.2.

IV. CONSULAR WARS, 200–167 (see p. 15).

Neither L. Cornelius Lentulus, *cos.* 199, nor Sex. Aelius Paetus, *cos.* 198, achieved anything *memorabile* in northern Italy according to Livy (xxxii. 7.8, 9.5, 26.1); in 198 the region was 'praeter spem quieta' (26.4). Paetus 'totum prope annum Cremonensibus Placentinisque cogendis redire in colonias, unde belli casibus dissipati erant, consumpsit' (26.1–3). However the reality of these two years was more complex. It should arouse suspicion that the stinging defeat inflicted by the Insubres in 199 is attributed to the praetor whose province was Ariminum (quite far away) rather than the consul whose province was Gallia. And presumably Paetus' re-establishment of Placentia (destroyed in 200 or 199) and Cremona required some military action against the Insubres, even if nothing *memorabile*, i.e. no sizable victories or defeats, resulted. Furthermore our only other narrative, Zonar. ix. 15–16, which is almost equally jejune, recounts that Paetus made an expedition against the Gauls, in which both sides suffered heavy casualties, καίριον δέ τι ἐπράχθη οὐδέν (ix. 16). Without discussing the problem in more detail, one can say that there was very probably some fighting for Paetus' army, and perhaps some for Lentulus'. Another important factor, which we shall observe again, is that in 199 and until late in 198 success was not known to be assured in another, less predictable, theatre of operations, the war against Philip V; it would not be surprising if the Senate consequently imposed a certain restraint on the commanders in northern Italy (cf. De Sanctis, *SR* iv. 1.413).

In 194 Scipio Africanus clearly wanted Macedonia as his province (Liv. xxxiv. 43.3–5) ('to avert war', according to H. H. Scullard's speculation, *Roman Politics*, 117), but was frustrated by a hostile Senate and assigned 'Italia', i.e. the north. Some sources known to Livy said that he conducted a plundering expedition among the Boii and Ligures, others that he did nothing *memorabile* (Liv. xxxiv. 48.1); both versions were probably correct. The expedition is summarily rejected by (among others) Scullard (o.c. 118 n. 2) and U. Schlag (*Regnum in Senatu* (Stuttgart, 1968), 48). However it seems unlikely that such an affair was invented to glorify the great Africanus, and as for the historicity of undistinguished plundering expeditions in general in this period, they are more likely to have been ignored by some annalists (who mostly wrote in a narrower compass than Livy) than invented by others to fill gaps. Such an expedition can only be understood in the context of contemporary attitudes towards plunder, on which see above, chapter II.

In 190 both consuls wanted the assignment of 'Graecia' (Liv. xxxvii. 1.7), but Laelius had to content himself with Italy (1.10), where the defeat of the Boii in the previous December (on the date: Liv. xxxvi. 38.5–39.1, *Acta Tr.*) left work of consolidation to be carried out (the reinforcement of Cremona and Placentia, the expulsion of many Boii (Strabo v. 213, 216; cf. Liv. xxxvi. 39.3), the foundation of Bononia in 189).

Of the consuls of 188 C. Livius Salinator seems to have continued this work in Gaul, while M. Valerius Messala returned from Liguria 'nulla memorabili in provincia gesta re, ut ea probabilis morae causa esset, quod solito serius ad comitia venisset' (Liv. xxxviii. 42.1). This is no evidence that his tenure was entirely peaceful, but it is likely that serious campaigns in Liguria were delayed until 187 because of preoccupation with events in the east.

Both consuls of 186 were assigned Liguria, but Sp. Postumius was detained by the Bacchanalia crisis, apparently for the whole year. The consuls of 184 did nothing *memorabile* (Liv. xxxix. 44.11) with their four legions in Liguria, to which they had been assigned 'quia bellum nusquam alibi erat' (38.1); but this is not the whole story, since one of them, L. Porcius Licinus, had his command prolonged into 183, and at some point in his campaign vowed an *aedes* to Venus Erycina (Liv. xl. 34.4); these are indications of real (but unsuccessful?) warfare. In 183 Q. Fabius Labeo did nothing *memorabile* in Liguria (Liv. xxxix. 56.3), but after reporting that the Apuani were contemplating 'rebellion' had his command extended. There is no way of telling whether such a notice conceals skirmishes, guerrilla warfare, Roman defeats, or total lack of contact with the enemy. The consuls of 181 had an 'otiosam provinciam' in Liguria (Liv. xl 35 1, cf. 37.9), partly because Aemilius Paullus (*cos.* 182) retained his command there; but with their commands prolonged into 180, they probably undertook some campaigning and were certainly awarded triumphs (against the comment of Liv. xl. 38.9 'hi omnium primi nullo bello gesto triumpharunt', see Scullard, o.c. 178 n. 5). Of the consuls of 179 Livy says that L. Manlius performed 'nihil memoria dignum' in Liguria (xl. 53.4). (For a case in which Livy probably through sheer ignorance reported peace in a promagistrate's province see xli. 26.1.) A lacuna in Livy conceals the provinces assigned to the consuls of 174, probably Liguria, and nothing is known of their activities. L. Postumius Albinus, *cos.* 172, spent the whole summer recovering public land in Campania without even going to his province of Liguria (Liv. xlii. 9.7). During the years 170–168 one consul was assigned Italy each year, and their activities were quite restrained, no doubt because of the war with Perseus (on 170: Liv. xliii. 9.1–3; on 168: xlv. 12.9). The war in Liguria was renewed immediately after the victory in Macedon.

Thus out of sixty-eight consuls who effectively held office in this period, eight did not command in active warfare, and eight others may not have done so; in four of five years there is a real indication that the restraint may have been involuntary. That is to say, more than three-quarters of the consuls were certainly active in war.

V. SCHUMPETER'S THEORY ON THE CAUSES OF ROME'S WARS (see p. 17).

Since *Imperialism and Social Classes* (New York–Oxford, 1951) is widely known, some comments are needed. The relevant essay first appeared in *Archiv für Sozialwissenschaft und Sozialpolitik*, xlvi (1919), and separately as *Zur Soziologie der Imperialismen* (Tübingen, 1919). It has, not surprisingly, received very little attention from Roman historians, and Schumpeter's own interest was not in Roman history but in establishing a general theory of imperialism. His interpretation of Roman imperialism is essentially that 'from the Punic Wars to Augustus' there was a time of imperialistic will to conquer, an unlimited aim which supposedly had no concrete objectives. He denies that the aristocracy had a 'specifically military orientation'. Hence it must have been 'domestic class interests' which created Roman imperialism, and since the only group which benefited extensively from imperialism was the landed aristocracy, it must have been they who brought it about in order to maintain and strengthen their own social and political position (*Zur Soziologie*, 39 = *Imperialism*, 51). This argument is presented in merely outline form.

Schumpeter's theory was criticized by P. A. Brunt (*Comparative Studies in Society and History*, vii (1964–5), 272) on two grounds: (a) that *unconscious* motives are of questionable validity. This is merely an obscurantist argument, hard though such motives are for the historian to identify; (b) that 'it was often not the governing class, but agrarian reformers or popular leaders who carried out annexations'—however it is war and the expansion of power, not annexation, that matter most (cf. above, p. 135), and in any case no act of annexation before the first century is to be attributed to an agrarian reformer (Ti. Gracchus was not responsible for the annexation of Asia: see p. 147) or a popular leader. The greatest weakness of Schumpeter's theory is that it grossly oversimplifies reality. Far from being 'objectless', Roman expansion produced some direct and important benefits, which are analysed as far as possible in chapters, I, II, and V. Schumpeter was aware of some of these benefits (the improved supply of slaves, for example), but he insisted quite artificially on making 'domestic class interests' the one fundamental factor. This theory is not very convincing for a period such as that between 287 and the 130s when the political system was remarkably stable and seldom caused aristocratic anxiety; and in the second half of the second century foreign wars, far from serving as a useful distraction from internal struggles, were—because of the manpower shortage (cf. pp. 49–50)—visibly one of their main causes.

One effect of the aristocracy's external policies was, as J. Bleicken has pointed out (*Staatliche Ordnung und Freiheit in der römischen Republik* (Kallmünz, 1972), 97), to absorb political energy and to promote internal stability. The question should be whether this was a result which the aristocracy intended. According to Bleicken, it was not—'sie hatte ja nicht das Bewusstsein von der Problematik ihrer Vorrangstellung.' However it is possible that in the 150s at least some aristocrats did regard war as a salutary preoccupation or distraction. The somewhat different but closely related theory of the *metus hostilis* (i.e. the theory that fear of foreign enemies ensured domestic stability) was being heard from Scipio Nasica (see p. 127) and also in a different form from Polybius (vi. 57.5–9; note especially οὐκέτι θελήσει [ὁ δῆμος] πειθαρχεῖν οὐδ᾽ ἴσον ἔχειν τοῖς προεστῶσιν, ἀλλὰ πᾶν καὶ τὸ πλεῖστον αὐτός (§ 8); cf. 18.5–8). At some point, perhaps not till the first century, annalistic writers began to claim that in early Rome aristocrats had sometimes regarded peace as politically dangerous (cf. Liv. ii. 28.5, 29.2, 52.2) and that tribunes had sometimes accused them of starting diversionary wars (Liv. iii. 10.10–14, iv. 58.11–14; cf. Sall. *Hist.* iii. 48.6). A war which may genuinely have been started partly as a diversion was the Gallic war of 125–121 (see p. 248). To go back to an earlier period, one can imagine that the aristocracy did see the Italian wars of the late fourth and early third centuries as useful distractions.

Yet the patrician–plebeian aristocracy was in no danger of social revolution, even during the Secession of 287. The causes of Rome's military initiatives in our period were more complex than Schumpeter allowed, and while it is true and important that the aristocrats sought 'the glory of victorious leadership' (*Zur Soziologie*, 40 = *Imperialism*, 52), they did so not to assert the pre-eminence of a class (this was scarcely questioned), but to assert their individual claims to be full members of that class.

VI. THE FAME OF VICTORIOUS COMMANDERS AS IT WAS REFLECTED IN THE MONUMENTS (see p. 20).

A surviving temple-dedication: *ILLRP* 122 (142 B.C.), describing the dedicator's victory. The very numerous temples dedicated in this period are listed by K. Latte, *Römische Religionsgeschichte*, 415–17. Renewals could also give opportunities for self-expression, as with the temple of Neptunus probably reconstructed by M. Antonius, censor in 97 and victor over pirates (cf. F. Coarelli, *DA* ii (1968), 302–68, iv–v (1970–1), 241–65); another case of reconstruction by a victorious commander was probably the contribution of M. Fulvius Flaccus (*cos.* 264), the conqueror of Volsinii, to the temple complex of Fortuna and Mater Matuta (Sant' Omobono), though the exact limits of what he did there are not clear (see M. Torelli's analysis of the donation epigraph, *Quaderni dell' Istituto di Topografia Antica della Università di Roma* v (1968), 71–5; the inscription was first published by A. Degrassi, *BCAR* lxxix (1963–4), 91–3 (= *AE* 1966 no. 13); see further F. Coarelli, *Guida archeologica di Roma* (n.p., 1974), 283). Only a magistrate with *imperium* was permitted to dedicate a temple, though this included *duoviri aedi dedicandae* appointed to fulfil a vow made by a holder of *imperium*. *Triumphatores* put up *tabulae* describing their feats (a text in Liv. xli. 28.8–9; and cf. the text in Liv. xl. 52.5–6, part of which is also quoted as from a *tabula triumphalis* by Caesius Bassus (*Grammatici Latini*, ed. Keil, vi), p. 265; lines from two other texts of this kind are given by Caesius Bassus, ibid., and Atilius Fortunatianus (*GL* vi. pp. 293–4), *ILLRP* 318 and *AE* 1964 no. 72 (= A. Degrassi, *BCAR* lxxviii (1961–2), 138–40) also fall into this category according to Degrassi (cf. *Acta of the Fifth International Congress of Greek and Latin Epigraphy, Cambridge 1967* (Oxford, 1971), 155; but on the latter inscription see J. Reynolds, *JRS* lxvi (1976), 177). For a later text of this kind (Pompey's) see Plin. *NH* vii. 98. Dedications of booty: *ILLRP* 100, 124, 221, 295, and the inscription from Sant' Omobono discussed by Torelli, l.c.; plus many from outside Rome— *ILLRP* 321, 321a, 322, 323, 326–32, E. Bizzarri, *Epigraphica* xxxv (1973), 140–2. The most elaborate republican text of this type is Pompey's dedication of 61 recorded in Diod. xl. 4 (cf. Plin. *NH* vii. 97). Cf. Liv. vi. 29.9, an important example (accompanying the statue of Iuppiter Imperator acquired from Praeneste) if it is authentically early. The ancient references to the particular monuments referred to in the text can easily be traced through S. B. Platner–T. Ashby, *TDAR*, and do not need to be listed here. The text of the Duillius inscription: *ILLRP* 319; the column of Aemilius was destroyed in 172 (Liv. xlii. 20.1). Three arches (*fornices*) were put up by L. Stertinius in 196, another by Scipio Africanus in 190, another by Q. Fabius Maximus after his triumph in 120 (cf. H. Kähler in *RE* s.v. Triumphbogen (1939), cols. 488–93, G. A. Mansuelli, *Aevum* xxii (1948), 75–84, A. Boethius in A. Boethius–J. B. Ward-Perkins,

Etruscan and Roman Architecture (London, 1970), 126). Statues in the forum area: Plin. *NH* xxxiv. 20–32 (not only military heroes); cf. Liv. xxiii. 19.18 for another example; such statues were commonly the result of a victory, Plu. *Cat. Mai.* 19.3. Epitaphs referring specifically to feats of war: *ILLRP* 309, 310, 313—but these are from the tomb of the Scipios, and other surviving epitaphs are jejune (however that of A. Atilius Caiatinus (*cos.* 258, 254) mentioned by Cicero, *De sen.* 61 (cf. W. Morel, *FPL* p. 7), must have referred to his victories). On paintings: Liv. xxiv. 16.19 (214 B.C.—a strange case), xli. 28.10 (177), Plin. *NH* xxxv. 19 (Fabius Pictor's work in 302: unfortunately no source tells us the subject of his *chef-d'oeuvre*, but it was probably military in some way (cf. De Sanctis, *SR* ii. 511), presumably a view of the triumphing dictator C. Iunius Bubulcus), 22–33 (264 B.C., 189, 146), Festus 228L (272, 264), Cic. *Quinct.* 25, Schol. Bob. (*Ciceronis Orationum Scholiastae*, ed. Stangl), p. 147 ('ad tabulam Sextiam', a reference to C. Sextius Calvinus, *cos.* 124: L. G. Pocock, *A Commentary on Cicero in Vatinium*, pp. 180–2); cf. De Sanctis, l.c. and iv. 2. 1.100– 3, G. Zinserling, *Wissenschaftliche Zeitschrift der Friedrich-Schiller-Universität Jena* ix (1959–60), 403–48 (not acceptable on all points). The function of the surviving painting from the Esquiline, datable to 300–250, was to decorate a tomb, but it is worth noting that it portrays scenes of war (it is best illustrated and described in *Rome Medio Repubblicana. Aspetti culturali di Roma e del Lazio nei secoli IV e III a. C.* (Rome, 1973), 200–8). As censor in 97 M. Antonius adorned the *rostra* with his *imperatoriae manubiae* from Cilicia (Cic. *De orat.* iii. 10).

VII. PRAETORIAN *TRIUMPHATORES* (see p. 32).

The exceptions who did not reach the consulship are (1) L. Aemilius Regillus (*pr.* 190), who celebrated a naval triumph in 188. He was not among the patrician candidates in 185, according to Liv. xxxix. 32.6 (L. Aemilius there is Paullus), and Liv. xl. 52.4 suggests that he was dead by 179 (otherwise he might be expected to have obtained an appointment as *duovir aedi dedicandae* and dedicated his temple at an earlier date). Liv. xlv. 22.11 may well be mistaken in implying that he was alive in 167 (cf. G. J. Szemler, *Priests of the Roman Republic* (Brussels, 1972), 109 n. 9). (2) L. Quinctius Crispinus (*pr.* 186), who triumphed from Hispania Citerior in 184 'magno patrum consensu' (Liv. xxxix. 42.2). He is not heard of after 183. (3) M. Titinius Curvus (*pr.* 178), who celebrated a triumph from Hispania Citerior in 175, sprang from a non-consular family, and probably suffered fatal damage to his reputation from the famous *repetundae* case of 171 (on which cf. H. H. Scullard, *Roman Politics*, 201–2), though he was acquitted. (4) L. Cornelius Dolabella (*RE* no. 138), who celebrated a triumph over the Lusitani in 98, is never heard of again, even in the Social War when so many former officers are known to have been in action; he may have died prematurely. On C. Cicereius, see p. 32 n. 3. Known praetorian *viri triumphales* who reached the consulship in this period (I leave aside two cases from the earlier period when the status of the praetorship was different): L. Furius Purpurio (196), Q. Minucius Thermus (193), Q. Fabius Labeo (183), C. Calpurnius Piso (180)*, Q. Fulvius Flaccus (179), Ti. Sempronius Gracchus (177), L. Postumius Albinus (173), Cn. Octavius (165)*, L. Anicius Gallus (160)*, L. Mummius (146)*, Q. Caecilius Metellus (143), Q. Servilius Caepio

(106), M. Antonius (99), T. Didius (98)*, P. Servilius Vatia (79). (Asterisks indicate those of non-consular descent.) Of course all these elections were influenced by other factors.

VIII. WAR-VOTES IN THE *COMITIA CENTURIATA* (see p. 41).

Though a vote of the *comitia centuriata* was still needed in Polybius' time (cf. Liv. (A.) xlv. 21.4–5, Polyb. vi. 14.10), the rule may not have been strictly adhered to. Cn. Manlius Vulso (*cos.* 189) attacked the Galatians without the authorization of a senatorial or comitial war-vote (Liv. xxxviii. 45.4–7, 46.13, 48.9, 50.1), presumably in the confidence—justified, as it turned out—that he would get away with it and even celebrate a triumph. A similar complaint was voiced about the Istrian war in 177, if Liv. xli. 7.8 is to be trusted (which is doubtful, especially since A. Manlius Vulso, the younger brother of Cnaeus, was one of the subjects of complaint). It seems most unlikely that every extension of Roman warfare to minor opponents was authorized by a comitial vote (cf., e.g., the war against Nabis and also Liv. xliii. 1.11); however J. W. Rich, *Declaring War in the Roman Republic in the Period of Transmarine Expansion* (Brussels, 1976), 15, is unduly confident that Livy mentioned all the comitial war-votes that took place in the period 218–167. No such votes are known after 171: even the Third Punic War may have lacked such authorization (cf. App. *Lib.* 75–6); the case of the Jugurthine War, argued by S. I. Oost, *AJPh* lxxv (1954), 151, is worse than doubtful; and App. *Mithr.* 22.83 scarcely shows that there was a comitial vote concerning Mithridates in 88, in spite of Rich, 14. A trace of late-republican controversy on the subject can be seen in Liv. iv. 30.15, and the *populus* maintained a nominal role (cf. Cic. *Pis.* 50). Mommsen limited himself to saying that comitial war-votes were no longer important in the late Republic (*R. Staatsrecht*, iii. 345). Cf. G. W. Botsford, *The Roman Assemblies* (New York, 1909), 231–2, L. R. Taylor, *Roman Voting Assemblies* (Ann Arbor, 1966), 100. Even in the days when there were comitial votes, no one could speak at the *contio* preceding the vote except on the invitation of the presiding magistrate (Mommsen, i³ 200–1), who commonly had a vested interest.

IX. ROMAN KILLING IN CAPTURED CITIES (see p. 52).

Further instances: at Minturnae, Vescia, and especially Ausona in 314 (Liv. ix. 25), at Saepinum in 293 (Liv. x. 45.14—the result of *ira*), (?) at Panormus in 254 (Diod. xxiii. 18.4), at Syracuse in 212 (Liv. xxv. 31.9—a relatively mild case), at Tarentum in 209 (Liv. xxvii. 16.5–7—worth mentioning since friends as well as rebels and enemies were apparently killed), at Oreus in Euboea in 208 (Liv. xxviii. 6.5), at Antipatrea on the western fringe of Macedon in 200 (Liv. (P.) xxxi. 27.4—all *puberes* killed), at Haliartus in Boeotia in 171 (Liv. (P.) xlii. 63.10), at Carthage in 146 (App. *Lib.* 128–130), at Corinth in 146 (Paus. vii. 16.8—women and children were kept for the slave market), in Numidia in 109 (Sall. *BJ* 54.6—killing of *puberes*). For a similar incident involving the Samnites in 320 see Liv. ix. 14.10–11 (but much is unhistorical in this section; the

Samnites were themselves often brutal, according to the Roman sources). It is worth registering the massacre at Henna in 214 of an unarmed ally population which showed signs of disloyalty (Liv. xxiv. 39.6: '. . . urbis captae modo fugaque et caedes omnia tenet . . .').

X. ROMAN SETTLEMENT OF ITALIAN LAND BEFORE THE SECOND PUNIC WAR (see p. 60).

Since the central fact cannot be disputed, the calculations will not be set out in full. Colonies: the twenty-one Latin colonies founded between 334 and 241 (listed by A. J. Toynbee, *Hannibal's Legacy*, i. 159–60) had *territoria* of just about 10,000 sq. km. (K. J. Beloch's figures, *Der italische Bund* (Leipzig, 1880), 138–45, with some necessary adjustments), of which a large proportion was assigned to Roman citizens (three-quarters according to P. A. Brunt's guess, *Italian Manpower*, 29). At least ten citizen colonies were founded between *c*. 350 and 241 (E. T. Salmon, *Roman Colonization under the Republic* (London, 1969), 70–81; but add Castrum Novum in Picenum). Though it is absurd to suppose on the basis of Liv. viii. 21.11 that the colonists were sustained on two *iugera* for each family (Toynbee, i. 185–6; he does not explain how they survived), the total of land confiscated for citizen colonies will only have been a few hundred sq. km. Individual assignment: Veii added 562 sq. km (most of it passing into Roman hands: W. V. Harris, *Rome in Etruria and Umbria*, 41–2); the territory of the eight new tribes created between 358 and 299 probably contained at least 1,000 sq. km. of land assigned to citizens (cf. L. R. Taylor, *The Voting Districts of the Roman Republic* (Rome, 1960), 47–68; the measurements are mainly Beloch's; cf. also Brunt, 28). Other major areas of individual assignment prior to 241: an indeterminate amount of Sabine territory (Taylor, 59–60, F. Cassola, *I gruppi politici romani*, 92), perhaps not very large if the assignments consisted of 7 *iugera* each; the tribe Velina, created in 241, probably contained men who received individual assignments in Praetuttian territory (which amounted to 1,089 sq. km.) and perhaps some individual settlers in Picenum. Early settlement of individual Romans may also have taken place in certain other regions.

XI. TALES ABOUT THE MODEST MEANS OF THE OLD ARISTOCRATS (see p. 66).

Dining habits: Samnite ambassadors found M'. Curius dining from a wooden dish (Val. Max. iv. 3.5), cooking a turnip (Plin. *NH* xix. 87), etc.; De Sanctis was quite unjustified in claiming (*SR* ii. 493) that even if it is untrue such a story shows how Romans thought in Curius' time. There was very little silver in the houses of C. Fabricius (on his alleged poverty cf. Val. Max. iv. 3.6, 4.10) and Q. Aemilius Papus (iv. 4.3). These two were censors in 275/4, when Fabricius was responsible for expelling P. Cornelius Rufinus (*cos.* 290, 277) from the Senate on the grounds that he possessed silver vessels weighing 10 lb. (the sources are listed in *MRR* i. 196, except for the important account of Gell. *NA* iv. 8); to some extent at least this was a pretext (cf. Cassola, *I gruppi politici romani*, 169–70). Sex. Aelius Catus (*cos.* 198) was allegedly found by Aetolian ambassadors dining *in fictilibus* (Plin. *NH* xxxiii. 142, with a confused version in Val. Max. iv. 3.7). Q. Aelius Tubero, Aemilius Paullus' son-in-law, never owned silver except for the little his father-in-law gave him after Pydna (Val. Max. iv. 4.9, Plin. *NH* xxxiii. 142—confusing him with Catus, as does Val. Max. iv. 3.7), a statement made highly suspect by among other things the great wealth eventually inherited by his wife Aemilia from her namesake, the widow of Scipio Africanus (Polyb. xxxiii. 26.2–5, 28.8–9). Whether the unseemly parsimony demonstrated by Tubero's son at the funeral banquet of Scipio Aemilianus (Cic. *Mur.* 75–6, Val. Max. vii. 5.1) stemmed from shortage of cash is uncertain; his philosophy may have been to blame. Aelii (cf. Val. Max. iv. 4.8) and Atilii seem to have been favourite subjects for fables of aristocratic frugality.

Doing the farmwork: Cic. *Rosc. Am.* 50, Val. Max. iv. 4.4, Plin. *NH* xviii. 19. As applied to an Atilius Serranus (sources: *MRR* i. 208 n. 1) the story is obviously apocryphal and derived from his *cognomen*; it is not even clear which Atilius is meant. Africanus labouring in retirement: Sen. *Ep.* 86.5.

Minuscule farms: seven *iugera* was the standard size in moralistic tales (Val. Max. iv. 4.11, cf. Plin. *NH* xviii. 18). This was allegedly the size of Atilius Regulus' *agellus* (Val. Max. iv. 4.6), as it had been that of Cincinnatus' (4.7). For the idealization of Atilius cf. P. Blättler, *Studien zur Regulusgeschichte* (diss. Freiburg, 1945), 45–55, A. Lippold, *Consules*, 39. Even if M'. Curius took only seven *iugera* of Sabine land, not the 50 offered by the Senate (Val. Max. iv. 3.5, cf. Front. *Strat.* iv. 3.12 etc.; for the modest character of this 'villa' the earliest source seems to be Cic. *Cat. Mai.* 55), it was obviously not his only property. Fabricius' small farm: Dion. Hal. xix. 15.1.

Few slaves: Dion. Hal. xix. 15.1, Val. Max. iv. 3.6, 4.6, Frontin. iv. 3.3, etc.

On further elaborations concerning Curius and Fabricius cf. F. Münzer's articles in *RE* s.v. Curius no. 9 (1901), cols. 1844–5, s.v. Fabricius no. 9 (1907), col. 1935.

XII. THE ANTIQUITY OF THE SECULAR PRAYER FOR INCREASED EMPIRE (see p. 121).

The essentials of the Augustan wording may have been devised in 249 B.C. In fact the phrase 'utique semper Latinus obtemperassit', restored to the Augustan *acta* from the new fragments of the Severan *acta* by J. Gagé (*REL* xi (1933), 179 = *Recherches sur les jeux séculaires* (Paris, 1934), 52), obviously points to an earlier date than 249 B.C. and specifically to 348 (in spite of P. Catalano, in *Scritti in onore di Edoardo Volterra* (Milan, 1971), iv. 803), but it would have been an intelligible thought in 249. There is no need to hold (as, e.g., Latte does, *Römische Religionsgeschichte*, 264 n. 4) that this phrase presupposes the oracular lines about the Latins preserved in Phlegon, *FGrH* 237 F37 (p. 1191, lines 5–6) (also in Zosimus, ii. 6), which he dates no earlier than the late second century (298 n. 5). Mommsen (*EE* viii (1899), 265 [→ Bibl.]) cited republican parallels for the Augustan prayer (note esp. Cato, *De agri cult.* cxli. 3, Liv. xxiii. 11.2–3, and the *lustrum* prayer from Valerius Maximus). The case for the prayer's republican date was expanded by E. Diehl, *RhM* lxxxiii (1934), 268–70, 357–69 (accepted by J. Vogt, *Ciceros Glaube an Rom* (Stuttgart, 1935), 74, E. Norden, *Aus altrömischen Priesterbüchern* (Lund, 1939), 104). It is clear that 'imperium maiestasque p.R.' was an old-established official phrase and that there is absolutely no reason to follow H. G. Gundel (*Historia* xii (1963), 301–2) in supposing that it entered the secular prayer only under Augustus; it is unlikely that it was at all new in the Aetolian treaty of 189 (Liv. (P.) xxxviii. 11.2), but the texts in which it might be expected to occur simply do not exist. Cic. *Rab. Perd.* 20 is interesting evidence for the solemnity of the phrase, even though Cicero was probably not quoting the official text of a *senatus consultum ultimum* there (S. Mendner, *Philologus* cx (1966), 261–4); cf. also Sall. *BJ* 24.10.

XIII. THE ALLEGED BEGINNINGS OF THE *METUS HOSTILIS* THEORY (see p. 127).

Q. Caecilius Metellus (*cos.* 206) is said by Val. Max. vii. 2.3 to have stated in the Senate, after the defeat of Carthage in 202, that he did not know whether the victory had brought the state more harm or good; and he went on to speak of the good effects of Hannibal's invasion in arousing Roman *virtus*. This is treated as historical by E. Malcovati (*ORF*[3] p. 11) and F. Cassola (*I gruppi politici romani*, 396). Wrongly. Metellus may have made some remarks about the *virtus* aroused by the invasion, but the theme of Valerius' story is anachronistic (cf. W. Hoffmann, *Historia* ix (1960), 320 [→ Bibl.]); and Metellus cannot have made a speech so derogatory to Scipio Africanus, with whom he was closely allied at this time (Liv. xxix. 20, xxx. 23.3–4, 27.2); and in any case the story is to be rejected because of the usual considerations applying to senatorial speeches in this period (see Additional Note 1; and there is no reason to think that Metellus' collected speeches were preserved).

The idea that the counterbalancing power of a foreign state would be beneficial to Rome is attributed, quite tentatively, by Appian to Scipio Africanus himself (*Lib.* 65): he led the Romans to make a moderate peace in 201 εἴτε τῶν εἰρημένων οὕνεκα λογισμῶν, εἴτε ὡς ἀρκοῦν Ῥωμαίοις ἐς εὐτυχίαν τὸ μόνην ἀφελέσθαι Καρχηδονίους τὴν ἡγεμονίαν· εἰσὶ γάρ, οἳ καὶ τόδε νομίζουσιν, αὐτὸν ἐς Ῥωμαίων σωφρονισμὸν ἐθελῆσαι γείτονα καὶ ἀντίπαλον αὐτοῖς φόβον ἐς ἀεὶ καταλιπεῖν, ἵνα μή ποτε ἐξυβρίσειαν ἐν μεγέθει τύχης καὶ ἀμεριμνίᾳ· καὶ τόδε οὕτω φρονῆσαι τὸν Σκιπίωνα οὐ πολὺ ὕστερον ἐξεῖπε τοῖς Ῥωμαίοις Κάτων, ἐπιπλήττων παρωξυμμένοις κατὰ Ῥόδου. But this too is anachronistic (K. Bilz, *Die Politik des P. Cornelius Scipio Aemilianus* (Stuttgart, 1936), 24–5, Hoffmann, o.c. 320, A. E. Astin, *Scipio Aemilianus*, 277 n. 2), and any moderation shown in 201 was dictated by circumstances (see above, p. 138). (However Hoffmann, o.c. 318–23, was wrong to try and simplify the problem by reading, witht he Vaticanus MS, τὸν Σκιπίωνα, ὃ οὐ πολύ, κτλ. The effect of this is to remove from Appian the claim that Cato, in addition to the vague 'some people', attributed the opinion to Africanus. The suggestion was accepted by F. W. Walbank, *JRS* lv (1965), 6. It is most unlikely, because (a) ὃ οὐ is a hiatus which Appian avoids (A. Zerdik, *Quaestiones Appianeae* (diss. Kiel, 1886), 52; Hoffmann's comments on this problem, o.c. 321, were uninformed); and (b) Hoffmann's text is excessively referential, assuming knowledge of Cato's *Pro Rhodiensibus* (cf. M. Gelzer, *KS* ii. 53 n. 31a)).

But in spite of Appian, Cato probably did not really attribute to Africanus, or endorse himself, the opinion that a counterbalancing external force should be maintained for Rome's own benefit. The nearest he came, as far as we know, was to describe the dangers of too much success (*ORF*[3] fr. 163; see p. 128 n. 5). Eventually some source of Appian's elaborated this into the argument, supposed to have been used by Scipio Nasica, that Rome needed a powerful neighbour—an argument entirely irrelevant to the speech on behalf of the Rhodians and not in any case likely to have appealed to Cato.

XIV. THE DATE OF THE ANNEXATION OF CYRENE (see p. 154).

Sall. *Hist.* ii. 43 dates it to early 75, App. *BC* i. 111.517 apparently to the Olympiad year 75/4, Eutrop. vi. 11 to about 67. G. Perl, *Klio* lii (1970), 321–5, shows clearly that on the existing evidence 75 is the best date for the establishment of the province. Badian apparently somewhat prefers Eutropius' date (*JRS* lv (1965), 119–20; cf. *RILR*[2] 36–7). This is largely because of some inscriptions published (in some cases republished) by J. Reynolds, *JRS* lii (1962), 97–103, which show that the Pompeian legate Cn. Cornelius Lentulus Marcellinus played an extraordinarily important part in the history of Cyrene, and in particular that his name formed part of a dating formula (in Reynolds no. 4, p. 98) in a way which would be surprising if there was a regular governor present in the province. (There remain material doubts about this, however, for the presence of Cn. Lentulus, rather than P. Lentulus, the quaestor who is said by Sallust to have been sent to the new province in 75, depends on the restoration of the *praenomen* in a damaged area of uncertain length in the inscription; see Reynolds, plate XIV (1).) We do not have enough evidence to disregard that of Sallust and Appian; and there is other testimony that Cyrene was in a sorry state, at least from the Roman point of view, by 67, for Diodorus states (xl. 4) that in the grandiose inscription that Pompey set up to commemorate his activities in the East he claimed to have conquered the province of Cyrene (ὑποτάξας . . . Κυρηναϊκὴν ἐπαρχίαν). It is possible, as P. Romanelli suggested (*La Cirenaica romana* (Verbania, 1943), 42 n. 7), that Eutropius erroneously dated the province to 67 because from that year it was put under the same governor as Crete—but there is much hypothesis here. There is, as far as I can see, no reason to doubt that there were regular governors of Cyrene before 67 (see further Perl, o.c. 325).

XV. WAR-DECLARATION PROCEDURES BETWEEN 281 AND 171 (see p. 167).

The case of Tarentum in 282/1 was probably a crucial one. L. Postumius Megellus may possibly have been sent in 282 *ad res repetendas* (cf. Val. Max. ii. 2.5, Zonar. viii. 2), but he seems not to have been empowered to declare war. On the other hand the consul of 281 who began the war, L. Aemilius Barbula, *was* provided with a conditional declaration of war (App. *Samn.* 7.3, Zonar. viii. 2). It looks as if the essential changes in the procedure had now been made, and given the remoteness of Tarentum from Rome, it may have been precisely in 281 that the change occurred. This hypothesis accords remarkably well with the information of Serv. Dan. *Aen.* ix. 52, according to which it was during, or probably at the start of, the war against Pyrrhus that the *fetiales* began the custom of casting their spear not into the actual territory of the enemy, but into a piece of quasi-hostile territory in the Circus Flaminius district (a custom attested by Ov. *Fast.* vi. 205–9). (K. Latte, *Römische Religionsgeschichte*, 122 n. 3, followed by W. Dahlheim, *Struktur und Entwicklung*, 175, objected that this story lacks legal logic. The complaint is that the commentator supposes that the Romans made a prisoner-of-war from Pyrrhus' army purchase a piece of land in Rome so that they could use it to declare war against Pyrrhus. The quibble is irrelevant, since religious Romans may well have continued to feel the need for a magical spear-throwing against Pyrrhus even after the war had begun. E. Rawson's arguments (*JRS* lxiii (1973), 167) against the authenticity of the fetials' spear-throwing in Rome are scarcely relevant.) Thus the first two parts of the fetial war-declaring procedure, as it is described by Livy, were replaced for practical reasons by the delivery of a conditional war-declaration by means of a *legatus*. The third part, the spear-throwing, would naturally be cherished by the *fetiales* and others as the most dramatic piece of magic in the whole programme; therefore it was not abolished, but adapted to the new circumstances, and this was done almost as soon as possible, in 280. How long the *fetiales* kept up this tradition we cannot know. Their attested later function in war-declarations is limited to giving procedural advice to magistrates (Liv. xxxi. 8.3, xxxvi. 3.7–12). It is fairly clear that in 264 the new procedure of conditional war-declaration was used against Hiero and Carthage: see Diod. xxiii. 1.4 (πρὸς δὲ τὸν Ἱέρωνα ...) (cf. F. W. Walbank on Polyb. i. 11.11). C. Cichorius suggested (*Römische Studien* (Berlin–Leipzig, 1922), 26–7) that Naevius' line 'scopas atque verbenas sagmina sumpserunt' (*Pun.* 2* [31] Strzelecki = 27 Warmington) referred to the declaration of war in 264, but much more probably it refers to treaty-making, either with Hiero or indeed with Carthage (cf. now K.-H. Schwarte, *Historia* xxi (1972), 206–23).

A mistaken notion has spread that the change did not take place until after the end of the First Punic War (cf. Dahlheim, l.c.). This seems to have resulted from Walbank's convincing demonstration (*CPh* xliv (1949), 16) that the 'new' procedure was used against Carthage in 238 (see Polyb. i. 88.10–12, iii. 10.3), as it was on some later occasions (see below). But though he discussed the change in procedure, Walbank for some reason neglected the earlier evidence. However, when he later came to comment on Polyb. i. 11.11, he granted that 'probably the revised procedure was employed.'

Later uses of the revised fetial procedure are as follows: 218: Polyb. iii. 20.6–21.8, 33.1–4, Liv. xxi. 18.1–14 (without the phrase 'ad res repetendas'). 200: Polyb. xvi. 34.3–7, Liv. (P.) xxxi. 18.1–4. 172–1: Liv. (A.) xlii. 25.1–2 reports on the embassy sent to Perseus 'ad res repetendas ... renuntiandamque amicitiam'; since H. Nissen, *Kritische Untersuchungen*, 246–7, this has sometimes been regarded as a spurious notice (cf. Walbank, o.c. 18 n. 19), but see *MRR* i. 415 n. 8, U. Bredehorn, *Senatsakten in der republikanischen Annalistik* (diss. Marburg, 1968), 196–200; it is significant that after the war-decision at Rome there remained a final, though merely nominal, possibility that Perseus would meet

Rome's demands (Liv. xlii. 30.11–31.1, 36.6). There seems to be no good evidence that the neo-fetial procedure was used to declare war against Queen Teuta in 230: see Walbank on Polyb. ii. 8.8.

XVI. SOME SECOND-CENTURY ROMAN CLAIMS TO HAVE FOUGHT JUST AND DEFENSIVE WARS (see p. 172).

Whether Scipio Africanus really told Hannibal, on the eve of Zama, that the gods had given the Romans the strength to win in Sicily and Spain, favouring οὐ τοῖς ἄρχουσι χειρῶν ἀδίκων, ἀλλὰ τοῖς ἀμυνομένοις (Polyb. xv. 8.2), must remain uncertain (it is self-defence and unjust deeds that are in question, not *fides*, as Walbank ad loc. states). Only the two generals and their interpreters were present (6.3). Walbank (n. on xv. 6.3–8.14) somewhat favours authenticity. In any case second-century Roman thinking about what Scipio should have said is revealed. Cf. Liv. (?P.) xxx. 16.9: 'populum Romanum et suscipere iuste bella et finire' (attributed to Scipio; on the source question see De Sanctis, *SR* iii. 2.651). According to Livy, L. Furius Purpurio claimed in 199 that the Romans had undertaken the First Macedonian War on behalf of the Aetolians (Liv. xxxi. 31.18, cf. 29.5); note also his words 'cum ad conquerendas Philippi iniurias in tot socias nobis urbes venissem' (31.2). When Livy makes Polybius' father Lycortas say to a Roman embassy in 184 'pro vobis igitur iustum piumque bellum suscepimus' (Liv. xxxix. 36.12), the source is presumably Polybius, and Lycortas was picking up the phraseology which he knew to be customary on the Roman side (concerning the authenticity of Lycortas' speech cf. the discussions listed by J. Deininger, *Der politische Widerstand gegen Rom im Griechenland, 217–86 v. Chr.* (Berlin–New York, 1971), 123 n. 28). But not many Greeks became convinced of Rome's political justice by 171: Liv. (P.) xlii. 30.3. For the propaganda campaign prior to the Third Macedonian War see esp. *RDGE* no. 40 (= *SIG*³ 643). Liv. xlv. 22.5 (the Rhodians are made to refer to the Roman habit of claiming that their wars are just) is annalistic and not reliable (H. Nissen, *Kritische Untersuchungen*, 275). Poseidonius, *FGrH* 87 F43 beginning, gives further evidence that second-century Romans advertised the supposed justice of Rome in war.

XVII. CASSIUS DIO'S SPURIOUS SENATORIAL DEBATE OF 218 (see p. 204).

See Dio fr. 55, Zonar. viii. 22. These speeches have been regarded as authentic reports of actual speeches by among others, H. H. Scullard (*Roman Politics*, 40–1), F. W. Walbank (*A Commentary on Polybius*, i. 332), F. Cassola (*I gruppi politici romani*, 275–8), A. Lippold (*Consules*, 139–40), but this is an error. Cf. now G. A. Lehmann, *EFH* xx (1974), 172. On the inaccessibility of early senatorial debates to historians see above, pp. 6–7. It is most improbable that Polybius, with his partly Roman audience, would have contradicted Fabius Pictor over such a matter and in such a tone (Walbank notwithstanding). If there really was such a debate, it is conceivable that Fabius would have felt embarrassed by, and would even have failed to mention, the pacific stance of Fabius Maximus (cf. M.

Gelzer, *Hermes* lxviii (1933), 162 [→ Bibl.])—but who then did record the debate? E. Täubler's suggestion (*Die Vorgeschichte des zweiten punischen Kriegs* (Berlin, 1921), 85), that Sosylus of Lacedaemon, who probably offered some senatorial speeches at this point in his narrative (cf. Polyb. iii. 20.5), as an ordinary Greek historian was bound to, actually used authentic material supplied to him by L. Cincius Alimentus when the former was a companion and the latter was a prisoner of Hannibal, presupposes among other things an unlikely degree of warmth between the pro-Carthaginian historian and the Roman senator. The only other person who might conceivably be the ultimate source is Cato, though he was not a senator in 218; but to mention only two difficulties, he is unlikely to have named debaters in this fashion (see above, p. 29 n. 3), and in any case the tone of Polybius' comments again means that Cato cannot possibly have reported such a debate (cf. De Sanctis, *SR* iii. 1.424 n. 86). The fact that Dio's account of the outbreak of the war is pro-Roman does precisely nothing to show that his speeches are derived from an early annalist (again *pace* Walbank). Dio shows no especially esoteric knowledge (even if he chances to be correct) in making Fabius Maximus, the Cunctator, an opponent of the war and L. Lentulus (probably the *princeps senatus*) its advocate; a similar story was already to be found in Silius Italicus, i. 675–94, which no scholar would want to treat as historical.

What matters most of all is the unimpressive character of the speeches themselves. Dio fr. 57.12 struck Cassola as particularly authentic, because he thought the argument (attributed to Fabius) that it is rash to attack enemies before putting internal affairs in order was 'del tutto estraneo alla topica della eloquenza greco-romana' (277). He should have considered Thuc. i. 82–3, Isocr. viii. 85, cf. Polyb. v. 104. Note also that Dio himself was hostile towards expansionist wars in his own time (F. Millar, *A Study in Cassius Dio* (Oxford, 1964), 141–3, 149). Neither side in the debate, as Millar points out (o.c. 82), 'makes any specific reference to the current situation'; in fact the speeches consist of the generalities typical of Dio's *invented* speeches (cf. Millar, o.c. 79–83), and they are no more authentic than the speech of Fabius Rullianus in fr. 36.1–5 or that of the Samnite in fr. 36.11–14. Scholars eager for information about the inner workings of Roman politics in 218 have grasped at a mirage.

Livy knows nothing of the debate, a point against its authenticity. He does pretend to describe (xxi. 16) the Roman state of mind immediately after the fall of Saguntum. But this passage is the merest confection, without an ounce of honest material in it; it ends appropriately with the grandiose and anachronistic claim that the Romans expected that they would have to fight the whole world 'in Italia ac pro moenibus Romanis'.

XVIII. M. POPILLIUS LAENAS AND THE STATELLATES
(see p. 226).

For another discussion see W. Eder, *Das vorsullanische Repetundenverfahren* (diss. Munich, 1969), 28–32. In 173 M. Popillius defeated the Statellates, and then enslaved some 10,000 of them (vague figure) after they had made a *deditio* (Liv. xlii. 8.3). Over this a political conflict arose which Livy embroiders with moralizing sentiments (xlii. 8.5–8, 21.3). Some may well have been voiced, but disapproval was far from unanimous, for M. Popillius' brother was elected consul for 172 (even though Marcus did not preside at the election), Marcus evidently had his *imperium* extended into 172 (cf. xlii. 21.2), he was not fined, and the Statellates did not recover their land (xlii. 22.5–6); and in 159 M. Popillius became censor. It is apparent that a major cause of the dispute was a rivalry with A. Atilius Serranus, the praetor who led the attack on Popillius. He presided over the election of the *decemviri* who had been appointed to distribute Ligurian and Gallic land (xlii. 4.3–4). Inaccurate statements have often had the effect of making the Senate seem more tender towards the Ligurians than it was; it did not, e.g., 'censure . . . [Popillius] for attacking without a just cause a tribe which had not been at war with Rome since 179', as H. H. Scullard (*Roman Politics*, 194) alleges (see xlii. 8.7–8). And the suggestion that Popillius' behaviour represented a trend towards violence and rapacity led by *novi homines* (Scullard, l.c.; cf. E. Will, *Histoire politique*, ii. 224) is fallacious. Admittedly the Popillii, though *nobiles*, had had no consuls in the family for many generations, and M. Popillius may have been a man of exceptional ambition. The lineage of L. Postumius Albinus (*cos.* 173) was impeccable; and P. Aelius Ligus (*cos.* 172) may have been related to the noble Aelii Paeti (in spite of the misleading comment of F. Münzer, *Römische Adelsparteien*, 220), for both lines liked the *praenomen* Publius. M. Popillius' offence, in so far as he was genuinely believed to have committed one, was to have achieved traditional ends by an untraditional, even if technically permissible, response to the Statellates' act of *deditio*. It is also possible that the Senate wished to quieten the Ligurian theatre in preparation for the imminent war in Macedonia. . . . The subsequent history of Roman settlement in southern Piedmont is obscure: A. J. Toynbee (*Hannibal's Legacy*, ii. 668) argues convincingly that Hasta and Valentia (significant names) were founded in 173/2; 159 is perhaps the most likely date for Forum Fulvii.

XIX. POLYBIUS' VIEW OF THE THIRD PUNIC WAR (see p. 237).

Appian is not taking his account from Polybius (see P. Pédech, *La Méthode historique de Polybe*, 195), nor is Plutarch (though this is often asserted, e.g. by M. Gelzer, *Philologus* lxxxvi (1931), 273 [→Bibl.], Pédech, o.c. 195–6). H. Nissen simply asserted (*Kritische Untersuchungen*, 296) that both accounts were Polybian. Gelzer argued from certain similarities between Polyb. xxxvi. 9.4 and Plu. *Cat. Mai.* 27.3, but they are not enough to establish a direct relationship, and in any case 9.4 is merely a Greek opinion Polybius mentions, not his own narrative account (see below). The fact that Polyb. xxxvi. 7.7 and Plu. 27.4 both say that Cato quoted *Odyssey* x. 495 in praise of Scipio Aemilianus proves nothing; Plutarch knew the story well (cf. *Mor.* 200a, 804f), and it appeared in Livy (*Per.* 49) and no doubt elsewhere.

　　How Polybius did explain Rome's Carthaginian policy remains obscure, all the more so because it probably forced him into a conflict with his own earlier and in some respects idealistic view of Roman imperialism (cf. F. W. Walbank, *Polybius*, 178–81). It is possible that he emphasized senators' defensive thinking, but Gelzer, o.c. 296, was incorrect to say that he shows this in xxxvi. 9.4 (the beginning of his list of Greek opinions on the destruction of Carthage). We do not know which, if any, of these Greek opinions were his own. In fact a good case can be made for taking the second of each pair of arguments as his—i.e. on the political question he answers §§ 3–4 (8 lines) with §§ 5–8 (15 lines), in effect arguing that it was not defensive thinking that mattered (cf. fr. 99B–W), but a new policy of extreme φιλαρχία which had since 168 replaced a more moderate policy of simply imposing obedience; while on the question of legalistic justification (not unimportant in his view, cf. xxxvi. 2.3) he answers §§ 9–11 (15 lines) with §§ 11–17 (27 lines), in effect arguing that the Carthaginian *deditio* put the Romans in the right. Cf. Pédech, o.c. 199. Walbank, o.c. 178–9, argues that §§ 5–8 cannot be Polybius' view because that would mean that—contrary to all likelihood—he rejected 'the Roman case over Carthage'. See further his remarks in *EFH* xx (1974), 14–18. However §§ 5–6 coincide with Polybius' view of Roman imperialism before 168 (as having been not utterly ruthless); and it was perhaps just because his own view was critical of Rome that he spent so much space on the part of Rome's case which he did accept (the legalistic justification). In any case we have no evidence that Polybius himself explained the war mainly as a result of defensive thinking in the Senate.

XX. THE THRACIAN WARS FROM 119 (see p. 245).

For the invasion of Macedonia in 119 see *SIG*³ 700 (Gauls, presumably Scordistae, lines 10–11, 21, and Maedi, line 11). When the Roman campaigns began is obscure. An army invaded Thrace and fought the Scordistae unsuccessfully in 114 (Liv. *Per.* 63; other sources are listed by *MRR* i. 533, where it is incorrectly stated that it was in Macedonia that the consul was defeated). But we do not know what had happened in the interval, or what had led to the assignment of Macedonia to one of the consuls in 116 (Q. Fabius Maximus: *MRR* ii. 644). Campaigns followed in every year from 113 to 106, mostly outside the province it seems (Flor. i. 39.5, Amm. Marc. xxvii. 4.10; but M. Livius Drusus, *cos.* 112, celebrated a triumph over the Scordistae and the 'Macedonians', *Acta Tr.* and cf. Fest. *Brev.* 9: 'Marcus Drusus [Thraces] intra fines continuit'). The positive results were booty (mainly slaves) and the addition of the Caeneic Chersonese to the province of Macedonia (the Cnidos inscription published by M. Hassall, M. Crawford, and J. Reynolds, *JRS* lxiv (1974), 195–220, shows that the 'Piracy Law' of 101/0 referred to this conquest and not to the conquest of all Thrace, as used to be inferred from *FIRA* (ed. Riccobono) i no. 9, lines 28–9). The security of Macedonia and Asia was also improved. None the less there were more invasions, by the Maedi in 92 (Obsequens 53) and by 'Thracians' in 89 (Liv. *Per.* 74, Oros. v. 18.30— probably exaggerating as so often; this was a *defectio* according to Cic. *Pis.* 84). During the Mithridatic war Thracians reached as far south as Dodona (Dio fr. 101) and Delphi (App. *Ill.* 5). On the Roman invasion of 85 see App. *Ill.* 5, *Mithr.* 55, Gran. Lic. 27–8 F, *De vir. ill.* 75.7.

XXI. THE ROMANS AND MITHRIDATES DOWN TO 89
(see p. 252).

This is not the place for a full re-examination of the history of Rome's relations with Mithridates before the war of 89. The sources are in any case inadequate, the events highly complex. In the very earliest phase, Mithridates *may* have been responsible for the death of Ariarathes VI of Cappadocia (so Justin xxxviii. 1.1; the date was about 116), who was a Roman friend. Later (in the period 107–104), having occupied part of Paphlagonia, he may have disobeyed the Senate's order to withdraw (Justin xxxvii. 4.5, Strabo xii. 541 and 544; but cf. Justin xxxviii. 5.6). His first seizure of power in Cappadocia (*c.* 100)—a territory to which he had some traditional claim (cf. P. Desideri, *Athenaeum* li (1973), 3 n. 3)—encouraged Marius to hope for war; the Senate, however, evidently felt greater fear of their colleague than of Mithridates (see above, p. 158). Not many years later the Senate apparently decided to bring Cappadocia within the sphere of Roman influence, and imposed a pro-Roman king on the Cappadocians, who had declined the offer of a republican constitution; the new king was Ariobarzanes, the date 96 or slightly later (I accept the basic reconstruction by E. Badian, *Athenaeum* xxxvii (1959), 279–303 = *Studies in Greek and Roman History*, 157–78). Appian (*Mithr.* 10) suggests that the Senate may have been nervous about the extent of Mithridates' empire (ἢ καὶ τὸ μέγεθος τῆς ἀρχῆς τοῦ Μιθριδάτου πολλῆς οὔσης ὑφορώμενοι), but this is simply conjecture. To install Ariobarzanes, Sulla took only a small force and relied mainly on allies (Plu. *Sull.* 5). This was the first armed conflict between Rome and troops representing Mithridates. In 91 Tigranes, king of Armenia, saw to the dethronement of Ariobarzanes (Justin xxxviii. 3.2–3, App. *Mithr.* 10), an action for which Mithridates may or may not have been responsible (cf. Desideri, o.c. 5 n. 5, 15); in any case the latter no doubt hoped that the Social War would prevent any forceful Roman response. Then in 89 M'. Aquillius organized the recovery both of Bithynia (which Mithridates had taken from Nicomedes IV) and of Cappadocia; Mithridates gave way, to the extent of putting to death his own claimant to the throne of Bithynia, Socrates Chrestus (Justin xxxviii. 5.8). But Aquillius, partly for personal gain (p. 90), provoked a war with Mithridates by forcing Nicomedes and Ariobarzanes to invade Pontus itself (the best detailed account of this is by T. J. Luce, *Historia* xix (1970), 186–90). Thus Rome was militarily inactive for a long period; distractions in other quarters played a part in this, as did apprehension about Marius. So probably did bribery (Diod. xxxvi. 15.1), and, as we have seen, there had in recent years been some decline in Roman enthusiasm for war. But the pressure from Mithridates' side should not be exaggerated. He is sometimes supposed to have planned from his earliest years to expel the Romans from the whole of Asia Minor (D. Magie, *Roman Rule in Asia Minor*, i. 195–6, E. Will, *Histoire politique*, ii. 397; hence the latter is puzzled by the king's actual behaviour, ii. 398). He did indeed work to expand his realm, but he sensibly avoided personal involvement in war against Rome until his home territory was invaded in 89.

BIBLIOGRAPHY

(Asterisks indicate works cited in their original languages that are also available in English.)

A. The following works are referred to simply by author and title, in most cases abbreviated title.

ASTIN, A. E., *Scipio Aemilianus* (Oxford, 1967).
BADIAN, E., *Foreign Clientelae, 264–70 B.C.* (Oxford, 1958).
—— *Studies in Greek and Roman History* (Oxford, 1964).
—— *Roman Imperialism in the Late Republic*² (Oxford, 1968) (= *RILR*²).
—— *Publicans and Sinners* (Ithaca, N.Y., 1972).
BENGTSON, H., *Grundriss der römischen Geschichte*² (Munich, 1970).
BRISSON, J.-P. (ed.), *Problèmes de la guerre à Rome* (Paris–The Hague, 1969).
BRUNT, P. A., *Italian Manpower, 225 B.C.–A.D. 14* (Oxford, 1971).
CASSOLA, F., *I gruppi politici romani nel III secolo a.C.* (Trieste, 1962).
CRAWFORD, M. H., *Roman Republican Coinage* (Cambridge, 1974) (= *RRC*).
DAHLHEIM, W., *Struktur und Entwicklung des römischen Völkerrechts im 3. und 2. Jahrhundert v. Chr.* (Munich, 1968).
DE SANCTIS, G., *Storia dei romani*, i–iv. 3 (Turin/Florence, 1907–64) (=*SR*).
FRAENKEL, E., *Elementi plautini in Plauto* (Florence, 1960), annotated trans. of *Plautinisches im Plautus* (Berlin, 1922).
FRANK, T., *Roman Imperialism* (New York, 1914).
—— *Economic Survey of Ancient Rome*, i–vi (Baltimore, 1933–40) (= *ESAR*).
GABBA, E., **Esercito e società nella tarda repubblica romana* (Florence, 1973).
GELZER, M., *Kleine Schriften*, i–iii (Wiesbaden, 1962–4) (= *KS*).
—— *The Roman Nobility* (Oxford, 1969), Eng. trans. of *Die Nobilität der römischen Republik* (Leipzig, 1912), reprinted in *KS* i (Wiesbaden, 1962).
HARRIS, W. V., *Rome in Etruria and Umbria* (Oxford, 1971).
HATZFELD, J., *Les Trafiquants Italiens dans l'Orient hellénique* (Paris, 1919).
HOLLEAUX, M., *Rome, la Grèce et les monarchies hellénistiques au IIIᵉ siècle avant J.-C. (273–205)* (Paris, 1921) (= *RGMH*).
—— *Études d'épigraphie et d'histoire grecques*, i–vi (1938–68) (= *Études*).
LATTE, K., *Römische Religionsgeschichte* (Munich, 1960).
LIPPOLD, A., *Consules, Untersuchungen zur Geschichte des römischen Konsulates von 264 bis 201 v. Chr.* (Bonn, 1963).
MAGIE, D., *Roman Rule in Asia Minor* (Princeton, 1950).
MOMMSEN, T., *Römisches Staatsrecht*, i³, ii³, iii (Leipzig, 1887) (= *R. Staatsrecht*).
—— **Römische Geschichte*, i–iii, v (twelfth edn., Berlin, 1920) (= *RG*).
MOREL, W., *Fragmenta Poetarum Latinorum Epicorum et Lyricorum* (Leipzig, 1927) (= *FPL*).
MÜNZER, F., *Römische Adelsparteien und Adelsfamilien* (Stuttgart, 1920).
NISSEN, H., *Kritische Untersuchungen über die Quellen der vierten und fünften Dekade des Livius* (Berlin, 1863).
OGILVIE, R. M., *A Commentary on Livy, Books 1–5* (Oxford, 1965).
PÉDECH, P., *La Méthode historique de Polybe* (Paris, 1964).

PLATNER, S. B., and ASHBY, T., *A Topographical Dictionary of Ancient Rome* (London, 1929) (= *TDAR*).

ROSTOVTZEFF, M., *A Social and Economic History of the Hellenistic World* (Oxford, 1941) (= *SEHHW*).

SCHMITT, H., *Die Staatsverträge des Altertums*, iii. *Die Verträge der griechisch-römischen Welt von 338 bis 200 v. Chr.* (Munich, 1969).

SCULLARD, H. H., *A History of the Roman World, 753–146 B.C.*[3] (London, 1961) (= *HRW*[3]).

—— *Roman Politics, 220–150 B.C.*[2] (Oxford, 1973).

SHERK, R. K., *Roman Documents from the Greek East* (Baltimore, 1969) (= *RDGE*).

TOYNBEE, A. J., *Hannibal's Legacy*, i–ii (Oxford, 1965).

WALBANK, F. W., *A Historical Commentary on Polybius*, i–ii (Oxford, 1957, 1967).

WILL, E., *Histoire politique du monde hellénistique*, i–ii (Nancy, 1966, 1967).

WISEMAN, T. P., *New Men in the Roman Senate, 139 B.C.–A.D. 14* (Oxford, 1971).

WISSOWA, G., *Religion und Kultus der Römer*[2] (Munich, 1912).

B. A list of all the other works cited in this book would probably help no more than a few readers. The following list consists of (a) works that have been republished in some form (so that bibliographical guidance may be needed), and (b) a limited number of other publications that are of special significance for the topics I have discussed.

ACCAME, S., *Il dominio romano in Grecia dalla guerra acaica ad Augusto* (Rome, 1946).

AFZELIUS, A., *Die römische Eroberung Italiens (340–264 v. Chr.)* (Copenhagen, 1942).

—— *Die römische Kriegsmacht* (Copenhagen, 1944).

ALFÖLDI, A., 'The Main Aspects of Political Propaganda on the Coinage of the Roman Republic', *Essays in Roman Coinage Presented to Harold Mattingly* (Oxford, 1956), 63–95.

—— *Early Rome and the Latins* (Ann Arbor, 1965).

ANDRESKI [= ANDRZEJEWSKI], S., *Military Organization and Society*[2] (London, 1968).

ASTIN, A. E., *The Lex Annalis before Sulla* (Brussels, 1958).

AYMARD, A., 'Deux anecdotes sur Scipion Emilien', *Mélanges de la Société toulousaine d'études classiques*, ii (1948), 101–20, repr. in *Etudes etc.*

—— 'L'interdiction des plantations de vignes en Gaule transalpine sous la République romaine', *Mélanges géographiques offerts en hommage à M. Daniel Faucher* (Toulouse, 1948), 227–47, repr. in *Etudes etc.*

—— *Etudes d'histoire ancienne* (Paris, 1967).

BADIAN, E., 'Notes on Roman Policy in Illyria', *PBSR* xx (1952), 72–93, repr. in *Studies etc.*

—— 'Notes on Provincial Governors from the Social War to Sulla's Victory', *PACA* i (1958), 1–18, repr. in *Studies etc.*

—— 'Rome and Antiochus the Great: a Study in Cold War', *CPh* liv (1959), 81–99, repr. in *Studies etc.*

—— 'Sulla's Cilician Command', *Athenaeum* xxxvii (1959), 279–303, repr. in *Studies etc.*

BADIAN, E., 'Notes on Provincia Gallia in the Late Republic', *Mélanges d'archéologie et d'histoire offerts à André Piganiol* (Paris, 1966), 901–18.
—— 'The Testament of Ptolemy Alexander', *RhM* cx (1967), 178–92.
—— *Titus Quinctius Flamininus, Philhellenism and Realpolitik* (Cincinnati, 1970).
BALSDON, J. P. V. D., 'Rome and Macedon, 205–200 B.C.', *JRS* xliv (1954), 30–42.
BAYET, J., 'Le rite du fécial et le cornouiller magique', *MEFR* lii (1935), 29–76.
BENOIT, F., *L'Epave du Grand Congloué à Marseille, Gallia*, Suppl. xiv (1961).
BERVE, H., *König Hieron II.*, *Abh. Bay. Ak. Wiss.* N.F. xlvii (1959).
BICKERMANN, E. J., 'Bellum Antiochicum', *Hermes* lxvii (1932), 47–76.
—— 'Les préliminaires de la seconde guerre de Macédoine', *RPh* lxi (1935), 59–81, 161–76.
—— 'Notes sur Polybe', *REG* l (1937), 217–39.
—— '*Bellum Philippicum:* some Roman and Greek Views concerning the Causes of the Second Macedonian War', *CPh* xl (1945), 137–48.
—— 'Notes sur Polybe. III. Initia belli Macedonici', *REG* lxvi (1953), 479–506.
BLEICKEN, J., review of E. Badian, *Foreign Clientelae*, *Gnomon* xxxvi (1964), 176–87.
—— *Staatliche Ordnung und Freiheit in der römischen Republik* (Kallmünz, 1972).
BOUTHOUL, G., *Traité de sociologie. Les guerres: éléments de polémologie* (Paris, 1951).
BREDEHORN, U., *Senatsakten in der republikanischen Annalistik* (diss. Marburg, 1968).
BRISCOE, J., 'Eastern Policy and Senatorial Politics 168–146 B.C.', *Historia* xviii (1969), 49–70.
—— *A Commentary on Livy, Books XXXI–XXXIII* (Oxford, 1973).
BRUNT, P. A., 'Reflections on British and Roman Imperialism', *Comparative Studies in Society and History*, vii (1964–5), 267–88.
—— 'The Equites in the Late Republic', *Second International Conference of Economic History* (Aix-en-Provence, 1962; publ. Paris–The Hague, 1965), 117–49, repr. in R. Seager (ed.), *The Crisis of the Roman Republic* (Cambridge, 1969).
CASSON, L., 'The Grain Trade of the Hellenistic World', *TAPhA* lxxxv (1954), 168–87.
CICHORIUS, C., *Römische Studien* (Berlin–Leipzig, 1922).
CLEMENTE, G., *I romani nella Gallia meridionale (II–I sec. a. C.)* (Bologna, 1974).
COARELLI, F., 'Classe dirigente romana e arti figurative', *DA* iv–v (1970–1), 241–65.
—— 'Il sepolcro degli Scipioni', *DA* vi (1972), 36–105.
—— 'Architettura e arti figurative in Roma: 150–50 a.C.', in P. Zanker (ed.), *Hellenismus in Mittelitalien* (Göttingen, 1976), 21–32.
D'ARMS, J. H., *Romans on the Bay of Naples* (Cambridge, Mass., 1970).
DAVIE, M. R., *The Evolution of War* (New Haven, 1929).
DEGRASSI, A., 'Nuovi miliari arcaici', *Hommages à A. Grenier* (Brussels, 1962), i. 499–513, repr. in *Scritti vari di antichità*, iii (Venice–Trieste, 1967).
—— 'L'epigrafia latina in Italia nell' ultimo quinquennio (1963–1967)', *Acta of*

the Fifth International Congress of Greek and Latin Epigraphy, Cambridge 1967 (Oxford, 1971), 153–74, repr. in *Scritti vari di antichità*, iv (Trieste, 1971), 39–64.

DE SANCTIS, G., *Problemi di storia antica* (Bari, 1932).

DIEHL, E., 'Das *saeculum*, seine Riten und Gebete', *RhM* lxxxiii (1934), 255–72, 348–72.

DREXLER, H., 'Gloria', *Helikon* ii (1962), 3–36.

EARL, D. C., *The Political Thought of Sallust* (Cambridge, 1961).

—— *Tiberius Gracchus, a Study in Politics* (Brussels, 1963).

ECKERT, K., '*ferocia*—Untersuchung eines ambivalenten Begriffs', *Der altsprachliche Unterricht* xiii (1970), 90–106.

EDER, W., *Das vorsullanische Repetundenverfahren* (diss. Munich, 1969).

EISEN, K. F., *Polybiosinterpretationen* (Heidelberg, 1966).

EISENHUT, W., *Virtus Romana* (Munich, 1973).

ERRINGTON, R. M., *The Dawn of Empire* (London, 1972).

FERGUSON, W. S., 'The Lex Calpurnia of 149 B.C.', *JRS* xi (1921), 86–100.

FRACCARO, P., 'I "decem stipendia" e le "leges annales" repubblicane', in P. Ciapessoni (ed.), *Per il XIV Centenario della codificazione giustinianea* (Pavia, 1934), 475–503, repr. in *Opuscula*, ii (Pavia, 1957).

FRANK, T., 'Mercantilism and Rome's Foreign Policy', *AHR* xviii (1912–13), 233–52.

FREDERIKSEN, M. W., review of E. T. Salmon, *Samnium and the Samnites*, *JRS* lviii (1968), 224–9.

—— 'The Contribution of Archaeology to the Agrarian Problem in the Gracchan Period', *DA* iv–v (1970–1), 330–57.

FUCHS, H., *Augustin und der antike Friedensgedanke* (Berlin, 1926).

GABBA, E., *'Le origini dell'esercito professionale in Roma: i proletari e la riforma di Mario', *Athenaeum* xxvii (1949), 173–209, repr. in *Esercito e società*.

—— *Appiani Bellorum Civilium Liber Primus* (Florence, 1958), . . . *Quintus* (Florence, 1970).

—— 'Mario e Silla', *ANRW* i. 1.764–805.

GAGÉ, J., 'Recherches sur les jeux séculaires', *REL* xi (1933), 172–202, 400–35, repr. separately (Paris, 1934).

GARLAN, Y., *La Guerre dans l'antiquité* (Paris, 1972).

GELZER, M., 'Nasicas Widerspruch gegen die Zerstörung Karthagos', *Philologus* lxxxvi (1931), 261–99, repr. in *Vom Römischen Staat*, i, and *KS* ii.

—— 'Römische Politik bei Fabius Pictor', *Hermes* lxviii (1933), 129–66, repr. in *KS* iii.

—— 'Die Anfänge des römischen Weltreichs', *Das Reich. Idee und Gestalt. Festschrift für Johannes Haller* (Stuttgart, 1940), 1–20, repr. in *Vom Römischen Staat*, i, and in *KS* ii.

—— 'Der Rassengegensatz als geschichtlicher Faktor beim Ausbruch der römisch-karthagischen Kriege', in J. Vogt (ed.), *Rom und Karthago* (Leipzig, 1943), 178–202, repr. in *Vom Römischen Staat*, i.

—— *Vom Römischen Staat* (Leipzig, 1943), i–ii.

GIANNELLI, G., *Trattato di storia romana*, i (Rome, 1953).

GLÜCK, J. J., 'Reviling and Monomachy as Battle-preludes in Ancient Warfare', *Acta Classica* vii (1964), 25–31.

GRUEN, E. S., *Roman Politics and the Criminal Courts, 149–78 B.C.* (Cambridge, Mass., 1968).

HAMMOND, N. G. L., 'Illyris, Rome and Macedon in 229–205 B.C.', *JRS* lviii (1968), 1–21.

HAMPL, F., '"Stoische Staatsethik" und frühes Rom', *HZ* clxxxiv (1957), 249–71, repr. in R. Klein (ed.), *Das Staatsdenken der Römer.*

—— 'Römische Politik in republikanischer Zeit und das Problem des "Sittenverfalls"', *HZ* clxxxviii (1959), 497–525, repr. in R. Klein (ed.), *Das Staatsdenken der Römer.*

—— 'Zur Vorgeschichte des ersten und zweiten Punischen Krieges', *ANRW* i. 1.412–41.

HARMAND, J., *L'Armée et le soldat à Rome* (Paris, 1967).

HARRIS, W. V., 'On War and Greed in the Second Century B.C.', *AHR* lxxvi (1971), 1371–85.

—— review of E. Badian, *Publicans and Sinners, AJPh* xcvi (1975), 433–6.

—— 'The Development of the Quaestorship, 267–81 B.C.', *CQ* N.S. xxvi (1976), 92–106.

HASSALL, M., CRAWFORD, M., and REYNOLDS, J., 'Rome and the Eastern Provinces at the End of the Second Century B.C.', *JRS* lxiv (1974), 195–220.

HAUSMANINGER, H., '"Bellum iustum" und "iusta causa belli" im älteren römischen Recht', *Österreichische Zeitschrift für öffentliches Recht,* N.F. xi (1961), 335–45.

HEINZE, R., *Von den Ursachen der Grösse Roms* (Leipzig, 1921), repr. in R. Heinze, *Vom Geist des Römertums*[3] (Stuttgart, 1960) and in H. Oppermann (ed.), *Römertum.*

HELLEGOUARC'H, J., *Le Vocabulaire latin des relations et des partis politiques sous la république* (Paris, 1963).

HEUSS, A., 'Der erste punische Krieg und das Problem des römischen Imperialismus', *HZ* clxix (1949–50), 457–513, repr. separately (third edition, Darmstadt, 1970).

—— *Römische Geschichte*[3] (Braunschweig, 1971).

HILL, H., *The Roman Middle Class in the Republican Period* (Oxford, 1952).

HOBSON, J. A., *Imperialism, A Study* (London, 1938 edn.).

HÖLSCHER, T., *Victoria Romana* (Mainz, 1967).

HOFFMANN, W., 'Die römische Politik des 2. Jahrhunderts und das Ende Karthagos', *Historia* ix (1960), 309–44, repr. in R. Klein (ed.), *Das Staatsdenken der Römer.*

—— 'Das Hilfegesuch der Mamertiner am Vorabend des ersten punischen Krieges', *Historia* xviii (1969), 153–180.

HOLLEAUX, M., 'Epigraphica II', *REG* xi (1898), 251–8, repr. in *Etudes,* ii.

—— 'Le prétendu recours des athéniens aux romains (en 201/200)', *REA* xxii (1920), 77–96, repr. in *Etudes,* v.

—— 'Les conférences de Lokride et la politique de T. Quinctius Flamininus', *REG* xxxvi (1923), 115–71, repr. in *Etudes,* v.

—— 'Notes sur Tite-Live, II', *RPh* lvii (1931), 193–208, repr. in *Etudes,* v.

HOYOS, B. D., 'Lex Provinciae and Governor's Edict', *Antichthon* vii (1973), 47–53.

JOLLIFFE, R. O., *Phases of Corruption in Roman Administration in the Last Half-Century of the Roman Republic* (diss. Chicago, 1919).

JONES, A. H. M., '[The Ancient Empires and the Economy:] Rome', *Third International Conference of Economic History, Munich, 1965* (Paris–The Hague, 1970), iii. 81–104, repr. in *The Roman Economy* (Oxford, 1974).

KIENAST, D., *Cato der Zensor* (Heidelberg, 1954).

KLEIN, R. (ed.), *Das Staatsdenken der Römer* (Darmstadt, 1966).

KLOTZ, A., *Livius und seine Vorgänger* (Stuttgart, 1940–1).

KNOCHE, U., 'Der römische Ruhmesgedanke', *Philologus* lxxxix (1934), 102–24, repr. in U. Knoche, *Vom Selbstverständnis der Römer* (Heidelberg, 1962), and in H. Oppermann (ed.), *Römische Wertbegriffe*.

KROLL, W., *Die Kultur der ciceronischen Zeit* (Leipzig, 1933).

KROMAYER, J.–VEITH, G., *Heerwesen und Kriegführung der Griechen und Römer* (Munich, 1928).

LA PENNA, A., 'L'interpretazione sallustiana della guerra contro Giugurta', *Ann. Sc. Norm. Pisa* xxviii (1959), 45–06, 243–04.

LATTE, K., 'Religiöse Begriffe im frührömischen Recht', *ZSS* lxvii (1950), 47–61, repr. in *KS*.

—— *Der Historiker L. Calpurnius Frugi*, *SB Berlin* no. 7 (1960), repr. in *KS*.

LEEMAN, A. D., *Gloria, Cicero's Waardering van de Roem en haar Achtergrond in de hellenistische Wijsbegeerte en de romeinse Samenleving* (diss. Leiden, 1949).

LEHMANN, G. A., *Untersuchungen zur historischen Glaubwürdigkeit des Polybios* (Münster, 1967).

—— 'Polybios und die ältere und zeitgenössische griechische Geschichtsschreibung: einige Bemerkungen', *EFH* xx (1974), 145–200.

LÉVÊQUE, P., 'La guerre à l'époque hellénistique', in J.-P. Vernant (ed.), *Problèmes de la guerre en Grèce ancienne* (Paris–The Hague, 1968), 261–87.

LIEBMANN-FRANKFORT, T., *La Frontière orientale dans la politique extérieure de la république romaine* (Brussels, 1969).

LOENEN, D., *Polemos (Med. Nederl. Akad.* xvi no. 3) (1953).

LUCE, T. J., 'Marius and the Mithridatic Command', *Historia* xix (1970), 161–94.

MARX, F., 'Animadversiones criticae in Scipionis Aemiliani historiam . . .', *RhM* xxxix (1884), 65–72.

MAZZARINO, S., *Il pensiero storico classico*, i–ii. 1–2 (Bari, 1966–8).

McDONALD, A. H.–WALBANK, F. W., 'The Origins of the Second Macedonian War', *JRS* xxvii (1937), 180–207.

MELONI, P., *Perseo e la fine della monarchia macedone* (Rome, 1953).

MOMIGLIANO, A., review of A. N. Sherwin-White, *The Roman Citizenship*, *JRS* xxxi (1941), 158–65, repr. in *Secondo contributo*.

—— 'Perizonius, Niebuhr and the Character of Early Roman Tradition', *JRS* xlvii (1957), 104–14, repr. in *Secondo contributo*.

—— 'Some Observations on Causes of War in Ancient Historiography', *Acta Congressus Madvigiani* (Copenhagen, 1958), i. 199–211, repr. in *Secondo contributo* and in *Studies in Historiography* (New York, 1966).

—— 'Linee per una valutazione di Fabio Pittore', *Rend. Acc. Linc.* ser. 8, xv (1960), 310–20, repr. in *Terzo contributo*.

—— *Secondo contributo alla storia degli studi classici* (Rome, 1960).

—— *Terzo contributo alla storia degli studi classici e del mondo antico* (Rome, 1966).

MOMMSEN, T., 'Commentaria ludorum saecularium quintorum et septimorum', *EE* viii (1899), 225–309, largely repr. in *Gesammelte Schriften* viii (Berlin, 1913).

MORGAN, M. G., 'Lucius Cotta and Metellus. Roman Campaigns in Illyria during the Late Second Century', *Athenaeum* xlix (1971), 271–301.

—— 'Pliny, N.H. III 129, the Roman Use of Stades and the Elogium of C. Sempronius Tuditanus (*cos.* 129 B.C.)' *Philologus* cxvii (1973), 29–48.

—— 'Cornelius and the Pannonians', *Historia* xxiii (1974), 183–216.

MUSTI, D., 'Polibio e la storiografia romana arcaica', *EFH* xx (1974), 105–39.

NICOLET, C., '"Consul togatus": remarques sur le vocabulaire politique de Cicéron et de Tite-Live', *REL* xxxviii (1960), 236–63.

—— 'Armée et société à Rome sous la république : à propos de l'ordre équestre', in J.-P. Brisson (ed.), *Problèmes de la guerre à Rome*, 117–56.

OOST, S. I., *Roman Policy in Epirus and Acarnania in the Age of the Roman Conquest of Greece* (Dallas, 1954).

—— 'Cyrene, 96–74 B.C.', *CPh* lviii (1963), 11–25.

OPPERMANN, H. (ed.), *Römertum* (Darmstadt, 1962).

—— (ed.), *Römische Wertbegriffe* (Darmstadt, 1967).

PERNA, R., *L'originalità di Plauto* (Bari, 1955).

PETZOLD, K.-E., *Studien zur Methode des Polybios und zu ihrer historischen Auswertung* (Munich, 1969).

PIANEZZOLA, E., *Traduzione e ideologia* (Bologna, 1969).

PIGHI, G. B., *De ludis saecularibus*[2] (Amsterdam, 1965).

RICH, J. W., *Declaring War in the Roman Republic in the Period of Transmarine Expansion* (Brussels, 1976).

RICHARDSON, J. S., 'The Triumph, the Praetors and the Senate in the Early Second Century B.C.', *JRS* lxv (1975), 50–63.

—— 'The Spanish Mines and the Development of Provincial Taxation in the Second Century B.C.', *JRS* lxvi (1976), 139–52.

ROLOFF, H., *Maiores bei Cicero* (diss. Göttingen, 1938)

Roma Medio Repubblicana. Aspetti culturali di Roma e del Lazio nei secoli IV e III a.C. (Rome, 1973).

SAUERWEIN, I., *Die leges sumptuariae als römische Massnahme gegen den Sittenverfall* (diss. Hamburg, 1970).

SCHLAG, U., *Regnum in Senatu* (Stuttgart, 1968).

SCHMITT, H. H., *Rom und Rhodos* (Munich, 1957).

SCHUMPETER, J., *Zur Soziologie der Imperialismen* (also in *Archiv für Sozialwissenschaft und Sozialpolitik* xlvi (1919)), transl. in *Imperialism and Social Classes* (New York–Oxford, 1951).

SCHWARTE, K.-H., 'Zum Ausbruch des zweiten Samnitenkrieges (326–304 v. Chr.)', *Historia* xx (1971), 368–75.

—— 'Naevius, Ennius und der Beginn des Ersten Punischen Krieges', *Historia* xxi (1972), 206–23.

SCHWERTFEGER, T., *Der achaiische Bund von 146 bis 27 v. Chr.* (Munich, 1974).

SHATZMAN, I., 'The Roman General's Authority over Booty', *Historia* xxi (1972), 177–205.

SHERWIN-WHITE, A. N., *The Roman Citizenship*[2] (Oxford, 1973).

SIMON, H., *Roms Kriege in Spanien, 154–133 v. Chr.* (Frankfurt-a.-M., 1962).

SMITH, R. E., *Service in the Post-Marian Roman Army* (Manchester, 1958).

ŠTAERMAN, E. M., *Die Blutezeit der Sklavenwirtschaft in der römischen Republik* (Wiesbaden, 1969), transl. of *Rastsvet rabovladelcheskikh otnoshenii v Rimskoi respublike* (Moscow, 1964).

STIER, H. E., *Roms Aufstieg zur Weltmacht und die griechische Welt* (Cologne–Opladen, 1957).

STRASBURGER, H., 'Poseidonios on Problems of the Roman Empire', *JRS* lv (1965), 40–53.

SUMNER, G. V., 'The Chronology of the Outbreak of the Second Punic War', *PACA* ix (1966), 5–30.

SYME, R., *Sallust* (Cambridge, 1964).

TAYLOR, L. R., 'New Light on the History of the Secular Games', *AJPh* lv (1934), 101–20.

—— *The Voting Districts of the Roman Republic* (Rome, 1960).

—— 'Forerunners of the Gracchi', *JRS* lii (1962), 19–27.

THIEL, J. H., *De Rol der Persoonlijkheid in de Geschiedenis der Romeinsche Republiek* (Groningen–The Hague, 1930).

—— *A History of Roman Sea-power before the Second Punic War* (Amsterdam, 1954).

TIBILETTI, G., 'Lo sviluppo del latifondo in Italia dall'epoca graccana al principio dell'impero', *Relazioni del X Congresso Internationale di Scienze Storiche* (Rome, 1955), ii. 235–92.

TURNEY-HIGH, H. H., *Primitive War* (Columbia, S.C., 1949).

VERNANT, J.-P. (ed.), *Problèmes de la guerre en Grèce ancienne* (Paris–The Hague, 1968).

VERSNEL, H. S., *Triumphus* (Leiden, 1970).

VEYNE, P., 'Y a-t-il eu un impérialisme romain?', *MEFRA* lxxxvii (1975), 793–855.

VOGT, J., *Orbis Romanus* (Tübingen, 1929), repr. in *Vom Reichsgedanken der Römer* and in *Orbis*.

—— *Vom Reichsgedanken der Römer* (Leipzig, 1942).

—— 'Pergamon und Aristonikos', *Atti del III Congresso internazionale di epigrafia greca e latina* (publ. Rome, 1959), 45–54, repr. in J. Vogt, **Sklaverei und Humanität* (Wiesbaden. 1965).

—— *Orbis* (Freiburg etc., 1960).

VOLKMANN, H., 'Griechische Rhetorik oder römische Politik?', *Hermes* lxxxii (1954), 465–76, repr. in R. Klein (ed.), *Das Staatsdenken der Römer.*

—— *Die Massenversklavungen der Einwohner eroberter Städte in hellenistisch-römischen Zeit (Abh. Mainz)* (1961).

VOLLMER, F., 'Laudationum funebrium Romanorum historia et reliquiarum editio', *Jahrbücher f. class. Philologie*, Suppl. xviii (1892), 449–528.

WALBANK, F. W., *Philip V of Macedon* (Cambridge, 1940).

—— 'Polybius, Philinus, and the First Punic War', *CQ* xxxviii (1945), 1–18.

—— 'Roman Declaration of War in the Third and Second Centuries', *CPh* xliv (1949), 15–19.

—— 'Polybius and Rome's Eastern Policy', *JRS* liii (1963), 1–13.

—— 'Three Notes on Polybius XII', *Miscellanea di studi alessandrini in memoria di Augusto Rostagni* (Turin, 1963), 203–13.

—— 'Political Morality and the friends of Scipio', *JRS* lv (1965), 1–16.

WALBANK, F. W., *Polybius* (Berkeley–Los Angeles–London, 1972).
—— 'Polybius between Greece and Rome', *EFH* xx (1974), 1–31.
WEINSTOCK, S., 'Victor and invictus', *HTR* l (1957), 211–47.
—— *Divus Julius* (Oxford, 1971).
WERNER, R., 'Das Problem des Imperialismus und die römische Ostpolitik im zweiten Jahrhundert v. Chr.', *ANRW* i. 1.501–63.
WESTINGTON, M. M., *Atrocities in Roman Warfare to 133 B.C.* (diss. Chicago, 1938).
WILLEMS, P., *Le Sénat de la république romaine*, i–ii (Louvain, 1878, 1883).
WILSON, A. J. N., *Emigration from Italy in the Republican Age of Rome* (Manchester, 1966).
WISEMAN, T. P., 'Roman Republican Road-building', *PBSR* xxxviii (1970), 122–52.

INDEX

I. Persons, Places, Wars

II. TOPICS